TRIVQUIZ

1001

TRIVIA QUESTIONS

ON THIS DAY IN
WORLD
FOOTBALL

FASCINATING FACTS! TRIVIA BRAINTEASERS!
WRITTEN AND ILLUSTRATED BY

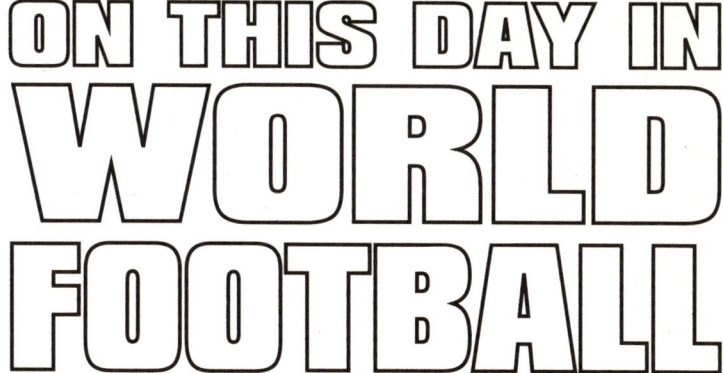

DESIGNED BY JOE McGARRY

First published by Pitch Publishing, 2021

Pitch Publishing
A2 Yeoman Gate
Yeoman Way
Worthing
Sussex
BN13 3QZ
www.pitchpublishing.co.uk
info@pitchpublishing.co.uk

ISBN: 978 1 80150 019 7

Typesetting and origination by Pitch Publishing
Printed and bound in India by Replika Press Pvt. Ltd.

1001 TRIVIA QUESTIONS: ON THIS DAY IN WORLD FOOTBALL

Other books in this series:

1001 TRIVIA QUESTIONS: ARSENAL
1001 TRIVIA QUESTIONS: MANCHESTER CITY
1001 TRIVIA QUESTIONS: MANCHESTER UNITED
1001 TRIVIA QUESTIONS: NEWCASTLE UNITED
1001 TRIVIA QUESTIONS: TOTTENHAM HOTSPUR
1001 TRIVIA QUESTIONS: WEST HAM UNITED

ACKNOWLEDGEMENTS

Thanks to Joe McGarry for his brilliant design work and his technical expertise. There would be no books without him!

Thanks to Debs McGarry for the research and art assistance.

Thanks to Luke McGarry for picking up the slack on the other features while we worked on this.

Thanks to all three for their patience!

Additional thanks to Tom and Andy at "Shoot! The Breeze" podcast and Rob Stokes for the additional research and scans!

ABOUT STEVE McGARRY

A former record sleeve designer, whose clients included Joy Division, Steve McGarry is one of the most prolific and widely-published cartoonists and illustrators that Britain has ever produced. In the UK alone, his national newspaper daily strips include "Badlands", which ran for a dozen years in The Sun, "The Diary of Rock & Pop" in the Daily Star, "Pop Culture" in Today and "World Soccer Diary" in The Sun.

Over his four-decade career he has regularly graced the pages of soccer magazines Match, Match of the Day and Shoot! and his comics work ranges from Romeo in the 1970s and Look-In, Tiger and Oink! in the 1980s, SI for Kids and FHM in the 1990s, through to the likes of Viz, MAD and Toxic! When The People launched his Steve McGarry's 20th Century Heroes series, they billed him as the world's top cartoonist.

His sports features have been published worldwide since 1982 and he currently has two features – "Biographic" and "Kid Town" – in newspaper syndication, with a client list that includes the New York Daily News and The Washington Post.

In recent years, he has also created story art for such movies as "Despicable Me 2", "The Minions" and "The Secret Life of Pets".

Although Manchester born and bred, Steve has been based in California since 1989. A two-term former President of the National Cartoonists Society, his honours include Illustrator of the Year awards from the NCS and the Australian Cartoonists Association, and he is a recipient of the prestigious Silver T-Square for "outstanding service to the profession of cartooning". In 2013, he was elected President of the NCS Foundation, the charitable arm of the National Cartoonists Society. He is also the founder and director of US comics festival NCSFest.

JANUARY

JAN 1

LEGEND HAS IT THAT **ROBERTO RIVELINO** ONCE SCORED A GOAL DIRECT FROM THE KICK-OFF WHEN HE SPOTTED THAT THE OPPOSITION GOALKEEPER WAS STILL ON HIS KNEES COMPLETING PRE-MATCH PRAYERS! BORN IN SÃO PAULO, BRAZIL, ON JANUARY 1, 1946, **RIVELINO** BEGAN HIS PLAYING CAREER AS A MIDFIELDER WITH **CORINTHIANS**, LATER MOVING TO **FLUMINESE**. WITH **GERSON** COMMANDING MIDFIELD IN THE 1970 WORLD CUP CAMPAIGN, **RIVELINO** WAS SWITCHED TO THE LEFT WING, WHERE HIS EXPLOSIVE SHOOTING AND LETHAL FREE KICKS WERE A MAJOR FACTOR IN **BRAZIL'S** TRIUMPH. HE WAS OUTSTANDING IN THE 1974 WORLD CUP AND WENT ON TO APPEAR IN THE 1978 FINALS, AFTER WHICH HE TOOK HIS SKILLS TO **AL-HILAL** IN SAUDI ARABIA. HE SCORED 26 GOALS IN 92 GAMES FOR **BRAZIL**, INCLUDING 6 GOALS IN 15 WORLD CUP APPEARANCES.

1. WHO COACHED **BRAZIL** AT THE WORLD CUP IN:
   A) 1970 AND 1974
   B) 1978

2. NAME TWO OF THE SEVEN PLAYERS WHO HAVE REPRESENTED **BRAZIL** IN FOUR WORLD CUP TOURNAMENTS.

JAN 2

BORN IN ABIDJAN, CÔTE D'IVOIRE, ON JANUARY 2, 1967, *BASILE BOLI* WAS RAISED IN FRANCE FROM AN EARLY AGE. BY HIS LATE TEENS, HE WAS A REGULAR FOR *AUXERRE* AND A *FRANCE* INTERNATIONAL, EVENTUALLY WINNING 45 CAPS. HE JOINED *OLYMPIQUE DE MARSEILLE* IN 1990, WHERE HE WON TWO LEAGUE TITLES AND THE UEFA CHAMPIONS LEAGUE. A SEASON IN SCOTLAND WITH *RANGERS* BROUGHT ANOTHER LEAGUE TITLE, BEFORE A RETURN TO FRANCE WITH *AS MONACO*. HE ENDED HIS CAREER WITH A SPELL IN JAPAN PLAYING FOR *URAWA RED DIAMONDS*.

1. *BOLI* SCORED THE ONLY GOAL IN THE 1993 EUROPEAN CHAMPIONS LEAGUE FINAL -- WHO DID *MARSEILLE* BEAT IN THAT GAME?

2. HE TEAMED UP WITH WHICH ENGLISH TEAMMATE AT *MARSEILLE* TO RECORD THE POP SONG *"WE'VE GOT A FEELING"*?

3. WHO WAS *BOLI'S* COACH AT *RANGERS* IN THE 1994/95 SEASON?

JAN 3 BORN IN SOUTHEND-ON-SEA, ON JANUARY 3, 1953, *PETER TAYLOR* WAS PLAYING IN THE THIRD TIER OF LEAGUE FOOTBALL WITH *CRYSTAL PALACE* WHEN HE WON THE FIRST OF FOUR *ENGLAND* CAPS. HE WENT ON TO PLAY FOR A NUMBER OF CLUBS, INCLUDING *TOTTENHAM HOTSPUR*, BEFORE ENTERING MANAGEMENT. HE SIGNED *ROBERTO MANCINI* WHILE IN CHARGE AT *LEICESTER CITY*, AND STEPPED IN AS THE CARETAKER MANAGER OF *ENGLAND* FOR ONE GAME, FOR WHICH HE HANDED *DAVID BECKHAM* THE CAPTAIN'S ARMBAND FOR THE FIRST TIME.

INCLUDING CARETAKERS, THERE HAVE BEEN 19 OTHER MANAGERS OF *ENGLAND* SINCE THE SECOND WORLD WAR - NAME THEM ALL.

JAMES PHILIP MILNER WAS BORN IN LEEDS, ON JANUARY 4, 1986. A PRODUCT OF THE **LEEDS UNITED** ACADEMY, HE MADE HIS PREMIER LEAGUE DEBUT AT THE AGE OF 16 YEARS AND 309 DAYS, AND BECAME THE YOUNGEST PREMIER LEAGUE SCORER A FEW DAYS BEFORE HIS 17TH BIRTHDAY. FOLLOWING RELEGATION IN 2004, HE WAS TRANSFERRED TO **NEWCASTLE UNITED**. AFTER **GRAEME SOUNESS** REPLACED **BOBBY ROBSON**, **MILNER'S** OPPORTUNITIES ON TYNESIDE WERE LIMITED AND HE WAS LOANED OUT TO **ASTON VILLA** FOR A SEASON. AFTER SPENDING THE NEXT SEASON BACK WITH **NEWCASTLE**, HE JOINED **VILLA** IN A PERMANENT DEAL IN 2008. TWO YEARS LATER, BY THIS TIME AN **ENGLAND** INTERNATIONAL, HE SIGNED FOR **MANCHESTER CITY**. THE 2010 PFA YOUNG PLAYER OF THE YEAR, HE WON TWO LEAGUE TITLES, THE FA CUP AND LEAGUE CUP BEFORE MOVING ON TO **LIVERPOOL** IN 2015, WHERE HE HAS ADDED THE UEFA CHAMPIONS LEAGUE, UEFA SUPER CUP, FIFA CLUB WORLD CUP AND ANOTHER PREMIER LEAGUE MEDAL TO HIS COLLECTION.

1. WHO MANAGED **MILNER** AT BOTH **LEEDS UNITED** AND **ASTON VILLA**?

2. WITH WHICH SECOND DIVISION CLUB DID **MILNER** PLAY ON LOAN DURING HIS **LEEDS UNITED** DAYS?

3. WHICH FORMER **ENGLAND** MANAGER GAVE **JAMES MILNER** HIS DEBUT AT **LEEDS UNITED**?

**JAN
5**

VINNIE JONES WAS BORN IN WATFORD ON JANUARY 5, 1965. HE WORKED AS A HOD CARRIER WHILE PLAYING WITH NON-LEAGUE **WEALDSTONE**, THEN SPENT A SEASON IN SWEDEN WITH **IFK HOLMSUND**, BEFORE SIGNING FOR **WIMBLEDON** IN 1986. TWO YEARS LATER, HE WAS A KEY MEMBER OF THE **"CRAZY GANG"** SIDE THAT BEAT **LIVERPOOL** IN THE FA CUP FINAL. AN AGGRESSIVE ENFORCER, HE COURTED CONTROVERSY ON AND OFF THE PITCH, BUT PLAYED FOR A NUMBER OF TOP ENGLISH CLUBS AND CAPTAINED **WALES**, BEFORE EMBARKING ON A SUCCESSFUL ACTING CAREER.

1. NAME THREE OF THE OTHER CLUBS THAT **VINNIE JONES** PLAYED FOR.

2. WHICH SUBSEQUENT **ENGLAND** INTERNATIONAL AND **ENGLAND U-21** MANAGER ALSO LAUNCHED HIS CAREER AT **WEALDSTONE**?

3. IN WHICH 1998 **GUY RITCHIE** CRIME COMEDY DID **VINNIE JONES** MAKE HIS FILM DEBUT PLAYING MOB ENFORCER **BIG CHRIS**?

JAN 6 THE FIRST PLAYER TO BE CAPPED AT EVERY INTERNATIONAL LEVEL FOR *ENGLAND* -- SCHOOLBOY, YOUTH, AMATEUR, UNDER-23 AND SENIOR -- *TERENCE FREDERICK VENABLES* WAS BORN IN DAGENHAM ON JANUARY 6, 1943. FOLLOWING A CAREER THAT TOOK HIM FROM *CHELSEA* TO *TOTTENHAM HOTSPUR, QUEENS PARK RANGERS* AND *CRYSTAL PALACE*, HE MADE THE TRANSITION TO COACHING, EVENTUALLY TAKING OVER THE REINS OF *ENGLAND*, WHOM HE STEERED TO THE SEMI-FINALS OF EURO 1996.

AWAY FROM FOOTBALL, HIS BUSINESS INTERESTS RAN THE GAMUT FROM BEING CHAIRMAN OF *PORTSMOUTH* FOOTBALL CLUB TO OWNING A HOTEL AND BAR IN SPAIN. HE CO-AUTHORED FIVE NOVELS, CO-CREATED THE SUCCESSFUL TV DETECTIVE SERIES *"HAZELL"*, DEVISED A BOARD GAME AND RECORDED A COVER VERSION OF *ELVIS PRESLEY'S "I CAN DREAM"* THAT REACHED THE UK TOP 30 IN 2010.

1. WITH WHICH CLUB DID *TERRY VENABLES* WIN THE FA CUP AS A PLAYER AND LATER AS MANAGER?

2. WHICH OTHER NATIONAL TEAM DID *VENABLES* COACH?

3. WHICH EUROPEAN CLUB DID *VENABLES* GUIDE TO A LEAGUE TITLE IN THE 1984-85 SEASON?

JAN 7

EDEN HAZARD WAS BORN IN LA LOUVIÈRE, BELGIUM, ON JANUARY 7, 1991. BOTH HIS PARENTS WERE FOOTBALLERS -- HIS DAD PLAYED FOR **R.A.A. LOUVIÉROISE** IN THE BELGIAN SECOND DIVISION, AND HIS MOTHER WAS A STRIKER IN THE BELGIAN WOMEN'S FIRST DIVISION. **EDEN** SIGNED FOR FRENCH CLUB **LILLE** AT THE AGE OF 14 AND WAS A FIRST TEAM PLAYER BY THE TIME HE WAS 16. THE FIRST NON-FRENCH PLAYER TO WIN THE UNFP YOUNG PLAYER OF THE YEAR AWARD -- AND THE FIRST TO WIN IT TWICE -- HE WENT ON TO WIN CONSECUTIVE UNFP PLAYER OF THE YEAR AWARDS AND HELP **LILLE** WIN A LEAGUE AND CUP DOUBLE. HE SIGNED FOR **CHELSEA** IN 2012, AND IN SEVEN YEARS IN LONDON HE WON TWO PREMIER LEAGUE TITLES, THE FA CUP, THE LEAGUE CUP AND THE UEFA EUROPA LEAGUE. HE JOINED **REAL MADRID** IN 2019, WINNING LA LIGA IN HIS DEBUT SEASON.

1. NAME THE SIX MANAGERS UNDER WHOM **HAZARD** PLAYED AT **CHELSEA**.

2. HE CAPTAINED **BELGIUM** TO THIRD PLACE AT THE 2018 WORLD CUP, WHERE HE WON THE SILVER BALL. WHICH CLUB AND COUNTRY TEAMMATE WON THE GOLDEN GLOVE?

3. NAME THE SIX MANAGERS OF **BELGIUM** UNDER WHOM **HAZARD** HAS PLAYED.

JAN 8

ON JANUARY 8, 2004, FLAMBOYANT 5' 6" GOALKEEPER *JORGE CAMPOS* ANNOUNCED HIS RETIREMENT. DESPITE HIS LACK OF HEIGHT, HE PLAYED 130 TIMES FOR *MEXICO*, INCLUDING THE 1994 AND 1998 WORLD CUP CAMPAIGNS. RENOWNED FOR THE GARISH NEON JERSEYS THAT HE DESIGNED AND SPORTED, HE WAS ALSO AN ACCOMPLISHED STRIKER, AND WOULD OFTEN TRANSFER UPFIELD IN THE LATTER STAGES OF A GAME. *CAMPOS* PLAYED WITH A NUMBER OF PRIMERA DIVISIÓN CLUBS IN MEXICO, AND PLAYED IN THE FIRST THREE SEASONS OF THE MLS.

1. *CAMPOS* PLAYED TWO SEASONS WITH THE *LOS ANGELES GALAXY* -- WHICH OTHER MLS TEAM DID HE PLAY FOR?

2. WHICH GOALKEEPER PLAYED FOR *MEXICO* IN FIVE WORLD CUPS?

3. THE *MEXICO* NATIONAL TEAM IS NICKNAMED *"EL TRICOLOR"*. WITH WHICH NATIONAL SIDE WOULD YOU ASSOCIATE THE NICKNAME:

   A) *"LES FENNECS"* (THE DESERT FOXES)

   B) *"BAFANA BAFANA"* (THE BOYS)

   C) *"THE BLACK STARS"*

   D) *"SUPER EAGLES"*

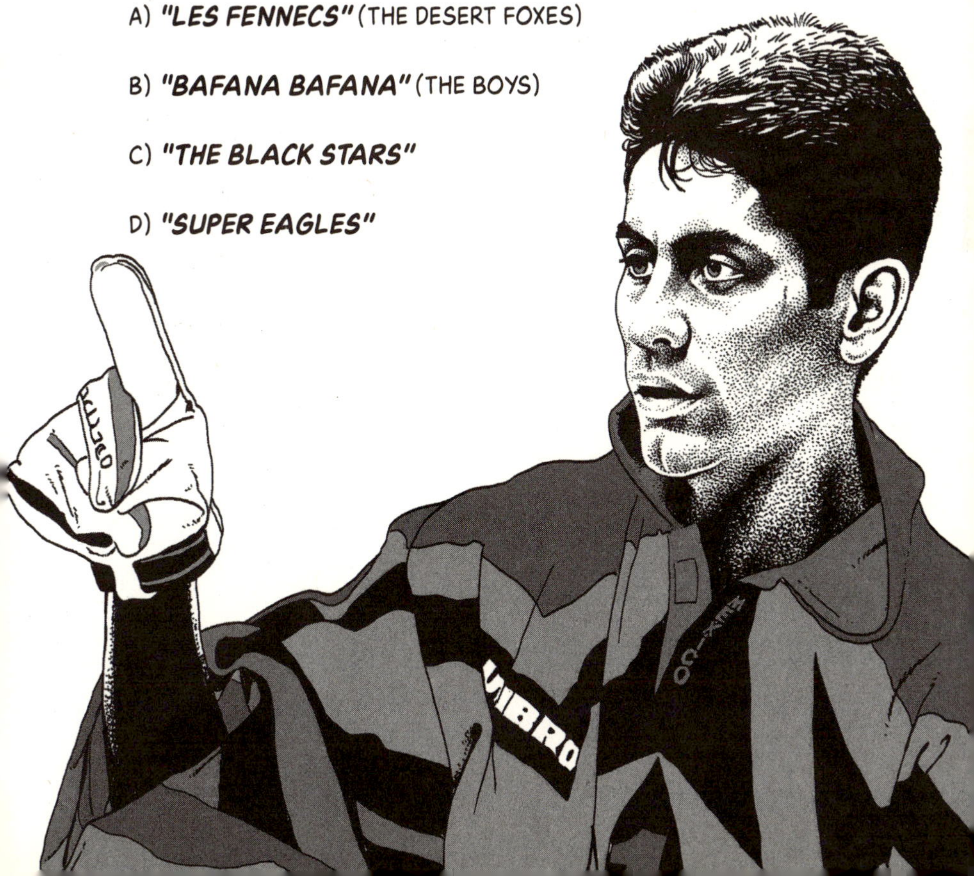

CLAUDIO PAUL CANIGGIA WAS BORN IN HENDERSON, ARGENTINA, ON JANUARY 9, 1967. HIS BLISTERING SPEED EARNED HIM THE NICKNAME *"EL HIJO DEL VIENTO" (THE SON OF THE WIND)* AND CULT HERO STATUS DURING A CAREER THAT SAW HIM PLAY FOR NINE CLUBS IN FIVE DIFFERENT COUNTRIES AND MAKE 50 APPEARANCES FOR **ARGENTINA**. HE WAS OUTSTANDING IN THE 1990 WORLD CUP BUT WAS SUSPENDED FOR THE FINAL, WHICH **ARGENTINA** LOST 1-0 TO GERMANY. A KEY PLAYER IN **ARGENTINA'S** 1994 WORLD CUP SIDE, HE WAS ABSENT FROM THE 1998 TOURNAMENT, PARTLY BECAUSE HE REFUSED TO CUT HIS FLOWING LOCKS TO MEET COACH **DANIEL PASSARELLA'S** DRESS CODE! HE WAS INCLUDED IN **MARCELO BIELSA'S** 2002 SQUAD AND, ALTHOUGH HE DIDN'T PLAY, HE MADE HISTORY WHEN HE RECEIVED A RED CARD FOR CURSING AT THE REFEREE FROM THE SIDELINES IN **ARGENTINA'S** LAST MATCH AGAINST **SWEDEN**, BECOMING THE FIRST PLAYER TO BE SENT OFF FROM THE BENCH IN A WORLD CUP!

NAME THREE OF THE CLUBS THAT **CANIGGIA** PLAYED FOR.

JAN 10 THE FIRST PLAYER TO SCORE IN SIX CONSECUTIVE EUROPEAN CHAMPIONS LEAGUE GAMES, **MAROUANE CHAMAKH** WAS BORN TO MOROCCAN PARENTS IN TONNEINS, FRANCE, ON JANUARY 10, 1984. HE ESTABLISHED HIS GOALSCORING PROWESS AT **BORDEAUX**, HELPING THE CLUB TO WIN A LEAGUE AND CUP DOUBLE IN 2009 AND WINNING THE CLUB'S 2010 PLAYER OF THE YEAR AWARD, BEFORE JOINING **ARSENAL**. ALTHOUGH HE PLAYED FOR **FRANCE** AT U-19 LEVEL, HE ELECTED TO PLAY FOR **MOROCCO**, MAKING HIS SENIOR INTERNATIONAL DEBUT AT THE AGE OF 19. HE PLAYED IN THREE AFRICA CUP OF NATIONS TOURNAMENTS, WINNING A RUNNERS-UP MEDAL IN 2004, AND EVENTUALLY WON 65 CAPS. FOLLOWING A SHORT LOAN SPELL WITH **WEST HAM UNITED**, HE SPENT THREE SEASONS AT **CRYSTAL PALACE**, BEFORE A BRIEF AND UNHAPPY SPELL AT **CARDIFF CITY**. HE RETIRED IN 2019 HAVING NOT PLAYED FOR ALMOST TWO AND A HALF YEARS.

NAME THE FORMER **BORDEAUX** PLAYER:

1. WON LEAGUE TITLES WITH **LEEDS UNITED** AND **MANCHESTER UNITED**.

2. THREE-TIME FIFA WORLD PLAYER OF THE YEAR AND WINNER OF THE BALLON D'OR.

3. REPLACED **LAURENT BLANC** AS **BORDEAUX** COACH IN 2010.

JAN 11

BORN IN CHESTER-LE-STREET, COUNTY DURHAM, ON JANUARY 11, 1957, **BRYAN ROBSON** CAPTAINED **ENGLAND** ON 65 OCCASIONS, SCORING 26 GOALS IN HIS 90 APPEARANCES. HE BEGAN HIS PLAYING CAREER AS AN APPRENTICE WITH **WEST BROMWICH ALBION** IN 1972 AND PROGRESSED THROUGH TO THE RANKS TO BECOME THE MOST EXPENSIVE PLAYER IN BRITISH FOOTBALL WHEN HE JOINED **MANCHESTER UNITED** IN 1981 FOR A TRANSFER FEE OF £1.5 MILLION. AN INSPIRATIONAL CAPTAIN FOR CLUB AND COUNTRY, IN 13 YEARS AT OLD TRAFFORD HIS TROPHY HAUL INCLUDED TWO LEAGUE TITLES, THREE FA CUPS, THE LEAGUE CUP, THE UEFA CUP WINNERS' CUP AND THE UEFA SUPER CUP. HE LEFT THE CLUB IN 1994 TO BECOME PLAYER/ MANAGER AT **MIDDLESBROUGH.**

1. NAME TWO OF THE TEAMS HE HAS SUBSEQUENTLY MANAGED.

2. **ROBSON** WAS ASSISTANT TO WHICH **ENGLAND** MANAGER BETWEEN 1994 AND 1996?

3. NAME TWO OF THE SIX MANAGERS THAT **ROBSON** WORKED UNDER AT **WEST BROMWICH ALBION.**

JAN 12

BORN IN SZCZECIN, POLAND, ON JANUARY 12, 1979, **GRZEGORZ RASIAK** BEGAN HIS CAREER IN THE POLISH LOWER LEAGUE WITH **WARTA POZNAŃ**, BEFORE PLAYING FOR A NUMBER OF BIGGER CLUBS, INCLUDING **DYSKOBOLIA GRODZISK WIELKOPOLSKI**. A 2004 TRANSFER TO ITALY'S **AC SIENA** FELL THROUGH AND HE MOVED TO ENGLAND TO JOIN **DERBY COUNTY**. HE WENT ON TO PLAY FOR **TOTTENHAM HOTSPUR, SOUTHAMPTON, BOLTON WANDERERS, WATFORD** AND **READING**, WITH VARYING DEGREES OF SUCCESS, BEFORE JOINING CYPRIOT SIDE **AEL LIMASSOL** IN 2010. HE ENDED HIS PLAYING CAREER BACK IN POLAND, AND WAS TOP SCORER AT HIS OLD CLUB, **WARTA POZNAŃ**, BEFORE RETIRING IN 2014. **RASIAK** WAS CAPPED 37 TIMES BY **POLAND**, SCORING 8 GOALS.

IDENTIFY THESE **POLAND** INTERNATIONALS WHO PLAYED IN ENGLAND:

1. GOALKEEPER WHO WON THE UEFA CHAMPIONS LEAGUE WITH **LIVERPOOL** IN 2005.

2. GOALKEEPER WHO JOINED **MANCHESTER UNITED** FROM **WEST BROMWICH ALBION** IN 2007, HE LATER PLAYED FOR **WATFORD, BRIGHTON & HOVE ALBION, WOLVERHAMPTON WANDERERS** AND **BIRMINGHAM CITY**.

3. ONE-TIME **MANCHESTER CITY** STAR WHO WAS KILLED IN A CAR CRASH IN SAN DIEGO IN 1989.

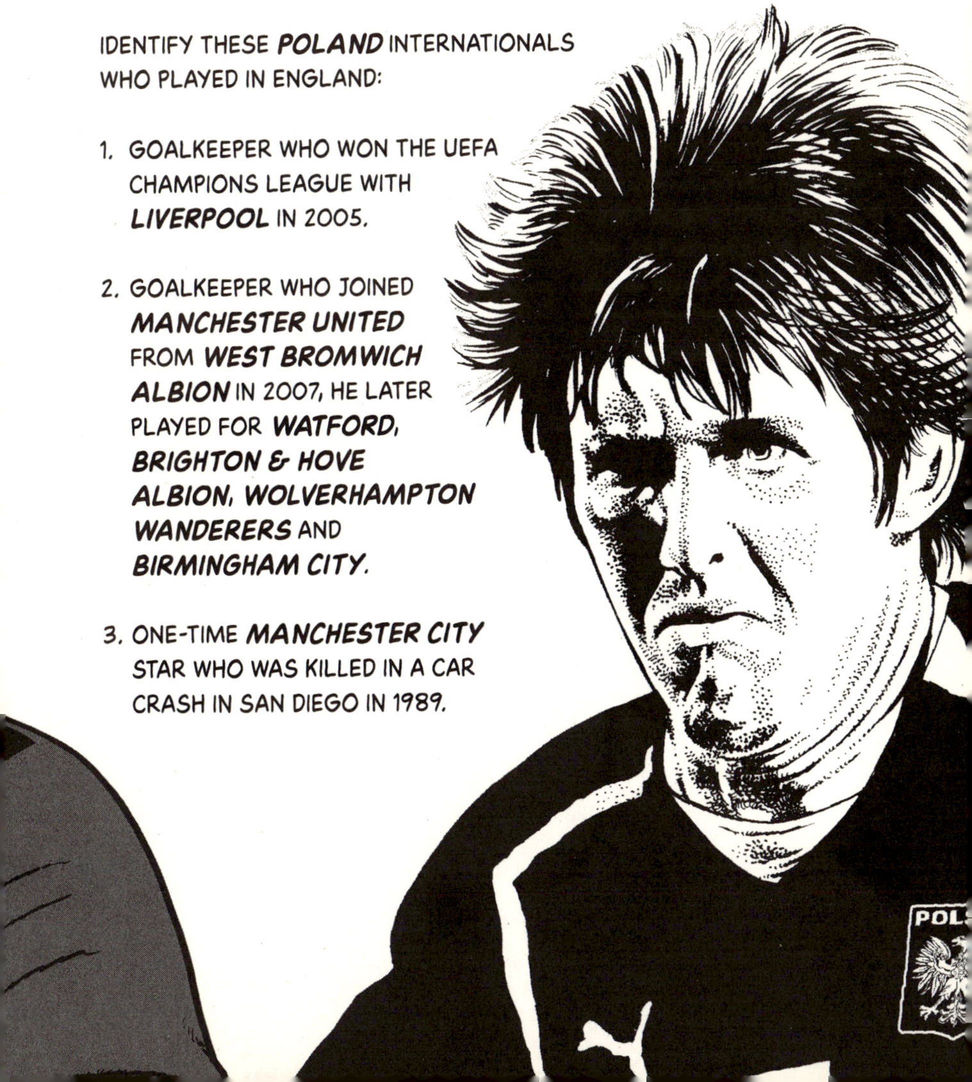

ON JANUARY 13, 1997, *MONACO* MANAGER *ARSÈNE WENGER* GAVE *THIERRY HENRY* HIS FIRST PROFESSIONAL CONTRACT. BY THEN, THE 19-YEAR-OLD WAS ALREADY A MAINSTAY OF THE TEAM, HAVING MADE HIS DEBUT IN 1994. *MONACO* WENT ON TO WIN THE LEAGUE TITLE THAT SEASON, AND IN JANUARY, 1999, HENRY JOINED *JUVENTUS* IN A £10.5 MILLION TRANSFER. A FEW MONTHS LATER, HE WAS REUNITED WITH *WENGER* AT *ARSENAL*, AND WENT ON TO CEMENT HIS PLACE IN CLUB LEGEND.

NAME THESE OTHER *MONACO* PLAYERS WHO WENT ON TO PLAY FOR *ARSENAL*:

1. SCORED THE THIRD GOAL IN *FRANCE'S* 1998 WORLD CUP FINAL VICTORY AND LATER PLAYED FOR *BARCELONA* AND *CHELSEA*.

2. WON TWO LEAGUE AND FA CUP DOUBLES WITH *ARSENAL* BEFORE BECOMING THE FIRST FRENCHMAN TO PLAY IN THE MLS WHEN HE SIGNED FOR *COLORADO RAPIDS*.

3. AFRICAN PLAYER OF THE YEAR, *TOGO* STRIKER WHOSE CLUBS INCLUDED *MANCHESTER CITY*, *TOTTENHAM HOTSPUR* AND *REAL MADRID*.

JAN 14

ON JANUARY 14, 1969, **SIR MATT BUSBY** ANNOUNCED THAT HE HAD DECIDED TO STEP ASIDE AS MANAGER OF **MANCHESTER UNITED** AT THE END OF THE SEASON. APPOINTED IN 1945, DURING HIS 24-YEAR REIGN **UNITED** WON THE FA CUP TWICE, THE LEAGUE FIVE TIMES AND, ON ONE OF THE MOST EMOTIONAL NIGHTS THE OLD WEMBLEY STADIUM EVER WITNESSED, BECAME THE FIRST ENGLISH SIDE TO WIN THE EUROPEAN CUP. IN 1958, RETURNING FROM A EUROPEAN CUP SEMI-FINAL IN YUGOSLAVIA, EIGHT OF **BUSBY'S** BRILLIANT YOUNG SIDE HAD BEEN KILLED WHEN THE PLANE BRINGING THEM BACK CRASHED ON TAKE-OFF AFTER REFUELLING IN MUNICH. **BUSBY** HIMSELF LAY AT DEATH'S DOOR FOR WEEKS, BUT HE SURVIVED AND WENT ON TO BUILD ANOTHER GREAT SIDE AROUND CRASH SURVIVOR **BOBBY CHARLTON**. TEN YEARS LATER, IN MAY, 1968, IT WAS INSPIRATIONAL CAPTAIN **CHARLTON** WHO, HAVING SCORED TWICE, FINALLY RAISED THE COVETED TROPHY WHEN **UNITED** BEAT **BENFICA** 4-1 IN THE FINAL. **BUSBY** JOINED THE BOARD OF DIRECTORS FOLLOWING HIS RETIREMENT, AND WAS EVENTUALLY MADE PRESIDENT IN 1982, TWELVE YEARS BEFORE HIS DEATH.

BUSBY WAS KNIGHTED IN 1969. NAME THE THREE MANAGERS OF THE **ENGLAND** TEAM WHO RECEIVED KNIGHTHOODS.

NAT LOFTHOUSE, THE BATTERING RAM FORWARD WHO SPENT HIS ENTIRE PLAYING CAREER WITH **BOLTON WANDERERS,** DIED ON JANUARY 15, 2011, AT THE AGE OF 84. HE SCORED 30 GOALS IN 33 APPEARANCES FOR **ENGLAND,** EARNING THE NICKNAME **"THE LION OF VIENNA"** AFTER ONE PARTICULARLY HEROIC PERFORMANCE AGAINST **AUSTRIA** IN 1952.

NAME THESE OTHER PLAYERS WHO PASSED AWAY IN 2011:

1. CAPTAINED **BRAZIL** AT THE 1982 WORLD CUP.

2. HUNGARIAN VOTED 1967 EUROPEAN FOOTBALLER OF THE YEAR.

3. MANAGER OF **SHEFFIELD UNITED** AND **WALES.**

JAN 16

AS A PLAYER, TWO-TIMES EUROPEAN FOOTBALLER OF THE YEAR *KEVIN KEEGAN* HAD SPENT THE FINAL TWO SEASONS OF HIS ILLUSTRIOUS CAREER WITH *NEWCASTLE UNITED*, LEADING THE CLUB BACK INTO THE TOP FLIGHT. ON HIS RETIREMENT IN 1984, HE LEFT THE FIELD BY HELICOPTER, STILL DRESSED IN HIS KIT! EIGHT YEARS LATER, HE RETURNED TO THE CLUB AS MANAGER, AND ONCE MORE PERFORMED MIRACLES! IN HIS ABSENCE, *NEWCASTLE* HAD BEEN RELEGATED AGAIN -- *"KING KEVIN"* INSPIRED THE CLUB TO PROMOTION AND THEN TWO CONSECUTIVE SECOND PLACE FINISHES IN THE PREMIER LEAGUE, BEFORE RESIGNING IN 1997. ELEVEN YEARS LATER, ON JANUARY 16, 2008, *KEEGAN* MADE A SURPRISE RETURN TO THE POST. UNFORTUNATELY, HIS SECOND PERIOD IN CHARGE ENDED IN ACRIMONY AFTER JUST NINE MONTHS.

1. NAME THE THREE OTHER TEAMS THAT *KEVIN KEEGAN* MANAGED.

2. NAME THREE OTHER TEAMS HE PLAYED FOR.

3. NAME FIVE OF THE TEN MEN WHO MANAGED *NEWCASTLE UNITED* BETWEEN **KEEGAN'S** TWO SPELLS IN CHARGE.

JAN 17

MEXICO'S LEGENDARY GOALSCORER **CUAUHTÉMOC BLANCO** WAS RENOWNED FOR A MOVE DUBBED THE **"CUAUHTEMIÑA",** IN WHICH HE GRIPPED THE BALL BETWEEN BOTH FEET AND LEAPED TO AVOID A TACKLE, BEFORE RELEASING THE BALL IN THE AIR AND CONTINUING HIS ATTACKING RUN! BORN IN MEXICO CITY ON JANUARY 17, 1973, HE MADE HIS DEBUT FOR **CLUB AMÉRICA** IN 1993 AND HIS INTERNATIONAL DEBUT 14 MONTHS LATER. HE JOINED SPAIN'S **REAL VALLADOLID** ON LOAN IN 2000, BUT RETURNED TO **AMÉRICA** TWO SEASONS LATER. HE ALSO SPENT TWO SEASONS IN THE UNITED STATES WITH THE **CHICAGO FIRE**. THE FIRST MEXICAN TO SCORE IN THREE WORLD CUPS, HE SCORED 39 GOALS IN 120 APPEARANCES FOR HIS COUNTRY. HE ENTERED POLITICS AFTER RETIRING FROM THE SPORT, AND IN 2018 WAS ELECTED GOVERNOR OF THE STATE OF MORELOS.

1. WHICH BALLON D'OR WINNER AND FIFA WORLD PLAYER OF THE YEAR WAS ELECTED PRESIDENT OF LIBERIA IN 2018?

2. WHO SERVED IN THE BELGIAN SENATE BEFORE RETURNING TO FOOTBALL, AND HAS SINCE MANAGED **BELGIUM, IVORY COAST** AND **IRAN**?

3. WHICH ITALIAN GREAT, KNOWN AS **"THE GOLDEN BOY"** IN HIS PLAYING DAYS, SERVED IN HIS COUNTRY'S PARLIAMENT BEFORE BECOMING A MEMBER OF THE EUROPEAN PARLIAMENT?

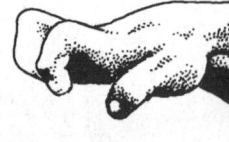

JAN 18

IVÁN "BAM BAM" ZAMORANO WAS BORN IN MAIPÙ, CHILE, ON JANUARY 18, 1967. HE BEGAN AT *TRASADINO*, BEFORE MOVING INTO THE TOP FLIGHT AT *COBRESAL*. HE LAUNCHED HIS EUROPEAN CAREER IN SWITZERLAND AT *ST. GALLEN* IN 1988. OVER THE NEXT DOZEN SEASONS HE WAS OUTSTANDING FOR *SEVILLA* AND *REAL MADRID* IN SPAIN, AND IN ITALY FOR *INTERNAZIONALE*. FOLLOWING A SEASON IN MEXICO WITH *CLUB AMÉRICA*, HE ENDED HIS PLAYING DAYS BACK HOME IN CHILE WITH *COLO-COLO*.

ZAMORANO WAS TOP SCORER IN SPAIN'S LA LIGA IN 1995 WITH 31 GOALS. IDENTIFY THESE OTHER CENTRAL OR SOUTH AMERICANS WHO TOPPED LA LIGA SCORING CHARTS:

1. MEXICAN SUPERSTAR WHO TOPPED THE CHARTS ONCE WITH *ATLÉTICO MADRID* AND FOUR TIMES WITH *REAL MADRID*.

2. *ARGENTINA'S* 1978 WORLD CUP STAR WHO TOPPED THE CHARTS TWICE WITH *VALENCIA*.

3. *BRAZIL* STAR WHO ACHIEVED THE FEAT WITH *BARCELONA* AND *REAL MADRID*.

4. URUGUAYAN WHO WON THE PREMIER LEAGUE WITH *MANCHESTER UNITED* AND THE GOLDEN BALL AT THE 2010 WORLD CUP, HE TOPPED THE CHARTS WITH *VILLAREAL* AND *ATLÉTICO MADRID*.

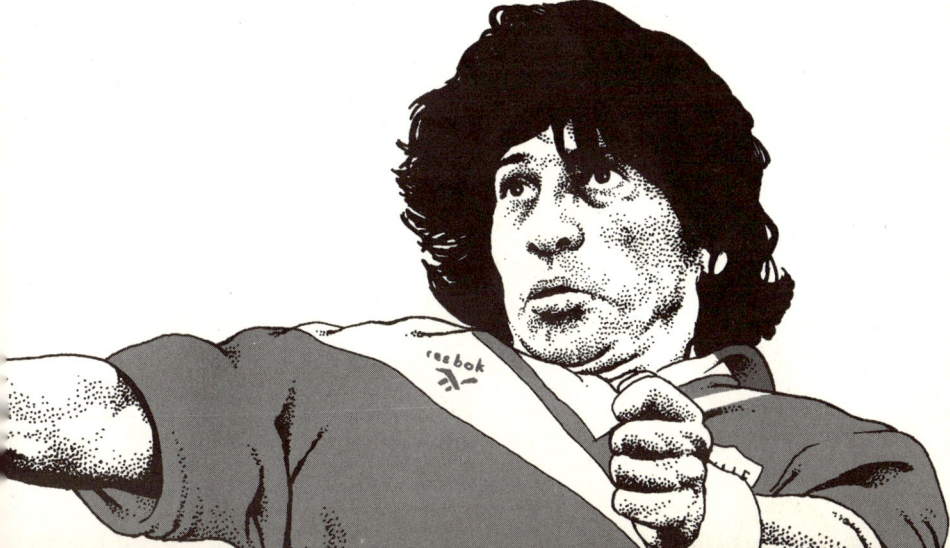

JAN 19

THE SON OF A CANADIAN SEMI-PROFESSIONAL ICE HOCKEY PLAYER, *LANDON DONOVAN'S* CAREER VERY NEARLY ENDED BEFORE IT HAD REALLY STARTED. WHEN HE WAS 17 AND PART OF *US SOCCER'S* YOUTH DEVELOPMENT RESIDENCY PROGRAMME IN FLORIDA, HE NARROWLY ESCAPED HAVING HIS FEET BITTEN BY AN ALLIGATOR WHILE PLAYING A ROUND OF GOLF WITH HIS COACHES! HAVING REPRESENTED THE *UNITED STATES* AT A NUMBER OF YOUTH LEVELS, HE MADE HIS DEBUT FOR THE SENIOR TEAM IN 2000. ON JANUARY 19, 2008, HIS PENALTY AGAINST *SWEDEN* MADE HIM THE NATIONAL TEAM'S ALL-TIME LEADING GOALSCORER.

1. NAME THREE TEAMS THAT *LANDON* PLAYED FOR.

2. *LANDON* IS ONE OF ONLY THREE *UNITED STATES* PLAYERS TO SCORE AT MULTIPLE WORLD CUP TOURNAMENTS -- WHO ARE THE OTHER TWO?

3. IN 2016, *LANDON* BECAME A PART-OWNER OF WHICH ENGLISH PREMIER LEAGUE CLUB?

ON JANUARY 20, 2006, AFTER JUST A HANDFUL OF GAMES AT SENIOR LEVEL, *THEO WALCOTT* BECAME THE MOST EXPENSIVE 16-YEAR-OLD IN BRITISH FOOTBALL HISTORY WHEN HE MOVED FROM *SOUTHAMPTON* TO *ARSENAL*, FOR A FEE THAT WOULD EVENTUALLY END UP AT £9 MILLION AFTER ADD-ON CLAUSES. THAT SUMMER, *ENGLAND* MANAGER *SVEN-GÖRAN ERIKSSON* STUNNED THE FOOTBALL WORLD BY NAMING *WALCOTT*, WHO HAD NOT YET EVEN MADE HIS *ARSENAL* DEBUT, IN HIS WORLD CUP SQUAD.

1. WHICH 17-YEAR-OLD WAS SIGNED BY *ARSENAL* FOR £12 MILLION FROM *SOUTHAMPTON* IN 2011?

2. WHICH WORLD CUP WINNER LEFT *ARSENAL* FOR *SOUTHAMPTON* IN 1976?

3. WHICH FORMER *SOUTHAMPTON* PLAYER SCORED 42 GOALS IN 41 LEAGUE GAMES TO WIN A CHAMPIONSHIP WITH *ARSENAL* ?

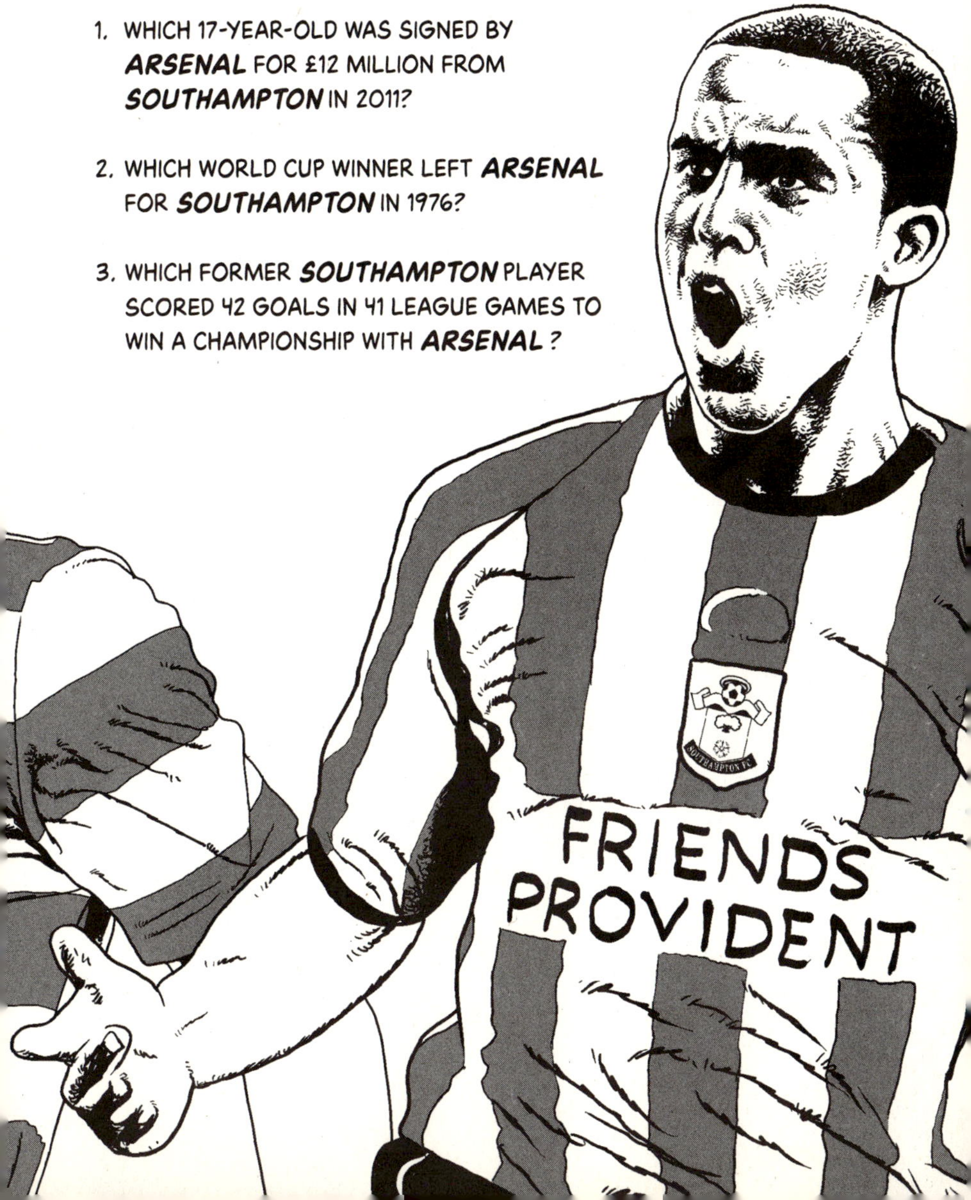

TWO OF THE GROUP OF YOUNG PLAYERS DUBBED **"FERGIE'S FLEDGLINGS"** SHARE A BIRTHDAY. **NICKY BUTT** WAS BORN ON JANUARY 21, 1975. PHIL NEVILLE WAS BORN TWO YEARS LATER. TOGETHER WITH **DAVID BECKHAM**, **PAUL SCHOLES**, **RYAN GIGGS** AND **PHIL'S** BROTHER, **GARY**, THEY WERE OUTSTANDING IN **MANCHESTER UNITED'S** 1996 DOUBLE-WINNING SIDE AND WENT ON TO BRING UNPRECEDENTED SUCCESS TO **ALEX FERGUSON'S** TEAM.

1. NAME ONE OF THE THREE CLUBS THAT **NICKY BUTT** PLAYED FOR AFTER LEAVING **UNITED**.

2. **PHIL NEVILLE** JOINED WHICH CLUB AFTER LEAVING **UNITED** IN 2005?

3. WHAT IS THE NAME OF THE CLUB THAT IS PART-OWNED BY ALL SIX OF **"FERGIE'S FLEDGLINGS"**?

JAN 22 ONE OF THE GREATEST PLAYERS THAT THE ASIAN GAME HAS EVER PRODUCED, *HIDETOSHI NAKATA* WAS BORN IN KOFU, IN JAPAN'S YAMANASHI PREFECTURE, ON JANUARY 22, 1977. TWICE NAMED ASIAN FOOTBALLER OF THE YEAR, HE SPENT MOST OF HIS CAREER IN ITALY, WHERE HE WON A SCUDETTO WITH *ROMA*, A COPPA ITALIA WITH *PARMA*, AND ALSO PLAYED FOR *PERUGIA*, *BOLOGNA* AND *FIORENTINA*, BEFORE ENDING HIS CAREER WITH A LOAN SPELL IN ENGLAND AT *BOLTON WANDERERS*. *NAKATA* REPRESENTED *JAPAN* AT NUMEROUS LEVELS, EVENTUALLY EARNING 77 CAPS AND PLAYING IN THREE WORLD CUP TOURNAMENTS AND TWO OLYMPICS.

IDENTIFY THESE ASIAN FOOTBALLER OF THE YEAR WINNERS:

1. CHINESE DEFENDER WHOSE CLUBS INCLUDED *CRYSTAL PALACE*, *DUNDEE* AND *CARDIFF CITY*.

2. IRANIAN LEGEND WHOSE 109 GOALS MADE HIM INTERNATIONAL FOOTBALL'S ALL-TIME LEADING GOALSCORER.

3. JAPANESE MIDFIELDER WHO WON THE 2002 UEFA CUP WITH *FEYENOORD*.

JAN 23

BORN IN BEDUM, NETHERLANDS, ON JANUARY 23, 1984, *ARJEN ROBBEN* BURST ONTO THE SCENE AS A TEENAGER WITH LOCAL CLUB *GRONINGEN*. NAMED THE CLUB'S PLAYER OF THE YEAR IN HIS FIRST FULL SEASON, HE WAS SNAPPED UP BY *PSV EINDHOVEN* IN 2002, WINNING A LEAGUE TITLE AND THE NETHERLANDS' YOUNG PLAYER OF THE YEAR AWARD THAT SEASON. HE WENT ON TO WIN TWO LEAGUE TITLES AND FA CUP AND LEAGUE CUP HONOURS WITH *CHELSEA*, AND LA LIGA AND SUPERCOPA DE ESPAÑA WITH *REAL MADRID*, BEFORE JOINING *BAYERN MUNICH* IN 2009. IN 10 SEASONS HE WON 20 TROPHIES, INCLUDING EIGHT LEAGUE TITLES AND THE UEFA CHAMPIONS LEAGUE, AND WAS NAMED GERMAN FOOTBALLER OF THE YEAR. HE RETURNED TO *GRONINGEN* IN 2020.

ROBBEN'S 96 APPEARANCES FOR THE *NETHERLANDS* MAKE HIM THE NINTH MOST-CAPPED PLAYER IN HIS COUNTRY'S HISTORY. HOW MANY OF THE EIGHT PLAYERS ABOVE HIM, ALL OF WHOM PLAYED MORE THAN 100 TIMES FOR THE DUTCH TEAM, CAN YOU NAME?

JAN 24

LUIS ALBERTO SUÁREZ DIAZ WAS BORN ON JANUARY 24, 1987, IN SALTO, URUGUAY, AND LIVED IN MONTEVIDEO FROM THE AGE OF 7. WHEN HE WAS 11, HE WAS SELECTED TO JOIN A URUGUAYAN YOUTH TEAM IN A TRAINING CAMP IN ARGENTINA, BUT HAD TO DROP OUT BECAUSE HIS FAMILY COULDN'T AFFORD THE EXPENSE. HE WENT ON TO BECOME ONE OF THE GREAT STRIKERS -- WINNING SOME OF THE GAME'S HIGHEST HONOURS, INCLUDING A UEFA CHAMPIONS LEAGUE AND A COPA AMÉRICA -- BUT A MAGNET FOR CONTROVERSY. HE WAS SENT OFF ON HIS INTERNATIONAL DEBUT IN 2007, EARNED A RED CARD AT THE 2010 WORLD CUP, WITH HIS DELIBERATE HANDBALL ON THE LINE IN EXTRA TIME OF THE QUARTER-FINAL, AND HAS RECEIVED LENGTHY BANS FOR BITING OPPONENTS!

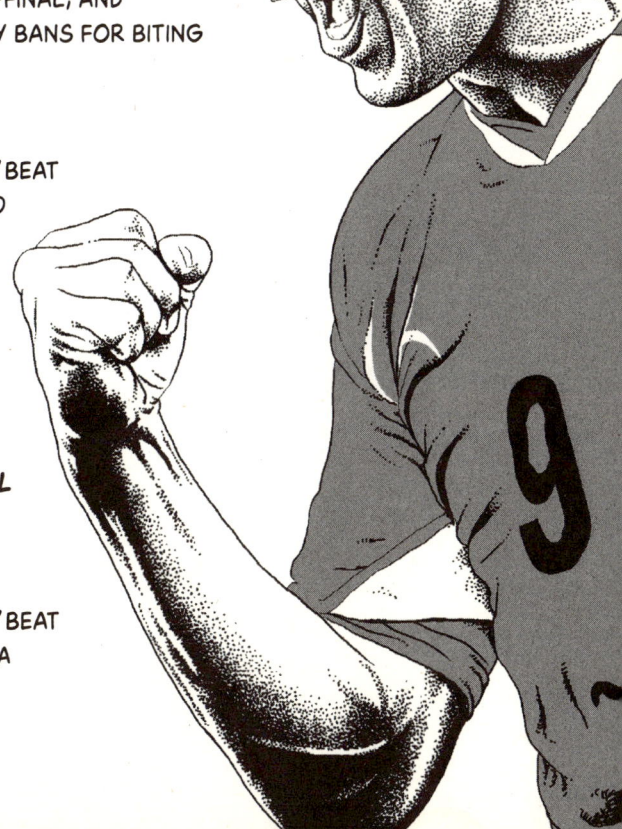

1. WHO DID **URUGUAY** BEAT IN THAT 2010 WORLD CUP QUARTER-FINAL?

2. NAME THREE CLUBS THAT **LUIS SUÁREZ** HAS PLAYED FOR SINCE LEAVING **NACIONAL MONTEVIDEO** FOR EUROPE IN 2006.

3. WHO DID **URUGUAY** BEAT 3-0 IN THE 2011 COPA AMÉRICA FINAL?

JAN 25

BORN ***ROBSON DE SOUZ***A IN SÃO VICENTE, SÃO PAULO STATE, BRAZIL, ON JANUARY 25, 1984, ***ROBINHO*** WAS 18 YEARS OLD WHEN HE BROKE INTO THE ***SANTOS*** FIRST TEAM AND HELPED THE CLUB WIN ITS FIRST LEAGUE TITLE SINCE 1968. HE INSPIRED ***SANTOS*** TO ANOTHER CHAMPIONSHIP IN 2004, BEFORE SIGNING FOR ***REAL MADRID***, WITH WHOM HE WON TWO LEAGUE TITLES, BEFORE MAKING A SENSATIONAL SWITCH TO ***MANCHESTER CITY*** IN 2008. HE FAILED TO SETTLE IN ENGLAND AND RETURNED TO ***SANTOS*** ON LOAN IN 2010, HELPING THE CLUB TO WIN THE COPA BRASIL FOR THE FIRST TIME IN HISTORY. LATER THAT YEAR, HE SIGNED FOR ***AC MILAN***, WINNING THE LEAGUE AND SUPERCOPPA ITALIANA IN HIS FIRST YEAR WITH THE CLUB, BUT BY 2014 HE WAS BACK ON LOAN AT ***SANTOS***. AFTER WINNING TITLES IN CHINA AND TURKEY, HE JOINED ***SANTOS*** ONCE MORE IN 2020.

IDENTIFY THESE FORMER ***SANTOS*** PLAYERS:

1. HAS SINCE WON MULTIPLE HONOURS WITH ***BARCELONA*** AND ***PARIS SAINT-GERMAIN***.

2. CHAMPIONS LEAGUE WINNER HAS WON TITLES WITH ***PORTO***, ***REAL MADRID***, ***MANCHESTER CITY*** AND ***JUVENTUS***.

3. ***ROBINHO'S*** TEAMMATE AT ***MANCHESTER CITY*** AFTER WINNING TITLES WITH ***SHAKHTAR DONETSK***.

BEFORE ESTABLISHING HIMSELF AS A TOP-FLIGHT COACH, *JOSÉ MOURINHO* WORKED AS A COACH AND TRANSLATOR FOR *SIR BOBBY ROBSON* AT *SPORTING CLUBE DE PORTUGAL* AND *PORTO* IN PORTUGAL, THEN AT *BARCELONA*. HE CONTINUED TO WORK IN THE SAME CAPACITY FOR *ROBSON'S* SUCCESSOR, *LOUIS VAN GAAL*. BORN ON JANUARY 26, 1963, IN SETÚBAL, THE SON OF A *PORTUGAL* INTERNATIONAL FOOTBALLER, *MOURINHO* ENJOYED A SHORT-LIVED CAREER AS A PLAYER BEFORE PURSUING A FUTURE IN COACHING.

WHO DID *JOSÉ MOURINHO* SUCCEED AS COACH OF:

1. *CHELSEA* (2004)

2. *INTERNAZIONALE* (2008)

3. *REAL MADRID* (2010)

4. *CHELSEA* (2013)

5. *MANCHESTER UNITED* (2016)

6. *TOTTENHAM HOTSPUR* (2019)

SOUTH KOREA SUPERSTAR **AHN JUNG-HWAN** WAS BORN IN PAJU, GYEONGGI, ON JANUARY 27, 1976. AFTER STARTING HIS CAREER WITH **BUSAN DAEWOO ROYALS** AND **BUSAN ICONS**, AND BEING NAMED 1999 K-LEAGUE PLAYER OF THE YEAR, HE JOINED ITALY'S **PERUGIA** IN 2000. INCREDIBLY, AFTER SCORING THE GOAL THAT KNOCKED **ITALY** OUT OF THE 2002 WORLD CUP AND SENT **SOUTH KOREA** INTO THE SECOND ROUND, **AHN'S** CONTRACT WAS CANCELLED BY **PERUGIA'S** IRATE OWNER! HE WENT ON TO PLAY FOR TEAMS IN JAPAN, FRANCE AND GERMANY, BEFORE RETURNING TO SOUTH KOREAN FOOTBALL AFTER PLAYING AND SCORING IN THE 2006 WORLD CUP. HE FINISHED HIS PLAYING CAREER WITH A TWO-YEAR SPELL IN CHINA.

IDENTIFY THESE OTHER **SOUTH KOREA** INTERNATIONALS:

1. THE FIRST SOUTH KOREAN TO SCORE IN THREE CONSECUTIVE WORLD CUPS, IN 2009 HE BECAME THE FIRST ASIAN PLAYER TO APPEAR IN A UEFA CHAMPIONS LEAGUE FINAL.

2. MOVED FROM **BAYER LEVERKUSEN** AND BECAME FIRST THE ASIAN PLAYER IN HISTORY TO SCORE MORE THAN 50 PREMIER LEAGUE GOALS.

3. ONCE DESCRIBED AS THE *"BEST LEFT-BACK IN HOLLAND"* BY **MARTIN JOL**, HE WON TWO LEAGUE TITLES WITH **PSV EINDHOVEN** AND A LEAGUE CUP WITH **TOTTENHAM HOTSPUR**.

JAN 28

GIANLUIGI BUFFON WAS BORN IN CARRARA ON JANUARY 28, 1978. HIS MOTHER WAS A DISCUS THROWER, HIS FATHER WAS A WEIGHTLIFTER, HIS TWO SISTERS PLAYED VOLLEYBALL AND HIS UNCLE PLAYED BASKETBALL. HE MADE HIS SENIOR DEBUT FOR ***PARMA*** IN 1995 AT THE AGE OF 17, GOING ON TO WIN THE UEFA CUP IN 1999. HE JOINED ***JUVENTUS*** IN 2001 IN A £32.6 MILLION TRANSFER, A WORLD RECORD FEE FOR A GOALKEEPER, AND HAS WON TEN SERIE A TITLES TO DATE. AT THE AGE OF 19, A YEAR AFTER WINNING THE 1996 UEFA UNDER-21 EUROPEAN CHAMPIONSHIP WITH ***ITALY***, HE MADE HIS FULL INTERNATIONAL DEBUT. A MEMBER OF THE 2006 WORLD CUP-WINNING TEAM, HIS 176 CAPS MAKE HIM ***ITALY'S*** MOST-CAPPED PLAYER.

1. NAME ONE OF THE THREE OTHER GOALKEEPERS WHO WON WORLD CUPS WITH ***ITALY***.

2. ***BUFFON*** EARNED A LIGUE 1 TITLE DURING A SEASON-LONG SOJOURN WITH WHICH CLUB IN 2018-19?

3. HE REPRESENTED HIS COUNTRY AT FIVE WORLD CUPS -- NAME ANOTHER PLAYER TO ACHIEVE THAT FEAT.

JAN 29 BORN IN THE JACAREZINHO AREA OF RIO DE JANEIRO ON JANUARY 29, 1966, **ROMÁRIO** FOUND EARLY SUCCESS WITH **VASCO DA GAMA**, BEFORE SIGNING FOR **PSV EINDHOVEN**, WITH WHOM HE WON THREE LEAGUE TITLES IN FIVE YEARS. HE WON LA LIGA IN HIS FIRST SEASON WITH **BARCELONA**, FINISHING TOP SCORER WITH 30 GOALS IN 33 GAMES. SUBSEQUENT TRAVELS TOOK HIM TO CLUBS IN SPAIN, QATAR, THE USA AND AUSTRALIA AND HE RETURNED TO **VASCO DA GAMA** THREE TIMES. AT INTERNATIONAL LEVEL, HE SCORED 56 GOALS IN 70 GAMES, INCLUDING FIVE AT THE 1994 WORLD CUP THAT EARNED HIM THE GOLDEN BALL AND HELPED WIN A FOURTH WORLD CUP FOR **BRAZIL**.

AT WHICH CLUB DID **ROMÁRIO** PLAY UNDER THESE COACHES:

1. **SIR BOBBY ROBSON**

2. **JOHAN CRUYFF**

3. **CLAUDIO RANIERI**

JAN 30

DIMITAR BERBATOV WAS BORN IN BLAGOEVGRAD, BULGARIA, ON JANUARY 30, 1981. THE SON OF A PROFESSIONAL FOOTBALLER, HE BEGAN HIS CAREER AT LOCAL CLUB **PIRIN BLAGOEVGRAD**, BEFORE JOINING HIS DAD'S OLD CLUB, **CSKA SOFIA**, AT THE AGE OF 17. HE WON THE BULGARIAN CUP IN HIS FIRST SEASON AND SCORED 14 GOALS IN 27 LEAGUE GAMES IN HIS SECOND SEASON. HAVING MADE HIS DEBUT FOR **BULGARIA** AT THE AGE OF 18, HE HOLDS HIS COUNTRY'S ALL-TIME GOALSCORING RECORD OF 48 GOALS.

1. WHILE PLAYING FOR **MANCHESTER UNITED**, **BERBATOV** WON THE 2010-11 PREMIER LEAGUE GOLDEN BOOT, AN AWARD HE SHARED WITH WHICH OTHER PLAYER?

2. **BERBATOV** WON THE BULGARIAN FOOTBALLER OF THE YEAR SEVEN TIMES, BREAKING THE RECORD OF FIVE SET BY WHICH LEGEND?

3. NAME TWO OTHER CLUBS THAT **BERBATOV** PLAYED FOR.

JAN 31 THE 2011 WINTER TRANSFER DEADLINE WINDOW CLOSED ON JANUARY 31 WITH *LIVERPOOL* DOING SOME RECORD-BREAKING BUSINESS. ON THE DAY THE CLUB SOLD STRIKER *FERNANDO TORRES* TO *CHELSEA* FOR AN UNDISCLOSED FEE -- REPORTED TO BE A BRITISH TRANSFER RECORD OF £50 MILLION -- *LIVERPOOL* MANAGER *KENNY DALGLISH* MADE *AJAX* FORWARD *LUIS SUÁREZ* THE CLUB'S MOST EXPENSIVE PLAYER. A FEW HOURS LATER, THAT RECORD WAS BROKEN WITH THE SIGNING OF *NEWCASTLE UNITED* STRIKER *ANDY CARROLL* FOR £35 MILLION.

IDENTIFY THESE OTHER SIGNINGS FROM THE 2011 JANUARY WINDOW:

1. *ENGLAND* INTERNATIONAL JOINED *WEST HAM UNITED* ON LOAN FROM *MANCHESTER CITY.*

2. NORWEGIAN STRIKER, A LEAGUE TITLE WINNER IN FRANCE AND SPAIN, JOINED *STOKE CITY* ON LOAN FROM *ASTON VILLA.*

3. *GHANA* STAR JOINED *SUNDERLAND* FROM *INTERNAZIONALE.*

FEBRUARY

FEB 1

THE FIRST PLAYER TO SCORE TWO HAT-TRICKS IN DIFFERENT WORLD CUPS, *GABRIEL BATISTUTA* WAS BORN IN RECONQUISTA, SANTA FE, ARGENTINA, ON FEBRUARY 1, 1969. THE PROLIFIC STRIKER BEGAN HIS CAREER WITH *NEWELL'S OLD BOYS*, BEFORE MOVING ON TO *RIVER PLATE* AND THEN THEIR ARCH-RIVALS, *BOCA JUNIORS*. FOLLOWING HIS PERFORMANCES WITH THE *ARGENTINA* TEAM THAT WON THE 1991 COPA AMÉRICA, HE WAS SIGNED BY *FIORENTINA*. "BATIGOL" BECAME A LEGEND IN ITALY, SETTING THE *FIORENTINA* SCORING RECORD OF 207 GOALS IN HIS 333 APPEARANCES, BEFORE JOINING *ROMA*, WITH WHOM HE WON THE SCUDETTO. LATER, FOLLOWING A LOAN SPELL AT *INTERNAZIONALE*, HE ENDED HIS PLAYING CAREER IN QATAR WITH *AL-ARABI*.

1. HE IS *ARGENTINA'S* ALL-TIME TOP SCORER AT THE WORLD CUP WITH 10 GOALS -- WHICH PLAYER HOLDS THE RECORD OF 6 GOALS SCORED FOR *ARGENTINA* IN A SINGLE WORLD CUP TOURNAMENT?

2. IN 2016, WHO SURPASSED *BATISTUTA'S ARGENTINA* GOALSCORING RECORD OF 54 GOALS IN 77 GAMES?

3. *BATISTUTA* PLAYED IN THREE WORLD CUPS -- WHICH THREE *ARGENTINA* PLAYERS APPEARED IN FOUR TOURNAMENTS?

BORN IN BARCELONA, ON FEBRUARY 2, 1987, **GERARD PIQUÉ** CAME THROUGH THE YOUTH RANKS AT **BARCELONA** BEFORE JOINING **MANCHESTER UNITED** IN 2004. ALTHOUGH HE ONLY PLAYED IN A HANDFUL OF GAMES, HE WON PREMIER LEAGUE AND UEFA CHAMPIONS LEAGUE MEDALS BEFORE REJOINING **BARCELONA** IN 2008. THAT FIRST SEASON BROUGHT A HISTORIC TREBLE, WITH LA LIGA AND COPA DEL REY TRIUMPHS FOLLOWED BY A VICTORY OVER **MANCHESTER UNITED** IN THE UEFA CHAMPIONS LEAGUE FINAL. HE HAS SINCE GONE ON TO WIN TWO MORE CHAMPIONS LEAGUES AND A HOST OF DOMESTIC HONOURS. A 2010 WORLD CUP AND 2012 EUROPEAN CHAMPIONSHIP WINNER, HE MADE 102 APPEARANCES FOR **SPAIN** AND RETIRED FROM THE NATIONAL TEAM IN 2018.

1. DURING HIS TIME WITH **MANCHESTER UNITED**, **PIQUÉ** SPENT TIME ON LOAN WITH WHICH SPANISH CLUB?

2. HE ALSO PLAYS FOR WHICH OTHER NATIONAL TEAM, WHICH REPRESENTS AN AREA OF NORTHEASTERN SPAIN?

3. **PIQUÉ** HAS TWO CHILDREN WITH WHICH COLOMBIAN POP STAR?

FEB 3

ONE OF THE GREATEST DEFENDERS THAT AUSTRIA HAS EVER PRODUCED, *BRUNO PEZZEY* WAS BORN IN LAUTERACH, ON FEBRUARY 3, 1955. A YOUTH TEAM PLAYER WITH *FC LAUTERACH*, HE STARTED HIS PROFESSIONAL CAREER AT *FC VORARLBERG*, BEFORE MOVING TO *WACKER INNSBRUCK* IN 1974. HE WON TWO LEAGUE TITLES AND THE AUSTRIAN CUP, BEFORE MOVING ON TO GERMANY'S *EINTRACHT FRANKFURT* IN 1978, WHERE HE ADDED THE UEFA CUP AND GERMAN CUP TO HIS HAUL. HE PLAYED FOR FOUR YEARS AT *WERDER BREMEN*, BEFORE RETURNING TO AUSTRIA IN 1987 TO WIN TWO LEAGUE TITLES AND AN AUSTRIAN CUP WITH *WAROVSKI TIROL*. HE MADE 84 APPEARANCES FOR *AUSTRIA*, REPRESENTING HIS COUNTRY AT THE 1978 AND 1982 WORLD CUPS.

BRUNO PEZZEY DIED OF HEART FAILURE IN 1994, JUST WEEKS SHORT OF HIS 40TH BIRTHDAY, LEAVING BEHIND A WIFE AND TWO DAUGHTERS. IDENTIFY THESE OTHER PLAYERS WHO PASSED AWAY IN 1994:

1. *COLOMBIA* INTERNATIONAL WHO WAS ASSASSINATED FOLLOWING AN OWN GOAL AT THE 1994 WORLD CUP.

2. LEGENDARY *MANCHESTER UNITED* MANAGER, DEAD AT THE AGE OF 84.

3. CAPTAIN OF *WOLVES* AND *ENGLAND*, WHO LATER MANAGED *ARSENAL*.

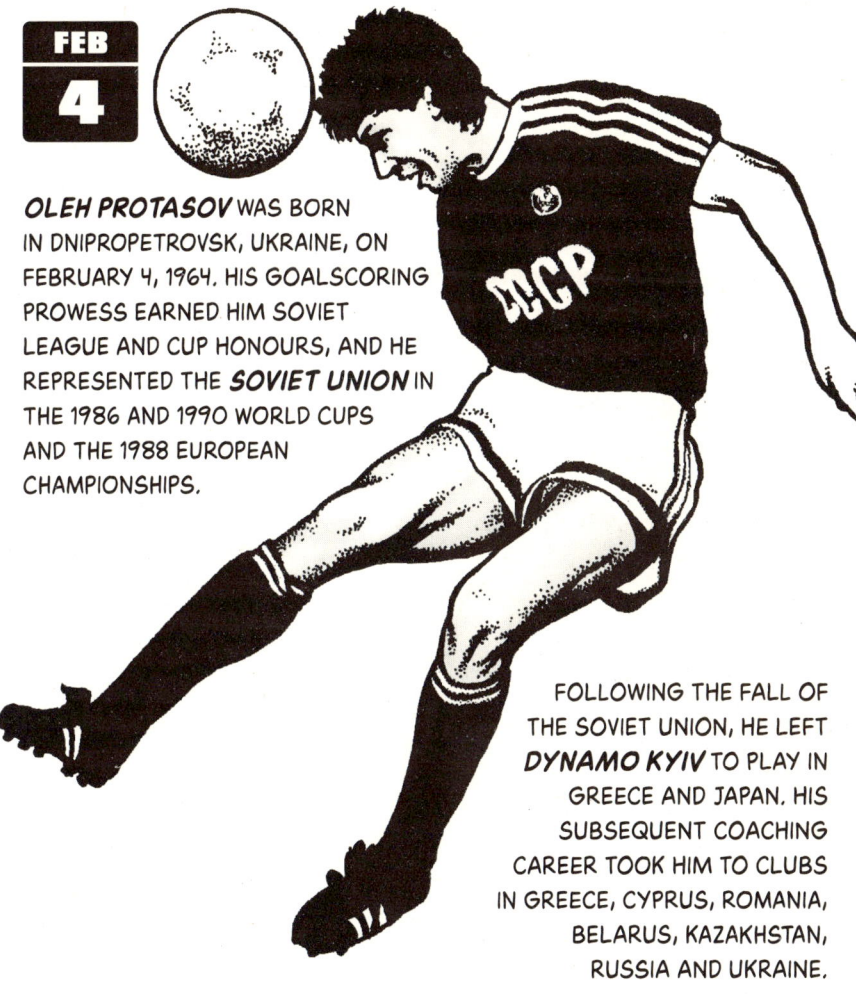

FEB 4

OLEH PROTASOV WAS BORN IN DNIPROPETROVSK, UKRAINE, ON FEBRUARY 4, 1964. HIS GOALSCORING PROWESS EARNED HIM SOVIET LEAGUE AND CUP HONOURS, AND HE REPRESENTED THE **SOVIET UNION** IN THE 1986 AND 1990 WORLD CUPS AND THE 1988 EUROPEAN CHAMPIONSHIPS.

FOLLOWING THE FALL OF THE SOVIET UNION, HE LEFT **DYNAMO KYIV** TO PLAY IN GREECE AND JAPAN. HIS SUBSEQUENT COACHING CAREER TOOK HIM TO CLUBS IN GREECE, CYPRUS, ROMANIA, BELARUS, KAZAKHSTAN, RUSSIA AND UKRAINE.

1. THE MOST-CAPPED SOVIET PLAYER WITH 112 APPEARANCES, HIS 42 GOALS MADE HIM THE **SOVIET UNION'S** ALL-TIME TOP SCORER.

2. THE MOST-CAPPED SOVIET GOALKEEPER, WHOSE CLUBS INCLUDED **SPARTAK MOSCOW** AND **SEVILLA**, HE REPRESENTED THE **SOVIET UNION** IN THREE WORLD CUP TOURNAMENTS.

3. HE CAPTAINED THE **USSR** TO VICTORY IN THE 1956 OLYMPICS AND THE 1960 EUROPEAN CHAMPIONSHIPS.

FEB 5

CRISTIANO RONALDO DOS SANTOS AVEIRO WAS BORN IN FUNCHAL, MADEIRA, PORTUGAL, ON FEBRUARY 5, 1985. HIS £80 MILLION TRANSFER FROM **MANCHESTER UNITED** TO **REAL MADRID** IN 2009 MADE HIM THE MOST EXPENSIVE PLAYER IN FOOTBALL HISTORY AT THAT TIME -- BUT A DECADE EARLIER, HIS CAREER HAD ALMOST BEEN ENDED BEFORE IT HAD BEGUN! AS A YOUNG TEEN, HE WAS DIAGNOSED WITH A HEART DEFECT AND HAD TO UNDERGO CORRECTIVE LASER SURGERY. FULLY RECOVERED, **RONALDO** BUILT HIS REPUTATION AT **SPORTING CLUBE DE PORTUGAL**, BEFORE BECOMING THE FIRST PORTUGUESE PLAYER TO PLAY FOR **MANCHESTER UNITED**.

1. **RONALDO** WAS THE FIRST PLAYER TO WIN THE EUROPEAN GOLDEN SHOE IN TWO DIFFERENT CHAMPIONSHIPS, WHEN HE FOLLOWED HIS **MANCHESTER UNITED** WIN WITH THE FIRST OF THREE HE WON WHILE WITH **REAL MADRID**. WHO IS THE ONLY OTHER PLAYER TO WIN WITH BOTH AN ENGLISH AND A SPANISH CLUB?

2. WHO IS THE ONLY OTHER PLAYER TO WIN THE EUROPEAN GOLDEN SHOE WHILE PLAYING FOR **REAL MADRID**?

3. THE 2013 TRANSFER OF WHICH PLAYER TO **REAL MADRID** FROM AN ENGLISH CLUB BROKE THE RECORD SET BY THE **RONALDO** TRANSFER?

FEB 6

SIR STANLEY MATTHEWS WAS THE FIRST WINNER OF THE EUROPEAN FOOTBALLER OF THE YEAR AWARD AND THE ONLY PLAYER TO HAVE BEEN KNIGHTED WHILE STILL PLAYING. HIS INCREDIBLE CAREER SPANNED 35 YEARS PLAYING FOR **STOKE CITY** AND **BLACKPOOL**, AND HIS TALLY OF 54 **ENGLAND** CAPS WOULD HAVE BEEN MUCH GREATER BUT FOR THE SECOND WORLD WAR HIATUS. HE PLAYED HIS LAST GAME FOR **ENGLAND** AT THE AGE OF 42 YEARS AND 104 DAYS. **"THE WIZARD OF THE WING"** MADE THE LAST OF NEARLY 700 ENGLISH LEAGUE APPEARANCES ON FEBRUARY 6, 1965, AT THE AGE OF 50 YEARS AND 5 DAYS, IN **STOKE CITY'S** 3-1 VICTORY OVER **FULHAM**.

1. WHO BECAME THE OLDEST PLAYER TO APPEAR IN A WORLD CUP TOURNAMENT WHEN HE REPRESENTED **EGYPT** AGAINST **SAUDI ARABIA**, AGED 45 YEARS AND 161 DAYS, IN 2018?

2. WHO PLAYED FOR **MANCHESTER CITY** AGAINST **QUEENS PARK RANGERS** IN 1995, AT THE AGE OF 43 YEARS AND 162 DAYS, TO BECOME THE OLDEST ENGLISH PREMIER LEAGUE PLAYER?

3. WITH HIS GOAL FOR **CAMEROON** AGAINST **RUSSIA** IN 1994, WHO BECAME, AT THE AGE OF 42 YEARS AND 39 DAYS, THE OLDEST WORLD CUP GOALSCORER?

ON FEBRUARY 7, 1970, RETURNING FROM A FOUR-WEEK SUSPENSION IMPOSED FOR KICKING A BALL OUT OF A REFEREE'S HANDS, *GEORGE BEST* SCORED 6 GOALS IN *MANCHESTER UNITED'S* 8-2 FA CUP DEMOLITION OF *NORTHAMPTON TOWN.* BY THE END OF THE GAME EVEN THE RIVAL FANS WERE APPLAUDING THE IRISH WIZARD'S MASTERCLASS.

1. WHO SCORED 6 GOALS FOR *MANCHESTER CITY* IN AN ABANDONED 1961 FA CUP TIE AGAINST *LUTON TOWN*?

2. WHO SCORED 10 GOALS IN ONE GAME FOR *LUTON TOWN* IN 1936?

3. WHO SCORED A WORLD CUP RECORD OF FIVE GOALS FOR *RUSSIA* IN A 6-1 VICTORY OVER *CAMEROON* IN THE 1994 TOURNAMENT?

FEB 8

HRISTO STOICHKOV, THE ORIGINAL BAD BOY OF BULGARIAN FOOTBALL, WAS BORN IN PLOVDIV, BULGARIA, ON FEBRUARY 8, 1966. WHILE PLAYING FOR **CSKA SOFIA** HIS INVOLVEMENT IN A FIGHT IN THE BULGARIAN CUP FINAL EARNED HIM A LIFELONG BAN, WHICH WAS LATER REDUCED TO A MONTH ON APPEAL. HE RETURNED TO WIN THE EUROPEAN GOLDEN SHOE, HITTING 38 GOALS IN 30 GAMES. HE MOVED TO **BARCELONA** -- WHERE HE PICKED UP A TWO-MONTH BAN FOR STAMPING ON THE FOOT OF A REFEREE -- THEN LED THEM TO EUROPEAN CUP TRIUMPH IN 1992. EUROPEAN FOOTBALLER OF THE YEAR IN 1994, HE WON FOUR LEAGUE TITLES WITH **BARCELONA**, SPENT A SEASON AT **PARMA**, THEN RETURNED TO **BARCELONA** TO WIN ANOTHER LEAGUE TITLE. HE SUBSEQUENTLY PLAYED FOR CLUBS IN ITALY, SAUDI ARABIA, JAPAN AND THE US, BEFORE HE MOVED INTO COACHING. HE MADE 83 APPEARANCES FOR **BULGARIA**, AND WAS JOINT TOP SCORER AT THE 1994 WORLD CUP, IN WHICH **BULGARIA** FINISHED FOURTH.

1. NAME ONE OF THE TWO MLS TEAMS HE PLAYED FOR IN THE STATES.

2. **STOICHKOV** MANAGED **BULGARIA** FOR THREE YEARS, BEFORE A DISAPPOINTING SPELL IN SPAIN AS COACH OF WHICH CLUB?

3. WHICH ITALIAN TEAM DID **STOICHKOV'S BARCELONA** DEFEAT 1-0 IN THE 1992 EUROPEAN CUP FINAL?

FEB 9

ANGELOS CHARISTEAS, THE STRIKER WHO SCORED THE WINNING GOAL FOR **GREECE** IN THE EURO 2004 FINAL, WAS BORN IN STRYMONIKO, SERRES, GREECE, ON FEBRUARY 9, 1980. HAVING STARTED HIS CAREER AT **ARIS THESSALONIKI**, HE PLAYED FOR CLUBS THROUGHOUT EUROPE AND IN SAUDI ARABIA, WINNING A LEAGUE AND CUP DOUBLE WITH **WERDER BREMEN**, AS WELL AS GERMAN CUPS WITH **BAYER LEVERKUSEN** AND **FC SCHALKE 04**, AND TWO CUP MEDALS WITH **AJAX**. HE MADE HIS DEBUT FOR **GREECE** IN 2001, SCORING TWICE IN A 3-3 DRAW WITH **RUSSIA**.

1. WHICH COUNTRY DID **GREECE** DEFEAT IN THE 2004 EUROPEAN CHAMPIONSHIP FINAL?

2. WHICH COUNTRY HOSTED THE 2004 EUROPEAN CHAMPIONSHIP TOURNAMENT?

3. WHICH COUNTRY WON THE FIRST EUROPEAN CHAMPIONSHIP IN 1960?

FEB 10

RADAMEL FALCAO WAS BORN IN SANTA MARTA, COLOMBIA, ON FEBRUARY 10, 1968, THE SON OF **COLOMBIA** INTERNATIONAL **RADAMEL GARCÍA**. **RADAMEL** STUDIED JOURNALISM AT UNIVERSITY IN BUENOS AIRES, ARGENTINA, BEFORE SIGNING FOR THAT CITY'S LEGENDARY **RIVER PLATE**. THE 19-YEAR-OLD EXPLODED IN ARGENTINIAN FOOTBALL, SCORING TWICE ON HIS DEBUT AND RACKING UP SEVEN GOALS IN HIS FIRST SEVEN STARTS -- BUT HIS PROGRESS WAS HALTED BY SERIOUS KNEE INJURIES THAT DERAILED HIS CAREER FOR ALMOST TWO YEARS. THE 2007-08 SEASON SAW HIM SCORE 19 GOALS IN ALL COMPETITIONS TO HELP FIRE **RIVER PLATE** TO A LEAGUE TITLE, WHILE ESTABLISHING HIMSELF AS A REGULAR FOR **COLOMBIA**. HE JOINED **PORTO** IN THE SUMMER OF 2009, AND SCORED 34 GOALS AND WON THE PORTUGUESE CUP IN HIS FIRST SEASON. HE WON PORTUGAL'S GOLDEN BALL IN 2010-11, HIS 37 GOALS HELPING **PORTO** TO A TREBLE OF LEAGUE, CUP AND UEFA EUROPA LEAGUE.

NAME THREE OF THE CLUBS FOR WHOM **RADAMEL FALCAO** HAS SUBSEQUENTLY PLAYED.

ON FEBRUARY 11, 1998, *MICHAEL OWEN* BECAME, AT THE AGE OF 18 YEARS AND 59 DAYS, THE YOUNGEST PLAYER TO REPRESENT *ENGLAND* IN THE 20TH CENTURY, WHEN HE MADE HIS INTERNATIONAL DEBUT IN THE 2-0 FRIENDLY LOSS TO *CHILE.* A FEW WEEKS LATER, HE OPENED HIS *ENGLAND* ACCOUNT WITH A GOAL AGAINST *MOROCCO* IN ANOTHER FRIENDLY, BEFORE HIS TWO GOALS IN THAT SUMMER'S WORLD CUP MADE HIM A NATIONAL HERO!

WHO NOW HOLDS THE RECORD AS *ENGLAND'S* YOUNGEST-EVER:
1. PLAYER?   2. GOALSCORER?   3. CAPTAIN?

FEB
12

JULIUS AGAHOWA WAS BORN IN BENIN CITY, NIGERIA, ON FEBRUARY 12, 1982. AFTER STARTING HIS CAREER AT **POLICE MACHINES**, A LOCAL POLICE TEAM, HE MOVED ON TO **BENDEL INSURANCE**. A TITLE-WINNING SEASON IN TUNISIA WITH **ESPÉRANCE** WAS FOLLOWED BY SIX SEASONS WITH **SHAKHTAR DONETSK**, WITH WHOM HE WON FOUR LEAGUE TITLES AND TWO UKRAINIAN CUPS. HE JOINED **WIGAN ATHLETIC** IN 2007 BUT IN 18 MONTHS IN ENGLAND HE FAILED TO SCORE A SINGLE GOAL. HE MOVED ON TO TURKEY'S **KAYSERISPOR**, BEFORE RETURNING TO **SHAKHTAR DONETSK** IN 2009. **NIGERIA'S** TOP SCORER AT THE 2002 AFRICAN CUP OF NATIONS, HE REPRESENTED HIS COUNTRY AT THE 2000 OLYMPICS AND THE 2002 WORLD CUP.

WHICH COUNTRIES HAVE THE FOLLOWING PAST AND PRESENT **WIGAN ATHLETIC** PLAYERS REPRESENTED:

1. **ANTOLÍN ALCARAZ**

2. **ALI AL HABSI**

3. **HENRI CAMARA**

4. **AROUNA KONÉ**

5. **JASON ROBERTS**

FEB 13

BORN IN ZAMORA, MICHOACÁN, MEXICO, ON FEBRUARY 13, 1979, *RAFAEL MÁRQUEZ* MADE HIS DEBUT FOR *ATLAS* AT THE AGE OF 17, AND WAS A *MEXICO* INTERNATIONAL BEFORE HIS 18TH BIRTHDAY. HE JOINED *MONACO* IN 1999 AND WON A LEAGUE TITLE IN HIS DEBUT SEASON. FOUR YEARS LATER, HE JOINED *BARCELONA*, WHERE HE WENT ON TO WIN FOUR LEAGUE TITLES AND BECOME THE FIRST MEXICAN PLAYER TO WIN THE UEFA CHAMPIONS LEAGUE. AFTER ADDING A SECOND CHAMPIONS LEAGUE IN 2009, HE JOINED *NEW YORK RED BULLS* IN 2010. HE SUBSEQUENTLY CAPTAINED *CLUB LEÓN* TO BACK-TO-BACK LIGA MX TITLES, HAD A SPELL IN ITALY'S SERIE A WITH *HELLAS VERONA*, AND ENDED HIS PLAYING CAREER BACK IN MEXICO WITH BOYHOOD CLUB *ATLAS*. HE MADE 147 APPEARANCES FOR *MEXICO* AND PLAYED IN FIVE WORLD CUP TOURNAMENTS.

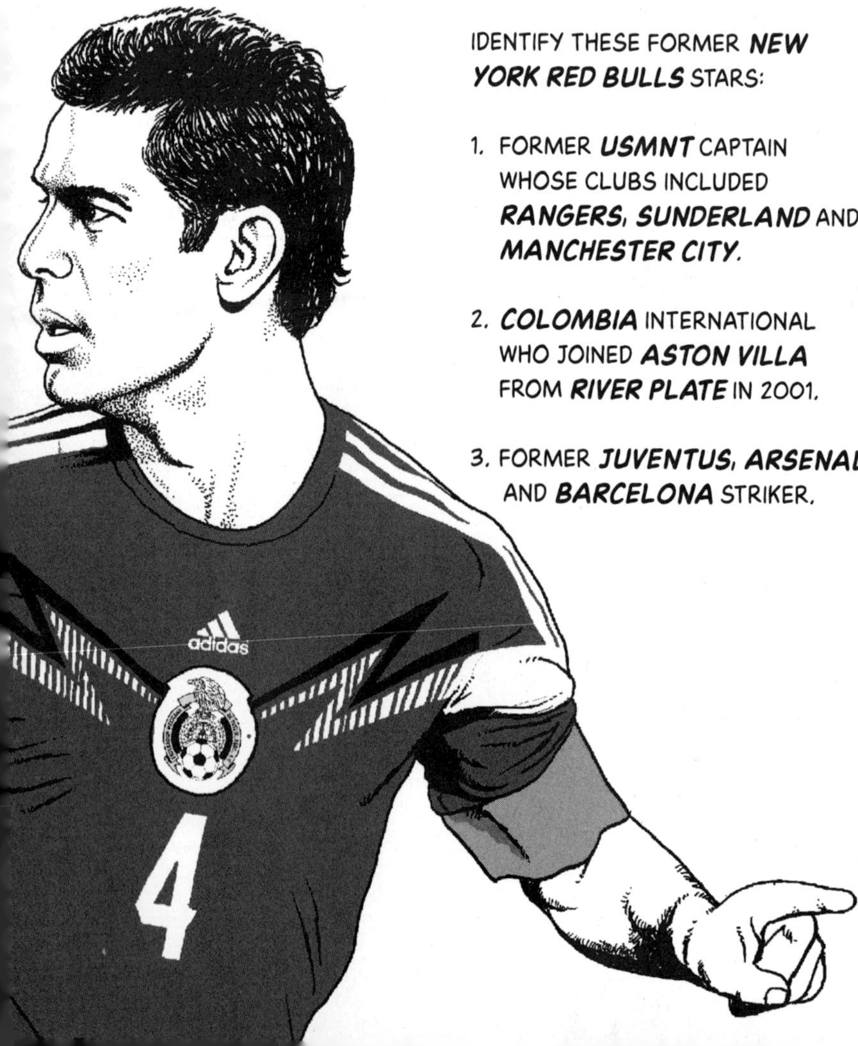

IDENTIFY THESE FORMER *NEW YORK RED BULLS* STARS:

1. FORMER *USMNT* CAPTAIN WHOSE CLUBS INCLUDED *RANGERS*, *SUNDERLAND* AND *MANCHESTER CITY*.

2. *COLOMBIA* INTERNATIONAL WHO JOINED *ASTON VILLA* FROM *RIVER PLATE* IN 2001.

3. FORMER *JUVENTUS*, *ARSENAL* AND *BARCELONA* STRIKER.

EDINSON CAVANI WAS BORN IN SALTO, URUGUAY, ON FEBRUARY 14, 1987. HE BEGAN HIS CAREER WITH **DANUBIO**, JOINING THE MONTEVIDEO CLUB'S YOUTH ACADEMY WHEN HE WAS 12 YEARS OLD. AFTER STARRING AT THE 2007 SOUTH AMERICAN YOUTH CHAMPIONSHIP, HE ATTRACTED THE INTEREST OF A NUMBER OF ITALIAN CLUBS, EVENTUALLY SIGNING FOR **PALERMO** IN EARLY 2007. A MOVE TO **NAPOLI** BROUGHT A COPPA ITALIA. HE ENDED THE 2012-13 SEASON AS SERIE A TOP SCORER, BEFORE SIGNING FOR **PARIS SAINT-GERMAIN** IN WHAT WAS THEN THE MOST EXPENSIVE TRANSFER IN FRENCH FOOTBALL HISTORY. HAVING WON SIX LIGUE 1 TITLES, FIVE COUPES DE LA LIGUE AND FOUR COUPES DE FRANCE, AND SET THE CLUB'S ALL-TIME GOALSCORING RECORD, HE JOINED **MANCHESTER UNITED** IN 2020.

1. **CAVANI** IS SECOND ONLY TO WHICH PLAYER AS THE **URUGUAY** NATIONAL TEAM'S TOP GOALSCORER?

2. **CAVANI** HAS MADE MORE THAN A CENTURY OF APPEARANCES FOR **URUGUAY** -- WHO HOLDS THE COUNTRY'S ALL-TIME APPEARANCE RECORD?

3. **CAVANI** WON THE 2011 COPA AMÉRICA WITH **URUGUAY** -- WHO DID THEY BEAT 3-0 IN THE FINAL?

FEB 15

A GOAL FROM STRIKER **LUIS HERNÁNDEZ** WAS ENOUGH TO BEAT THE **USA** IN THE 1998 CONCACAF GOLD CUP FINAL, HELD ON FEBRUARY 15, 1998, IN THE LOS ANGELES MEMORIAL COLISEUM, AND GIVE **MEXICO** A THIRD CONSECUTIVE TITLE. IT WAS A FOURTH GOAL IN THE TOURNAMENT FOR **HERNÁNDEZ**, WHO HAD PREVIOUSLY SCORED THE ONLY GOAL OF THE GAME IN THE SEMI-FINAL VICTORY OVER **BRAZIL**, AND MEANT THAT HE TIED WITH **COSTA RICA'S PAULO WANCHOPE** AS TOURNAMENT TOP SCORER.

1. WHICH **MANCHESTER UNITED** STRIKER WAS TOP SCORER AT THE 2011 CONCACAF GOLD CUP?

2. NAME THE TWO FORMER **EVERTON** PLAYERS WHO HAVE TOPPED THE CONCACAF GOLD CUP GOALSCORING CHARTS.

3. WHICH **FULHAM** AND **TOTTENHAM HOTSPUR** STAR WAS TOP SCORER AT THE 2015 CONCACAF GOLD CUP?

FEB 16

BEBETO, THE 1989 SOUTH AMERICAN FOOTBALLER OF THE YEAR, WAS BORN **JOSÉ ROBERTO GAMA DE OLIVEIRA** IN SALVADOR, BRAZIL, ON FEBRUARY 16, 1964. **BEBETO** PLAYED IN THREE WORLD CUPS -- WINNING THE TROPHY IN 1994 -- AND TWO OLYMPICS, IN WHICH HE FOLLOWED HIS 1998 SILVER WITH BRONZE IN 1996. HE PLAYED FOR CLUBS IN BRAZIL, SPAIN, MEXICO, JAPAN AND SAUDI ARABIA BEFORE BECOMING AN ELECTED POLITICIAN BACK HOME IN BRAZIL.

IDENTIFY THESE WORLD CUP WINNERS WHO HAVE PLAYED IN THE ENGLISH PREMIER LEAGUE:

1. FRENCH GOALKEEPER WHO PLAYED FOR **MANCHESTER UNITED**.

2. FRENCH STRIKER WHO WON THREE FA CUPS WITH **ARSENAL** AND THE UEFA EUROPA LEAGUE WITH **CHELSEA**.

3. FORMER **MANCHESTER CITY** DEFENDER WHO HAS WON TWO UEFA CHAMPIONS LEAGUES WITH **BAYERN MUNICH**.

FEB
17

ENRIQUE OMAR SÍVORI -- 1961 EUROPEAN FOOTBALLER OF THE YEAR -- BEGAN HIS CAREER AT **RIVER PLATE**, WITH WHOM HE WON TWO ARGENTINIAN TITLES, BEFORE HE JOINED **JUVENTUS** FOR A WORLD RECORD TRANSFER FEE OF £91,000 IN 1957. IN HIS FOUR YEARS IN TURIN, HE WON THREE LEAGUE TITLES. HAVING WON THE 1957 COPA AMÉRICA WITH **ARGENTINA**, FOR WHOM HE SCORED 9 GOALS IN 19 GAMES, HE WAS BANNED FROM THE NATIONAL TEAM FOLLOWING HIS MOVE TO EUROPE. HIS ITALIAN ANCESTRY MADE HIM ELIGIBLE TO PLAY FOR **ITALY** AND HE WENT ON TO SCORE 8 GOALS IN 9 GAMES FOR THE **"AZZURRI"**, AND REPRESENTED HIS ADOPTED COUNTRY AT THE 1962 WORLD CUP. HE ENDED HIS CAREER WITH A SPELL AT **NAPOLI**, BEFORE HE SUBSEQUENTLY MOVED INTO COACHING BACK IN ARGENTINA. HE DIED ON FEBRUARY 17, 2005 AT THE AGE OF 69.

SÍVORI COACHED **ARGENTINA** FROM 1972 TO 1974. NAME THREE OTHER **ARGENTINA** INTERNATIONALS WHO HAVE COACHED THE **ARGENTINA** TEAM SINCE THEN.

FEB 18

BORN IN BURY, GREATER MANCHESTER, ON FEBRUARY 18, 1975, *GARY NEVILLE* JOINED *MANCHESTER UNITED* STRAIGHT FROM SCHOOL, CAPTAINING THE CLUB TO VICTORY IN THE FA YOUTH CUP FINAL IN HIS FIRST SEASON. ALONG WITH HIS YOUNGER BROTHER, *PHIL*, HE WAS A KEY MEMBER OF *"FERGIE'S FLEDGLINGS"*, THE GROUP OF YOUNG PLAYERS WHO PROPELLED *ALEX FERGUSON'S* SIDE TO UNPRECEDENTED GLORY IN THE 1990S. HE MADE 85 APPEARANCES FOR *ENGLAND* AND WON A HOST OF TROPHIES WITH *UNITED*, INCLUDING EIGHT LEAGUE TITLES, FIVE DOMESTIC CUPS AND THE UEFA CHAMPIONS LEAGUE. HE RETIRED IN 2011 AND CARVED OUT A CAREER AS A NEWSPAPER PUNDIT AND A GAME ANALYST ON TV.

1. *GARY NEVILLE* IS *ENGLAND'S* MOST-CAPPED RIGHT BACK, A RECORD PREVIOUSLY HELD BY WHICH FORMER *LIVERPOOL* AND *BOLTON WANDERERS* PLAYER?

2. THE *NEVILLES* HAVE 144 *ENGLAND* CAPS BETWEEN THEM, BEATING THE TALLY OF 141 SET BY WHICH OTHER PAIR OF ENGLISH BROTHERS?

3. *GARY'S* SISTER, *TRACEY*, PLAYED WHICH SPORT FOR *ENGLAND*?

FEB 19

ROUTINELY HAILED AS THE GREATEST PLAYER IN THE HISTORY OF THE WOMEN'S GAME, *MARTA* WAS BORN *MARTA VIEIRA DA SILVA* IN DOIS RIACHOS, ALAGOAS, BRAZIL ON FEBRUARY 1, 1986. SIX TIMES FIFA WORLD PLAYER OF THE YEAR, SHE WAS THE FIRST FOOTBALLER OF EITHER GENDER TO SCORE IN FIVE WORLD CUP TOURNAMENTS. SHE ALSO THE TOP *BRAZIL* GOALSCORER, MALE OR FEMALE, OF ALL TIME AND WON THE GOLDEN BALL AND THE GOLDEN BOOT AT THE 2007 WOMEN 'S WORLD CUP.

WHICH COUNTRIES DO THESE PLAYERS REPRESENT:

1. *HOMARE SAWA*

2. *ABBY WAMBACH*

3. *LUCY BRONZE*

4. *PERNILLE HARDER*

5. *ADA HEGERBERG*

FEB
20

JIMMY GREAVES MADE A HABIT OF SCORING ON HIS DEBUT FOR EVERY TEAM IN WHICH HE PLAYED. BORN IN LONDON, ON FEBRUARY 20, 1940, HE MADE HIS DEBUT FOR **CHELSEA** IN 1957 AND WAS THE LEAGUE'S TOP GOALSCORER TWICE IN HIS FOUR YEARS AT THE CLUB. FOLLOWING A BRIEF SPELL IN ITALY WITH **AC MILAN**, HE JOINED **TOTTENHAM HOTSPUR** IN 1961 FOR A FEE OF £99,999, A FIGURE INTENDED TO RELIEVE HIM OF THE PRESSURE OF BECOMING THE FIRST £100,000 FOOTBALLER. **GREAVES** WON TWO FA CUPS AND THE EUROPEAN CUP WINNERS' CUP WITH **SPURS**. HE SCORED 44 TIMES IN 57 APPEARANCES FOR **ENGLAND**, FAMOUSLY LOSING HIS PLACE IN THE 1966 WORLD CUP-WINNING TEAM. HE LATER PLAYED FOR **WEST HAM UNITED**, WHERE HE TOOK HIS GOALS TALLY TO A RECORD 357 GOALS IN 516 TOP-FLIGHT LEAGUE GAMES.

NAME THE 11 PLAYERS ON **ENGLAND'S** 1966 WORLD CUP-WINNING TEAM.

FEB
21

GEORGIOS SAMARAS WAS BORN IN HERAKLION, ON THE GREEK ISLAND OF CRETE, ON FEBRUARY 21, 1985. HE LAUNCHED HIS CAREER AS A 10-YEAR-OLD AT **CRETE** -- WHERE HIS DAD WAS ON THE BOOKS -- THEN JOINED DUTCH CLUB **HEERENVEEN** IN 2001. ALTHOUGH HE WAS ELIGIBLE TO PLAY FOR HIS DAD'S NATIVE **AUSTRALIA**, **GEORGIOS** CHOSE TO PLAY FOR THE COUNTRY OF HIS BIRTH AND MADE HIS FULL INTERNATIONAL DEBUT FOR **GREECE** IN 2006, ONE WEEK AFTER HIS 21ST BIRTHDAY, AND THREE WEEKS AFTER SIGNING FOR **MANCHESTER CITY**. HE JOINED **CELTIC** IN 2008, WHERE HE WON A LEAGUE AND LEAGUE CUP DOUBLE IN HIS FIRST SEASON. HE GAINED FURTHER HONOURS IN SCOTLAND, INCLUDING THREE MORE LEAGUE TITLES, BUT FARED POORLY IN SUBSEQUENT SPELLS AT **WEST BROMWICH ALBION** AND IN SAUDI ARABIA, SPAIN, THE UNITED STATES AND TURKEY. CAPPED 81 TIMES BY **GREECE**, HE RETIRED IN 2018.

NAME THE **GREECE** INTERNATIONAL:

1. 2003 GREEK FOOTBALLER OF THE YEAR, WAS A EURO 2004 CHAMPION WHILE PLAYING AT **BOLTON WANDERERS**.

2. WON A LEAGUE AND CUP DOUBLE WITH **RANGERS**, HAD TWO SEASONS AT **LIVERPOOL** AND A LOAN SPELL WITH **SUNDERLAND**.

3. GERMAN-BORN DEFENDER SPENT FIVE SEASONS WITH **WATFORD**, HE WAS ABLE TO PLAY IN THE 2019 FA CUP FINAL WHEN A PRIOR RED CARD WAS RESCINDED.

FEB 22

FOUR TIMES DANISH FOOTBALLER OF THE YEAR, **BRIAN LAUDRUP** WAS OUTSTANDING IN THE **DENMARK** TEAM THAT TRIUMPHED, AGAINST ALL EXPECTATIONS, AT EURO 1992. BORN ON FEBRUARY 22, 1969, IN VIENNA, AUSTRIA, WHERE HIS FATHER WAS PLAYING FOR **WIENER SPORT-CLUB, BRIAN** STARTED HIS CAREER AT **BRØNDBY**, WHERE HE WON TWO LEAGUE TITLES WHILE STILL IN HIS TEENS. HE WENT ON TO PLAY FOR CLUBS THROUGHOUT EUROPE, WINNING A NUMBER OF HONOURS, INCLUDING THE UEFA CHAMPIONS LEAGUE AND A SERIE A TITLE WITH **AC MILAN**, THREE SCOTTISH LEAGUE TITLES WITH **RANGERS** AND THE UEFA SUPER CUP WITH **CHELSEA**. HE SCORED 21 GOALS IN 82 INTERNATIONALS, AND ALONG WITH HIS OLDER BROTHER, **MICHAEL**, IS REGARDED AMONG THE GREATEST PLAYERS THAT **DENMARK** HAS EVER PRODUCED. WHICH EURO 1992 WINNER WON:

1. THE 1994 EUROPEAN CUP WINNERS' CUP WITH **ARSENAL**?

2. THE 1999 CHAMPIONS LEAGUE WITH **MANCHESTER UNITED**?

3. THE 1983 UEFA CUP WITH **ANDERLECHT**?

BORN IN HASTINGS, SUSSEX, ON FEBRUARY 23, 1981, *GARETH BARRY* CAME THROUGH THE YOUTH RANKS AT *BRIGHTON & HOVE ALBION*, BEFORE JOINING *ASTON VILLA* AS A TRAINEE IN 1997. HE MADE HIS SENIOR DEBUT AT 17, IN THE SAME YEAR THAT HE ESTABLISHED HIMSELF IN THE *ENGLAND UNDER-21* SIDE. HE WON THE FIRST OF HIS 53 *ENGLAND* CAPS IN 2000. IN 2007, AGED 26 YEARS AND 247 DAYS, HE BECAME THE YOUNGEST PLAYER TO APPEAR IN 300 PREMIER LEAGUE GAMES. HE WAS HEAVILY LINKED WITH A MOVE TO *LIVERPOOL*, BUT JOINED *MANCHESTER CITY* IN 2009, WINNING THE FA CUP IN 2011. THE FOLLOWING SEASON, HE HELPED THE CLUB TO A FIRST LEAGUE TITLE IN 44 YEARS. HE WENT ON TO PLAY FOR *EVERTON* AND *WEST BROMWICH ALBION* AND RETIRED IN 2020.

IDENTIFY THE FOLLOWING PLAYERS WHO JOINED *MANCHESTER CITY* AFTER PLAYING FOR *ASTON VILLA:*

1. HIS PREVIOUS CLUBS INCLUDE *LEEDS UNITED* AND *NEWCASTLE UNITED*, AND HE SUBSEQUENTLY SIGNED FOR *LIVERPOOL*.

2. EURO 1992 AND 1999 UEFA CHAMPIONS LEAGUE WINNER.

3. *ENGLAND* INTERNATIONAL WHO JOINED *ANKARAGÜCÜ* IN TURKEY AFTER LEAVING *CITY*, BEFORE SIGNING FOR *LEICESTER CITY*.

FÁBIO CÉSAR MONTEZINE WAS BORN IN LONDRINA, BRAZIL, ON FEBRUARY 24, 1979. AS A SCHOOLBOY HE HAD TRIALS IN ITALY BUT EVENTUALLY SIGNED ON AS A YOUTH PLAYER IN BRAZIL WITH **SÃO PAULO**, WHERE HE PLAYED ALONGSIDE THE LIKES OF **KAKÁ** AND **JULIO BAPTISTA**. HIS PROFESSIONAL CAREER TOOK TO HIM TO CZECH SIDE **FC VIKTORIA PLZEN**, BEFORE HE SPENT FOUR YEARS IN ITALY WITH **UDINESE**, **NAPOLI** AND **AVELLINO**. HE SUBSEQUENTLY PLAYED HIS CLUB FOOTBALL IN QATAR AND, AS A NATURALISED CITIZEN, WAS A KEY MEMBER OF THE **QATAR** NATIONAL TEAM, MAKING 28 APPEARANCES.

IDENTIFY THE FOLLOWING WORLD STARS WHO HAVE PLAYED IN QATAR:

1. COSTA RICAN WHOSE PREVIOUS CLUBS INCLUDE **DERBY COUNTY**, **MANCHESTER CITY**, **FC TOKYO** AND **CHICAGO FIRE**.

2. 1998 WORLD CUP AND 2000 EUROPEAN CHAMPIONSHIP WINNER WHOSE CLUBS INCLUDED **MARSEILLE**, **AC MILAN** AND **CHELSEA**.

3. **BARCELONA** AND **SPAIN** STAR WHOSE SUBSEQUENT CAREER IN COACHING HAS BROUGHT TITLES IN SPAIN, GERMANY AND ENGLAND.

4. THE MOST-CAPPED **NETHERLANDS** PLAYER OF ALL TIME.

FEB 25 ONE OF THE MOST DECORATED ASIAN FOOTBALLERS OF ALL TIME, *SOUTH KOREA* SUPERSTAR *PARK JI-SUNG* WAS BORN IN SEOUL, ON FEBRUARY 25, 1981. HE WON A SECOND TIER TITLE AND AN EMPEROR'S CUP IN JAPAN WITH *KYOTO PURPLE SANGA*, BEFORE JOINING *PSV EINDHOVEN* IN 2002. HE WON TWO LEAGUE TITLES IN THE NETHERLANDS, INCLUDING A LEAGUE AND CUP DOUBLE IN 2005, FOLLOWING WHICH HE SIGNED FOR *MANCHESTER UNITED*, WITH WHOM HE WON FOUR PREMIER LEAGUE TITLES AND THREE LEAGUE CUPS, AND BECAME THE FIRST ASIAN PLAYER TO WIN THE UEFA CHAMPIONS LEAGUE AND THE FIFA CLUB WORLD CUP. CAPPED 100 TIMES BY *SOUTH KOREA*, HE WAS THE FIRST ASIAN PLAYER TO SCORE IN THREE CONSECUTIVE WORLD CUP TOURNAMENTS, AND WAS A MEMBER OF THE TEAM THAT FINISHED FOURTH AT THE 2002 WORLD CUP.

1. NAME ONE OF THE CLUBS THAT *PARK JI-SUNG* PLAYED FOR AFTER LEAVING *MANCHESTER UNITED*.

2. WHO COACHED *PARK JI-SUNG* AT THE 2002 WORLD CUP AND AT *PSV EINDHOVEN*?

3. *PARK'S* 2009 CHAMPIONS LEAGUE FINAL APPEARANCE CAME IN THE 2-0 LOSS TO WHICH CLUB?

FEB 26

SHEYI EMMANUEL ADEBAYOR WAS BORN IN LOMÉ, TOGO, ON FEBRUARY 26, 1984. AT THE AGE OF 15 HE WAS SIGNED BY FRENCH CLUB **METZ**, AND BROKE INTO THE FIRST TEAM IN THE 2001-02 SEASON. A **TOGO** INTERNATIONAL SINCE 2000, **ADEBAYOR** SCORED 11 GOALS TO HELP HIS COUNTRY QUALIFY FOR THE 2006 AFRICAN CUP OF NATIONS AND HE PLAYED IN ALL THREE OF **TOGO'S** GAMES AT THE 2006 WORLD CUP. HE WON FOUR CONSECUTIVE TOGO FOOTBALLER OF THE YEAR AWARDS BETWEEN 2005 AND 2008, AND WAS THE FIRST TOGOLESE TO BE NAMED AFRICAN FOOTBALLER OF THE YEAR. TRAGEDY STRUCK IN 2010, WHEN THREE PEOPLE WERE KILLED WHEN A BUS CARRYING THE **TOGO** TEAM WAS ATTACKED IN ANGOLA. THE NEARLY MAN OF CLUB SOCCER, HAVING REACHED CUP FINALS WITH A NUMBER OF TEAMS, HIS ONLY MAJOR HONOUR WAS THE COPA DEL REY HE WON DURING A LOAN SPELL WITH **REAL MADRID** IN 2011.

HE WAS ON THE LOSING SIDE PLAYING FOR WHICH TEAM IN THE FOLLOWING FINALS?

1. UEFA CHAMPIONS LEAGUE FINAL, 2004: A 3-0 LOSS TO **PORTO**.

2. FOOTBALL LEAGUE CUP FINAL, 2007: A 2-1 LOSS TO **CHELSEA**.

3. FA CUP FINAL, 2016: A 2-1 LOSS TO **MANCHESTER UNITED**.

FEB
27

BAYERN MUNICH, THE MOST SUCCESSFUL CLUB IN THE HISTORY OF GERMAN FOOTBALL, WAS FOUNDED ON FEBRUARY 27, 1900, BY MEMBERS OF A LOCAL GYMNASTICS CLUB. IT WAS THE MID-1960S BEFORE **BAYERN MUNICH** JOINED THE BUNDESLIGA, BUT BY THE END OF THE FOLLOWING DECADE, THE TEAM HAD WON THREE EUROPEAN CUPS IN A ROW AND DOMINATED THE GERMAN GAME. SOME OF THE MOST ILLUSTRIOUS NAMES IN GERMAN FOOTBALL HAVE PLAYED FOR THE TEAM.

1. WHICH **BAYERN MUNICH** LEGEND WON THE WORLD CUP AS BOTH A PLAYER AND A COACH?

2. NAME THE THREE PLAYERS WHO WERE VOTED EUROPEAN FOOTBALLER OF THE YEAR WHILE PLAYING FOR **BAYERN MUNICH**.

3. NAME THE THREE MEN WHO WERE VOTED **IFFHS** WORLD'S BEST GOALKEEPER WHILE PLAYING FOR **BAYERN MUNICH**.

FEB 28

WHEN *ITALY* CAPTAIN *DINO ZOFF* LIFTED THE WORLD CUP TROPHY IN 1982, THE VETERAN GOALKEEPER BECAME, AT THE AGE OF 40 YEARS, 4 MONTHS AND 13 DAYS, THE COMPETITION'S OLDEST WINNER. BORN IN MARIANO DEL FRIULI, ON FEBRUARY 28, 1942, HE LAUNCHED HIS CAREER AT *UDINESE*, BEFORE MOVING ON TO *MANTOVA*. HE JOINED *NAPOLI* IN 1967, AND MADE HIS FULL INTERNATIONAL DEBUT SOON AFTER. HE WON THE 1968 EUROPEAN CHAMPIONSHIPS IN HIS FOURTH APPEARANCE FOR THE *"AZZURRI"*. HE JOINED *JUVENTUS* IN 1972, GOING ON TO WIN SIX LEAGUE TITLES, TWO COPPA ITALIA AND THE UEFA CUP. AFTER MOVING INTO MANAGEMENT, HE WON ANOTHER COPPA ITALIA AND A UEFA CUP WITH *JUVENTUS*, COACHED *LAZIO* AND *FIORENTINA* AND STEERED *ITALY* TO THE 2000 EUROPEAN CHAMPIONSHIP FINAL.

WHICH MANAGER OF *ITALY*:

1. MANAGED *MANCHESTER CITY* TO A PREMIER LEAGUE TITLE?

2. MANAGED *CHELSEA* TO A PREMIER LEAGUE TITLE?

3. MANAGED THE 2006 WORLD CUP WINNERS?

BORN IN MINNEAPOLIS, MINNESOTA, USA, ON FEBRUARY 29, 1980, *TAYLOR TWELLMAN* FIRST MADE AN IMPACT AT THE 1999 WORLD YOUTH CHAMPIONSHIP, WHEN HIS FOUR GOALS ALERTED A NUMBER OF CLUBS TO HIS TALENTS. HE SUBSEQUENTLY SIGNED FOR *1860 MUNICH* BUT AFTER TWO UNHAPPY YEARS IN GERMANY, HE RETURNED TO THE STATES AND WAS DRAFTED BY THE *NEW ENGLAND REVOLUTION*. THE 2005 MAJOR LEAGUE SOCCER MVP AND WINNER OF THE MLS GOLDEN BOOT, HIS CAREER WAS CURTAILED BY NECK AND HEAD INJURIES AND HE ANNOUNCED HIS RETIREMENT IN 2010, HAVING SCORED SIX GOALS IN 30 APPEARANCES FOR HIS COUNTRY. HE CURRENTLY WORKS AS A TV SOCCER ANALYST.

IDENTIFY THESE FORMER *NEW ENGLAND REVOLUTION* PLAYERS:

1. PLAYING FOR *FULHAM* IN 2012, HE BECAME THE FIRST AMERICAN TO SCORE AN ENGLISH PREMIER LEAGUE HAT-TRICK.

2. FIRST AMERICAN TO PLAY IN THE ENGLISH PREMIER LEAGUE, HIS OTHER CLUBS INCLUDED *SHEFFIELD WEDNESDAY* AND *DERBY COUNTY*.

3. *ENGLAND* CENTRE-BACK WHO WON HONOURS WITH *NEWCASTLE UNITED* AND *MANCHESTER CITY* AND PLAYED FOR *LEICESTER CITY* AND *BOLTON WANDERERS*.

MARCH

MAR 1

ON MARCH 1, 1921, *JULES RIMET*, PRESIDENT OF THE *FRENCH FOOTBALL FEDERATION*, BECAME THE THIRD PRESIDENT OF *FIFA*. NINE YEARS LATER, HE ACHIEVED A LONG-CHERISHED AMBITION WITH THE INAUGURAL WORLD CUP TOURNAMENT. AS A TRIBUTE TO HIS DRIVING FORCE, THE ORIGINAL WORLD CUP AWARD WAS NAMED THE *JULES RIMET TROPHY. BRAZIL* WON THE TROPHY OUTRIGHT IN 1970 WHEN THEY WON IT FOR A THIRD TIME, AND IT WAS REPLACED BY THE FIFA WORLD CUP TROPHY THAT IS STILL PLAYED FOR TO THIS DAY. *RIMET* SERVED AS *FIFA* PRESIDENT UNTIL 1946, AND DIED TEN YEARS LATER.

THE FIRST WORLD CUP TOURNAMENT WAS HELD IN URUGUAY, AND HAS SUBSEQUENTLY BEEN STAGED EVERY FOUR YEARS IN VARIOUS COUNTRIES AROUND THE WORLD, EXCEPT FOR A 12-YEAR BREAK BECAUSE OF THE SECOND WORLD WAR.

NAME THE HOST COUNTRIES OF THE TOURNAMENTS SINCE 1930.

MAR 2

BORN ON MARCH 2, 1982, IN RIO DE JANEIRO, BRAZIL, TO A GERMAN-HUNGARIAN FATHER AND A PANAMANIAN MOTHER, **KEVIN KURÁNYI** SPENT HIS FORMATIVE YEARS PLAYING FOR CLUBS IN BRAZIL AND PANAMA, BEFORE MOVING TO GERMANY WHEN HE WAS 15 TO SIGN FOR **VFB STUTTGART.** BY THE TIME HE JOINED **SCHALKE 04** IN 2005, HE WAS A **GERMANY** INTERNATIONAL PLAYER. CAPPED 52 TIMES, HIS INTERNATIONAL CAREER WAS CURTAILED IN 2008 AFTER HE FELL OUT WITH **GERMANY** COACH **JOACHIM LÖW**. AFTER A FIVE-YEAR SPELL WITH **DYNAMO MOSCOW**, **KURÁNYI** PLAYED A SEASON WITH **1899 HOFFENHEIM** BEFORE RETIRING.

THE FOLLOWING PLAYERS WERE ALSO BORN IN **BRAZIL** BUT CAPPED BY ANOTHER COUNTRY:

1. WINNER OF LEAGUE TITLES IN TWO SPELLS WITH **PORTO**, THREE-TIME UEFA CHAMPIONS LEAGUE WINNER WITH **REAL MADRID**, HE WON THE EUROPEAN CHAMPIONSHIP WITH **PORTUGAL** IN 2016.

2. **CROATIA'S** THIRD ALL-TIME LEADING GOALSCORER, HE WON HONOURS WITH **DINAMO ZAGREB**, **SHAKHTAR DONETSK** AND **LEGIA WARSAW** AND SUFFERED A TERRIBLE LEG INJURY PLAYING FOR **ARSENAL**.

3. WINNER OF MULTIPLE HONOURS WITH **ATLÉTICO MADRID** AND **CHELSEA**, HE PLAYED FOR **SPAIN** IN THE 2014 WORLD CUP IN BRAZIL ... AND WAS BOOED BY **BRAZIL** FANS!

MAR 3

OF THE FINEST PLAYERS IN THE HISTORY OF SERBIAN AND YUGOSLAVIAN FOOTBALL, *DRAGAN STOJKOVIĆ* WAS BORN IN NIS, IN THE FORMER YUGOSLAVIA, ON MARCH 3, 1965. NICKNAMED *"PIKSI"*, HE FIRST FOUND INTERNATIONAL ACCLAIM AT *RED STAR BELGRADE*, TWICE WINNING THE YUGOSLAV MVP AWARD, BEFORE JOINING *OLYMPIQUE DE MARSEILLE* IN 1990. HE WAS A MEMBER OF THE SIDE THAT LOST TO HIS OLD CLUB, *RED STAR BELGRADE*, IN THE 1991 EUROPEAN CUP FINAL. HE JOINED JAPAN'S *NAGOYA GRAMPUS EIGHT* IN 1994, AND THE FOLLOWING YEAR, THE TEAM WON THE EMPEROR'S CUP, WITH *STOJKOVIĆ* NAMED J. LEAGUE MVP AND JAPANESE FOOTBALLER OF THE YEAR. CAPPED 84 TIMES, HE RETIRED AFTER SPENDING SEVEN SEASONS IN JAPAN AND BECAME PRESIDENT OF THE SERBIAN FOOTBALL ASSOCIATION, THEN *RED STAR* PRESIDENT, BEFORE COACHING *NAGOYA GRAMPUS EIGHT* TO THE J. LEAGUE TITLE IN 2010. AFTER SPENDING FOUR SEASONS AT THE HELM OF CHINA'S *GUANGZHOU R&F*, HE WAS APPOINTED *SERBIA* MANAGER IN 2021.

1. WHICH SUBSEQUENT ENGLISH PREMIER LEAGUE-WINNING MANAGER SIGNED *STOJKOVIĆ* TO *NAGOYA GRAMPUS EIGHT?*

2. WHICH *NAGOYA GRAMPUS EIGHT* STRIKER HAD PREVIOUSLY WON THE GOLDEN SHOE AT THE 1986 WORLD CUP?

3. WHICH FORMER *PRESTON NORTH END, LIVERPOOL* AND *WIGAN ATHLETIC* PLAYER COACHED *NAGOYA GRAMPUS EIGHT* IN 1994?

MAR 4

BORN IN LEDESMA, JUJUY, ON MARCH 4, 1974, *ARIEL ORTEGA* PLAYED IN THREE WORLD CUPS FOR *ARGENTINA*. HE WAS FAMOUSLY RED-CARDED FOR HEADBUTTING GOALKEEPER *EDWIN VAN DER SAR* IN THE 1998 QUARTER-FINAL AGAINST *NETHERLANDS*. HE BEGAN HIS CAREER AT *RIVER PLATE*, BEFORE SIGNING FOR SPAIN'S *VALENCIA* IN 1997. HE WENT ON TO PLAY IN ITALY FOR *SAMPDORIA* AND *PARMA*, AND WAS HEAVILY PENALISED AND BANNED FROM THE SPORT FOR FOUR MONTHS AFTER FAILING TO REPORT BACK TO HIS TURKISH CLUB, *FENERBAHÇE*, FROM INTERNATIONAL DUTY. HE EVENTUALLY RETURNED TO FOOTBALL BACK HOME IN ARGENTINA, WHERE HE SUBSEQUENTLY PLAYED FOR A NUMBER OF CLUBS, INCLUDING *NEWELL'S OLD BOYS* AND *RIVER PLATE*.

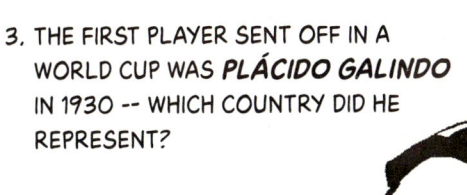

1. NAME THE THREE *ENGLAND* PLAYERS DISMISSED IN WORLD CUP TOURNAMENTS.

2. NAME THREE OF THE FIVE PLAYERS DISMISSED IN A WORLD CUP FINAL.

3. THE FIRST PLAYER SENT OFF IN A WORLD CUP WAS *PLÁCIDO GALINDO* IN 1930 -- WHICH COUNTRY DID HE REPRESENT?

MAR 5

BORN IN SHEFFIELD ON MARCH 5, 1993, *HARRY MAGUIRE* CAME THROUGH THE RANKS AT *SHEFFIELD UNITED* TO BE NAMED CLUB PLAYER OF THE YEAR THREE TIMES IN A ROW. TRANSFERRED TO *HULL CITY* IN 2014, HE WAS LOANED OUT TO *WIGAN ATHLETIC* AFTER A HANDFUL OF APPEARANCES. HE RETURNED TO *HULL* AND WAS NAMED PLAYER OF THE SEASON IN 2016/17, BUT THE CLUB'S RELEGATION PROMPTED HIS SALE TO *LEICESTER CITY*. TWO SEASONS OF OUTSTANDING PERFORMANCES EARNED THE *ENGLAND* REGULAR HIS RECORD-BREAKING £80 MILLION TRANSFER TO *MANCHESTER UNITED* IN 2019.

NAME THESE OTHER *SHEFFIELD UNITED* PLAYER OF THE YEAR WINNERS:

1. CENTRE-BACK WHO PLAYED 385 GAMES FOR *EVERTON* BEFORE RETURNING TO *"THE BLADES"* IN 2019.

2. GOALKEEPER WHO PLAYED 675 GAMES FOR THE CLUB BETWEEN 1954 AND 1971.

3. *ENGLAND* INTERNATIONAL, SCORER OF THE FIRST-EVER GOAL IN THE ENGLISH PREMIER LEAGUE IN 1992.

REAL MADRID WAS FOUNDED AS **SOCIEDAD MADRID FC** ON MARCH 6, 1902. ROYAL FAVOUR WAS CONFERRED ON THE CLUB BY **KING ALFONSO XIII** IN 1929, AND THE CLUB CHANGED ITS NAME TO **REAL MADRID**. THE MOST SUCCESSFUL CLUB IN SPAIN, THEY HAVE WON 34 LEAGUE TITLES AND HAVE BEEN CHAMPIONS OF EUROPE A RECORD 13 TIMES. THEY WON THE EUROPEAN CUP FIVE TIMES IN A ROW BETWEEN 1956 AND 1960, AND WON THE LEAGUE EIGHT TIMES OUT OF TEN IN THE 1960S.

1. **CRISTIANO RONALDO** HOLDS THE **REAL MADRID** GOALSCORING RECORD. WHO HOLDS THE CLUB APPEARANCE RECORD?

2. WHICH **NORWAY** INTERNATIONAL WAS **REAL MADRID'S** YOUNGEST-EVER FIRST TEAM PLAYER, AGED 16 YEARS, 157 DAYS?

3. IN 1974, WHICH MIDFIELDER BECAME THE FIRST PLAYER TO WIN A WORLD CUP WITH HIS COUNTRY WHILE PLAYING FOR **REAL MADRID?**

MAR 7

JORDAN PICKFORD WAS BORN IN WASHINGTON ON MARCH 7, 1994. HAVING JOINED SUNDERLAND'S ACADEMY AT THE AGE OF 8, HIS ROUTE TO THE TOP INVOLVED A LENGTHY SLOG THROUGH THE LOWER REACHES OF THE ENGLISH GAME. OVER A FOUR-YEAR PERIOD HE WAS LOANED OUT TO DARLINGTON, ALFRETON TOWN, BURTON ALBION, CARLISLE UNITED, BRADFORD CITY AND PRESTON NORTH END -- BY THE TIME HE WAS 21 HE HAD PLAYED IN THE TOP FIVE LEAGUES OF ENGLISH FOOTBALL. HAVING ESTABLISHED HIMSELF IN THE SUNDERLAND FIRST TEAM, HIS £25 MILLION TRANSFER TO EVERTON IN 2017, RISING TO £30 MILLION WITH ADD-ONS, MADE HIM THE MOST EXPENSIVE BRITISH GOALKEEPER IN HISTORY. LATER THAT SAME YEAR, HAVING REPRESENTED HIS COUNTRY AT EVERY LEVEL FROM U-16, HE MADE HIS FULL ENGLAND DEBUT AND WAS HIS COUNTRY'S FIRST CHOICE GOALKEEPER AT THE 2018 WORLD CUP.

1. WHO IS THE ONLY ENGLAND PLAYER TO WIN THE GOLDEN GLOVE, AWARDED TO THE BEST GOALKEEPER AT A WORLD CUP TOURNAMENT?

2. WHICH GOALKEEPER HOLDS THE ENGLAND WORLD CUP APPEARANCE RECORD, HAVING PLAYED 17 GAMES OVER THREE TOURNAMENTS?

3. ENGLAND'S FIRST WORLD CUP WAS THE 1950 TOURNAMENT. WHICH WOLVERHAMPTON WANDERERS GOALKEEPER PLAYED IN ALL THREE GAMES, INCLUDING THE INFAMOUS 1-0 LOSS TO THE UNITED STATES?

MAR 8

THE FIRST AMERICAN TO PLAY IN THE ENGLISH PREMIER LEAGUE, *JOHN HARKES* WAS BORN IN KEARNY, NEW JERSEY, ON MARCH 8, 1967. AFTER PLAYING FOR THE *UNIVERSITY OF VIRGINIA*, HE LAUNCHED HIS PROFESSIONAL CAREER IN THE AMERICAN SOCCER LEAGUE WITH THE *ALBANY CAPITALS*, BEFORE MOVING TO ENGLAND TO JOIN *SHEFFIELD WEDNESDAY* IN 1990. HE WAS ON THE LOSING SIDE IN AN FA CUP FINAL AND THE WINNING SIDE IN A LEAGUE CUP FINAL, BEFORE GOING ON TO PLAY FOR *DERBY COUNTY* AND *WEST HAM UNITED*. HE RETURNED TO THE STATES FOR THE LAUNCH OF MAJOR LEAGUE SOCCER AND PLAYED FOR *D.C. UNITED*, *NEW ENGLAND REVOLUTION* AND *COLUMBUS CREW*. *HARKES* WON A TOTAL OF 90 *USA* CAPS AND WAS A STAR OF THE 1990 AND 1994 WORLD CUPS. ALTHOUGH HE WAS NATIONAL TEAM CAPTAIN, HE WAS CONTROVERSIALLY DROPPED FROM THE 1998 SQUAD AMID RUMOURS OF PERSONAL CONFLICTS BEHIND THE SCENES.

NAME THREE MEMBERS OF THE *UNITED STATES* 1990 OR 1994 WORLD CUP SQUADS WHO ALSO PLAYED FOR ENGLISH CLUBS.

**MAR
9**

WITH HIS THREE GOALS IN **FULHAM'S** 5-2 VICTORY OVER **NEWCASTLE UNITED** IN EARLY 2012, **CLINT DEMPSEY** BECAME THE FIRST AMERICAN TO SCORE A HAT-TRICK IN THE ENGLISH PREMIER LEAGUE. BORN ON MARCH 8, 1983, IN NACOGDOCHES, TEXAS, **DEMPSEY** LAUNCHED HIS PROFESSIONAL CAREER WITH **NEW ENGLAND REVOLUTION** AND JOINED **FULHAM** IN 2007, THE FIRST AMERICAN TO APPEAR IN A MAJOR EUROPEAN FINAL -- **FULHAM'S** 2010 UEFA EUROPA LEAGUE LOSS TO **ATLÉTICO MADRID** -- HE WAS THE SECOND AMERICAN, AFTER **BRIAN MCBRIDE**, TO SCORE IN MULTIPLE WORLD CUP TOURNAMENTS. FOLLOWING A SEASON WITH T**OTTENHAM HOTSPUR,** HE RETURNED TO THE STATES IN 2013 TO PLAY FOR **SEATTLE SOUNDERS**. HE ANNOUNCED HIS RETIREMENT IN 2018.

NAME THREE MANAGERS THAT **CLINT DEMPSEY** PLAYED UNDER AT **FULHAM**.

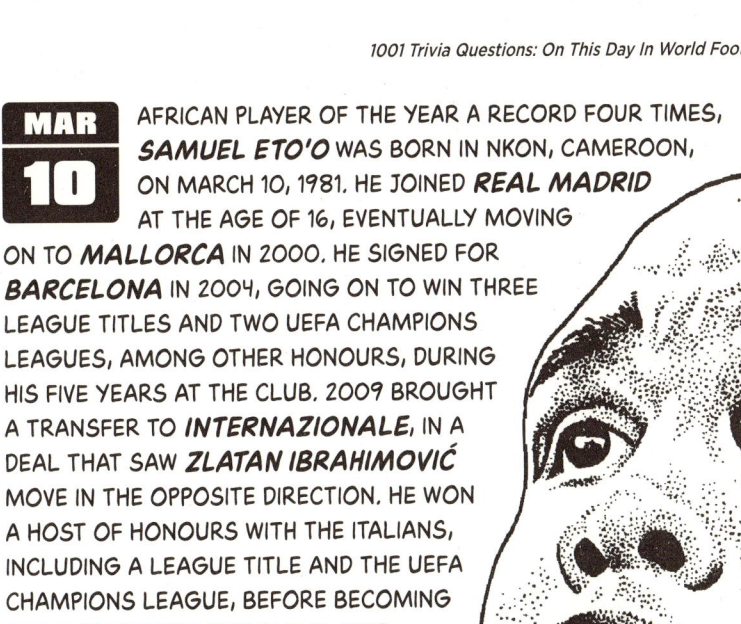

MAR 10

AFRICAN PLAYER OF THE YEAR A RECORD FOUR TIMES, *SAMUEL ETO'O* WAS BORN IN NKON, CAMEROON, ON MARCH 10, 1981. HE JOINED *REAL MADRID* AT THE AGE OF 16, EVENTUALLY MOVING ON TO *MALLORCA* IN 2000. HE SIGNED FOR *BARCELONA* IN 2004, GOING ON TO WIN THREE LEAGUE TITLES AND TWO UEFA CHAMPIONS LEAGUES, AMONG OTHER HONOURS, DURING HIS FIVE YEARS AT THE CLUB. 2009 BROUGHT A TRANSFER TO *INTERNAZIONALE*, IN A DEAL THAT SAW *ZLATAN IBRAHIMOVIĆ* MOVE IN THE OPPOSITE DIRECTION. HE WON A HOST OF HONOURS WITH THE ITALIANS, INCLUDING A LEAGUE TITLE AND THE UEFA CHAMPIONS LEAGUE, BEFORE BECOMING THE WORLD'S HIGHEST PAID PLAYER WITH HIS 2011 MOVE TO RUSSIA'S *ANZHI MAKHACHKALA*. HIS SUBSEQUENT TRAVELS TOOK HIM TO ENGLAND, WITH SPELLS AT *CHELSEA* AND *EVERTON*, ITALY'S *SAMPDORIA*, AND TURKEY, WHERE HE SPENT TWO AND A HALF YEARS AT *ANTALYASPOR* -- HE WAS INTERIM PLAYER-MANAGER FOR A WHILE -- BEFORE JOINING RIVALS *KONYASPOR*. HE ENDED HIS PLAYING CAREER WITH A YEAR AT *QATAR SC*.

1. *ETO'O* IS *CAMEROON'S* TOP ALL-TIME GOALSCORER -- WHICH FORMER *LIVERPOOL* AND *WEST HAM STAR* HOLDS THE COUNTRY'S APPEARANCE RECORD?

2. *ETO'O* WAS THE FOURTH PLAYER TO WIN THE UEFA CHAMPIONS LEAGUE TWO YEARS IN A ROW WITH DIFFERENT TEAMS -- NAME ONE OF THE FIRST THREE.

3. IN WHICH YEAR DID *ETO'O* WIN OLYMPIC GOLD?

MAR 11 BORN IN THE CÔTE D'IVOIRE CAPITAL OF ABIDJAN, ON MARCH 11, 1978, *DIDIER DROGBA* SPENT MUCH OF HIS CHILDHOOD IN FRANCE, WHERE HE LIVED WITH HIS UNCLE, SOCCER PROFESSIONAL *MICHEL GOBA. DIDIER* BEGAN HIS CAREER IN YOUTH FOOTBALL AS A FULL-BACK, BUT SOON FOUND HIMSELF PLAYING AS A STRIKER. BY THE TIME HE WAS 15, HE WAS LIVING NEAR PARIS WITH HIS PARENTS AND SIX SIBLINGS AND BEGINNING TO MAKE A NAME FOR HIMSELF AS A JUNIOR WITH LOCAL CLUB *LEVALLALOIS*. HE BEGAN HIS PROFESSIONAL CAREER AT LIGUE 2 CLUB *LE MANS*, MOVING ON TO LIGUE 1 SIDE *GUINGAMP*, BEFORE SIGNING FOR *MARSEILLE*, WHERE HE BECAME A CLUB LEGEND, SCORING 32 GOALS IN ONE SEASON AND WINNING THE FRENCH FOOTBALLER OF THE YEAR AWARD. HE SIGNED FOR *CHELSEA* IN 2004 AND IN HIS DEBUT SEASON, HE HELPED THE CLUB WIN A FIRST LEAGUE TITLE IN 50 YEARS! HE WENT ON TO ADD TWO MORE LEAGUE TITLES, FOUR FA CUPS AND THE UEFA CHAMPIONS LEAGUE TO HIS TALLY BEFORE JOINING CHINA'S *SHANGHAI SHENHUA* IN 2012. AFTER WINNING FURTHER HONOURS IN TURKEY WITH *GALATASARAY*, HE RETURNED TO LONDON TO HELP *CHELSEA* WIN ANOTHER LEAGUE TITLE. HE FOLLOWED TWO SEASONS IN THE MLS WITH *MONTREAL IMPACT* BEFORE ENDING HIS PLAYING DAYS AS A PLAYER-OWNER OF UNITED SOCCER LEAGUE SIDE *PHOENIX RISING*. HE RETIRED AT THE AGE OF 40.

NAME THREE OF THE COACHES THAT *DIDIER DROGBA* PLAYED UNDER AT *CHELSEA*.

THE ONLY COACH EVER TO WIN TWO WORLD CUPS, **VITTORIO POZZO** WAS BORN IN TURIN, ON MARCH 12, 1886. HE PLAYED PROFESSIONALLY IN SWITZERLAND AND FRANCE, BEFORE HELPING FOUND **TORINO FC** IN 1906. HE PLAYED FOR AND LATER MANAGED THE TEAM, AND MANAGED **ITALY'S** 1912 OLYMPIC SIDE, BEFORE TAKING A JOB OUTSIDE FOOTBALL WITH **PIRELLI**. HE RETURNED TO COACH THE 1934 AND 1938 WORLD CUP-WINNING TEAMS, AS WELL AS THE SIDE THAT WON GOLD AT THE 1936 OLYMPIC GAMES.

1. WHICH COUNTRY HOSTED THE WORLD CUP IN:
   A) 1934
   B) 1938

2. WHO COACHED **ITALY** TO VICTORY IN THE WORLD CUP IN:
   A) 1982
   B) 2006

3. WHICH OTHER COUNTRIES HAVE WON THE WORLD CUP MORE THAN ONCE?

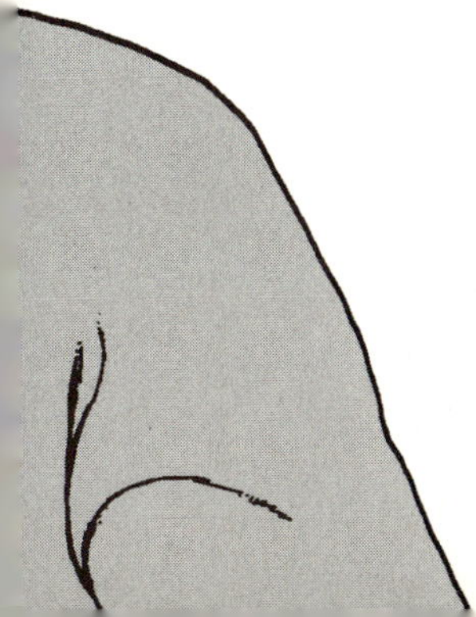

MAR 13

EDGAR DAVIDS WAS BORN IN PARAMARIBO, SURINAME, ON MARCH 13, 1973. INSTANTLY RECOGNISABLE ON THE FIELD, THANKS TO HIS DREADLOCKED HAIR AND THE GOGGLES HE WORE DUE TO HIS GLAUCOMA, HE FIRST CAME TO PROMINENCE WITH **AJAX**, WHERE HIS MEDAL HAUL INCLUDED THREE CONSECUTIVE LEAGUE TITLES, THE UEFA CHAMPIONS LEAGUE AND THE UEFA CUP. A SPELL AT **AC MILAN** WAS FOLLOWED BY SIX YEARS AT **JUVENTUS**, WHERE HE WON THREE LEAGUE TITLES, BUT HIS TIME THERE WAS MARRED BY A FIFA BAN FOLLOWING A POSITIVE TEST FOR THE BANNED STEROID, NANDRALONE. HE SUBSEQUENTLY PLAYED FOR **BARCELONA, INTERNAZIONALE, TOTTENHAM HOTSPUR** AND **AJAX** AGAIN, BEFORE ENDING HIS CAREER AT **CRYSTAL PALACE**, HAVING MADE 74 APPEARANCES FOR THE **NETHERLANDS** NATIONAL TEAM.

IDENTIFY THE FOLLOWING SURINAME-BORN PLAYERS:

1. WON THE UEFA CHAMPIONS LEAGUE FOUR TIMES WITH THREE DIFFERENT CLUBS.

2. EURO 1998 WINNER WHO WON THE UEFA CUP WITH BOTH **AJAX** AND **INTERNAZIONALE.**

3. **LEEDS UNITED, CHELSEA** AND **MIDDLESBROUGH** STRIKER.

MARK FISH WAS BORN IN CAPE TOWN, ON MARCH 14, 1974. HE STARTED HIS PROFESSIONAL CAREER AS A STRIKER WITH **JOMO COSMOS**, BUT BY THE TIME HE JOINED **ORLANDO PIRATES** IN 1994, HE HAD BEEN CONVERTED INTO A CENTRAL DEFENDER. HIS PERFORMANCES IN **SOUTH AFRICA'S** HISTORIC 1996 AFRICAN CUP OF NATIONS TRIUMPH EARNED HIM A TRANSFER TO ITALY'S **LAZIO**. HE MOVED ON TO ENGLAND, WHERE HE SPENT THREE YEARS AT **BOLTON WANDERERS** AND FIVE YEARS AT **CHARLTON ATHLETIC**. A SEVERE CRUCIATE LIGAMENT INJURY IN 2005 WHILE ON LOAN AT **IPSWICH TOWN** FORCED HIS RETIREMENT.

IDENTIFY THE FOLLOWING **SOUTH AFRICA** INTERNATIONALS WHO JOINED ENGLISH PREMIER LEAGUE CLUBS:

1. **SOUTH AFRICA'S** ALL-TIME LEADING GOALSCORER, HE WON LEAGUE TITLES IN THE NETHERLANDS AND PORTUGAL, AND WON THE UEFA CHAMPIONS LEAGUE WITH **PORTO**, BEFORE SPENDING FOUR YEARS AT **BLACKBURN ROVERS**.

2. CAPTAIN OF **LEEDS UNITED** AND THE 2002 **SOUTH AFRICA** WORLD CUP TEAM.

3. DEFENDER WHO SPENT SEVEN YEARS WITH **MANCHESTER UNITED** BEFORE JOINING **BOLTON WANDERERS**.

MAR 15

IN 1884, *EVERTON FC* BEGAN TO PLAY THEIR GAMES AT THE ANFIELD ROAD GROUND IN LIVERPOOL. A YEAR LATER, THE CLUB'S PRESIDENT, *JOHN HOULDING*, BOUGHT THE GROUND OUTRIGHT. A FOUNDING MEMBER OF THE FOOTBALL LEAGUE IN 1888, *EVERTON* WON THE TITLE IN 1891 -- BUT *HOULDING'S* DECISION TO IMPOSE A STEEP INCREASE IN RENT CAUSED A RIFT. ON MARCH 15, 1892, *HOULDING* FOUNDED A NEW CLUB TO USE ANFIELD. ORIGINALLY NAMED *EVERTON ATHLETIC*, THE NEW CLUB SOON CHANGED ITS NAME TO *LIVERPOOL FC.*

AS OF 2021, *LIVERPOOL* HAVE WON HOW MANY:

1. LEAGUE TITLES?

2. FA CUPS?

3. EUROPEAN TROPHIES?

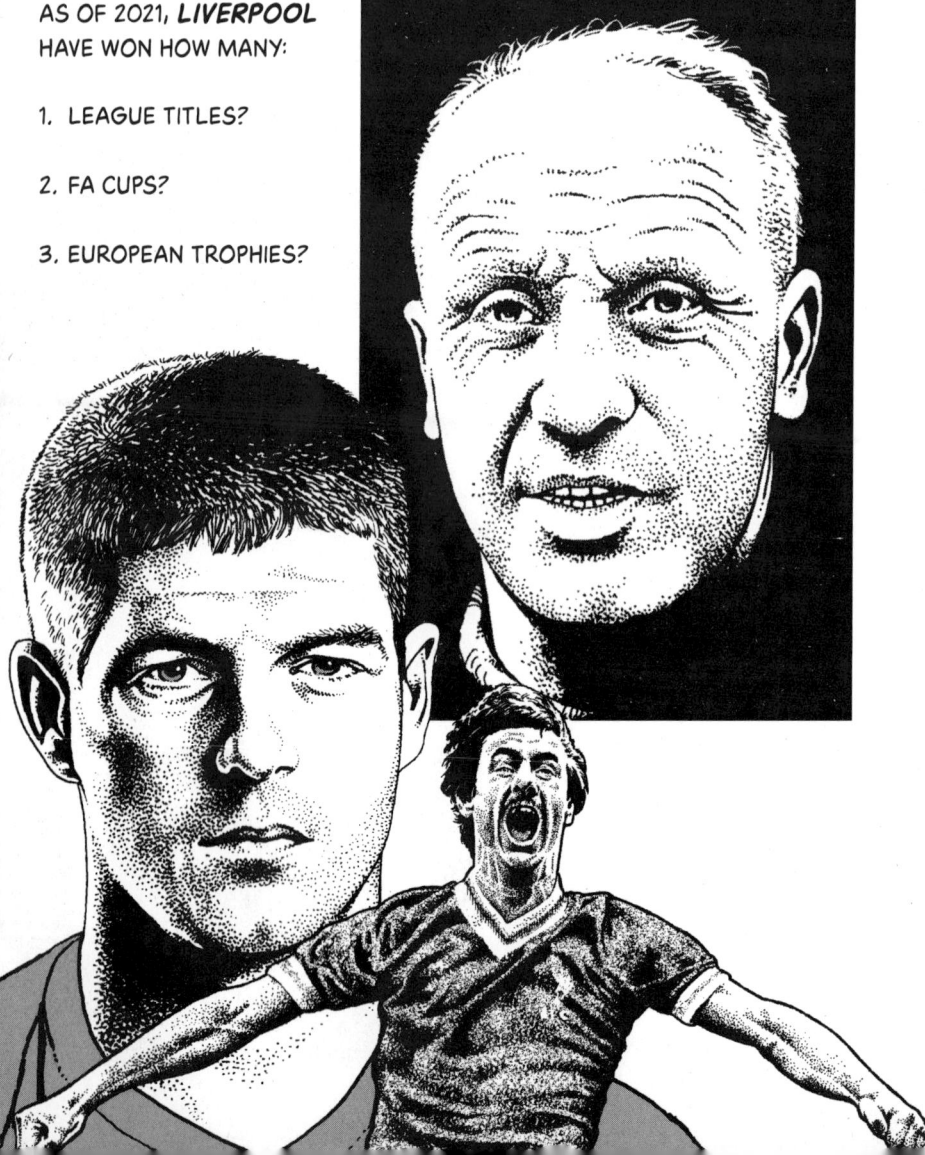

MAR 16

WHEN 16-YEAR-OLD **THEO WALCOTT** MADE HIS SENIOR DEBUT FOR **HARRY REDKNAPP'S SOUTHAMPTON** ON THE FIRST DAY OF THE 2005-06 SEASON, HE BECAME THE CLUB'S YOUNGEST-EVER PLAYER -- AND COMPLETED ONE OF FOOTBALL'S MOST METEORIC RISES! BORN IN THE STANMORE AREA OF LONDON, ON MARCH 16, 1989, AND RAISED IN A SMALL VILLAGE NEAR NEWBURY, BERKSHIRE, **THEO** HADN'T EVEN PLAYED FOOTBALL UNTIL HE WAS 10 YEARS OLD! HE WAS SNAPPED UP BY **ARSENAL** TWO MONTHS BEFORE HIS 17TH BIRTHDAY, AND LATER THAT YEAR, THE FOOTBALL WORLD WAS STUNNED WHEN HE WAS INCLUDED IN **ENGLAND'S** WORLD CUP SQUAD -- BEFORE HE HAD EVEN PLAYED FOR THE **ARSENAL** FIRST TEAM! IN 2008, IN HIS SECOND INTERNATIONAL APPEARANCE, **WALCOTT** BECAME THE YOUNGEST PLAYER TO SCORE A HAT-TRICK FOR **ENGLAND**.

1. NAME ONE OF THE THREE PLAYERS SINCE **WALCOTT** TO SCORE AN **ENGLAND** HAT-TRICK.

2. NAME THE ONLY PLAYER SINCE THE SECOND WORLD WAR TO SCORE 5 GOALS IN ONE GAME FOR **ENGLAND**.

3. WHO IS **ENGLAND'S** ALL-TIME LEADING GOALSCORER?

**MAR
17**

TWO-TIME OLYMPIC GOLD MEDAL WINNER AND TWO-TIME FIFA WOMEN'S WORLD CUP CHAMPION, *MIA HAMM* WAS ONE OF THE FIRST SUPERSTARS OF WOMEN'S SOCCER. BORN IN SELMA, ALABAMA, ON MARCH 17, 1972, SHE WORE CORRECTIVE SHOES AS A TODDLER, HAVING BEEN BORN WITH A CLUB FOOT! TWICE NAMED FIFA WORLD PLAYER OF THE YEAR, SHE IS CO-OWNER OF *LOS ANGELES FC*, A GLOBAL AMBASSADOR FOR *BARCELONA* AND IS ON THE BOARD OF DIRECTORS OF *AS ROMA*.

NAME THE THREE OTHER COUNTRIES BESIDES THE *USA* TO HAVE WON THE FIFA WOMEN'S WORLD CUP.

MAR 18

NAMED AFTER A HERO OF GREEK MYTHOLOGY, *AFC AJAX* WAS FOUNDED IN AMSTERDAM ON MARCH 18, 1900. THE CLUB HAS GONE ON TO WIN A HOST OF HONOURS, INCLUDING 35 EREDIVISIE LEAGUE TITLES, 20 KNVB CUPS AND FOUR UEFA EUROPEAN CUPS/CHAMPIONS LEAGUES. MANY OF THE WORLD'S GREATEST PLAYERS, INCLUDING *SUÁREZ*, *SNEIJDER* AND *VAN BASTEN*, HAVE WORN THE *AJAX* SHIRT. IN 2007, THE CLUB RETIRED THE NUMBER 14 SHIRT OF THE LEGENDARY TRIPLE BALLON D'OR WINNER, *JOHAN CRUYFF*.

IDENTIFY THE PLAYERS HONOURED
BY THESE RETIRED NUMBERS:

1. *MANCHESTER CITY* -- 23

2. *WEST HAM UNITED* -- 6

3. *AC MILAN* -- 3

4. *BRESCIA* -- 10

ON MARCH 19, 2008, **CRISTIANO RONALDO** SCORED BOTH GOALS IN **MANCHESTER UNITED'S** 2-0 WIN OVER **BOLTON WANDERERS**, TAKING HIS TALLY IN ALL COMPETITIONS FOR THE SEASON TO 33. THIS SURPASSED **GEORGE BEST'S** TALLY OF 32 GOALS, SET IN THE 1967-68 SEASON. **UNITED** ENDED THE SEASON AS CHAMPIONS, CLAIMING THEIR 18TH LEAGUE TITLE, AND **RONALDO** FINISHED ON 42 GOALS, JUST FOUR GOALS SHY OF **DENIS LAW'S** CLUB RECORD OF 46 IN ALL COMPETITIONS.

WHO HOLDS THESE **UNITED** RECORDS:

1. SCORING IN 10 CONSECUTIVE LEAGUE MATCHES IN 2003.

2. MOST LEAGUE GOALS IN A SEASON - 32 GOALS IN 1959-60.

3. ALL-TIME TOP GOALSCORER (253 GOALS).

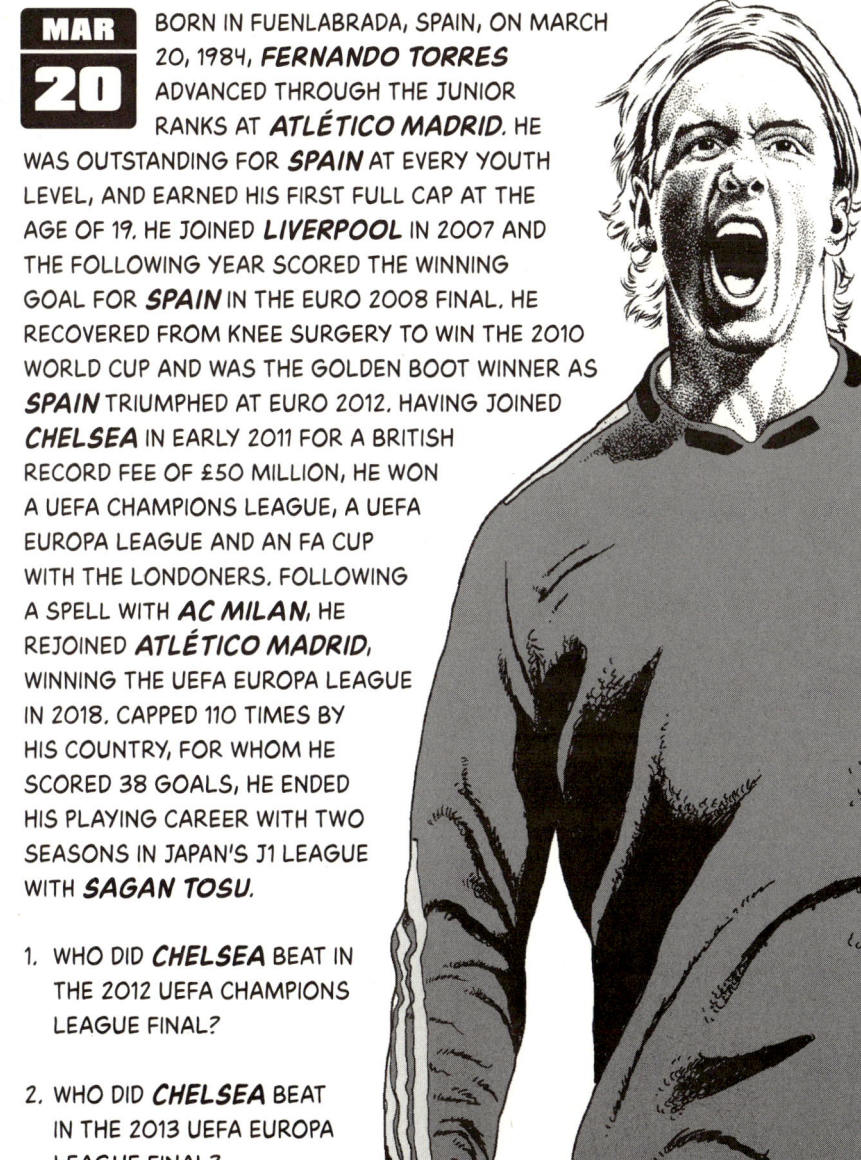

MAR 20

BORN IN FUENLABRADA, SPAIN, ON MARCH 20, 1984, *FERNANDO TORRES* ADVANCED THROUGH THE JUNIOR RANKS AT *ATLÉTICO MADRID*. HE WAS OUTSTANDING FOR *SPAIN* AT EVERY YOUTH LEVEL, AND EARNED HIS FIRST FULL CAP AT THE AGE OF 19. HE JOINED *LIVERPOOL* IN 2007 AND THE FOLLOWING YEAR SCORED THE WINNING GOAL FOR *SPAIN* IN THE EURO 2008 FINAL. HE RECOVERED FROM KNEE SURGERY TO WIN THE 2010 WORLD CUP AND WAS THE GOLDEN BOOT WINNER AS *SPAIN* TRIUMPHED AT EURO 2012. HAVING JOINED *CHELSEA* IN EARLY 2011 FOR A BRITISH RECORD FEE OF £50 MILLION, HE WON A UEFA CHAMPIONS LEAGUE, A UEFA EUROPA LEAGUE AND AN FA CUP WITH THE LONDONERS. FOLLOWING A SPELL WITH *AC MILAN*, HE REJOINED *ATLÉTICO MADRID*, WINNING THE UEFA EUROPA LEAGUE IN 2018. CAPPED 110 TIMES BY HIS COUNTRY, FOR WHOM HE SCORED 38 GOALS, HE ENDED HIS PLAYING CAREER WITH TWO SEASONS IN JAPAN'S J1 LEAGUE WITH *SAGAN TOSU*.

1. WHO DID *CHELSEA* BEAT IN THE 2012 UEFA CHAMPIONS LEAGUE FINAL?

2. WHO DID *CHELSEA* BEAT IN THE 2013 UEFA EUROPA LEAGUE FINAL?

3. WHO DID *ATLÉTICO MADRID* BEAT IN THE 2018 UEFA EUROPA LEAGUE FINAL?

MAR 21

BORN IN PORTO ALEGRE, BRAZIL, ON MARCH 21, 1980, **RONALDINHO GAÚCHO** FIRST MADE HEADLINES AT THE AGE OF 13 WHEN HE SCORED ALL 23 GOALS IN A 23-0 WIN FOR HIS LOCAL TEAM. HE FOLLOWED IN THE FOOTSTEPS OF HIS OLDER BROTHER, **ROBERTO**, AND BEGAN HIS PROFESSIONAL CAREER AT **GRÊMIO**. *(WHEN INJURY CURTAILED HIS CAREER, **ROBERTO** BECAME **RONALDINHO'S** MANAGER.)* TWO-TIMES FIFA WORLD PLAYER OF THE YEAR, HE WAS A WORLD CUP WINNER WITH **BRAZIL** IN 2002, AND CAPTAINED HIS COUNTRY TO GLORY IN THE 2005 CONFEDERATIONS CUP. HE SCORED 33 GOALS IN HIS 97 APPEARANCES FOR HIS COUNTRY.

EUROPEAN FOOTBALLER OF THE YEAR IN 2005, HE WON A HOST OF HONOURS IN EUROPEAN FOOTBALL BEFORE RETURNING TO BRAZIL IN 2011 TO SIGN FOR **FLAMENGO**. 20,000 FANS TURNED OUT TO WELCOME HIM AT HIS UNVEILING, AND HE SOON CELEBRATED HIS RETURN HOME BY HELPING THE CLUB TO CAPTURE THE CAMPEONATO CARIOCA LEAGUE TITLE.

HE MOVED ON TO **ATLÉTICO MINEIRO** IN 2012 AND ADDED MORE TROPHIES TO HIS HAUL. HE SUBSEQUENTLY PLAYED FOR **QUERÉTARO** IN MEXICO, BEFORE A SHORT, UNHAPPY RETURN TO BRAZIL WITH **FLUMINESE**. FOLLOWING A SPELL PLAYING FUTSAL IN INDIA, HE ANNOUNCED HIS RETIREMENT IN 2018.

NAME THE THREE EUROPEAN CLUBS THAT HE PLAYED FOR.

BORN IN CARDIFF, WALES, ON MARCH 22, 1949, *JOHN TOSHACK* BECAME *CARDIFF CITY'S* YOUNGEST PLAYER WHEN HE MADE A GOALSCORING DEBUT FOR THE CLUB AT THE AGE OF 16 YEARS AND 236 DAYS, A RECORD THAT STOOD FOR 41 YEARS. HE JOINED *LIVERPOOL* IN 1970, WHERE HE SUBSEQUENTLY STRUCK UP A FAMOUS GOALSCORING PARTNERSHIP WITH *KEVIN KEEGAN*. HAVING WON A HOST OF HONOURS AT THE CLUB, INCLUDING THREE LEAGUE TITLES AND TWO UEFA CUPS, HE BECAME PLAYER-MANAGER AT *SWANSEA CITY* IN 1978. IN A THREE-YEAR SPELL, HE STEERED THE CLUB FROM THE FOURTH DIVISION TO THE FIRST, AND AT ONE POINT, THEY WERE ACTUALLY TOP OF THE LEAGUE. *TOSHACK* WAS AWARDED THE MBE FOR HIS SERVICES TO FOOTBALL AND TIPPED AS THE NEXT *LIVERPOOL* MANAGER. UNFORTUNATELY, *SWANSEA* WERE RELEGATED IN 1983, AND BY YEAR'S END, WITH THE CLUB FLOUNDERING AT THE FOOT OF THE SECOND DIVISION, *TOSHACK* RESIGNED -- ONLY TO REJOIN EIGHT WEEKS LATER! THIS TIME THERE WERE NO MIRACLES AND BY THE END OF THE SEASON, *SWANSEA* WERE BACK IN THE THIRD TIER AND THE BIG MAN WAS OUT OF A JOB.

TOSHACK SUBSEQUENTLY ENJOYED AN ILLUSTRIOUS COACHING CAREER, WINNING TROPHIES IN SPAIN, TURKEY, AZERBAIJAN AND MOROCCO, AND ENJOYING TWO SPELLS AS MANAGER OF *WALES*. NAME THREE OF THE OTHER TEAMS HE COACHED.

MAR 23

BORN IN VÉLEZ-MÁLAGA, ON MARCH 23, 1968, *FERNANDO RUIZ HIERRO* BEGAN HIS PROFESSIONAL CAREER AT *VALLADOLID*, JOINING *REAL MADRID* AFTER TWO SEASONS. HE SPENT 14 YEARS IN MADRID, WHERE HIS HONOURS INCLUDED THREE UEFA CHAMPIONS LEAGUES AND FIVE LEAGUE TITLES, AND HE AMASSED AN IMPRESSIVE GOAL TALLY FOR A DEFENDER, SCORING 102 GOALS IN 439 APPEARANCES. A SEASON IN QATAR WITH *AL RAYYAN SPORTS CLUB* WAS FOLLOWED BY A SEASON WITH *BOLTON WANDERERS*, FOLLOWING WHICH HE RETIRED FROM PLAYING. HE MADE 89 APPEARANCES FOR *SPAIN*, REPRESENTING HIS COUNTRY IN FOUR WORLD CUPS AND TWO EUROPEAN CHAMPIONSHIPS. HE BRIEFLY COACHED THE NATIONAL TEAM IN 2018.

IDENTIFY THE FOLLOWING INTERNATIONAL STARS WHO HAVE PLAYED IN QATAR:

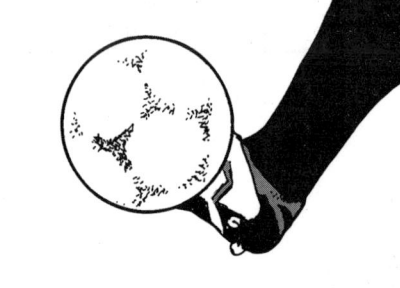

1. FOUR TIMES UEFA CHAMPIONS LEAGUE WINNER WITH *BARCELONA*, WORLD CUP WINNER WITH *SPAIN*, PLAYED FOR *AL-SADD* BEFORE TAKING OVER AS CLUB MANAGER.

2. *CHELSEA* CENTRAL DEFENDER WHO WON THE 1998 WORLD CUP WITH *FRANCE*.

3. THE MOST-CAPPED *NETHERLANDS* PLAYER OF ALL TIME.

MAR 24

CHRISTOPHE JÉRÔME DUGARRY WAS BORN IN LORMONT, FRANCE, ON MARCH 24, 1972. A PRODUCT OF THE **BORDEAUX** YOUTH SYSTEM, HE WON A LIGUE 2 TITLE AND A LEAGUE CUP WITH THE CLUB BEFORE MOVING TO **AC MILAN** IN 1996. A YEAR LATER, HE JOINED **BARCELONA**, WHERE HE WON A LEAGUE TITLE BEFORE SIGNING FOR **MARSEILLE**. A WORLD CUP WINNER IN 1998 AND A EUROPEAN CHAMPIONSHIP WINNER IN 2000, HE WAS CAPPED 55 TIMES BY **FRANCE**. HE RETURNED TO **BORDEAUX** IN 2003, EARNED FOLK HERO STATUS DURING A SPELL WITH **BIRMINGHAM CITY**, AND RETIRED IN 2005 AFTER A BRIEF STAY AT **QATAR SC**, IN WHICH HE MADE NO APPEARANCES.

NAME FIVE OTHER PLAYERS WHO WERE MEMBERS OF BOTH THE 1998 WORLD CUP AND EURO 2000 TRIUMPHANT **FRANCE** SQUADS.

MAR 25

BORN IN CAMBERWELL ON MARCH 25, 2000, *JADON SANCHO* WAS WITH *WATFORD'S* ACADEMY FROM THE AGE OF SEVEN. *MANCHESTER CITY* PAID £66,000 TO SIGN HIM AT 14, IN A DEAL WITH THE POTENTIAL TO REACH £500,000 WITH ADD-ONS. THREE YEARS LATER, IMPATIENT FOR SUCCESS, HE PUSHED FOR A MOVE THAT WOULD GUARANTEE FIRST-TEAM ACTION, AND JOINED *BORUSSIA DORTMUND* IN 2017 FOR A FEE OF £8 MILLION. BY THE END OF 2018, HE WAS A FULL *ENGLAND* INTERNATIONAL AND HAD WON THE BUNDESLIGA PLAYER OF THE MONTH AWARD.

IDENTIFY THESE *ENGLAND* INTERNATIONALS WHO PLAYED IN GERMANY:

1. CANADIAN-BORN CHAMPIONS LEAGUE WINNER WITH *BAYERN MUNICH*, PLAYED FOR BOTH *MANCHESTER UNITED* AND *CITY*.

2. TWO-TIME BALLON D'OR WINNER, WON LEAGUE TITLES WITH *LIVERPOOL* AND *HAMBURG*.

3. EUROPEAN CUP WINNER WITH *NOTTINGHAM FOREST*, HE HAD TWO SPELLS IN GERMANY WITH *FC KÖLN*.

MAR 26

DENMARK CAPTAIN **SIMON KJÆR** WAS BORN IN HORSENS, DENMARK, ON MARCH 26, 1989. HE GRADUATED THROUGH THE YOUTH RANKS AT DANISH SUPERLIGA CLUB FC **MIDTJYLLAND** TO MAKE HIS SENIOR DEBUT IN 2006, BEFORE MOVING TO ITALY'S **PALERMO** IN 2008. AFTER PLAYING FOR **DENMARK** AT THE 2010 WORLD CUP, HE SIGNED FOR **VFL WOLFSBURG**, BUT WAS SOON LOANED OUT TO **ROMA**. HE SUBSEQUENTLY PLAYED FOR **LILLE**, **FENERBAHÇE**, **SEVILLA** AND **ATALANTA**, BEFORE JOINING **AC MILAN** IN 2020.

IDENTIFY THESE COACHES FOR WHOM **KJÆR** HAS PLAYED:

1. FORMER **ENGLAND** MANAGER WHO SIGNED HIM FOR **VFL WOLFSBURG**.

2. FORMER **ITALY** GOALKEEPER WHO WON TWO UEFA CUPS AS AN **INTERNAZIONALE** PLAYER, COACHED **KJÆR** AT **PALERMO**.

3. **KJÆR'S** COACH AT **ROMA**, HE WAS A LEAGUE CHAMPION WITH **REAL MADRID** AND **BARCELONA**, AND WON AN OLYMPIC GOLD MEDAL WITH **SPAIN** IN 1992.

MAR
27

MANUEL NEUER WAS BORN IN GELSENKIRCHEN, WEST GERMANY, ON MARCH 27, 1986. HE GREW UP IN THE SHADOW OF **SCHALKE 04'S** OLD PARKSTADION, WAS GIVEN HIS FIRST BALL AT THE AGE OF TWO AND WAS SIGNED TO THE CLUB BY THE AGE OF FOUR. HE INITIALLY PLAYED AS A STRIKER BUT QUICKLY SHOWED AN APTITUDE FOR GOALKEEPING. PROGRESSING THROUGH THE YOUTH RANKS WITH CLUB AND COUNTRY, HE MADE HIS FIRST TEAM DEBUT FOR **SCHALKE 04** IN THE OPENING WEEKS OF THE 2006-07 SEASON. AROUND THE SAME TIME, THE 20-YEAR-OLD ALSO ESTABLISHED HIMSELF IN **GERMANY'S U-21** TEAM. HE PLAYED EVERY MINUTE OF **SCHALKE'S** 2007-08 BUNDESLIGA SEASON AND IN 2009, HE HELPED **GERMANY** WIN THE UEFA EUROPEAN U-21 FOOTBALL CHAMPIONSHIP. NAMED **SCHALKE** CAPTAIN FOR THE 2010-11 SEASON, HE LED THE TEAM TO ITS FIRST UEFA CHAMPIONS LEAGUE SEMI-FINAL AND VICTORY IN THE GERMAN CUP FINAL. HE JOINED **BAYERN MUNICH** IN 2011, BY WHICH TIME HE WAS THE AUTOMATIC FIRST CHOICE FOR **GERMANY.**

NEUER KEPT GOAL IN THE **GERMANY** SIDE THAT WON THE 2014 WORLD CUP. WHO KEPT GOAL FOR **GERMANY** IN THESE WORLD CUP FINAL WINS:

1. 1954?

2. 1974?

3. 1990?

MAR 28 BENJAMIN PAVARD, BORN ON MARCH 28, 1992 IN MAUBEUGE, LAUNCHED HIS CAREER AT *LILLE*, HAVING ENTERED THE CLUB'S ACADEMY AS A NINE-YEAR-OLD. HE JOINED *VFB STUTTGART* IN 2016, AND THE TEAM WAS PROMOTED TO THE TOP FLIGHT IN HIS DEBUT SEASON. HIS OUTSTANDING FORM EARNED HIM A MOVE TO *BAYERN MUNICH* IN 2019, BY WHICH TIME HE WAS A WORLD CUP WINNER WITH *FRANCE*.

PAVARD WAS ONE OF ONLY TWO GERMANY-BASED PLAYERS, ALONG WITH *BAYERN MUNICH'S CORENTIN TOLISSO*, IN THE *FRANCE* SQUAD THAT WON THE 2018 WORLD CUP. CAN YOU NAME THE FIVE SQUAD PLAYERS WHO PLAYED THEIR FOOTBALL IN THE ENGLISH PREMIER LEAGUE AT THAT TIME?

BORN IN AMADORA, PORTUGAL, ON MARCH 29, 1972, *RUI COSTA* GRADUATED THROUGH THE YOUTH RANKS AT *BENFICA*. FOLLOWING A SEASON ON LOAN AT *FAFE*, HE ESTABLISHED HIMSELF IN THE *BENFICA* FIRST TEAM. AFTER WINNING A PORTUGUESE CUP AND A LEAGUE TITLE, HE MOVED TO *FIORENTINA*, WHERE HE WON TWO COPPA ITALIAS AND A SUPERCOPPA ITALIANA. SEVEN YEARS LATER, AS *FIORENTINA* EXPERIENCED FINANCIAL PROBLEMS, *COSTA* WAS SOLD TO *AC MILAN*. THE CLUB'S RECORD SIGNING AT THAT TIME, HE WON A HOST OF HONOURS WITH THE *"ROSSONERI"*, INCLUDING A SERIE A TITLE AND A UEFA CHAMPIONS LEAGUE. A FIFA U-20 WORLD CUP WINNER AS A TEENAGER, HE MADE 94 APPEARANCES FOR *PORTUGAL*, SCORING 26 GOALS. HE ENDED HIS PLAYING CAREER BACK AT *BENFICA*, RETIRING IN 2008 TO TAKE UP A POSITION AS THE CLUB'S DIRECTOR OF FOOTBALL.

TO DATE, ONLY SIX PLAYERS HAVE SCORED MORE THAN *COSTA'S* 26 GOALS FOR *PORTUGAL* -- CAN YOU NAME THREE OF THEM?

MAR 30

HAVING LEARNED HIS TRADE WITH **SEVILLA**, **SERGIO RAMOS** -- BORN IN CAMAS ON MARCH 30, 1986 -- JOINED **REAL MADRID** IN 2005. NAMED LA LIGA'S BEST DEFENDER A RECORD FIVE TIMES, HE WON A MULTITUDE OF HONOURS WITH **"LOS MERENGUES"**, INCLUDING FIVE LEAGUE TITLES AND FOUR UEFA CHAMPIONS LEAGUES. THE MOST-CAPPED PLAYER IN **SPAIN'S** HISTORY, HE WAS A MEMBER OF THE TEAMS THAT WON THE 2010 WORLD CUP AND THE 2008 AND 2012 EUROPEAN CHAMPIONSHIPS. HE IS ALSO THE MOST CARDED PLAYER IN THE HISTORY OF LA LIGA AND THE UEFA CHAMPIONS LEAGUE!

THE **SPAIN** SQUAD THAT WON THE 2010 WORLD CUP WAS DRAWN ENTIRELY FROM **REAL MADRID** AND **BARCELONA**, WITH THE EXCEPTION OF THREE PLAYERS, TWO FROM **LIVERPOOL** AND ONE FROM **ARSENAL**, WHO PLAYED IN THE ENGLISH PREMIER LEAGUE. CAN YOU NAME THEM?

MAR 31 CAPTAIN OF THE 1990 **CAMEROON** WORLD CUP TEAM THAT BECAME THE FIRST AFRICAN NATION TO REACH THE QUARTER-FINALS OF THE COMPETITION, **STEPHEN TATAW** WAS BORN IN YAOUNDÉ, ON MARCH 31, 1963. HE ALSO CAPTAINED HIS COUNTRY AT THE 1994 WORLD CUP, THE SAME YEAR HE JOINED **TOSU FUTURES**, BECOMING THE FIRST AFRICAN PLAYER TO PLAY FOR A JAPANESE CLUB.

WHO CAPTAINED THESE COUNTRIES AT THE 1990 WORLD CUP?

1. **ARGENTINA** -- FIFA WORLD PLAYER OF THE CENTURY.

2. **NETHERLANDS** -- 1987 EUROPEAN FOOTBALLER OF THE YEAR AND CAPTAIN OF THE TEAM THAT WON THE 1988 EUROPEAN CHAMPIONSHIPS.

3. **WEST GERMANY** -- FIFA WORLD PLAYER OF THE YEAR, BALLON D'OR WINNER, PLAYED IN 5 WORLD CUPS, WON 7 LEAGUE TITLES WITH **BAYERN MUNICH** AND THE UEFA CUP WITH **INTERNAZIONALE**.

4. **REPUBLIC OF IRELAND** -- BORN IN ENGLAND, HE PLAYED FOR **IRELAND** 57 TIMES AND MANAGED THE 2002 WORLD CUP TEAM.

APRIL

APR 1

CLARENCE SEEDORF WAS BORN IN PARAMARIBO, SURINAME, ON APRIL 1, 1976. HE MADE HIS DEBUT WITH *AJAX* AGED 16 AND HELPED THE CLUB WIN A DOMESTIC TREBLE IN HIS SECOND SEASON. AT 19, HE WAS A EUROPEAN CUP WINNER AND WON A SECOND LEAGUE TITLE. A SPELL AT *SAMPDORIA* WAS FOLLOWED BY FOUR YEARS AT *REAL MADRID*, WHERE HE ADDED ANOTHER LEAGUE TITLE AND A SECOND EUROPEAN CUP TO HIS TALLY. HE SIGNED FOR *INTERNAZIONALE* IN 1999 BUT TWO YEARS LATER JOINED ARCH-RIVALS *AC MILAN*, WITH WHOM HE GAINED A HOST OF HONOURS, INCLUDING TWO SERIE A TITLES AND A EUROPEAN CUP, MAKING HIM THE FIRST PLAYER TO WIN EUROPE'S MOST-COVETED TROPHY WITH THREE DIFFERENT CLUBS. HE ENDED HIS PLAYING CAREER WITH TWO SEASONS AT BRAZIL'S *BOTAFOGO*, WINNING THE 2013 CAMPEONATO CARIOCA. HE RETIRED TO TAKE OVER AS *AC MILAN* HEAD COACH BUT HIS TENURE WAS SHORT-LIVED. SUBSEQUENT SPELLS AT THE HELM OF CHINA'S *SHENZHEN FC*, BRAZIL'S *ATLÉTICO PARANAENSE* AND *DEPORTIVO DE LA CORUÑA* IN SPAIN WERE EQUALLY BRIEF AND HIS TIME AS HEAD COACH OF THE *CAMEROON* NATIONAL TEAM LASTED LESS THAN A YEAR.

SEEDORF IS TIED ON 87 *NETHERLANDS* CAPS WITH *JOHN HEITINGA*. NAME THREE PLAYERS WHO HAVE MADE MORE APPEARANCES FOR THE DUTCH NATIONAL TEAM.

APR 2

FERENC PUSKÁS WAS BORN IN BUDAPEST, HUNGARY, ON APRIL 2, 1927. AS A PLAYER, HIS HONOURS INCLUDED OLYMPIC GOLD, THREE EUROPEAN CUPS AND 10 LEAGUE TITLES. AS A COACH, HE WON LEAGUE TITLES IN THREE COUNTRIES. HE MADE 85 APPEARANCES FOR **HUNGARY**, SCORING 84 GOALS, INCLUDING ONE IN THE 3-2 LOSS TO **WEST GERMANY** IN THE 1954 WORLD CUP FINAL. ON TOUR WITH **HONVÉD** AT THE TIME OF THE 1956 UPRISING, HE ELECTED NOT TO RETURN TO HUNGARY, EARNING HIMSELF A TWO-YEAR BAN FROM UEFA. HE LATER SIGNED FOR **REAL MADRID**, WITH WHOM HE WON FIVE LEAGUE TITLES AND THREE EUROPEAN CUPS IN EIGHT SEASONS. HE ALSO PLAYED FOR **SPAIN** AT THE 1962 WORLD CUP.

1. AFTER MOVING INTO COACHING, **PUSKÁS** GUIDED WHICH GREEK CLUB TO THE EUROPEAN CUP FINAL IN 1971?

2. WITH HIS 11 GOALS, WHICH HUNGARIAN WAS THE 1954 WORLD CUP TOP SCORER?

3. **PUSKÁS** SCORED FOUR GOALS FOR **REAL MADRID** IN 1960'S 7-3 EUROPEAN CUP FINAL WIN OVER WHICH TEAM?

APR 3

GABRIEL JESUS WAS BORN IN SÃO PAULO, BRAZIL, ON APRIL 3, 1997. HE BURST ONTO THE SCENE AS A TEEN WITH **PALMEIRAS**, HELPING THE CLUB TO WIN THE COPA DO BRASIL AND A FIRST NATIONAL LEAGUE TITLE IN 22 YEARS. HAVING BEEN A MEMBER OF THE **BRAZIL** TEAM THAT REACHED THE FINAL OF THE 2015 FIFA U-20 WORLD CUP, HE WON A GOLD MEDAL AT THE 2016 OLYMPICS. HE JOINED **MANCHESTER CITY** IN EARLY 2017. IN 2018, HE WON A LEAGUE AND LEAGUE CUP DOUBLE AND SCORED THE WINNING GOAL IN **CITY'S** FINAL LEAGUE GAME OF THE SEASON THAT GAVE THE CLUB A RECORD 100 POINTS! THE FOLLOWING SEASON, HE HELPED **CITY** WIN A DOMESTIC TREBLE!

IDENTIFY THESE **BRAZIL** INTERNATIONALS WHO SIGNED FOR **MANCHESTER CITY:**

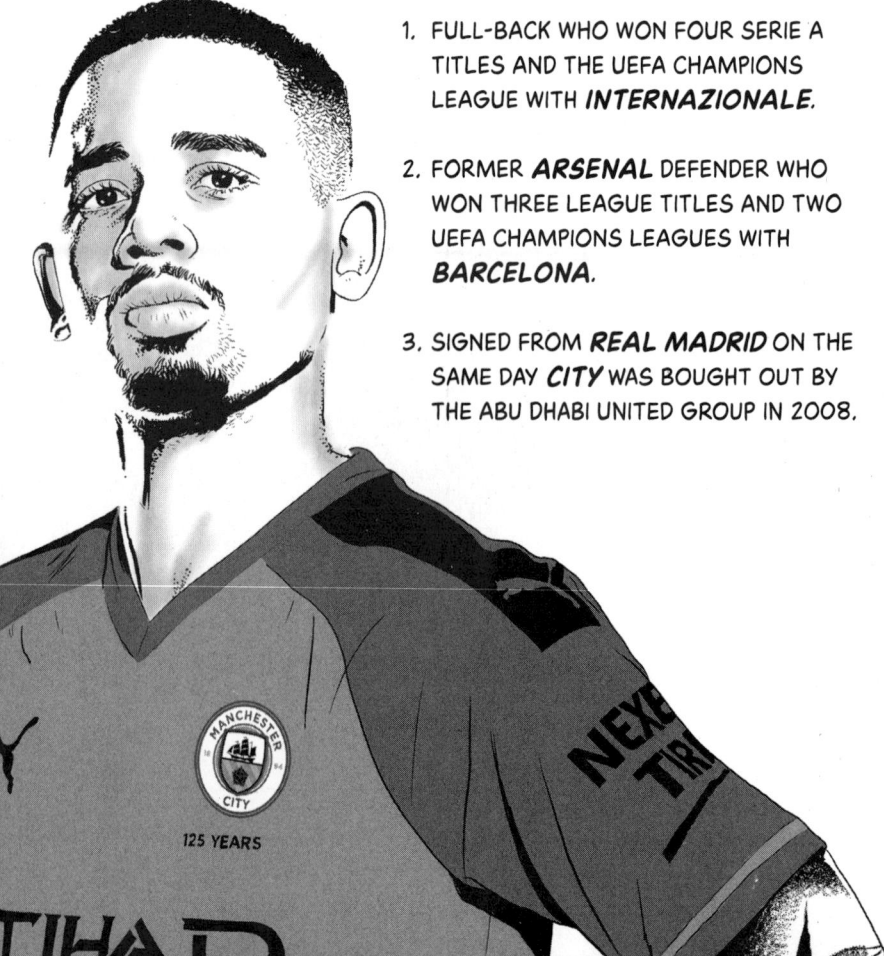

1. FULL-BACK WHO WON FOUR SERIE A TITLES AND THE UEFA CHAMPIONS LEAGUE WITH **INTERNAZIONALE**.

2. FORMER **ARSENAL** DEFENDER WHO WON THREE LEAGUE TITLES AND TWO UEFA CHAMPIONS LEAGUES WITH **BARCELONA**.

3. SIGNED FROM **REAL MADRID** ON THE SAME DAY **CITY** WAS BOUGHT OUT BY THE ABU DHABI UNITED GROUP IN 2008.

APR 4

BORN IN MONTEVIDEO, URUGUAY, ON NOVEMBER 26, 1898, *HÉCTOR SCARONE* WAS 19 YEARS OLD WHEN HE SCORED THE GOAL THAT MADE *URUGUAY* SOUTH AMERICAN CHAMPIONS IN 1917. HE WON THE TITLE THREE MORE TIMES -- IN 1923, 1924 AND 1926 -- AND WAS A GOLD MEDAL WINNER AT THE 1924 AND 1928 OLYMPIC GAMES. AT CLUB LEVEL, HE WON EIGHT URUGUAYAN LEAGUE TITLES WITH *NACIONAL* AND PLAYED IN EUROPE WITH *BARCELONA* AND *INTERNAZIONALE*. HIS CROWNING ACHIEVEMENT WAS HIS PART IN *URUGUAY'S* 1930 TRIUMPH IN THE INAUGURAL WORLD CUP. HE RETIRED FROM INTERNATIONAL FOOTBALL SOON AFTER, HIS RECORD OF 31 GOALS IN 52 GAMES REMAINING UNSURPASSED UNTIL 2011. *HÉCTOR SCARONE* WENT ON TO COACH *REAL MADRID* AND *NACIONAL*, AND DIED ON APRIL 4, 1967.

1. WHO BROKE *SCARONE'S* RECORD OF 31 GOALS FOR *URUGUAY* IN OCTOBER, 2011?

2. SINCE *SCARONE*, ONLY TWO OTHER WORLD CUP-WINNING PLAYERS -- A CHAMPION WITH *ARGENTINA* IN 1986 AND A WINNER IN 1998 -- HAVE COACHED *REAL MADRID*. CAN YOU NAME THEM?

3. WHO DID *URUGUAY* DEFEAT IN THE 1930 WORLD CUP FINAL?

APR 5

LEGENDARY **PRESTON NORTH END** AND **ENGLAND** WINGER **TOM FINNEY** WAS BORN IN PRESTON ON APRIL 5, 1922. TWICE VOTED FOOTBALLER OF THE YEAR, HE SCORED 187 GOALS FOR **PRESTON** IN 433 LEAGUE APPEARANCES. HIS OVERSEAS SERVICE DURING THE SECOND WORLD WAR, AND THE PRESENCE OF **STANLEY MATTHEWS**, KEPT HIM OUT OF THE **ENGLAND** TEAM, BUT HE EVENTUALLY WON 76 CAPS, SCORING 30 GOALS. HE DIED IN 2014.

ONLY EIGHT OTHER PLAYERS HAVE
SCORED 30 OR MORE GOALS
FOR **ENGLAND** --
CAN YOU NAME THEM?

APR 6

BORN IN KINSHASA, ZAIRE, ON APRIL 6, 1988, *FABRICE MUAMBA* WAS RAISED IN BRITAIN FROM THE AGE OF 11. A PRODUCT OF THE YOUTH SYSTEM AT *ARSENAL*, HE REPRESENTED *ENGLAND* AT ALL YOUTH LEVELS AND CAPTAINED THE UNDER-19 SIDE. HE ESTABLISHED HIS REPUTATION AS A DYNAMIC CENTRAL MIDFIELDER WITH *BIRMINGHAM CITY*, MOVING ON TO *BOLTON WANDERERS* IN 2008. DURING AN FA CUP GAME AGAINST *TOTTENHAM HOTSPUR* IN 2012, FABRICE SUFFERED A CARDIAC ARREST AND COLLAPSED. AFTER PROLONGED ATTEMPTS TO REVIVE HIM FAILED, THE GAME WAS ABANDONED, AND HE WAS RUSHED TO A NEARBY HOSPITAL. IT WAS LATER REVEALED THAT HIS HEART HAD STOPPED FOR 78 MINUTES. AS HE BATTLED FOR LIFE, HE AND HIS FAMILY RECEIVED A WORLDWIDE OUTPOURING OF SUPPORT FROM PLAYERS AND FANS ALIKE. FORTUNATELY, HE RECOVERED -- BUT RETIRED FROM THE GAME ON MEDICAL ADVICE.

IDENTIFY THESE OTHER NATURALISED BRITISH CITIZENS WHO ALSO REPRESENTED *ENGLAND* AT YOUTH OR UNDER-21 LEVELS:

1. BORN IN NIGERIA, HE JOINED *QUEENS PARK RANGERS* FROM *MANCHESTER CITY* AFTER A LOAN SPELL AT *SUNDERLAND*, AND ENDED HIS CAREER IN THE MLS WITH *REAL SALT LAKE*.

2. NIGERIA-BORN, HE JOINED *WIGAN ATHLETIC* FROM *CRYSTAL PALACE*, EARNED MULTIPLE HONOURS WITH *CHELSEA*, AND REPRESENTED *NIGERIA* IN THE 2014 AND 2018 WORLD CUPS.

3. HE SPENT 14 YEARS WITH *NEWCASTLE UNITED*, AND WAS ANOTHER *ENGLAND* JUNIOR WHO OPTED TO PLAY FOR *NIGERIA*, REPRESENTING HIS HOMELAND AT THE 2014 WORLD CUP.

APR 7

FRANCK RIBÉRY WAS BORN IN BOULOGNE-SUR-MER, FRANCE, ON APRIL 7, 1983. HE SPENT THE EARLY YEARS OF HIS CAREER IN THE LOWER DIVISIONS OF THE FRENCH LEAGUE WITH **BOULOGNE, OLYMPIQUE ALÈS** AND **STADE BREST**, EVENTUALLY JOINING **FC METZ** IN THE TOP FLIGHT. A SPELL WITH **GALATASARAY** WAS FOLLOWED BY A RETURN TO FRANCE WITH **MARSEILLE**, ALTHOUGH THE TRANSFER WAS UNSUCCESSFULLY CONTESTED IN THE INTERNATIONAL COURT OF ARBITRATION BY THE TURKISH CLUB. STAR OF THE 2006 WORLD CUP FOR **FRANCE**, HE JOINED **BAYERN MUNICH** IN 2007, GOING ON TO WIN TWO LEAGUE AND CUP DOUBLES AND THE 2008 GERMAN FOOTBALLER OF THE YEAR AWARD. HE HAS BEEN NAMED FRENCH PLAYER OF THE YEAR THREE TIMES.

1. **RIBÉRY** IS ONE OF ONLY SIX NON-GERMANS TO BE NAMED GERMAN FOOTBALLER OF THE YEAR -- NAME ONE OF THE OTHERS.

2. NAME ONE OF THE TEN COACHES **RIBÉRY** PLAYED UNDER AT **BAYERN MUNICH**.

3. WHICH ITALIAN CLUB SIGNED **RIBÉRY** IN 2019?

APR 8

BORN IN MALBORK, POLAND, ON APRIL 8, 1950, *GRZEGORZ LATO* MADE THE FIRST OF HIS CENTURY OF APPEARANCES FOR *POLAND* IN 1971 AND WAS A MEMBER OF THE SQUAD WHICH WON OLYMPIC GOLD IN 1972. AN OUTSTANDING STRIKER, HE WAS THE LEADING SCORER IN THE 1974 WORLD CUP FINALS, WHEN HIS SEVEN GOALS HELPED *POLAND* INTO THIRD PLACE. FOUR YEARS LATER, AFTER LEADING *POLAND'S* ATTACK AT THE 1978 WORLD CUP, HE WAS REWARDED WITH A TRANSFER TO BELGIUM'S *KSC LOKEREN*, HAVING WON THE POLISH LEAGUE TITLE TWICE WITH *STAL MIELEC*. DROPPING BACK FROM ATTACK TO MIDFIELD, *LATO* TURNED IN ANOTHER SERIES OF MAGNIFICENT DISPLAYS IN *POLAND'S* 1982 WORLD CUP CAMPAIGN, WHERE THE POLES WERE, ONCE AGAIN, PLACED THIRD. HE BOWED OUT OF THE INTERNATIONAL SCENE TWO YEARS LATER -- HAVING SCORED 45 GOALS FOR *POLAND* -- AND ENDED HIS CAREER IN MEXICO WITH *ATLANTE*.

NAME THE SUBSEQUENT WORLD CUP GOLDEN SHOE WINNERS SINCE *LATO* FINISHED AS TOP SCORER AT THE 1974 TOURNAMENT.

**APR
9**

ROBBIE FOWLER WAS
BORN IN LIVERPOOL ON
APRIL 9, 1975. DURING
TWO SPELLS WITH
LIVERPOOL HE WON
TWO FA CUPS, TWO
LEAGUE CUPS, THE
UEFA CUP AND THE UEFA
SUPER CUP, SCORING 183
GOALS, 128 OF WHICH WERE
IN THE PREMIER LEAGUE. HE
WAS VOTED PFA YOUNG PLAYER
OF THE YEAR IN 1995 AND 1996.
CAPPED 26 TIMES BY ***ENGLAND***,
FOR WHOM HE SCORED 7 GOALS, HE
PLAYED FOR A NUMBER OF BRITISH
CLUBS, BEFORE MOVING TO AUSTRALIA
IN 2009. FOLLOWING SPELLS WITH ***NORTH
QUEENSLAND FURY*** AND ***PERTH GLORY***,
HE SIGNED FOR THAI CLUB ***MUANGTHONG
UNITED*** IN 2011, BECOMING PLAYER-MANAGER
SOON AFTER. HE COACHED AUSTRALIA'S
BRISBANE ROAR BEFORE TAKING THE
REINS OF INDIAN SUPER LEAGUE CLUB
EAST BENGAL IN 2020.

1. NAME THE FOUR OTHER BRITISH
   CLUBS FOR WHOM HE PLAYED.

2. NAME THE THREE OTHERS, TWO FROM ***MANCHESTER UNITED***
   AND ONE FROM ***TOTTENHAM HOTSPUR***, WHO WERE NAMED PFA
   YOUNG PLAYER OF THE YEAR IN TWO CONSECUTIVE SEASONS.

3. ***ROBBIE FOWLER*** SCORED NINE PREMIER LEAGUE HAT-TRICKS. WHO
   HOLDS THE RECORD OF 12 HAT-TRICKS IN THE PREMIER LEAGUE?

APR 10 CAPPED 125 TIMES BY **BRAZIL**, WITH WHOM HE WON THE 2002 WORLD CUP AND TWO COPA AMÉRICAS, **ROBERTO CARLOS** WAS BORN IN GARÇA, SÃO PAULO, BRAZIL, ON APRIL 10, 1973, HE WON TWO LEAGUE TITLES WITH **PALMEIRAS**, BEFORE SPENDING A SEASON IN ITALY WITH **INTERNAZIONALE**. MOVING ON TO **REAL MADRID**, HE WON A HOST OF HONOURS OVER THE NEXT 11 SEASONS, INCLUDING FOUR LEAGUE TITLES AND THREE UEFA CHAMPIONS LEAGUES, HE WENT ON TO WIN TWO TURKISH SUPER CUPS WITH **FENERBAHÇE** AND PLAYED BRIEFLY BACK IN BRAZIL WITH **CORINTHIANS**, BEFORE ENDING HIS PLAYING DAYS IN RUSSIA WITH **ANZHI MAKHACHKALA**.

IDENTIFY THESE FORMER **ANZHI MAKHACHKALA** PLAYERS:

1. FRENCH-BORN CONGO INTERNATIONAL DEFENDER WHO SPENT FIVE YEARS AT **BLACKBURN ROVERS**.

2. **RUSSIA** INTERNATIONAL WHO WON A LEAGUE AND CUP DOUBLE WITH **CHELSEA** IN 2010.

3. FOUR TIMES AFRICAN PLAYER OF THE YEAR WHO WON THE UEFA CHAMPIONS LEAGUE WITH TWO DIFFERENT CLUBS.

APR 11

DELE ALLI WAS BORN **BAMIDELE JERMAINE ALLI** IN MILTON KEYNES, ON APRIL 11, 1996. HE CAME THROUGH THE YOUTH SYSTEM AT LOCAL CLUB **MILTON KEYNES DONS**, MAKING HIS SENIOR DEBUT AT THE AGE OF 16. HE WAS SIGNED BY **TOTTENHAM HOTSPUR** IN EARLY 2015 AND LOANED BACK TO **MK DONS** FOR THE REMAINDER OF THE SEASON. HE WAS VOTED FOOTBALL LEAGUE YOUNG PLAYER OF THE YEAR, HIS PERFORMANCES HELPING **"THE DONS"** GAIN PROMOTION TO THE CHAMPIONSHIP. IN EACH OF HIS FIRST TWO SEASONS WITH **SPURS**, HE WAS VOTED PFA YOUNG PLAYER OF THE YEAR.

IDENTIFY THE FOLLOWING WHO HAVE PLAYED FOR **MK DONS:**

1. FORMER **LEEDS UNITED**, **MANCHESTER UNITED** AND **NEWCASTLE UNITED** MIDFIELDER WHO HAD A SPELL AS CARETAKER MANAGER OF **NOTTS COUNTY**.

2. **GERMANY** MIDFIELDER WHO WON HONOURS WITH **BAYERN MUNICH** AND **LIVERPOOL** AND PLAYED FOR **BOLTON WANDERERS** AND MANCHESTER CITY.

3. STRIKER CAPPED 76 TIMES BY **NORWAY**, HE WON NUMEROUS HONOURS WITH **CHELSEA** AND PLAYED FOR **RANGERS, SUNDERLAND** AND **LEEDS UNITED**.

APR 12

THE OUTPOURING OF GRIEF THAT FOLLOWED THE END OF *BOBBY MOORE'S* BATTLE WITH CANCER IN 1993 WAS A MEASURE OF HIS HERO STATUS. THE INSPIRATIONAL CAPTAIN OF *ENGLAND'S* VICTORIOUS 1966 WORLD CUP SIDE WAS BORN IN BARKING, ESSEX, ON APRIL 12, 1941 AND SIGNED FOR *WEST HAM UNITED* AS A TEENAGER. HE WON THE FIRST OF HIS 108 CAPS IN 1962 -- HIS SECOND CAP COMING IN *ENGLAND'S* OPENING GAME OF THE 1962 WORLD CUP FINALS. HE WAS APPOINTED *ENGLAND'S* YOUNGEST CAPTAIN THE FOLLOWING YEAR, AND IN 1964 WAS VOTED FOOTBALLER OF THE YEAR. HE LED *WEST HAM* TO FA CUP AND EUROPEAN CUP-WINNERS' CUP TRIUMPHS, SETTING A CLUB RECORD FOR THAT TIME OF 642 LEAGUE AND CUP APPEARANCES, BEFORE JOINING *FULHAM* IN 1974. FOLLOWING SPELLS IN THE NASL WITH SAN *ANTONIO THUNDER* AND *SEATTLE SOUNDERS, MOORE* BRIEFLY PLAYED FOR DENMARK'S *HERNING FC* BEFORE MANAGING *OXFORD CITY*, HONG KONG'S *EASTERN AA* AND *SOUTHEND UNITED.*

BOBBY MOORE CAPTAINED *ENGLAND* 90 TIMES, AS DID HIS PREDECESSOR, *BILLY WRIGHT.* HOW MANY OF THE SEVEN OTHER PLAYERS WHO HAVE CAPTAINED *ENGLAND* AT LEAST 30 TIMES CAN YOU NAME?

APR 13

RUDI VÖLLER SCORED 47 GOALS IN 90 GAMES FOR *GERMANY*, WAS A WORLD CUP WINNER IN 1990, AND WAS A MEMBER OF THE TEAMS THAT FINISHED RUNNERS-UP AT THE 1986 WORLD CUP AND EURO 92. AS A COACH, HE STEERED HIS COUNTRY TO THE FINAL OF THE 2002 WORLD CUP, WHERE *GERMANY* LOST TO *BRAZIL*. BORN IN HANAU, ON APRIL 13, 1960, *VÖLLER* WAS TOP BUNDESLIGA SCORER DURING HIS TIME WITH *WERDER BREMEN*, WAS A LEAGUE CHAMPION WITH *ROMA*, AND WON THE UEFA CHAMPIONS LEAGUE WITH *MARSEILLE*.

1. NAME ONE OF THE CLUBS THAT *VÖLLER* MANAGED.

2. IN 1986, *VÖLLER* BECAME THE THIRD SUBSTITUTE IN HISTORY TO SCORE IN A WORLD CUP FINAL. NAME ONE OF THE THREE OTHERS WHO HAVE ACHIEVED THIS FEAT.

3. WHO DID *GERMANY* DEFEAT IN THE 1990 WORLD CUP FINAL?

APR 14

ON APRIL 14, 1999, IN EXTRA TIME OF A TELEVISED FA CUP SEMI-FINAL, *RYAN GIGGS* SLALOMED THROUGH THE *ARSENAL* DEFENCE AND BLASTED THE BALL PAST *DAVID SEAMAN* TO SEND *MANCHESTER UNITED* TO WEMBLEY AND KEEP THEM ON COURSE FOR THEIR HISTORIC TREBLE OF LEAGUE, FA CUP AND UEFA CHAMPIONS LEAGUE. THE GOAL WAS SUBSEQUENTLY VOTED THE GREATEST IN HISTORY IN A POLL. *SIR ALEX FERGUSON* WAS THE MANAGER WHO STEERED *MANCHESTER UNITED* TO THAT HISTORIC TREBLE. TO DATE, ONLY SIX OTHER CLUBS HAVE ACHIEVED THE FEAT OF A CONTINENTAL TREBLE -- DOMESTIC LEAGUE AND CUP AND EUROPEAN CUP/ CHAMPIONS LEAGUE -- WITH TWO CLUBS DOING IT TWICE.

WHICH CLUB WAS MANAGED TO A CONTINENTAL TREBLE BY:

1. *JOCK STEIN* IN 1967
2. *STEFAN KOVÁCS* IN 1972
3. *GUUS HIDDINK* IN 1988
4. *PEP GUARDIOLA* IN 2009
5. *JOSÉ MOURINHO* IN 2010
6. *JUPP HEYNCKES* IN 2013
7. *LUIS ENRIQUE* IN 2015
8. *HANS-DIETER FLICK* IN 2020

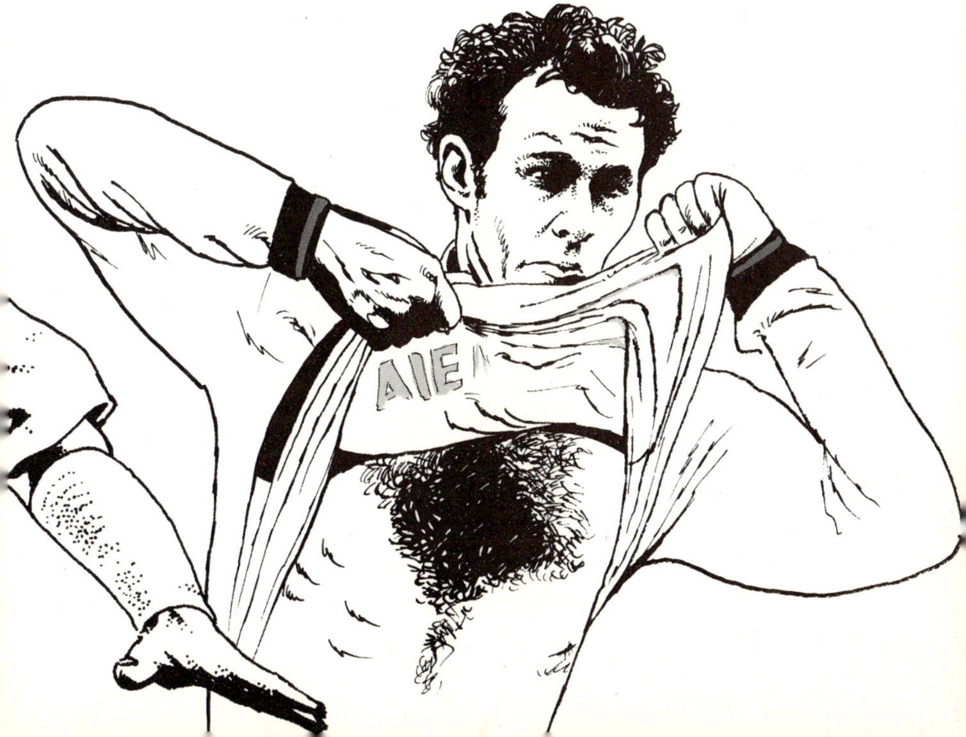

APR 15

SCOTLAND INTERNATIONAL **DAVID HERD** WAS BORN IN HAMILTON ON APRIL 15, 1934. AS A TEEN AT THE OUTSET OF HIS CAREER, HE MADE HISTORY IN 1951 WHEN HE PLAYED IN THE SAME **STOCKPORT COUNTY** TEAM AS HIS FATHER, **ALEX**, A VETERAN WHO HAD WON THE LEAGUE WITH **MANCHESTER CITY** IN 1937. **DAVID HERD** JOINED **ARSENAL** IN 1954 AND WAS THE CLUB'S TOP GOALSCORER IN FOUR CONSECUTIVE SEASONS. HIS GOALSCORING PROWESS PERSUADED **MANCHESTER UNITED** TO PAY £35,000 TO TAKE HIM TO OLD TRAFFORD IN 1961. HE WON AN FA CUP AND TWO LEAGUE TITLES WITH THE **"RED DEVILS"** -- AND WAS A MEMBER OF THE SQUAD THAT WON THE 1968 EUROPEAN CUP -- BEFORE SIGNING FOR **STOKE CITY**. HE ENDED HIS CAREER WITH A SEASON IN IRELAND PLAYING FOR **WATERFORD**.

IDENTIFY THESE FAMOUS FATHERS AND SONS:

1. AS A PLAYER, HE WON ALL UEFA CLUB COMPETITIONS AND AS MANAGER OF THE **NETHERLANDS** TEAM, SELECTED HIS EUROPA LEAGUE-WINNING SON.

2. BOTH CAPTAINS OF **AC MILAN**, THE FATHER MANAGED THE 1998 **ITALY** WORLD CUP TEAM CAPTAINED BY HIS SON.

3. TWO GENERATIONS OF GOALKEEPERS WHO BOTH REPRESENTED **DENMARK** AND EACH WON PREMIER LEAGUE TITLES.

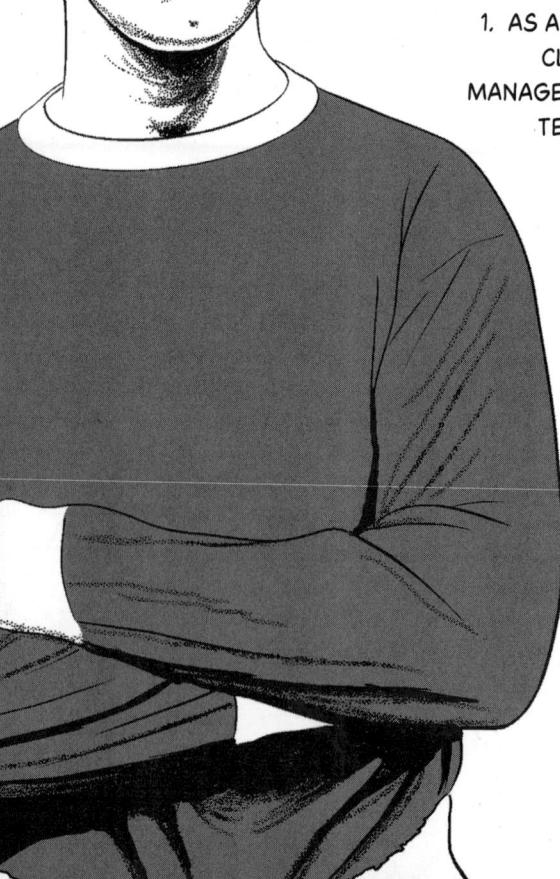

APR 16

FORMER **SWEDEN** CAPTAIN **FREDDIE LJUNGBERG** WAS BORN IN VITTSJÖ, ON APRIL 16, 1977. HE EXCELLED AT SPORTS, PLAYING HOCKEY AND EARNING A CALL-UP TO THE NATIONAL HANDBALL TEAM, BUT HIS PASSION WAS FOOTBALL, AND HE PLAYED FOR **HALMSTADS BK** FROM THE AGE OF 5. HE GRADUATED TO THE SENIOR TEAM IN 1994, AND AFTER WINNING THE LEAGUE AND SWEDISH CUP WITH THE CLUB, JOINED **ARSENAL** IN 1998. HE SPENT NINE YEARS WITH **"THE GUNNERS"**, WINNING TWO LEAGUE TITLES AND THREE FA CUPS, DURING WHICH TIME HE WAS TWICE NAMED SWEDISH FOOTBALLER OF THE YEAR. HE WENT ON TO PLAY FOR **WEST HAM UNITED, SEATTLE SOUNDERS** AND **CHICAGO FIRE**, WON THE SCOTTISH CUP WITH **CELTIC** AND ENDED HIS CAREER IN JAPAN WITH **SHIMIZU S-PULSE**.

LJUNGBERG WAS A MEMBER OF THE **ARSENAL** TEAM THAT COMPLETED A LEAGUE AND FA CUP DOUBLE IN 2002 -- CAN YOU NAME THE SEVEN OTHER CLUBS TO ACHIEVE THIS FEAT?

APR 17

HORST HRUBESCH WAS ONLY CALLED INTO **WEST GERMANY'S** SQUAD FOR EURO 1980 AFTER **KLAUS FISCHER** BROKE A LEG, AND THE FINAL WAS ONLY HIS FIFTH APPEARANCE FOR HIS COUNTRY -- BUT THE BURLY STRIKER'S TWO GOALS WERE ENOUGH TO CROWN **WEST GERMANY** CHAMPIONS. BORN IN HAMM, ON APRIL 17, 1951, **HRUBESCH** WAS A LATE DEVELOPER, PLAYING IN THE LOWER REACHES OF GERMAN FOOTBALL BEFORE HE WAS SIGNED BY **HAMBURGER SV** AT THE AGE OF 24. NICKNAMED **"THE HEADER BEAST"** FOR HIS AERIAL PROWESS, HE WON THREE LEAGUE TITLES AND THE EUROPEAN CUP IN HIS FIVE YEARS AT THE CLUB, AND WAS THE BUNDESLIGA TOP SCORER IN 1982. HE WENT ON TO PLAY FOR **STANDARD LIÈGE** AND **BORUSSIA DORTMUND**, BEFORE MOVING INTO A COACHING CAREER THAT HAS INCLUDED SPELLS IN GERMANY, AUSTRIA AND TURKEY. SINCE 2000, HE HAS BEEN INVOLVED IN THE COACHING OF THE NATIONAL TEAM, AND HAS WON EUROPEAN CHAMPIONSHIPS WITH **GERMANY'S UNDER-19** AND **UNDER-21** TEAMS. HAVING COACHED HIS COUNTRY TO A SILVER MEDAL AT THE 2016 OLYMPICS, HE WAS APPOINTED AS HEAD COACH OF THE **GERMANY WOMEN'S** NATIONAL TEAM IN 2018.

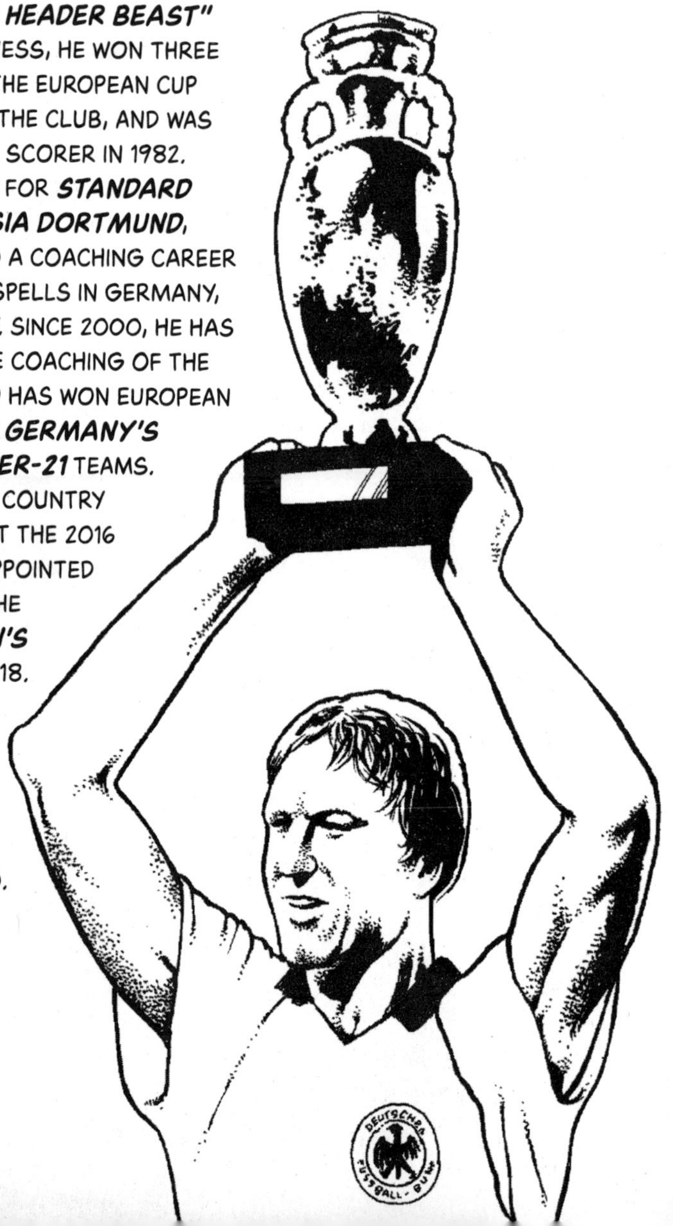

NAME THE WINNERS OF THE EUROPEAN CHAMPIONSHIPS SINCE THE FIRST TOURNAMENT IN 1960.

APR 18

WEST HAM UNITED AND **POLAND** GOALKEEPER **LUKASZ FABIANSKI** WAS BORN IN KOSTRZYN NAD ODRA ON APRIL 18, 1985. AFTER LEARNING HIS TRADE AT YOUTH LEVEL WITH A NUMBER OF CLUBS, HE SIGNED PROFESSIONAL TERMS WITH **LECH POZNAŃ** AT THE AGE OF 19. **FABIANSKI** FIRST REPRESENTED HIS COUNTRY AT U-15 LEVEL AND PROGRESSED THROUGH THE JUNIOR RANKS BEFORE WINNING HIS FIRST FULL CAP IN 2006. HE REPRESENTED **POLAND** AT THE 2006 FIFA WORLD CUP, UEFA EURO 2008, EURO 2016 AND 2018 FIFA WORLD CUP.

1. HE SPENT TWO SEASONS AT **LEGIA WARSAW**, WHERE HE COMPETED WITH WHICH OTHER **POLAND** INTERNATIONAL FOR THE GOALKEEPER SPOT BEFORE HIS RIVAL'S TRANSFER TO **CELTIC**?

2. **FABIANSKI** WON AN FA CUP WITH **ARSENAL** IN 2014 -- WHO WERE THE OPPONENTS IN THAT FINAL?

3. **FABIANSKI** WAS RELEGATED FROM THE PREMIER LEAGUE WITH WHICH CLUB IN 2018?

APR
19

BORN ***RIVALDO VÍTOR BORBA FERREIRA*** IN PAULISTA, PERNAMBUCO, BRAZIL, ON APRIL 19, 1972, ***RIVALDO*** OVERCAME GREAT ADVERSITY TO BECOME A WORLD CUP-WINNING SUPERSTAR. RAISED IN EXTREME POVERTY, MALNOURISHMENT CAUSED HIS BOWLEGGED GAIT AND RESULTED IN A LOSS OF SOME TEETH, AND JUST MONTHS BEFORE HE SIGNED HIS FIRST PROFESSIONAL CONTRACT IN 1989, HIS FATHER WAS KILLED IN A ROAD ACCIDENT. AFTER WINNING A BRAZILIAN SÉRIE A TITLE AND TWO STATE CHAMPIONSHIPS WITH ***PALMEIRAS***, ***RIVALDO*** ENJOYED HUGE SUCCESS IN EUROPE, WINNING SILVERWARE IN SPAIN, ITALY AND GREECE. HIS ZENITH WAS REACHED IN 1999, WHEN HE WAS NAMED FIFA WORLD PLAYER OF THE YEAR, EUROPEAN FOOTBALLER OF THE YEAR, WORLD SOCCER PLAYER OF THE YEAR AND SPANISH LEAGUE FOOTBALLER OF THE YEAR, WON THE ONZE D'OR AND BALLON D'OR, AND WAS COPA AMÉRICA TOP SCORER AND MVP. A WORLD CUP WINNER IN 2002, HE SCORED 34 GOALS IN 74 APPEARANCES FOR ***BRAZIL***.

1. WITH WHICH SPANISH CLUB DID ***RIVALDO*** WIN TWO LEAGUE TITLES?

2. ***RIVALDO*** WAS A UEFA CHAMPIONS LEAGUE WINNER WITH WHICH ITALIAN CLUB?

3. WITH WHICH CLUB DID HE WIN THREE GREEK SUPER LEAGUES?

APR 20

THE SECOND MOST-CAPPED **REPUBLIC OF IRELAND** PLAYER OF ALL TIME, **SHAY GIVEN** WAS BORN IN LIFFORD, COUNTY DONEGAL, ON APRIL 20, 1976. ALTHOUGH HE CONCEDED SEVEN GOALS ON HIS DEBUT, AT THE AGE OF 14, FOR LOCAL AMATEUR SIDE **LIFFORD CELTIC**, HE WAS SOON ON HIS WAY TO SCOTLAND TO SIGN FOR HIS BOYHOOD IDOLS, **CELTIC**. HIS PERFORMANCES IN **CELTIC'S** YOUTH TEAM EARNED HIM A TRANSFER TO **BLACKBURN ROVERS**. AFTER LOAN SPELLS AT **SWINDON TOWN** AND **SUNDERLAND** -- WHERE HIS PERFORMANCES HELPED EARN **"THE BLACK CATS"** PROMOTION TO THE PREMIER LEAGUE -- HE WAS SNAPPED UP BY **NEWCASTLE UNITED**. HE SPENT EIGHT YEARS WITH THE CLUB AND WAS JUST 34 GAMES AWAY FROM BREAKING THE ALL-TIME APPEARANCE RECORD WHEN HE JOINED **MANCHESTER CITY** IN 2009. DESPITE HIS EXCELLENT DISPLAYS, INJURY AND THE EMERGENCE OF **JOE HART** AS FIRST CHOICE SAW HIM INCREASINGLY SIDELINED, AND HE MOVED ON TO **ASTON VILLA** IN 2011. A SHORT LOAN SPELL WITH **MIDDLESBROUGH** IN 2013 WAS FOLLOWED BY A MOVE TO **STOKE CITY** IN 2015. HE ANNOUNCED HIS RETIREMENT A FEW DAYS AFTER HIS 42ND BIRTHDAY IN 2018.

1. WHO WAS THE MANAGER WHO SIGNED **GIVEN** TO **NEWCASTLE UNITED** IN THE SUMMER OF 1997?

2. **GIVEN** PLAYED FOR **NEWCASTLE UNITED** IN THE 1998 FA CUP FINAL. WHO WERE THE WINNING OPPONENTS?

3. **GIVEN** WAS AGAIN ON THE LOSING SIDE IN AN FA CUP FINAL IN 2015 WHEN **ASTON VILLA** LOST 4-0 TO WHICH TEAM?

APR 21

BORN *FRANCISCO ROMÁN ALARCÓN SUÁREZ* IN BENALMÁDENA, SPAIN, ON APRIL 21, 1992, *ISCO* PROGRESSED THROUGH THE JUNIOR RANKS AT *VALENCIA* BEFORE JOINING *MÁLAGA* IN 2011. AFTER WINNING THE GOLDEN BOY AWARD, A PRESTIGIOUS HONOUR GIVEN TO THE BEST YOUNG PLAYER IN EUROPEAN FOOTBALL, HE SIGNED FOR *REAL MADRID* IN 2013 AND HAS WON MULTIPLE TROPHIES WITH THE CLUB. HE WON THE 2013 UEFA EUROPEAN UNDER-21 CHAMPIONSHIP WITH *SPAIN*, THE SAME YEAR THAT HE MADE HIS FULL INTERNATIONAL DEBUT.

IDENTIFY THESE OTHER RECIPIENTS OF THE GOLDEN BOY AWARD:

1. 2017: NAMED BEST YOUNG PLAYER AT THE 2018 WORLD CUP, WHERE HE BECAME THE SECOND TEENAGER TO SCORE IN A WORLD CUP FINAL, HIS TRANSFER FROM *MONACO* TO *PSG* MADE HIM THE GAME'S MOST EXPENSIVE TEENAGER.

2. 2013: WON IN THE YEAR THAT HE WAS A SERIE A WINNER WITH *JUVENTUS* AND AWARDED THE GOLDEN BALL FOR HIS DISPLAYS AS *FRANCE* WON THE FIFA U-20 WORLD CUP.

3. 2014: HE LEFT *LIVERPOOL* FOR *MANCHESTER CITY* THE FOLLOWING SEASON.

APR 22 BORN *RICARDO IZECSON DOS SANTOS LEITE* IN GAMA, BRAZIL, ON APRIL 22, 1982, *KAKÁ* BEGAN HIS CAREER WITH *SÃO PAULO* AT THE AGE OF EIGHT. HE SUFFERED A SPINAL FRACTURE IN A SWIMMING POOL ACCIDENT WHEN HE WAS 18 THAT THREATENED TO END HIS CAREER, BUT RECOVERED IN TIME TO MAKE HIS SENIOR DEBUT FOR *BRAZIL* IN 2002, AND WAS A MEMBER OF THE WORLD CUP-WINNING SQUAD THAT YEAR. HE SIGNED FOR *AC MILAN* IN 2003, WHERE HE WON A NUMBER OF HONOURS IN HIS SIX YEARS AT THE CLUB, INCLUDING A SERIE A TITLE AND THE UEFA CHAMPIONS LEAGUE. BALLON D'OR WINNER AND FIFA WORLD PLAYER OF THE YEAR IN 2007, HE JOINED *REAL MADRID* IN 2009. A LEAGUE AND COPA DEL REY WINNER WITH *"LOS BLANCOS"*, HIS 2013 SHORT-LIVED RETURN TO *AC MILAN* WAS FOLLOWED BY A MOVE TO *ORLANDO CITY* THAT MADE HIM THE HIGHEST-PAID PLAYER IN MLS HISTORY! HE RETIRED IN 2017.

THE FOLLOWING ALSO PLAYED FOR *AC MILAN* AND *REAL MADRID*:

1. HIS OTHER CLUBS INCLUDE *SANTOS* AND *MANCHESTER CITY*.

2. WON SIX LEAGUE TITLES AND THE UEFA CHAMPIONS LEAGUE WITH *MANCHESTER UNITED*, HIS OTHER CLUBS INCLUDE *LA GALAXY* AND *PSG*.

3. NICKNAMED *"EL PIPITA"*, HIS OTHER CLUBS INCLUDE *NAPOLI, JUVENTUS* AND *CHELSEA*.

APR 23

LEE YOUNG-PYO MADE 127 APPEARANCES FOR **SOUTH KOREA**, HELPING HIS COUNTRY TO FOURTH PLACE AT THE 2002 WORLD CUP AND THIRD PLACE IN THE AFC ASIAN CUP IN BOTH 2000 AND 2011. BORN IN HONGCHEON, GANGWON, ON APRIL 23, 1977, HE BEGAN HIS CAREER AT **FC SEOUL**, THEN KNOWN AS **ANYANG LG CHEETAHS**, IN THE KOREAN K LEAGUE. HE WENT ON TO PLAY IN THE NETHERLANDS, ENGLAND, GERMANY AND SAUDI ARABIA, BEFORE ENDING HIS CAREER IN CANADA WITH **VANCOUVER WHITECAPS**.

1. UNDER WHICH DUTCH COACH DID **LEE YOUNG-PYO** PLAY FOR **SOUTH KOREA** AT THE 2002 WORLD CUP, BEFORE JOINING HIM AT **PSV EINDHOVEN**, WHERE THEY WON TWO LEAGUE TITLES TOGETHER?

2. UNDER WHICH DUTCH COACH DID **LEE YOUNG-PYO** PLAY AT **SPURS**?

3. **LEE YOUNG-PYO** LEFT **TOTTENHAM HOTSPUR** TO JOIN WHICH GERMAN CLUB IN 2008?

APR 24 AFTER FAILING A TRIAL WITH *QUEENS PARK RANGERS* AND REJECTING AN OFFER FROM *HULL CITY*, *STUART PEARCE* -- BORN IN SHEPHERD'S BUSH, LONDON ON APRIL 24, 1962 -- WORKED AS AN ELECTRICIAN WHILE PLAYING SEMI-PRO FOR HIS LOCAL TEAM, NON-LEAGUE *WEALDSTONE*. HE TURNED PROFESSIONAL IN 1983, WHEN HE WAS TRANSFERRED TO TOP-FLIGHT TEAM *COVENTRY CITY*. HE WENT ON TO ENJOY A STELLAR PLAYING CAREER WITH A SUCCESSION OF BIG CLUBS AND WAS CAPPED 78 TIMES BY *ENGLAND*. MOVING INTO COACHING AND MANAGEMENT, HIS SUBSEQUENT PATH INCLUDES MANAGING THE *GREAT BRITAIN* OLYMPIC TEAM, *ENGLAND UNDER-21* TEAM AND CARETAKER MANAGER OF *ENGLAND* FOR ONE GAME IN 2012.

1. NAME THREE OF THE CLUBS FOR WHOM *PEARCE* PLAYED AFTER LEAVING *COVENTRY CITY*.

2. *PEARCE'S* COACHING CAREER HAS TAKEN IN SPELLS AT *PORTSMOUTH* AND *WEST HAM UNITED* -- BUT WHICH TWO CLUBS DID HE MANAGE?

3. WHAT WAS *PEARCE'S* NICKNAME AS A PLAYER?

APR 25

THE FIRST DUTCHMAN TO BE VOTED EUROPEAN FOOTBALLER OF THE YEAR AND, SUBSEQUENTLY, THE FIRST MAN TO WIN THAT TITLE THREE TIMES, *JOHAN CRUYFF* WAS BORN ON APRIL 25, 1947, IN AMSTERDAM, NEAR THE *AJAX* STADIUM WHERE HIS MOTHER WORKED AS A CLEANER. RECRUITED BY THE CLUB AT THE AGE OF 12, HE MADE HIS DEBUT FOR *AJAX* IN 1964 AND WON THE FIRST OF HIS 48 CAPS FOR *NETHERLANDS* TWO YEARS LATER, SCORING THE FIRST OF HIS 33 INTERNATIONAL GOALS. HE CAPTAINED HIS COUNTRY TO THE 1974 WORLD CUP FINAL, WHERE THEY WERE NARROWLY BEATEN BY *WEST GERMANY*, *CRUYFF* WINNING THE GOLDEN BALL AS THE TOURNAMENT'S BEST PLAYER. AFTER FINISHING THIRD AT EURO 76, HE REFUSED TO GO TO THE 1978 WORLD CUP TOURNAMENT IN PROTEST AT ARGENTINA'S MILITARY REGIME.

1. NAME TWO OF THE CLUBS THAT *CRUYFF* PLAYED FOR AFTER LEAVING *AJAX* IN 1973.

2. NAME THE TWO OTHER DUTCH PLAYERS WHO WON THE BALLON D'OR, THE EUROPEAN FOOTBALLER OF THE YEAR AWARD.

3. AFTER COACHING *AJAX* TO VICTORY IN THE UEFA CUP WINNERS' CUP, *CRUYFF* TOOK HIS COACHING SKILLS TO *BARCELONA*, WHERE HE WON FOUR LEAGUE TITLES, THE UEFA CUP WINNERS' CUP AND A LONG-AWAITED EUROPEAN CUP TRIUMPH. NAME TWO OF THE OTHER DUTCHMEN WHO HAVE COACHED *BARCELONA*.

APR 26

PLAGUED BY FINANCIAL WOES, SECOND DIVISION TEAM *NEWTON HEATH* WAS ON THE VERGE OF EXTINCTION ... UNTIL FOUR INVESTORS RAISED £2,000 TO RESCUE THE CLUB. ON APRIL 26, 1902, HAVING REJECTED SUGGESTIONS OF *MANCHESTER CENTRAL* AND *MANCHESTER CELTIC*, THE NEW OWNERS RENAMED THE CLUB *MANCHESTER UNITED*, ADOPTING RED SHIRTS WITH WHITE SHORTS TO ACCOMPANY THE CHANGE OF IDENTITY.

WHICH CLUB WAS ORIGINALLY KNOWN AS:

1. *SMALL HEATH ALLIANCE*

2. *ST. DOMINGO FC*

3. *BOSCOMBE ST. JOHN'S LADS' INSTITUTE*

4. *DIAL SQUARE*

APR 27 WHEN *MARTIN CHIVERS* JOINED *TOTTENHAM HOTSPUR* IN EARLY 1968, THE £125,000 FEE MADE HIM THE MOST EXPENSIVE BRITISH PLAYER AT THAT TIME. IN EIGHT SEASONS AT *WHITE HART LANE*, THE *ENGLAND* INTERNATIONAL WON TWO LEAGUE CUPS AND THE UEFA CUP, SCORING 174 GOALS IN 367 FIRST TEAM APPEARANCES. HE SUBSEQUENTLY PLAYED FOR *SERVETTE*, *NORWICH CITY, BRIGHTON & HOVE ALBION, DORCHESTER TOWN, FRANKSTON CITY, VARD HAUGESUND* AND *BARNET*.

1. *CHIVERS* JOINED *TOTTENHAM HOTSPUR* FROM WHICH CLUB?

2. WHO WAS THE MANAGER WHO SIGNED *CHIVERS* FOR *SPURS* IN 1968?

3. *MARTIN CHIVERS* WAS THE LEADING *TOTTENHAM* GOALSCORER IN EUROPEAN COMPETITION FOR 39 YEARS UNTIL HE WAS OVERTAKEN BY WHICH PLAYER IN 2013?

APR 28

THE FIRST **PORTUGAL** NATIONAL TEAM PLAYER NEVER TO HAVE PLAYED AT THE PORTUGUESE TOP LEVEL -- HE SPENT THE MAJORITY OF HIS CAREER IN SPAIN AND FRANCE --**PAULETA** SCORED 47 GOALS IN 88 MATCHES FOR **PORTUGAL**, A NATIONAL RECORD AT THE TIME OF HIS RETIREMENT. BORN **PEDRO MIGUEL CARREIRO RESENDES** IN PONTA DELGADA ON APRIL 28, 1973, AFTER WINNING SPAIN'S LA LIGA WITH **DEPORTIVO**, HE WON HONOURS IN FRANCE WITH **BORDEAUX** AND **PARIS SAINT-GERMAIN** AND WAS LIGUE 1 TOP SCORER THREE TIMES.

1. WHICH **SWEDEN** STRIKER WAS LIGUE 1 TOP SCORER THREE TIMES DURING HIS TIME WITH **PSG** BETWEEN 2012 AND 2016?

2. WHICH **URUGUAY** STRIKER WAS LIGUE 1 TOP SCORER WITH **PARIS SAINT-GERMAIN** IN 2017 AND 2018?

3. NAME ONE OF THE TWO ARGENTINE PLAYERS WHO EACH FINISHED LIGUE 1 TOP SCORER FIVE TIMES IN THE 1970S AND 1980S -- ONE WHO BECAME THE FIRST COACH TO WIN THE COPA LIBERTADORES FOUR TIMES, THE OTHER WHO SET THE RECORD FOR ALL-TIME HIGHEST GOALSCORER IN LIGUE 1 HISTORY.

APR 29

BORN IN WESTHOUGHTON ON APRIL 29, 1944, *FRANCIS LEE* MADE HIS NAME AT LOCAL CLUB *BOLTON WANDERERS* BEFORE *MANCHESTER CITY* PAID A CLUB RECORD £60,000 TO SIGN HIM IN 1967. *CITY* MANAGER *JOE MERCER'S* ASSERTION THAT *LEE* WAS *"THE FINAL PIECE OF THE JIGSAW"* WAS BORNE OUT WHEN THE BARREL-CHESTED STRIKER'S 16 GOALS IN 31 APPEARANCES HELPED CITY WIN THE LEAGUE IN HIS DEBUT SEASON. *"FRANNY"* WENT ON TO WIN THE FA CUP, THE LEAGUE CUP AND UEFA CUP WINNERS' CUP BEFORE HE WAS SOLD TO *DERBY COUNTY* IN 1974, WHERE HE ADDED ANOTHER LEAGUE TITLE TO HIS HAUL. CAPPED 27 TIMES BY *ENGLAND*, *LEE'S* POST-PLAYING CAREER SAW HIM BECOME A VERY SUCCESSFUL BUSINESSMAN AND RACEHORSE TRAINER. HE BECAME CHAIRMAN OF *MANCHESTER CITY* IN 1994 BUT STEPPED DOWN IN 1998, WITH THE CLUB ON THE BRINK OF RELEGATION TO THE THIRD TIER.

LEE WAS INDUCTED INTO THE ENGLISH FOOTBALL HALL OF FAME IN 2010, THE SAME YEAR AS:

1. *ENGLAND* GOALKEEPER WHO PLAYED FOR *SCUNTHORPE UNITED, LIVERPOOL* AND *SPURS*.

2. *REPUBLIC OF IRELAND* MIDFIELDER WHO WON THE FA CUP WITH *MANCHESTER UNITED*, MULTIPLE HONOURS WITH *LEEDS UNITED* AND SUCCESSFULLY SUED OVER THE WAY HE WAS PORTRAYED IN THE BOOK *"THE DAMNED UNITED"*.

3. *ENGLAND* INTERNATIONAL WINGER WHO SET THE *LIVERPOOL* APPEARANCE RECORD OF 857 GAMES BETWEEN 1959 AND 1978.

ON APRIL 30, 1993, A MONTH AFTER ANNOUNCING HIS RETIREMENT, 30-YEAR-OLD **TOMMY CATON** DIED SUDDENLY OF A HEART ATTACK AT HIS OXFORDSHIRE HOME. THE FATHER OF THREE YOUNG CHILDREN HAD LONG BATTLED ALCOHOL ADDICTION. LIVERPUDLIAN **CATON** MADE HIS SENIOR **MANCHESTER CITY** DEBUT AT THE AGE OF 16 AND PLAYED 100 GAMES FOR THE CLUB BEFORE HIS 20TH BIRTHDAY. **CITY** DROPPING DOWN A TIER IN 1983 PROMPTED **CATON'S** MOVE TO **ARSENAL**, WHERE HE WAS A REGULAR UNDER **DON HOWE**. HE FELL OUT OF FAVOUR UNDER SUBSEQUENT MANAGER **GEORGE GRAHAM** AND WAS TRANSFERRED TO **OXFORD UNITED** IN 1987, BEFORE JOINING **CHARLTON ATHLETIC** A YEAR LATER.

IDENTIFY THESE OTHER 1993 DEATHS IN SOCCER:

1. **SCOTLAND** DEFENDER SIGNED TO **MANCHESTER UNITED** FROM **SHREWSBURY TOWN** BY **TOMMY DOCHERTY**, HIS SUBSEQUENT CLUBS INCLUDED **SUNDERLAND** AND **COVENTRY CITY**, DEAD AT THE AGE OF 42.

2. **ENGLAND'S** WORLD CUP-WINNING CAPTAIN.

3. IRISHMAN WHO CAPTAINED THE **TOTTENHAM HOTSPUR** DOUBLE-WINNERS OF 1961.

MAY

SCORER OF THE FIRST GOLDEN GOAL IN HISTORY, WHICH WON THE EURO 1996 FINAL FOR *GERMANY, OLIVER BIERHOFF* WAS BORN IN KARLSRUHE, ON MAY 1, 1968. HE PLAYED FOR NINE CLUBS IN FOUR DIFFERENT LEAGUES AND FOUND HIS GREATEST SUCCESS OUTSIDE HIS HOMELAND. A POWERFUL STRIKER, RENOWNED FOR HIS HEADING ABILITY, HE WAS SERIE A TOP SCORER WITH *UDINESE* IN 1997-98 AND WON A SERIE A TITLE WITH *AC MILAN* THE FOLLOWING SEASON. *BIERHOFF* IS THE ONLY GERMAN PLAYER TO TOP THE SERIE A SCORING CHARTS.

1. WHO IS THE ONLY SERIE A TOP SCORER BORN IN THE FOLLOWING COUNTRIES:
    A) BOSNIA AND HERZEGOVINA (2016-17)
    B) WALES (1957-58)

2. *GUNNAR NORDAHL* WAS TOP SERIE A SCORER FIVE TIMES, IN WHICH COUNTRY WAS HE BORN?

3. WHICH DUTCH STRIKER TOPPED THE SERIE A SCORING CHARTS TWICE DURING HIS TIME WITH *AC MILAN*?

MAY 2

BORN IN LONDON, ON MAY 2, 1975, *DAVID BECKHAM* GREW UP FOOTBALL-CRAZY AND A *MANCHESTER UNITED* FANATIC! HE PLAYED WITH A NUMBER OF CLUBS AT JUNIOR LEVEL, BEFORE SIGNING SCHOOLBOY FORMS WITH *UNITED* AT THE AGE OF 14. HE MADE HIS FIRST TEAM DEBUT AGED 17, GOING ON TO WIN A HOST OF HONOURS, INCLUDING A TREBLE OF LEAGUE, FA CUP AND UEFA CHAMPIONS LEAGUE IN 1999. IN 2003, SHORTLY AFTER WINNING A SIXTH LEAGUE TITLE WITH *UNITED* AND RECEIVING AN OBE AWARD, HE SIGNED FOR *REAL MADRID*. A LEAGUE TITLE IN SPAIN WAS FOLLOWED BY A SENSATIONAL SWITCH TO THE MLS IN 2007 TO JOIN THE *LOS ANGELES GALAXY*. HE SPENT FIVE YEARS IN CALIFORNIA, INTERRUPTED BY TWO LOAN SPELLS WITH *AC MILAN*, AND ADDED TWO MLS CUPS TO HIS TALLY, BEFORE HEADING TO *PARIS SAINT-GERMAIN* IN 2013, WHERE HE BECAME THE FIRST ENGLISH PLAYER TO WIN LEAGUE TITLES IN FOUR DIFFERENT COUNTRIES!

CAPPED 115 TIMES, *DAVID BECKHAM* IS ONE OF 13 PLAYERS WHO HAVE PLAYED FOR *ENGLAND* IN THREE WORLD CUPS -- HOW MANY OF THOSE OTHER 12 PLAYERS CAN YOU NAME?

MAY 3

CAPPED 135 TIMES BY **HONDURAS**, **NOEL VALLADARES** KEPT GOAL FOR HIS COUNTRY IN THE 2010 AND 2014 WORLD CUP TOURNAMENTS. BORN IN COMAYAGUA ON MAY 3, 1977, HE SPENT HIS ENTIRE CLUB CAREER IN LIGA NACIONAL, THE HIGHEST DIVISION IN HONDURAN FOOTBALL.

IDENTIFY THESE **HONDURAS** INTERNATIONALS:

1. THE MOST-CAPPED PLAYER IN THE COUNTRY'S HISTORY, HE HAD SPELLS WITH **WIGAN ATHLETIC** AND **HULL CITY**, BEFORE PLYING HIS TRADE IN MLS SOCCER.

2. LEFT-BACK WHO WON SIX LEAGUE TITLES IN HIS FIRST SPELL AT **CELTIC**, RETURNING TO THE CLUB IN 2018 -- AFTER A YEAR IN SAUDI ARABIA WITH **AL-FAYHA** -- TO WIN A SEVENTH TITLE.

3. PLAYED FOR **BIRMINGHAM CITY**, **WIGAN ATHLETIC**, **TOTTENHAM HOTSPUR** AND **STOKE CITY**.

CAPPED 110 TIMES BY HIS COUNTRY, **CESC FÀBREGAS** WON THE WORLD CUP AND TWO EUROPEAN CHAMPIONSHIPS WITH SPAIN. BORN IN ARENYS DE MAR ON MAY 4, 1987, HE LEFT **BARCELONA'S** FAMED LA MASIA ACADEMY AT 16 TO JOIN **ARSENAL** AND BECAME THE CLUB'S YOUNGEST-EVER PLAYER WHEN HE MADE HIS SENIOR DEBUT AGED 16 YEARS AND 177 DAYS. AN FA CUP WINNER WITH **ARSENAL**, HE RETURNED TO **BARCELONA** IN 2011 AND WON A NUMBER OF HONOURS, INCLUDING LA LIGA AND THE FIFA CLUB WORLD CUP, BEFORE HEADING BACK TO LONDON IN 2014 TO JOIN **CHELSEA**, WITH WHOM HE WON TWO PREMIER LEAGUES, AN FA CUP, A LEAGUE CUP AND THE UEFA EUROPA LEAGUE. HE JOINED **MONACO** IN 2018.

FÀBREGAS WAS THE FIRST SPANISH PLAYER TO WIN THE PFA YOUNG PLAYER OF THE YEAR AWARD. WHO WAS THE FIRST WINNER FROM:

1) GERMANY   2) PORTUGAL   3) AUSTRALIA

DURING THE 1950S, MUCH WAS MADE OF THE **"WEMBLEY HOODOO"** OF SERIOUS INJURIES THAT PLAGUED THE FA CUP FINAL IN THE DAYS BEFORE SUBSTITUTES WERE PERMITTED. PERHAPS THE MOST NOTABLE CASUALTY WAS **MANCHESTER CITY** GOALKEEPER **BERT TRAUTMANN,** WHO -- ON MAY 5, 1956 -- PLAYED ON IN THE FINAL WITH A BROKEN NECK HE RECEIVED IN A COLLISION WITH **BIRMINGHAM CITY** FORWARD **PETER MURPHY.**

WHO WAS THE HOODOO'S VICTIM IN THE FOLLOWING FA CUP FINALS:

1. 1952 -- KNEE LIGAMENTS

2. 1953 -- TORN MUSCLE

3. 1955 -- KNEE LIGAMENTS

4. 1957 -- FRACTURED CHEEKBONE

5. 1959 -- BROKEN LEG

6. 1960 -- BROKEN LEG

GARY SPEED MADE HIS DEBUT FOR **LEEDS UNITED** AT THE AGE OF 19, ON MAY 6, 1998. HE HELPED THE CLUB WIN A CHAMPIONSHIP IN THE SECOND TIER OF THE LEAGUE IN 1990, AND THE LEAGUE TITLE TWO YEARS LATER.

NAME THE FOUR CLUBS FOR WHOM **SPEED** SUBSEQUENTLY PLAYED.

JOSÉ LÁZARO ROBLES, BEST KNOWN AS **PINGA**, DIED ON MAY 7, 1996 AT THE AGE OF 72. A PROLIFIC GOALSCORER, HE SCORED TWICE IN **BRAZIL'S** OPENING GAME OF THE 1954 WORLD CUP TOURNAMENT. AT CLUB LEVEL, HE SCORED 250 GOALS IN 466 GAMES.

IDENTIFY THESE OTHER 1996 DEATHS:

1. HE WON THREE EUROPEAN CUPS, THE UEFA CUP AND SIX LEAGUE TITLES AS MANAGER OF **LIVERPOOL**.

2. HE SCORED 22 GOALS IN 23 GAMES FOR **ENGLAND**, WAS A LEAGUE WINNER WITH **EVERTON**, AND HIS OTHER CLUBS INCLUDED **CHELSEA, ARSENAL** AND **NOTTS COUNTY**.

3. COACHED **WEST GERMANY** TO VICTORY IN THE 1974 WORLD CUP AND THE 1972 EUROPEAN CHAMPIONSHIPS.

MAY 8

FRANCO BARESI WAS BORN IN TRAVAGLIATO ON MAY 8, 1960. HE SPENT HIS ENTIRE CAREER WITH **AC MILAN**, WITH WHOM HE WON THREE UEFA CHAMPIONS LEAGUE TITLES, SIX SERIE A TITLES, FOUR SUPERCOPPA ITALIANA TITLES, TWO EUROPEAN SUPER CUPS AND TWO INTERCONTINENTAL CUPS. A NON-PLAYING MEMBER OF **ITALY'S** 1982 WORLD CUP SQUAD, HE WAS OMITTED COMPLETELY FROM THE 1986 LINEUP -- BUT HIS FORTUNES CHANGED IN THE MID-1980S. **BARESI'S** PERFORMANCES AT THE EURO '88 AND ITALIA '90 ESTABLISHED HIM AS ONE OF THE BEST SWEEPERS IN THE WORLD, BUT FOLLOWING **ITALY'S** FAILURE TO QUALIFY FOR THE 1992 EUROPEAN CHAMPIONSHIPS, **BARESI** RETIRED FROM THE INTERNATIONAL GAME. HOWEVER, HE WAS PERSUADED TO RETURN TO THE FOLD FOR THE 1994 WORLD CUP AND CAPTAINED **ITALY** TO THE FINAL, WHERE A PENALTY SHOOT-OUT DENIED HIM A WINNER'S MEDAL. HE MADE ONE MORE APPEARANCE FOR THE NATIONAL TEAM. AFTER HIS FINAL SEASON AT **AC MILAN** IN 1997, THE CLUB RETIRED HIS SHIRT NUMBER 6.

1. **BARESI** PLAYED UNDER NINE COACHES WITH THE **"ROSSONERI"** INCLUDING:
   A) WHICH SUBSEQUENT MANAGER OF THE **ENGLAND** TEAM?
   B) WHICH MANAGER WHO COACHED **BARESI** AT CLUB AND COUNTRY LEVEL?

2. NAME **FRANCO BARESI'S** OLDER BROTHER, WHO PLAYED 18 TIMES FOR **ITALY** AND SPENT THE MAJORITY OF HIS CLUB CAREER WITH **AC MILAN'S** CROSS-CITY RIVALS **INTERNAZIONALE**.

3. WHO SUCCEEDED **FRANCO BARESI** AS **AC MILAN** CAPTAIN, AND LATER ECLIPSED **BARESI** AS HOLDER OF THE CLUB APPEARANCE RECORD?

MAY 9

CAPPED 91 TIMES BY **CZECHOSLOVAKIA**, FOR WHOM HE SCORED 31 GOALS, **ZDENEK NEHODA** WAS BORN IN HULIN ON MAY 9, 1952. A STAR OF THE CZECH TEAM THAT WON EURO 1976, HE SPENT THE MAJORITY OF HIS CAREER WITH **DUKLA PRAGUE**, WINNING THREE LEAGUE TITLES. TWICE VOTED CZECHOSLOVAK FOOTBALLER OF THE YEAR, HE PLAYED THE LATTER PART OF HIS CAREER WITH CLUBS IN GERMANY, BELGIUM AND FRANCE.

1. WHO DID **CZECHOSLOVAKIA** BEAT IN THE 1976 EUROPEAN CHAMPIONSHIPS FINAL?

2. WHO SCORED THE WINNING PENALTY IN THE EURO '76 FINAL SHOOTOUT WITH A SOFTLY-CHIPPED BALL UP THE MIDDLE OF THE GOAL AS THE GOALKEEPER DIVED AWAY -- A STYLE OF PENALTY THAT NOW BEARS HIS SURNAME?

3. NAME **CZECHOSLOVAKIA'S** EURO 1976 GOALKEEPER, A FIVE-TIME WINNER OF THE CZECHOSLOVAK FOOTBALLER OF THE YEAR AWARD, A TWO-TIME WINNER OF THE EUROPEAN GOALKEEPER OF THE YEAR AWARD, WHO PLACED THIRD IN THE 1976 BALLON D'OR.

MAY 10

THE SON OF AN ELECTRICIAN, *DENNIS NICOLAAS MARIA BERGKAMP* WAS BORN IN AMSTERDAM ON MAY 10, 1969. HE GRADUATED THROUGH THE YOUTH RANKS AT *AJAX* TO WIN A LEAGUE TITLE, TWO KNVB CUPS, THE UEFA CUP WINNERS' CUP AND THE UEFA CUP. TWICE VOTED DUTCH FOOTBALLER OF THE YEAR, HE TOPPED THE EREDIVISE SCORING CHARTS THREE YEARS IN A ROW, BEFORE JOINING *INTERNAZIONALE*, HIS GOALS HELPING THE ITALIANS WIN THE UEFA CUP. HE MOVED TO *ARSENAL* IN 1995 AND BECAME ONE OF THE CLUB'S GREATEST PLAYERS, HIS 120 GOALS IN 424 APPEARANCES HELPING THEM WIN THREE LEAGUE TITLES AND FOUR FA CUPS. HE PLAYED 79 TIMES FOR THE *NETHERLANDS* NATIONAL TEAM, HIS 37 GOALS MAKING HIM HIS COUNTRY'S RECORD GOALSCORER AT THAT TIME.

IDENTIFY THE FOLLOWING PLAYERS WHO LEFT *INTERNAZIONALE* FOR ENGLAND:

1. ITALIAN INTERNATIONAL STRIKER WHO JOINED *MANCHESTER CITY* IN 2010 AND WHOSE SUBSEQUENT CLUBS INCLUDED *LIVERPOOL, AC MILAN* AND *MARSEILLE.*

2. UEFA CHAMPIONS LEAGUE WINNER WITH *AJAX*, THREE TIMES SERIE A WINNER WITH *JUVENTUS*, JOINED *TOTTENHAM HOTSPUR* IN 2005 AND LATER PLAYED FOR *CRYSTAL PALACE* AND *BARNET.*

3. *SWITZERLAND* INTERNATIONAL WHO JOINED *STOKE CITY* FROM *INTER* IN 2015 BEFORE SIGNING FOR *LIVERPOOL.*

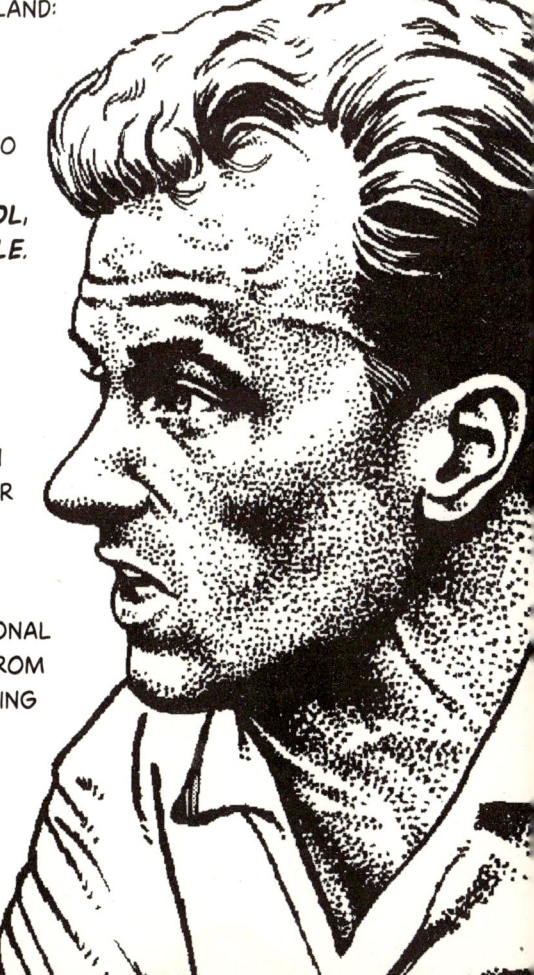

MAY 11

IN 1999, **ANDRÉS INIESTA** CAPTAINED THE **BARCELONA** UNDER-15 TEAM TO VICTORY IN THE NIKE PREMIER CUP, A GLOBAL TOURNAMENT FOR THE BEST YOUTH TEAMS IN THE WORLD. HE SCORED THE WINNING GOAL IN THE LAST MINUTE OF THE FINAL AND WAS NAMED THE PLAYER OF THE TOURNAMENT. THE TROPHY WAS PRESENTED BY **BARCELONA** STAR **PEP GUARDIOLA**, WHO GAVE **ANDRÉS** A SIGNED PHOTO DEDICATED TO *"THE BEST PLAYER I'VE EVER SEEN"*. WITHIN A FEW YEARS, **GUARDIOLA** WOULD BECOME **BARCELONA** COACH AND MAKE **INIESTA** THE HEART OF HIS TEAM.

BORN IN THE SMALL VILLAGE OF FUENTEALBILLA ON MAY 11, 1984, **INIESTA** MAINLY PLAYED FUTSAL GROWING UP DUE TO A LACK OF LOCAL FOOTBALL PITCHES. HE WENT ON TO BECOME THE MOST DECORATED SPANISH FOOTBALLER OF ALL TIME, WINNING 35 TROPHIES, INCLUDING NINE LA LIGAS AND FOUR UEFA CHAMPIONS LEAGUE TITLES. WITH THE NATIONAL TEAM HE WON THE EUROPEAN CHAMPIONSHIPS IN 2008 AND 2012, AND SCORED THE GOAL THAT WON THE 2010 WORLD CUP.

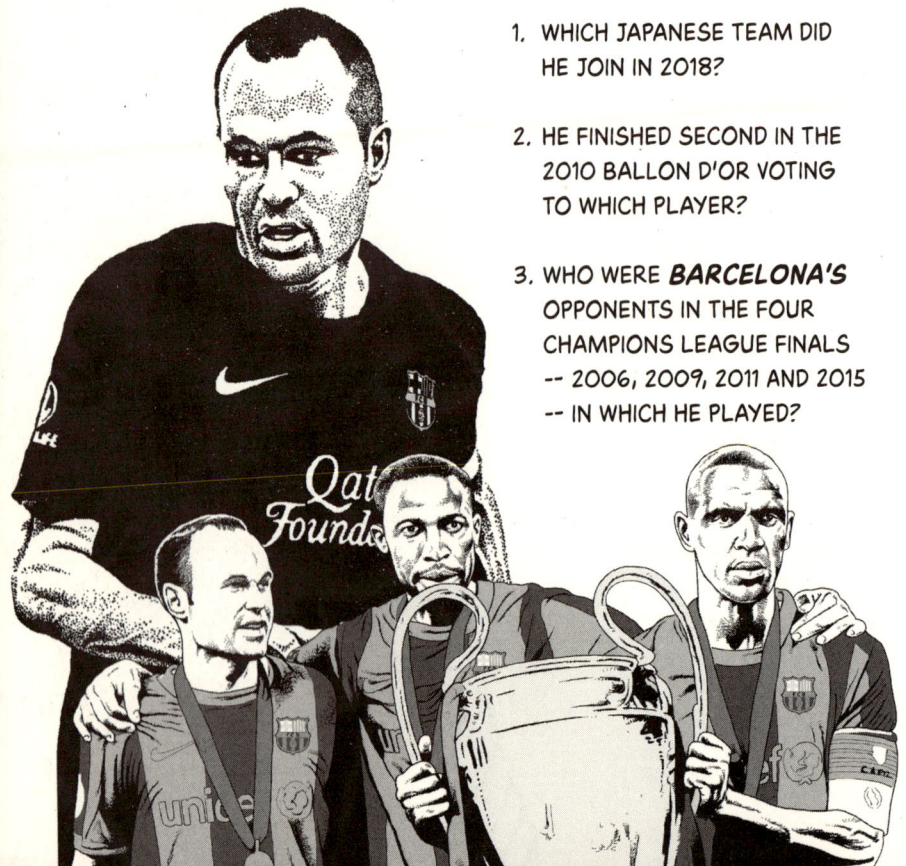

1. WHICH JAPANESE TEAM DID HE JOIN IN 2018?

2. HE FINISHED SECOND IN THE 2010 BALLON D'OR VOTING TO WHICH PLAYER?

3. WHO WERE **BARCELONA'S** OPPONENTS IN THE FOUR CHAMPIONS LEAGUE FINALS -- 2006, 2009, 2011 AND 2015 -- IN WHICH HE PLAYED?

ON MAY 12, 2001, FOR THE FIRST TIME IN THE COMPETITION'S HInStory, THE FA CUP FINAL WAS STAGED OUTSIDE ENGLAND. WITH THE ONGOING RECONSTRUCTION OF WEMBLEY STADIUM, *ARSENAL* AND *LIVERPOOL* JOINED BATTLE AT THE MILLENNIUM STADIUM IN CARDIFF. TWO GOALS FROM *MICHAEL OWEN* WERE ENOUGH TO WIPE OUT *ARSENAL'S* LEAD AND GIVE *LIVERPOOL* A 2-1 VICTORY, SECURING THE SECOND PART OF A UNIQUE TREBLE OF LEAGUE CUP, FA CUP AND UEFA CUP. *OWEN'S* PERFORMANCES THAT SEASON SAW HIM BECOME THE FIRST *LIVERPOOL* PLAYER TO WIN THE EUROPEAN FOOTBALLER OF THE YEAR AWARD.

1. WHO SCORED THE OPENING GOAL FOR *ARSENAL* IN THE 2001 FA CUP FINAL?

2. WHO WERE THE MANAGERS OF THE TWO TEAMS?

3. THE NEXT FIVE FA CUP FINALS WERE ALSO PLAYED IN CARDIFF. WHO DID THE FOLLOWING DEFEAT IN THOSE FINALS:

   A) 2002: *ARSENAL*

   B) 2003: *ARSENAL*

   C) 2004: *MANCHESTER UNITED*

   D) 2005: *ARSENAL*

   E) 2006: *LIVERPOOL*

MAY 13 PERHAPS THE GREATEST FOOTBALLER THAT THE NETHERLANDS HAS EVER PRODUCED, THREE-TIME EUROPEAN FOOTBALLER OF THE YEAR *JOHAN CRUYFF* SPEARHEADED THE DUTCH REVOLUTION THAT SWEPT THE GAME IN THE 1970S. HE LED *AJAX* TO UNPRECEDENTED GLORY, WINNING MULTIPLE HONOURS THAT INCLUDED SIX EREDIVISIE TITLES AND THREE EUROPEAN CUPS, BEFORE TAKING HIS SKILLS TO *BARCELONA*, THE NORTH AMERICAN SOCCER LEAGUE AND BACK TO SPAIN WITH *LEVANTE*. HE RETURNED TO *AJAX* AND HELPED THE CLUB WIN TWO MORE TITLES, BUT WHEN *AJAX* DECIDED NOT TO RENEW HIS CONTRACT, *CRUYFF* WAS SO INCENSED THAT HE SIGNED FOR ARCHRIVALS *FEYENOORD* --AND INSPIRED THEM TO A LEAGUE AND CUP DOUBLE! *CRUYFF* PLAYED HIS LAST GAME IN THE EREDIVISIE ON MAY 13, 1984, SIGNING OFF WITH A GOAL AGAINST *PEC ZWOLLE*. HE WENT ON TO ENJOY GREAT SUCCESS AS MANAGER OF *AJAX* AND *BARCELONA*.

1. WHO ARE THE TWO OTHER DUTCH PLAYERS WHO WON THE EUROPEAN FOOTBALLER OF THE YEAR AWARD?

2. *CRUYFF* PLAYED FOR WHICH TWO NASL CLUBS DURING HIS TIME IN THE UNITED STATES?

3. NAME *JOHAN CRUYFF'S* SON, WHOSE PLAYING CAREER TOOK IN SPELLS WITH A NUMBER OF CLUBS, INCLUDING *BARCELONA* AND *MANCHESTER UNITED.*

MAY 14

ON MAY 14, 1938, **ENGLAND** PLAYED **GERMANY** IN BERLIN. BEFORE THE GAME, THERE WAS A HUGE DEBATE BETWEEN THE BRITISH GOVERNMENT AND THE FOOTBALL ASSOCIATION AS TO WHETHER THE PLAYERS SHOULD GIVE THE NAZI SALUTE. AT THE 1936 OLYMPICS IN GERMANY THE ATHLETES HAD REFUSED, BUT BY NOW THE BRITISH GOVERNMENT WAS PURSUING THE POLICY OF APPEASEMENT AND IT WAS DECIDED THAT THE SALUTE SHOULD BE GIVEN AS A *"COURTESY"* TO THE HOST NATION. BEFORE A CROWD OF 100,000, THE UNHAPPY PLAYERS DID AS THEY WERE TOLD AND RAISED THEIR RIGHT ARMS IN SALUTE. **ENGLAND'S** 6-3 VICTORY WAS SMALL COMPENSATION FOR WHAT ONE PLAYER TERMED *"THE WORST MOMENT IN MY LIFE"*.

1. WHICH TWO SOUTH AMERICAN COUNTRIES WENT TO WAR WITH EACH OTHER FOLLOWING VIOLENT CLASHES BETWEEN FANS DURING QUALIFYING GAMES FOR THE 1970 WORLD CUP?

2. WHICH *"WUNDERTEAM"* QUALIFIED FOR THE 1938 WORLD CUP BUT WAS FORCED TO WITHDRAW WHEN THE COUNTRY WAS INVADED AND ANNEXED?

3. ONE OF THE MOST POLITICALLY CHARGED GAMES IN HISTORY SAW **IRAN** DEFEAT THE **USA** 2-1 IN WHICH WORLD CUP TOURNAMENT?

MAY 15 THE SECOND MOST-CAPPED OUTFIELD PLAYER IN THE HISTORY OF THE **NETHERLANDS** NATIONAL TEAM, **FRANK DE BOER** WAS BORN IN HOORN ON MAY 15, 1970. TOGETHER WITH TWIN BROTHER **RONALD**, HE WON THE EUROPEAN CUP WITH **AJAX** IN 1995. FOLLOWING A BITTER TRANSFER WRANGLE, THEY BOTH JOINED **BARCELONA** THREE YEARS LATER. LA LIGA WINNERS IN 1989, THEY WENT ON TO PLAY TOGETHER AT **RANGERS**, **AL-RAYYAN** AND **AL-SHAMAL**, AND WERE BOTH STALWARTS OF THE DUTCH NATIONAL TEAM.

1. WHICH TURKISH CLUB DID **FRANK** SIGN FOR IN 2003, BEFORE JOINING HIS BROTHER AT **RANGERS** THE FOLLOWING YEAR?

2. **FRANK** WAS APPOINTED MANAGER OF **NETHERLANDS** IN 2020. NAME THREE OF THE FOUR CLUBS HE PREVIOUSLY MANAGED.

3. THE **DE BOER** TWINS PLAYED IN THE 1994 AND 1998 WORLD CUPS ... BUT CAN YOU NAME THE TWINS WHO REPRESENTED **NETHERLANDS** AT THE 1974 AND 1978 TOURNAMENTS?

MAY 16

ON MAY 16, 1998, GOALS FROM **MARC OVERMARS** AND TEENAGE STRIKER **NICOLAS ANELKA** GAVE **ARSENAL** A 2-0 VICTORY OVER **NEWCASTLE UNITED** IN THE FA CUP FINAL AT WEMBLEY, SECURING A LEAGUE AND CUP DOUBLE FOR THE LONDONERS. IT WAS **ARSÈNE WENGER'S** FIRST FA CUP FINAL TRIUMPH. HE WENT ON TO WIN SIX MORE FINALS IN A 22-YEAR SPELL AT THE CLUB TO BECOME THE COMPETITION'S MOST SUCCESSFUL MANAGER.

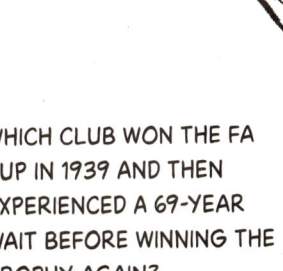

1. WHICH CLUB WON THE FA CUP IN 1939 AND THEN EXPERIENCED A 69-YEAR WAIT BEFORE WINNING THE TROPHY AGAIN?

2. WHICH TWO CLUBS SHARE THE UNWANTED RECORD OF EIGHT FA CUP FINAL DEFEATS?

3. WHICH PLAYER HOLDS THE RECORD OF MOST FA CUP FINAL WINS, HAVING WON THREE TIMES WITH **ARSENAL** AND FOUR TIMES WITH **CHELSEA?**

WITH **CHELSEA'S** FA CUP FINAL VICTORY OVER **MIDDLESBROUGH** ON MAY 17, 1997, **RUUD GULLIT** BECAME THE FIRST FOREIGN MANAGER TO LIFT THE TROPHY.

1. WHO ARE THE TWO OTHER DUTCH MANAGERS TO WIN THE FA CUP?

2. WHO ARE THE FOUR SPANISH MANAGERS TO ACHIEVE THE FEAT?

3. WHO WAS THE FIRST ITALIAN MANAGER TO WIN THE FA CUP?

MAY 18

NOBBY STILES, THE PINT-SIZED TERRIER WHO PLAYED EVERY MINUTE OF **ENGLAND'S** VICTORIOUS 1966 WORLD CUP CAMPAIGN, WAS BORN IN THE CELLAR OF HIS FAMILY HOME IN MANCHESTER, DURING A WAR-TIME AIR RAID, ON MAY 18, 1942. IN 11 YEARS WITH **MANCHESTER UNITED** HE WON TWO LEAGUE TITLES AND THE EUROPEAN CUP, BEFORE SIGNING FOR **MIDDLESBROUGH** IN 1971. TWO YEARS LATER, HE BECAME PLAYER/COACH AT **PRESTON NORTH END** WHEN **BOBBY CHARLTON** WAS APPOINTED MANAGER. HE SUBSEQUENTLY MANAGED **PRESTON**, **VANCOUVER WHITECAPS** AND **WEST BROMWICH ALBION**, BEFORE RETURNING TO OLD TRAFFORD TO TAKE ON THE ROLE OF **MANCHESTER UNITED** YOUTH TEAM COACH.

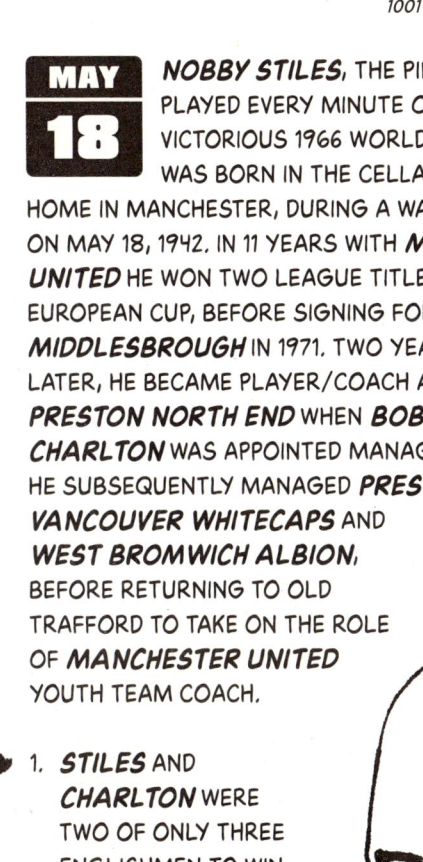

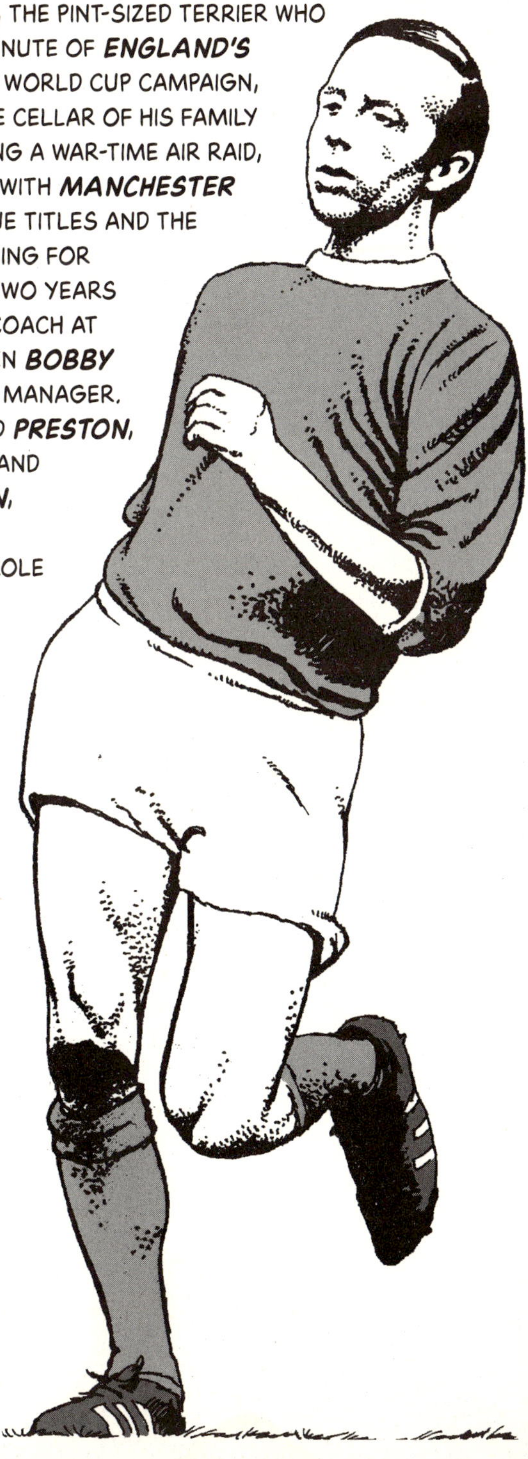

1. **STILES** AND **CHARLTON** WERE TWO OF ONLY THREE ENGLISHMEN TO WIN THE WORLD CUP AND THE EUROPEAN CUP -- WHO WAS THE OTHER?

2. WHO WAS **NOBBY'S** INTERNATIONAL FOOTBALLER BROTHER-IN-LAW?

MAY 19

CAPPED 116 TIMES BY HIS COUNTRY, LEGENDARY PLAYMAKER *ANDREA PIRLO* EARNED THE BRONZE BALL FOR HIS OUTSTANDING PERFORMANCES IN *ITALY'S* TRIUMPHANT 2006 WORLD CUP CAMPAIGN. BORN IN FIERO ON MAY 19, 1979, HE WON A SERIE B TITLE WITH LOCAL CLUB *BRESCIA* BEFORE SIGNING FOR *INTERNAZIONALE* IN 1988. AFTER FAILING TO ESTABLISH HIMSELF WITH THE *"NERAZZURRI"*, HE JOINED RIVALS *AC MILAN* IN 2001, WHERE HE DEVELOPED INTO A WORLD-CLASS STAR, WINNING TWO SERIE A TITLES, TWO UEFA CHAMPIONS LEAGUES, TWO UEFA SUPER CUPS, A FIFA CLUB WORLD CUP, A COPPA ITALIA, AND A SUPERCOPPA ITALIANA. MORE GLORY FOLLOWED HIS FREE TRANSFER TO *JUVENTUS* IN 2011, *PIRLO* ADDING FOUR SERIE A TITLES AND CUP HONOURS TO HIS MEDAL TALLY. HE ENDED HIS PLAYING CAREER IN THE MLS AND WAS APPOINTED HEAD COACH OF SERIE C CLUB *JUVENTUS U23* IN 2020. HE TOOK CHARGE OF THE FIRST TEAM ONLY NINE DAYS LATER!

1. WHICH MLS TEAM DID *PIRLO* PLAY FOR?

2. NAME THE *ITALY* CAPTAIN WHO WAS AWARDED THE SILVER BALL AT THE 2006 WORLD CUP.

3. ONLY FOUR PLAYERS HAVE MADE MORE APPEARANCES THAN *ANDREA PIRLO* FOR *ITALY*. HOW MANY CAN YOU NAME?

MAY 20

BORN IN MADRID ON MAY 20, 1981, *IKER CASILLAS* MADE HIS DEBUT FOR *REAL MADRID* AT THE AGE OF 16 AND BECAME THE YOUNGEST GOALKEEPER TO PLAY IN A UEFA CHAMPIONS LEAGUE FINAL, IN THE 3-0 WIN OVER *VALENCIA* IN 2000, JUST DAYS AFTER HIS 19TH BIRTHDAY. A FEW DAYS LATER, HE MADE HIS DEBUT FOR *SPAIN*. HE CAPTAINED HIS COUNTRY TO VICTORY AT EURO 2008, THE 2010 WORLD CUP AND EURO 2012. THE SECOND MOST-CAPPED *SPAIN* PLAYER OF ALL TIME, HE WON A HOST OF HONOURS WITH *REAL MADRID*, INCLUDING FIVE LEAGUE TITLES AND THREE UEFA CHAMPIONS LEAGUES, BEFORE SIGNING FOR *PORTO* IN 2015. HE HELPED THE CLUB WIN A LEAGUE TITLE IN 2018 BUT HIS CAREER WAS CUT SHORT FOLLOWING A HEART ATTACK, AND IN 2020 *CASILLAS* ANNOUNCED HIS RETIREMENT. *CASILLAS* WON THE GOLDEN GLOVE AT THE 2010 WORLD CUP.

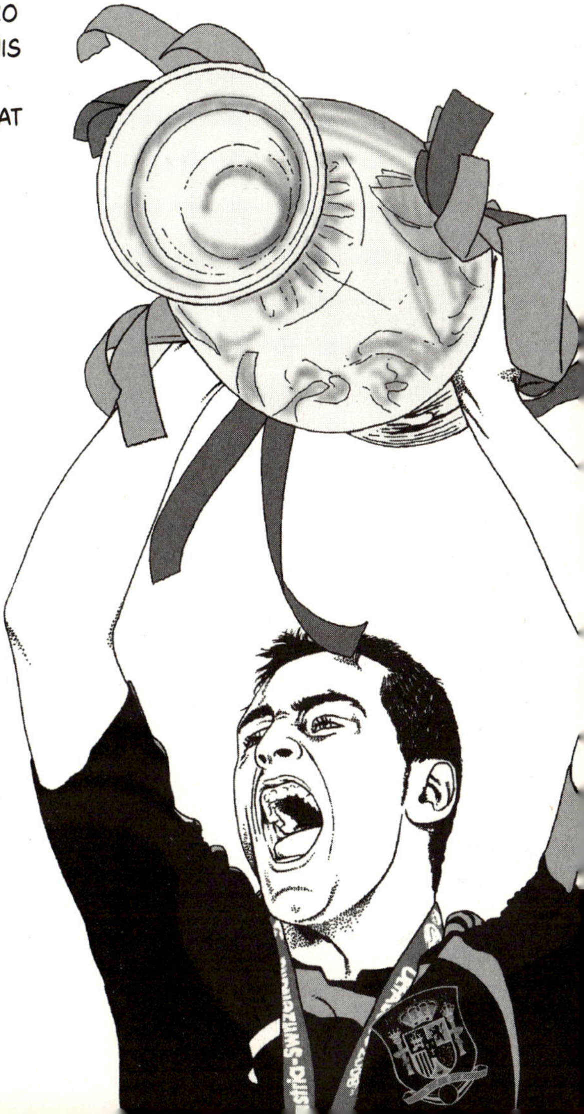

NAME THE GOALKEEPER WHO WON THE AWARD AT THESE TOURNAMENTS:

1. 1994 *(BELGIUM)*

2. 1998 *(FRANCE)*

3. 2002 *(GERMANY)*

4. 2006 *(ITALY)*

5. 2014 *(GERMANY)*

6. 2018 *(BELGIUM)*

MAY 21

FRANÇOIS OMAM-BIYIK CEMENTED HIS LEGENDARY STATUS IN **CAMEROON** FOOTBALL HISTORY WHEN HE SCORED THE GOAL THAT GAVE THE **"INDOMITABLE LIONS"** THEIR HISTORIC 1-0 VICTORY OVER **ARGENTINA** IN THE OPENING GAME OF THE 1990 WORLD CUP. HE ALSO SCORED AGAINST **SWEDEN** IN THE 1994 WORLD CUP AND CAPTAINED THE TEAM IN THE 1998 TOURNAMENT. BORN IN SACKBAYENE ON MAY 21, 1966, HE PLAYED HIS CLUB FOOTBALL IN FRANCE, ITALY AND MEXICO BEFORE EMBARKING ON A COACHING CAREER THAT HAS SEEN HIM MANAGE CLUBS IN MEXICO, FRANCE, TOGO AND GABON, AND TWICE SERVE AS ASSISTANT COACH OF THE **CAMEROON** NATIONAL TEAM.

1. WHICH FORMER **LIVERPOOL, WEST HAM UNITED** AND **GALATASARAY** DEFENDER IS THE MOST-CAPPED **CAMEROON** PLAYER?

2. WHICH **REAL MADRID, CHELSEA, NEWCASTLE UNITED** AND **MIDDLESBROUGH** STAR WAS THE FIRST **CAMEROON** PLAYER TO WIN THE UEFA CHAMPIONS LEAGUE?

3. WHICH FOUR-TIME AFRICAN PLAYER OF THE YEAR HOLDS THE ALL-TIME **CAMEROON** GOALSCORING RECORD?

MAY 22 HAVING WON THREE LEAGUE TITLES WITH *COLO-COLO* IN HIS NATIVE CHILE, TENACIOUS MIDFIELDER *ARTURO VIDAL* RELOCATED TO EUROPE, PLAYING FOUR SEASONS IN THE BUNDESLIGA WITH *BAYER LEVERKUSEN*. HE MOVED ON TO *JUVENTUS* IN 2011 AND STARTED A WINNING STREAK OF EIGHT CONSECUTIVE LEAGUE TITLES IN THREE DIFFERENT COUNTRIES, HIS FOUR IN ITALY FOLLOWED BY THREE IN GERMANY WITH *BAYERN MUNICH* AND THE 2019 LA LIGA IN SPAIN WITH *BARCELONA*. HE JOINED *INTERNAZIONALE* IN 2020 AND ADDED ANOTHER LEAGUE TITLE TO HIS ACCOMPLISHMENTS IN HIS DEBUT SEASON. BORN IN SANTIAGO ON MAY 22, 1987, *VIDAL* HAS MADE MORE THAN A CENTURY OF APPEARANCES FOR HIS COUNTRY AND WAS A MEMBER OF THE TEAMS THAT WON THE COPA AMÉRICA IN 2015 AND 2016.

1. WHICH PLAYER HOLDS BOTH THE *CHILE* NATIONAL TEAM APPEARANCE AND GOALSCORING RECORDS?

2. WHO IS *CHILE'S* MOST-CAPPED GOALKEEPER, A UEFA CHAMPIONS LEAGUE WINNER WITH *BARCELONA*?

3. WHICH SUBSEQUENT PREMIER LEAGUE MANAGER WAS IN CHARGE OF THE *CHILE* NATIONAL TEAM BETWEEN 2007 AND 2011?

MAY 23

IT WAS HIS GOAL AGAINST *ISRAEL* THAT SECURED *NORTHERN IRELAND'S* BERTH AT ESPAÑA 82, THE COUNTRY'S FIRST WORLD TOURNAMENT APPEARANCE IN 24 YEARS ... AND, WITH HIS TEAM REDUCED TO TEN MEN, IT WAS *WATFORD* STRIKER *GERRY ARMSTRONG* WHO ALSO SCORED THE VITAL GOAL AGAINST HOST NATION *SPAIN* THAT SAW THE IRISHMEN SECURE A 1-0 WIN TO TOP THEIR GROUP AND ADVANCE TO THE NEXT PHASE. BORN IN BELFAST ON MAY 23, 1954, *ARMSTRONG* SPENT MOST OF HIS CAREER IN ENGLAND -- ALTHOUGH THAT FAMOUS WORLD CUP GOAL DID HELP EARN A TRANSFER TO *REAL MALLORCA* IN 1983, WHERE HE WAS REGULARLY SHOWERED WITH ABUSE FROM UNFORGIVING OPPOSITION FANS!

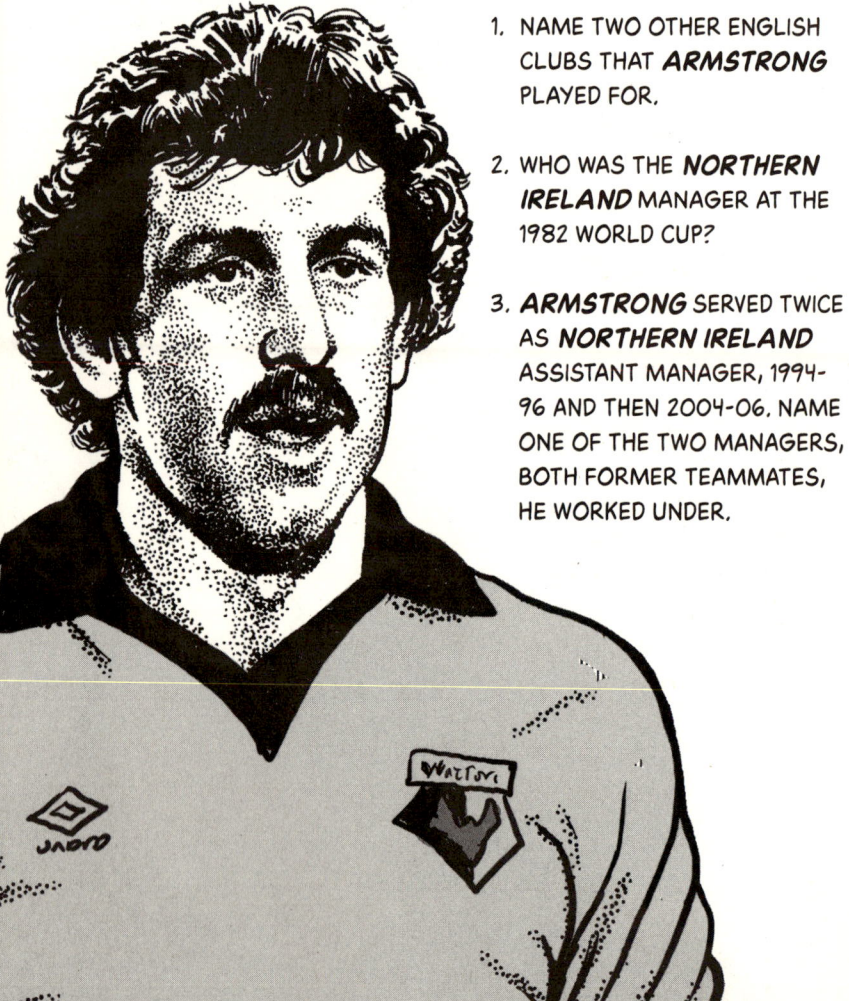

1. NAME TWO OTHER ENGLISH CLUBS THAT *ARMSTRONG* PLAYED FOR.

2. WHO WAS THE *NORTHERN IRELAND* MANAGER AT THE 1982 WORLD CUP?

3. *ARMSTRONG* SERVED TWICE AS *NORTHERN IRELAND* ASSISTANT MANAGER, 1994-96 AND THEN 2004-06. NAME ONE OF THE TWO MANAGERS, BOTH FORMER TEAMMATES, HE WORKED UNDER.

MAY 24

BORN IN MARSEILLE ON MAY 24, 1966, **ERIC CANTONA** BEGAN HIS CAREER WITH AUXERRE AT THE AGE OF 14. PRONE TO ERUPTIONS OF TEMPER, THE MOODY MISFIT WAS BOUNCED FROM CLUB TO CLUB IN FRANCE. HE RECEIVED FINES AND LENGTHY SUSPENSIONS AT **AUXERRE**, **MARSEILLE** AND **MONTPELLIER** AND WAS BANNED FROM THE **FRANCE** TEAM FOR SWEARING AT THE COACH. SENT OFF WHILE PLAYING FOR **NIMES** IN 1991, HE INSULTED THE DISCIPLINARY BOARD, WHO PROMPTLY DOUBLED HIS SUSPENSION, PROMPTING **ERIC** TO ANNOUNCE HIS RETIREMENT. HE RELENTED AND REVIVED HIS CAREER IN ENGLAND. HAVING HELPED **LEEDS UNITED** CLINCH THE LEAGUE TITLE IN 1992, HE MOVED ON TO **MANCHESTER UNITED** FOR A FEE OF £1.2 MILLION AND INSPIRED THEM TO A FIRST TITLE IN 26 YEARS IN 1993, AND THE LEAGUE AND FA CUP DOUBLE THE FOLLOWING YEAR. HIS INFAMOUS KUNG FU KICK ATTACK ON A SPECTATOR IN EARLY 1995 ALMOST LANDED HIM IN PRISON AND EARNED HIM AN EIGHT-MONTH BAN. HE RETURNED TO HELP **UNITED** TO A SECOND LEAGUE AND FA CUP DOUBLE IN 1996, AND ADDED ANOTHER LEAGUE TITLE THE FOLLOWING YEAR BEFORE RETIRING AT THE AGE OF 30.

1. BEFORE JOINING **LEEDS UNITED**, **CANTONA** HAD A TRIAL AT **SHEFFIELD WEDNESDAY** THAT FAILED TO RESULT IN A DEAL. WHO WAS **WEDNESDAY** MANAGER AT THAT TIME?

2. THE KUNG FU ATTACK OCCURRED IN A GAME AGAINST WHICH OPPOSITION?

3. WHO WAS **CANTONA'S** MANAGER AT **LEEDS UNITED?**

MAY 25

"EL GRAN CAPITÁN" DANIEL PASSARELLA WAS BORN IN CHACABUCO ON MAY 25, 1963. HAVING CAPTAINED THE *ARGENTINA* TEAM THAT WON THE 1978 WORLD CUP ON HOME SOIL AND STARRED AT THE 1982 TOURNAMENT, HE WAS SIDELINED IN THE 1986 WORLD CUP BUT AS A MEMBER OF THE SQUAD, HE BECAME THE ONLY PLAYER TO FEATURE IN BOTH OF HIS COUNTRY'S WORLD CUP-WINNING CAMPAIGNS. HE LEFT *RIVER PLATE* FOR ITALY IN 1982, PLAYING FOR *FIORENTINA* AND *INTERNAZIONALE* BEFORE ENDING HIS CAREER BACK AT *RIVER PLATE*. HE WAS SUBSEQUENTLY APPOINTED CLUB COACH AND WENT ON TO MANAGE A NUMBER OF TEAMS AND THE NATIONAL SIDES OF *ARGENTINA* AND *URUGUAY*. IN 2009, HE WAS ELECTED *RIVER PLATE* PRESIDENT.

WHICH MEMBER OF *ARGENTINA'S* 1978 WORLD CUP-WINNING TEAM:

1. WENT ON TO MANAGE *SWINDON TOWN*, *NEWCASTLE UNITED*, *WEST BROMWICH ALBION* AND *TOTTENHAM HOTSPUR* AMONG OTHERS?

2. TOPPED LA LIGA SCORING CHARTS TWICE WHILE PLAYING FOR *VALENCIA?*

3. SCORED THE GOAL THAT WON THE 1981 FA CUP FOR *TOTTENHAM HOTSPUR?*

MAY 26 THE FIRST ITALIAN PLAYER EVER TO WIN THE EUROPEAN GOLDEN SHOE, THE AWARD PRESENTED TO THE TOP SCORER ACROSS EVERY TOP DIVISION IN EUROPEAN LEAGUES, *LUCA TONI* PLAYED FOR A DOZEN DIFFERENT ITALIAN TEAMS DURING HIS CAREER, AS WELL AS *BAYERN MUNICH* IN GERMANY AND *AL-NASR* IN DUBAI. BORN IN PAVULLO NEL FRIGNANO ON MAY 26, 1977, HE WAS SERIE A TOP SCORER TWICE. A WORLD CUP WINNER IN 2006, HE SCORED 16 GOALS IN 47 APPEARANCES FOR *ITALY*.

LIONEL MESSI AND *CRISTIANO RONALDO* HAVE PRETTY MUCH MONOPOLISED THE EUROPEAN GOLDEN SHOE IN RECENT YEARS. CAN YOU IDENTIFY THESE OTHER WINNERS:

1. 34 GOALS FOR *RANGERS* IN BOTH 1991-92 AND 1992-93.

2. 32 GOALS FOR *ATLÉTICO MADRID* IN 2008-09.

3. 30 GOALS FOR *SUNDERLAND* IN 1999-2000.

GOALS FROM **SAMUEL ETO'O** AND **LIONEL MESSI** WERE ENOUGH TO GIVE **BARCELONA** VICTORY OVER DEFENDING CHAMPIONS **MANCHESTER UNITED** IN THE UEFA CHAMPIONS LEAGUE FINAL AT THE STADIO OLIMPICO IN ROME, ON MAY 27, 2009. THE WIN MADE **PEP GUARDIOLA'S** SIDE THE FIRST SPANISH TEAM IN HISTORY TO WIN THE TREBLE OF LA LIGA, THE COPA DEL REY AND THE CHAMPIONS LEAGUE.

IDENTIFY THE FOLLOWING PLAYERS WHO CONTESTED THE GAME:

1. **BARCELONA** DEFENDER WHO WOULD GO ON TO WIN THREE PREMIER LEAGUE TITLES AND THE FA CUP.

2. HE ALSO WON HONOURS WITH **MONACO, ARSENAL, NEW YORK RED BULLS** AND **FRANCE.**

3. FIVE TIMES WINNER OF THE BALLON D'OR AND THE FIRST EUROPEAN TO SCORE 100 INTERNATIONAL GOALS.

MAY 28

NEWCASTLE UNITED'S PAUL GASCOIGNE, THE PFA YOUNG PLAYER OF THE YEAR, JOINED **TOTTENHAM HOTSPUR** FOR A BRITISH RECORD FEE OF £2.2 MILLION ON JULY 7, 1988. THE NEWS CAME AS A SURPRISE TO **MANCHESTER UNITED** BOSS **ALEX FERGUSON**, WHO HAD GONE ON HOLIDAY TO MALTA AFTER RECEIVING ASSURANCES FROM **GASCOIGNE** THAT HE WOULD BE SIGNING FOR **UNITED**.

1. WHO WAS THE MANAGER WHO SIGNED **GASCOIGNE** TO **TOTTENHAM HOTSPUR?**

2. FOUR YEARS LATER, **GASCOIGNE** JOINED WHICH ITALIAN CLUB?

3. NAME THE ONLY CLUB WITH WHOM **GASCOIGNE** WON A LEAGUE TITLE.

MAY 29

BORN IN LENINGRAD (NOW CALLED ST. PETERSBURG) ON MAY 29, 1981, *ANDREI ARSHAVIN* WAS ENROLLED IN THE *FC ZENIT* ACADEMY FROM THE AGE OF SEVEN. VOTED THE 2006 RUSSIAN FOOTBALLER OF THE YEAR, HIS HONOURS WITH *FC ZENIT* INCLUDED THREE LEAGUE TITLES AND THE UEFA CUP. DESPITE INTEREST FROM A NUMBER OF OTHER CLUBS, *ANDREI* -- WHO WAS A BREAKOUT STAR AT EURO 2008 -- SIGNED FOR *ARSENAL* IN EARLY 2009. HIS EARLY PROMISE IN LONDON WAS UNFULFILLED, AND BY 2013 HE WAS AN *FC ZENIT* PLAYER ONCE MORE. AN UNHAPPY SPELL WITH *KUBAN KRASNODAR* WAS FOLLOWED BY A MOVE TO *KAZAKHSTAN'S FC KAIRAT* IN 2016. CAPPED 75 TIMES BY *RUSSIA*, HE RETIRED IN 2018.

IDENTIFY THESE OTHER *RUSSIA* INTERNATIONALS WHO PLAYED IN THE ENGLISH PREMIER LEAGUE:

1. WINGER WHO WON TWO LEAGUE TITLES WITH *MANCHESTER UNITED* BEFORE MOVING ON TO *EVERTON, FIORENTINA, RANGERS, MANCHESTER CITY, SOUTHAMPTON* AND MORE.

2. WON A PREMIER LEAGUE WITH *CHELSEA* BEFORE PLAYING FOR *PORTSMOUTH, CHARLTON ATHLETIC* AND *FULHAM.*

3. GOALKEEPER WHO WON MULTIPLE HONOURS IN SEVEN SEASONS WITH *CHELSEA* BEFORE JOINING *CELTIC.*

MAY 30

STEVEN GEORGE GERRARD WAS BORN IN WHISTON, MERSEYSIDE, ON MAY 30, 1980. HE PLAYED ON THE SAME JUNIOR TEAM AS **TONY HIBBERT**, BUT WHILE **TONY** WAS RECRUITED BY **EVERTON**, **STEVEN** WAS SPOTTED BY SCOUTS OF RIVALS **LIVERPOOL**, AND HE JOINED THE CLUB'S ACADEMY AT THE AGE OF NINE. IN HIS 17 SEASONS AT ANFIELD, HE WON TWO FA CUPS, THREE LEAGUE CUPS, THE UEFA CHAMPIONS LEAGUE, UEFA CUP AND UEFA SUPER CUP. TWO YEARS PLAYING IN THE MLS WERE FOLLOWED BY A MOVE INTO COACHING. APPOINTED MANAGER OF **RANGERS** IN 2018, HE LED THE TEAM TO A FIRST SCOTTISH PREMIERSHIP TITLE IN TEN YEARS.

1. WHICH MLS TEAM DID HE PLAY FOR?

2. NAME THREE OF THE SIX MANAGERS HE PLAYED UNDER AT **LIVERPOOL**.

3. **GERRARD** WAS CAPPED 114 TIMES BY **ENGLAND** -- NAME THREE OF THE MANAGERS HE PLAYED UNDER.

MAY 31

ON MAY 31, 2006, *UKRAINE* CAPTAIN *ANDRIY SHEVCHENKO* COMPLETED HIS £30 MILLION MOVE TO *CHELSEA* FROM *AC MILAN*. INFORMED OPINION HAD IT THAT THE TRANSFER WAS AT THE BEHEST OF *CHELSEA* OWNER *ROMAN ABRAMOVICH*, NOT MANAGER *JOSÉ MOURINHO*. THE MOVE DIDN'T WORK OUT. THE BALLON D'OR WINNER WAS SOON PLAYING SECOND FIDDLE TO *DIDIER DROGBA* AND WAS SIDELINED FOR MUCH OF HIS UNHAPPY STAY IN LONDON.

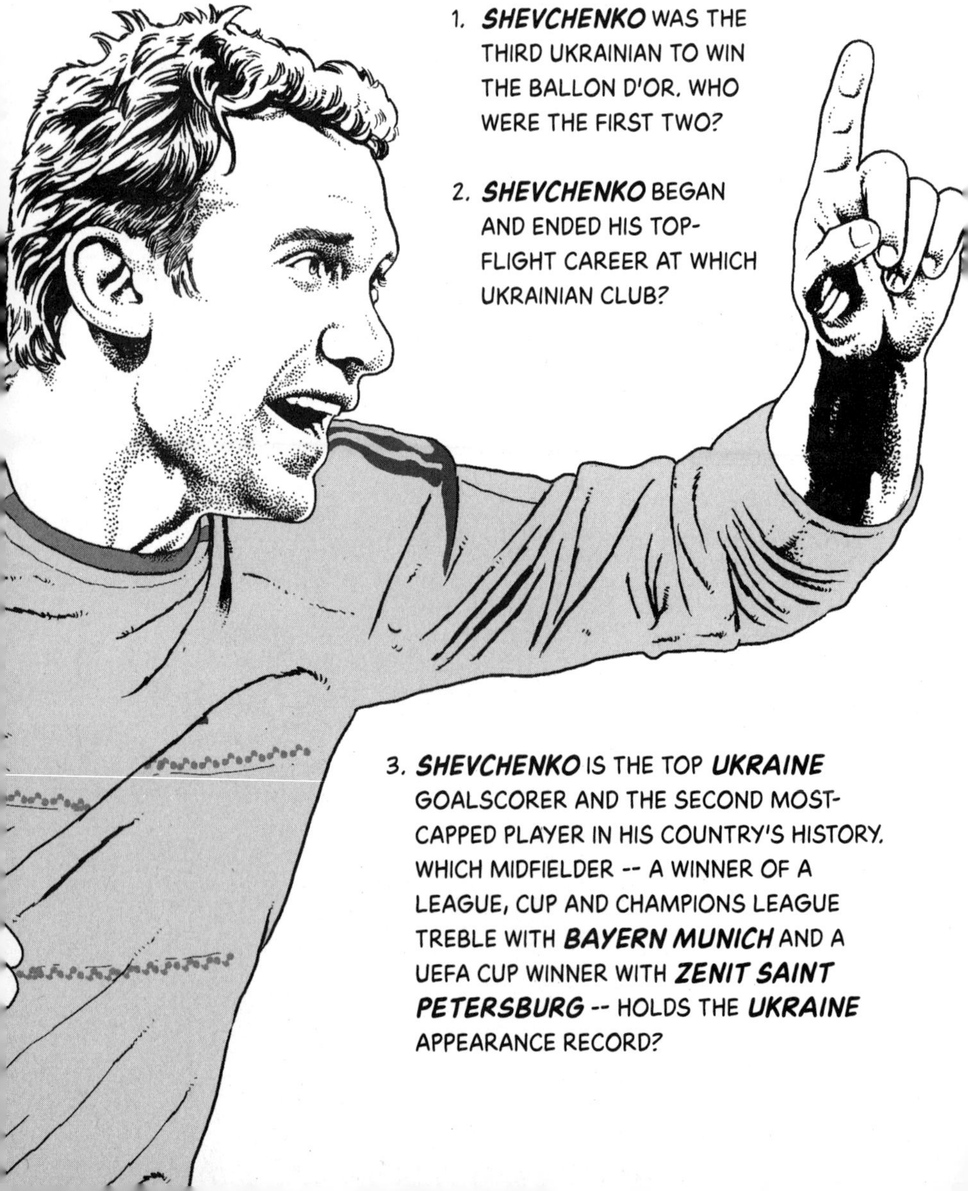

1. *SHEVCHENKO* WAS THE THIRD UKRAINIAN TO WIN THE BALLON D'OR. WHO WERE THE FIRST TWO?

2. *SHEVCHENKO* BEGAN AND ENDED HIS TOP-FLIGHT CAREER AT WHICH UKRAINIAN CLUB?

3. *SHEVCHENKO* IS THE TOP *UKRAINE* GOALSCORER AND THE SECOND MOST-CAPPED PLAYER IN HIS COUNTRY'S HISTORY. WHICH MIDFIELDER -- A WINNER OF A LEAGUE, CUP AND CHAMPIONS LEAGUE TREBLE WITH *BAYERN MUNICH* AND A UEFA CUP WINNER WITH *ZENIT SAINT PETERSBURG* -- HOLDS THE *UKRAINE* APPEARANCE RECORD?

JUNE

JUN 1

JAVIER HERNÁNDEZ BALCÁZAR WAS BORN ON JUNE 1, 1988, IN GUADALAJARA, MEXICO. HE TURNED PROFESSIONAL AT AGE 15.

JAVIER EARNED THE NICKNAME "CHICHARITO" BECAUSE HIS FATHER, WHO WAS A MEMBER OF THE MEXICO 1986 WORLD CUP SQUAD, WAS NICKNAMED "CHICHARO" -- IT MEANS "PEA" IN SPANISH -- DUE TO HIS GREEN EYES. JAVIER'S GRANDFATHER PLAYED FOR "EL TRICOLOR" IN THE 1954 WORLD CUP, WHERE HE SCORED AGAINST FRANCE.

1. CHICHARITO BEGAN HIS CAREER AT GUADALAJARA -- NAME THREE OTHER TEAMS HE HAS PLAYED FOR.

2. HE IS THE TOP SCORER IN THE HISTORY OF THE MEXICO TEAM, HAVING BROKEN THE RECORD SET BY WHICH FORMER BOLTON WANDERERS STRIKER?

JUN 2

BORN IN BUENOS AIRES, ARGENTINA, ON JUNE 2, 1988, *SERGIO AGÜERO* WAS GIVEN HIS *"KUN"* NICKNAME AT AN EARLY AGE BY HIS GRANDPARENTS. IT IS DERIVED FROM *"KUM-KUM"*, A CHARACTER ON HIS FAVOURITE ANIMATED CARTOON SHOW. AGED 15 YEARS AND 35 DAYS, HE BECAME THE YOUNGEST PLAYER TO DEBUT IN THE ARGENTINIAN PRIMERA DIVISIÓN, BREAKING THE RECORD PREVIOUSLY SET BY *DIEGO MARADONA* IN 1976.

1. NAME THE *COLOMBIA* STAR, LATER TO PLAY FOR *EVERTON*, WHO SET THE RECORD FOR YOUNGEST EXPATRIATE IN THE ARGENTINIAN PRIMERA DIVISIÓN WHEN HE WAS 17 YEARS OLD IN 2008.

2. NAME THE CAPTAIN OF THE 1978 WORLD CUP-WINNING *ARGENTINA* TEAM WHOSE 99 GOALS IS A PRIMERA DIVISIÓN RECORD FOR A DEFENDER.

3. NAME THE PARAGUAYAN GOALKEEPER WHO SCORED A RECORD 36 GOALS IN THE ARGENTINIAN PRIMERA DIVISIÓN.

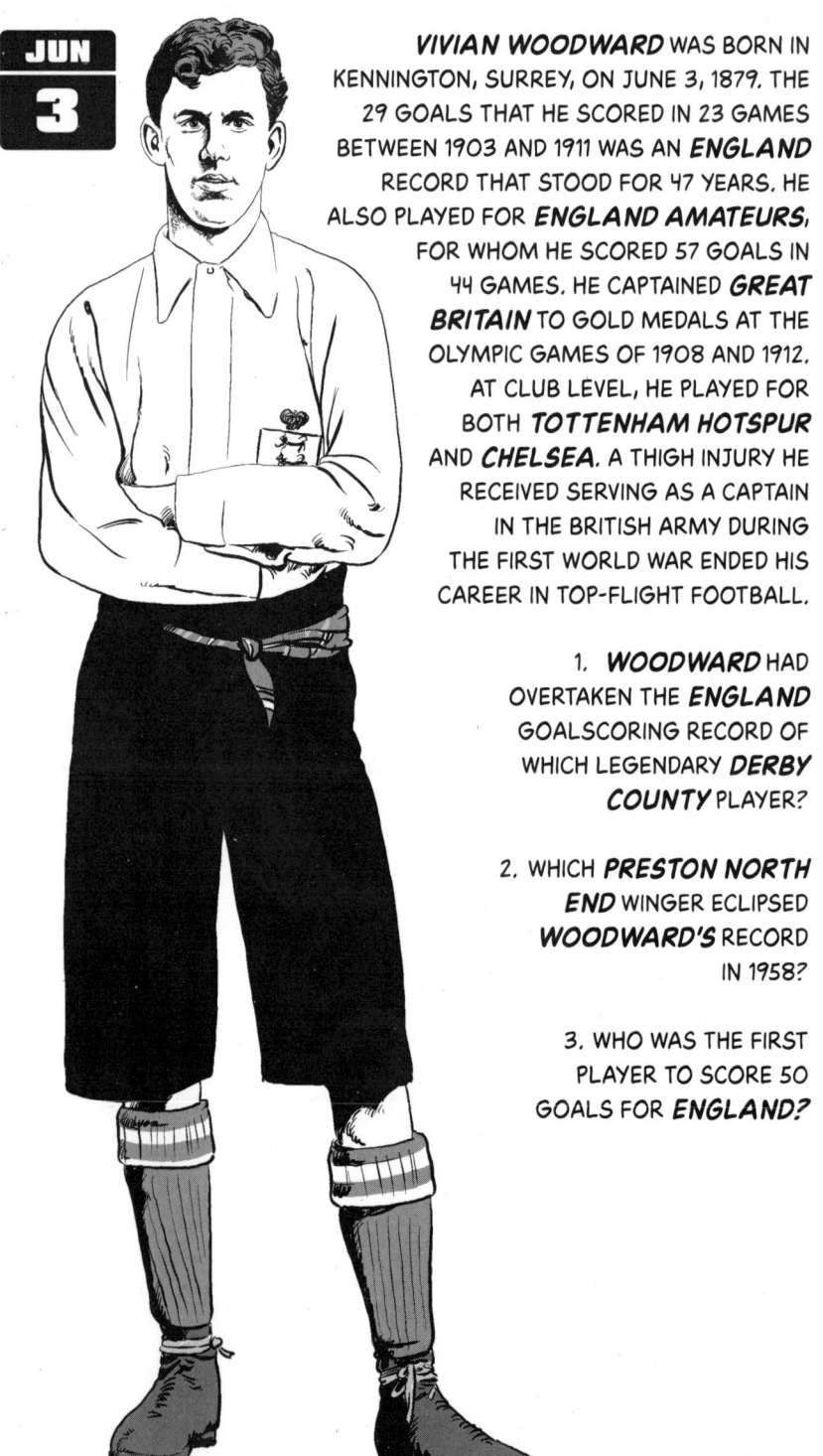

JUN 3

VIVIAN WOODWARD WAS BORN IN KENNINGTON, SURREY, ON JUNE 3, 1879. THE 29 GOALS THAT HE SCORED IN 23 GAMES BETWEEN 1903 AND 1911 WAS AN **ENGLAND** RECORD THAT STOOD FOR 47 YEARS. HE ALSO PLAYED FOR **ENGLAND AMATEURS**, FOR WHOM HE SCORED 57 GOALS IN 44 GAMES. HE CAPTAINED **GREAT BRITAIN** TO GOLD MEDALS AT THE OLYMPIC GAMES OF 1908 AND 1912. AT CLUB LEVEL, HE PLAYED FOR BOTH **TOTTENHAM HOTSPUR** AND **CHELSEA**. A THIGH INJURY HE RECEIVED SERVING AS A CAPTAIN IN THE BRITISH ARMY DURING THE FIRST WORLD WAR ENDED HIS CAREER IN TOP-FLIGHT FOOTBALL.

1. **WOODWARD** HAD OVERTAKEN THE **ENGLAND** GOALSCORING RECORD OF WHICH LEGENDARY **DERBY COUNTY** PLAYER?

2. WHICH **PRESTON NORTH END** WINGER ECLIPSED **WOODWARD'S** RECORD IN 1958?

3. WHO WAS THE FIRST PLAYER TO SCORE 50 GOALS FOR **ENGLAND?**

BORN IN GLIWICE, POLAND, ON JUNE 4, 1985, *LUKAS PODOLSKI* WAS RAISED IN GERMANY FROM THE AGE OF TWO. HE JOINED *1. FC KÖLN* AT THE AGE OF 10 AND BY 18 HE WAS A FIRST TEAM REGULAR. HAVING BEEN REJECTED BY THE *POLAND* TEAM, HE OPTED TO PLAY FOR *GERMANY*, AND WENT ON TO BECOME THE THIRD MOST-CAPPED PLAYER IN GERMAN HISTORY. HE SCORED THREE GOALS AND WAS NAMED BEST YOUNG PLAYER AT THE 2006 WORLD CUP, WON THE SILVER BOOT AT EURO 2008, SCORED TWICE AT THE 2010 WORLD CUP, ADDED ONE MORE GOAL TO HIS IMPRESSIVE OVERALL TALLY AT EURO 2012 AND WAS A WORLD CUP WINNER IN 2014.

IDENTIFY THESE *GERMANY* INTERNATIONALS WHO WERE ALSO BORN IN POLAND, OR AN AREA SUBSEQUENTLY PART OF POLAND:

1. SCORED THE LAST-MINUTE EQUALISER FOR *WEST GERMANY* THAT TOOK THE 1966 WORLD CUP FINAL INTO EXTRA TIME.

2. *GERMANY'S* ALL-TIME TOP GOALSCORER AND ONE OF FEW PLAYERS TO WIN GOLD, SILVER AND BRONZE MEDALS IN THE WORLD CUP.

3. AS A MANAGER, HE LED *DENMARK* TO THEIR FIRST-EVER WORLD CUP PARTICIPATION IN THE 1986 TOURNAMENT.

JUN 5

ON JUNE 5, 1938, *POLAND'S* FIRST-EVER WORLD CUP GAME ENDED IN A 6-5 LOSS TO *BRAZIL* AFTER EXTRA TIME. *BRAZIL* STAR *LEONIDAS DA SILVA* SCORED A HAT-TRICK, BUT HE WAS OUTSCORED BY POLISH MAVERICK *ERNST WILLIMOWSKI*, WHOSE FOUR GOALS CEMENTED HIS PLACE IN *"EAGLES"* LEGEND.

1. NAME TWO OF THE OTHER FIVE PLAYERS WHO HAVE SCORED FOUR GOALS IN A SINGLE WORLD CUP GAME.

2. WHO IS THE ONLY PLAYER TO SCORE 5 GOALS IN ONE GAME AT THE WORLD CUP?

JUN 6

SEBASTIAN LARSSON WAS BORN IN ESKILSTUNA, SWEDEN, ON JUNE 6, 1985. HAVING JOINED **ARSENAL** AS A TEENAGER, HE PLAYED MOST OF HIS SENIOR CLUB FOOTBALL IN ENGLAND. A LOAN MOVE TO **BIRMINGHAM CITY** WAS SUBSEQUENTLY MADE PERMANENT, AND IN THE 2010-11 SEASON, HE ENJOYED THE HIGH OF BEATING **ARSENAL** IN THE LEAGUE CUP FINAL BEFORE EXPERIENCING THE LOW POINT OF RELEGATION. IT WAS THE SECOND TIME THAT HE HAD BEEN RELEGATED FROM THE TOP FLIGHT WITH **BIRMINGHAM**, AND LATER THAT SUMMER HE JOINED **SUNDERLAND**. HIS SIX YEARS WITH **"THE BLACK CATS"** ENDED IN THE SUMMER OF 2017 AND THE CLUB'S RELEGATION FROM THE PREMIER LEAGUE. FOLLOWING A SEASON IN THE CHAMPIONSHIP WITH **HULL CITY**, HE RETURNED TO SWEDEN TO SIGN FOR **AIK**, HELPING THE CLUB WIN THE LEAGUE TITLE IN HIS DEBUT SEASON. AN EVER-PRESENT FOR THE NATIONAL TEAM, HE EARNED HIS 100TH **SWEDEN** CAP IN 2018.

1. UNDER WHICH MANAGER DID **SEB LARSSON** PLAY AT BOTH **BIRMINGHAM CITY** AND **SUNDERLAND**?

2. **LARSSON** WAS IN THE **SUNDERLAND** SIDE THAT LOST TO WHICH TEAM IN THE 2011 LEAGUE CUP FINAL?

3. WHICH SWEDISH CITY IS HOME TO **AIK**?

JUN 7

ON JUNE 7, 1970, REIGNING WORLD CHAMPIONS *ENGLAND* TOOK ON EVENTUAL TROPHY WINNERS *BRAZIL* IN A WORLD CUP GROUP GAME THAT IS REGARDED AS ONE OF THE TOURNAMENT'S GREATEST. DECIDED IN *BRAZIL'S* FAVOUR BY A *JAIRZINHO* GOAL, THE MATCH IS REMEMBERED IN PART FOR AN INCREDIBLE SAVE THAT GOALKEEPER *GORDON BANKS* MADE TO DENY THE GREAT *PELÉ*. AT THE FINAL WHISTLE, *PELÉ* RUSHED TO EMBRACE AND EXCHANGE SHIRTS WITH *ENGLAND* CAPTAIN *BOBBY MOORE*, LATER SAYING HE WAS THE GREATEST DEFENDER HE HAD EVER PLAYED AGAINST.

1. WHO WERE THE MANAGERS OF THE TWO TEAMS?

2. WHO CAPTAINED THE 1970 *BRAZIL* WORLD CUP TEAM?

3. WHICH COUNTRY ELIMINATED *ENGLAND* IN THE QUARTER-FINALS?

BY THE THIRD TOURNAMENT, THE EUROPEAN NATIONS CUP HAD BECOME THE EUROPEAN CHAMPIONSHIPS AND A STRAIGHT KNOCKOUT SYSTEM HAD BEEN REPLACED BY GROUPS. THE FINAL STAGES WERE HELD IN ITALY, AND THE SEMI-FINAL BETWEEN *ITALY* AND THE *USSR* IN ROME WAS DECIDED BY THE TOSS OF A COIN. WORLD CHAMPIONS *ENGLAND* WENT OUT TO A SINGLE *YUGOSLAVIA* GOAL IN FLORENCE IN THE OTHER SEMI-FINAL. ON JUNE 8, 1968, AFTER EXTRA TIME, THE FINAL ENDED IN A 1-1 DRAW. IT WAS REPLAYED TWO DAYS LATER, *ITALY* INTRODUCING FIVE NEW PLAYERS AGAINST A WEARY *YUGOSLAVIA* AND COASTING TO A COMFORTABLE VICTORY.

1. THE TOURNAMENT SAW THE FIRST-EVER SENDING OFF OF AN *ENGLAND* PLAYER WHILE REPRESENTING HIS COUNTRY. WHO WAS THAT PLAYER?

2. WHO CAPTAINED *ITALY* TO VICTORY IN 1968?

3. IN WHICH YEAR WAS THE EUROPEAN CHAMPIONSHIP FINAL HELD IN ITALY AGAIN?

JUN 9

BORN IN UTRECHT ON JUNE 9, 1984, **WESLEY SNEIJDER** WAS STILL IN HIS TEENS WHEN HE ESTABLISHED HIMSELF AS A REGULAR FOR BOTH **AJAX** AND THE **NETHERLANDS**. HAVING WON LEAGUE AND CUP HONOURS WITH **AJAX**, HE SIGNED FOR **REAL MADRID** IN 2007 AND WON A LEAGUE TITLE IN HIS FIRST SEASON.

HE MOVED ON TO **INTERNAZIONALE** IN 2009, WINNING A TREBLE OF SERIE A TITLE, COPPA ITALIA AND UEFA CHAMPIONS LEAGUE IN HIS FIRST SEASON IN ITALY. HE JOINED **GALATASARAY** IN 2013, AND WAS A TURKISH SÜPER LIG WINNER IN HIS FIRST SEASON, ADDING A LEAGUE AND CUP DOUBLE IN 2016. HE BECAME HIS COUNTRY'S MOST-CAPPED PLAYER ON HIS 33RD BIRTHDAY ON JUNE 9, 2017.

FOLLOWING A BRIEF SPELL IN FRANCE WITH **NICE**, HE ENDED HIS PLAYING CAREER WITH A SEASON PLAYING FOR QATARI SIDE **AL GHARAFA**.

1. WHICH GOALKEEPER DID HE OVERTAKE TO BECOME THE MOST-CAPPED **NETHERLANDS** PLAYER?

2. HE WAS ONE OF FOUR PLAYERS WHO SCORED 5 GOALS AT THE 2010 WORLD CUP. NAME ONE OF THE OTHERS.

JUN 10

HAVING FAILED TO MAKE THE GRADE AT **MANCHESTER UNITED**, **DAVID PLATT** -- BORN IN CHADDERTON, LANCASHIRE, ON JUNE 10, 1966 -- RESURRECTED HIS CAREER AT FOURTH DIVISION **CREWE ALEXANDRA**. HE JOINED **ASTON VILLA** IN 1988, HELPING THE CLUB RETURN TO THE TOP FLIGHT IN HIS DEBUT SEASON AND PLAYING HIS WAY INTO **BOBBY ROBSON'S ENGLAND** TEAM. AT ITALIA '90, HE CAME ON AS A SUBSTITUTE AND SCORED A MEMORABLE VOLLEY -- HIS FIRST GOAL FOR HIS COUNTRY -- TO ELIMINATE **BELGIUM** AND PUT **ENGLAND** IN THE QUARTER-FINALS.

1. NAME TWO OF THE THREE CLUBS IN ITALY FOR WHOM **DAVID PLATT** PLAYED.

2. WHICH MANAGER SIGNED **PLATT** TO **ARSENAL** IN THE SUMMER OF 1995?

3. HE SPENT THREE YEARS AS PLAYER/MANAGER OF WHICH CLUB BEFORE TAKING THE REINS OF THE **ENGLAND U21** TEAM?

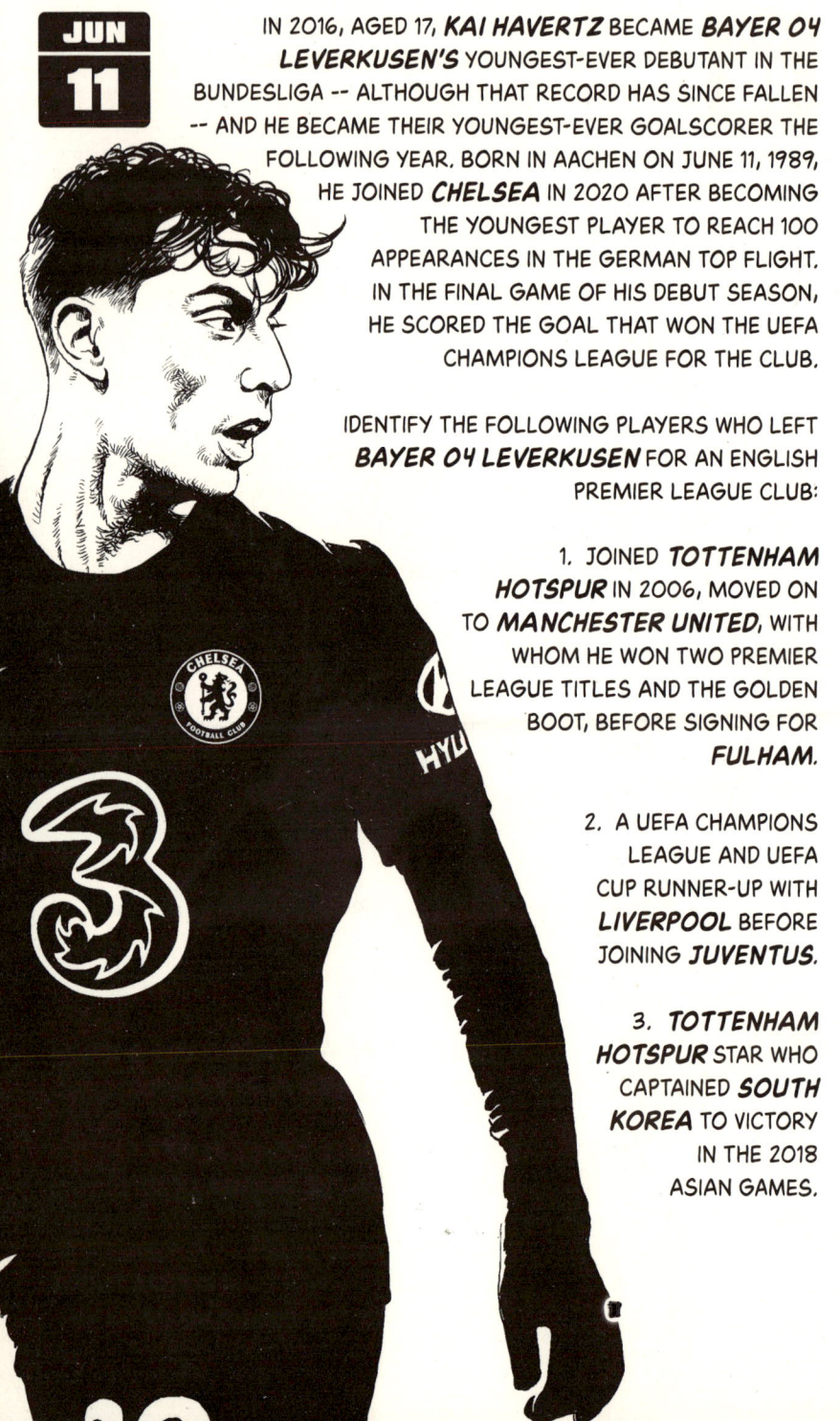

JUN 11

IN 2016, AGED 17, **KAI HAVERTZ** BECAME **BAYER O4 LEVERKUSEN'S** YOUNGEST-EVER DEBUTANT IN THE BUNDESLIGA -- ALTHOUGH THAT RECORD HAS SINCE FALLEN -- AND HE BECAME THEIR YOUNGEST-EVER GOALSCORER THE FOLLOWING YEAR. BORN IN AACHEN ON JUNE 11, 1989, HE JOINED **CHELSEA** IN 2020 AFTER BECOMING THE YOUNGEST PLAYER TO REACH 100 APPEARANCES IN THE GERMAN TOP FLIGHT. IN THE FINAL GAME OF HIS DEBUT SEASON, HE SCORED THE GOAL THAT WON THE UEFA CHAMPIONS LEAGUE FOR THE CLUB.

IDENTIFY THE FOLLOWING PLAYERS WHO LEFT **BAYER O4 LEVERKUSEN** FOR AN ENGLISH PREMIER LEAGUE CLUB:

1. JOINED **TOTTENHAM HOTSPUR** IN 2006, MOVED ON TO **MANCHESTER UNITED**, WITH WHOM HE WON TWO PREMIER LEAGUE TITLES AND THE GOLDEN BOOT, BEFORE SIGNING FOR **FULHAM**.

2. A UEFA CHAMPIONS LEAGUE AND UEFA CUP RUNNER-UP WITH **LIVERPOOL** BEFORE JOINING **JUVENTUS**.

3. **TOTTENHAM HOTSPUR** STAR WHO CAPTAINED **SOUTH KOREA** TO VICTORY IN THE 2018 ASIAN GAMES.

JUN 12

BORN IN FREDERICIA, DENMARK, ON JUNE 12, 1976, **THOMAS SØRENSEN** CAME THROUGH THE YOUTH RANKS AT **ODENSE BK** BEFORE JOINING **SUNDERLAND** IN 1998, WHERE HE HELPED THE CLUB WIN PROMOTION TO THE ENGLISH TOP FLIGHT IN HIS DEBUT SEASON. HE MADE THE FIRST OF HIS 101 APPEARANCES FOR **DENMARK** IN 1999. HAVING REPRESENTED HIS COUNTRY AT THE 2002 AND 2010 WORLD CUPS AND EURO 2004, HE RETIRED FROM THE NATIONAL TEAM IN 2012.

1. BEFORE JOINING **STOKE CITY** IN 2008, HE SPENT FIVE YEARS AT WHICH PREMIER LEAGUE CLUB?

2. **SØRENSEN** WAS KEPT OUT OF **DENMARK'S** EURO 2000 TEAM BY WHICH LEGENDARY GOALKEEPER?

3. HE FINISHED HIS PLAYING CAREER WITH A TWO-YEAR SPELL AT WHICH AUSTRALIAN A-LEAGUE CLUB?

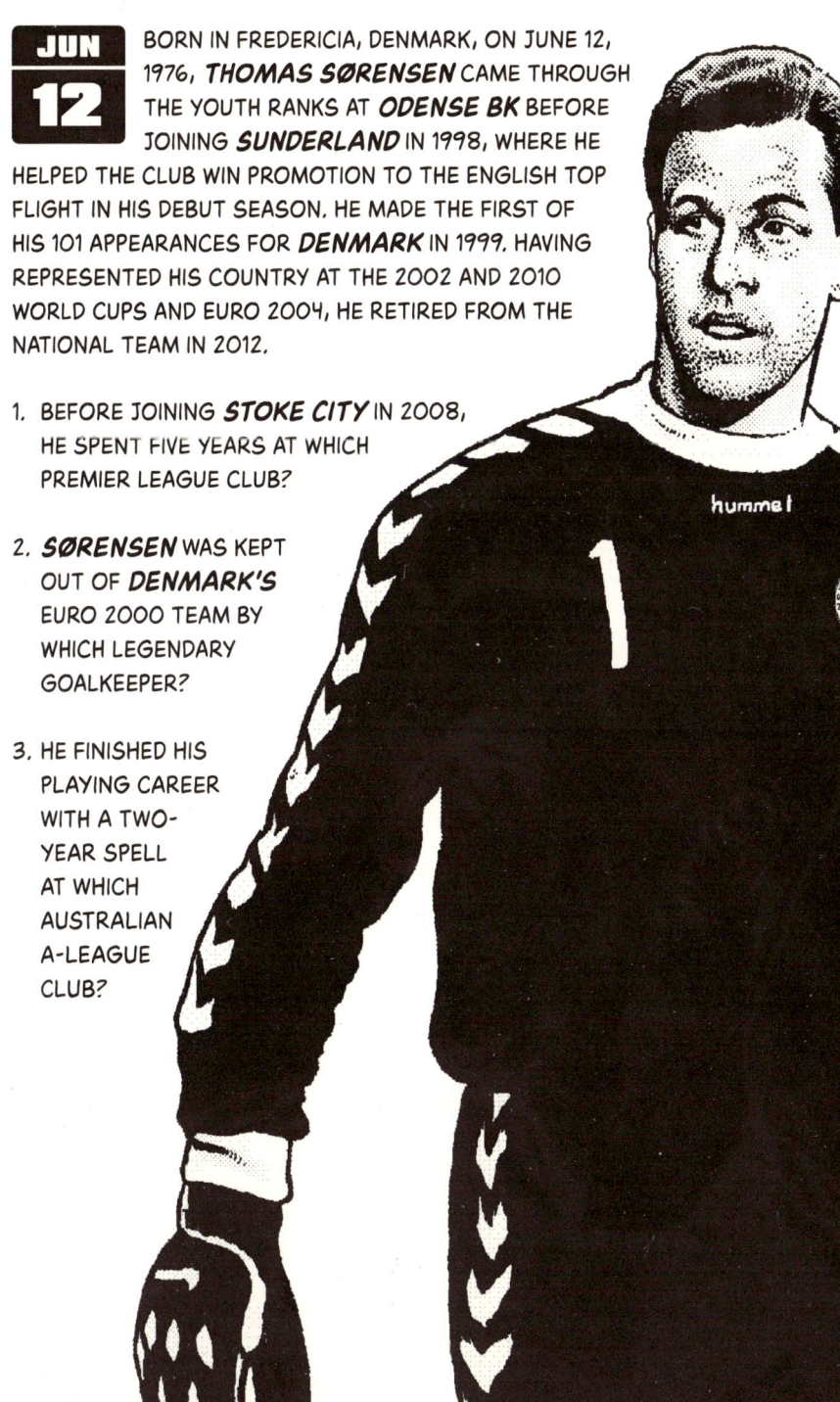

JUN 13

JAPANESE FOOTBALLER OF THE YEAR IN 2010, *KEISUKE HONDA* WAS NAMED MVP AT THE 2011 AFC ASIAN CUP AND BEST PLAYER IN ASIA IN 2013. BORN IN SETTSU, OSAKA, ON JUNE 13, 1986, HE LAUNCHED HIS SENIOR CAREER AT *NAGOYA GRAMPUS* BEFORE HEADING TO THE NETHERLANDS IN 2008 TO JOIN EREDIVISIE SIDE *VVV-VENIO* -- WHO WERE PROMPTLY RELEGATED! THE FOLLOWING SEASON, *HONDA* HIT 16 GOALS IN 36 LEAGUE GAMES TO HELP THEM BOUNCE BACK TO THE TOP FLIGHT, EARNING HIMSELF THE NICKNAME *"EMPEROR KEISUKE"* IN THE PROCESS. HIS TRAVELS HAVE TAKEN HIM TO PLAY FOR CLUBS AS FAR AFIELD AS MEXICO, PORTUGAL, AUSTRALIA, BRAZIL AND AZERBAIJAN. ALTHOUGH STILL PLAYING PROFESSIONALLY, HE WAS APPOINTED MANAGER OF *CAMBODIA* IN 2018.

1. HE WON FOUR TROPHIES, INCLUDING A LEAGUE AND CUP DOUBLE, IN FOUR YEARS WITH WHICH RUSSIAN CLUB?

2. HE JOINED WHICH ITALIAN SERIE A CLUB IN 2014?

3. *KEISUKE HONDA* SCORED TWO GOALS AT THE 2010 WORLD CUP -- NAME ONE OF THE OPPOSING TEAMS.

JUN 14

A GOAL FROM LEFT-BACK *PAUL BREITNER* GAVE HOSTS *WEST GERMANY* VICTORY OVER *CHILE* AND A WINNING START TO THEIR WORLD CUP CAMPAIGN ON JUNE 14, 1974. THE GAME SAW THE FIRST RED CARD EVER ISSUED IN A WORLD CUP WHEN *CARLOS CASZELY* WAS DISMISSED FOR A FOUL ON *BERTI VOGTS*. THE GERMANS WENT ON TO WIN THE TROPHY, WITH *BREITNER* ADDING TWO MORE TO HIS TALLY, INCLUDING A GOAL IN THE FINAL.

1. *BREITNER* IS ONE OF FOUR PLAYERS TO SCORE IN TWO WORLD CUP FINALS -- NAME THE OTHER THREE.

2. IN WHICH YEAR DID *BREITNER* WIN A UEFA EUROPEAN CHAMPIONSHIP WITH *WEST GERMANY*?

3. *BREITNER* WON A UEFA EUROPEAN CUP WITH WHICH CLUB TEAM?

JUN 15

NICKNAMED **"THE TITAN"**, **OLIVER KAHN** IS THE ONLY GOALKEEPER TO HAVE WON THE WORLD CUP GOLDEN BALL, THE AWARD GIVEN TO THE TOURNAMENT'S BEST PLAYER. HE WON IN 2002, IN THE SAME TOURNAMENT THAT HE WON THE GOLDEN GLOVE. TWICE GERMAN FOOTBALLER OF THE YEAR, **KAHN** -- WHO WAS BORN IN KARLSRUHE ON JUNE 15, 1969 -- WON A HOST OF HONOURS WITH **BAYERN MUNICH**, INCLUDING EIGHT LEAGUE TITLES, THE UEFA CHAMPIONS LEAGUE AND THE UEFA CUP. HE ALSO CAPTAINED **GERMANY** 49 TIMES IN 86 APPEARANCES.

NAME THREE OTHER GOALKEEPERS WHO HAVE BEEN NAMED GERMAN FOOTBALLER OF THE YEAR.

JUN 16

ON JUNE 16, 1982, **ENGLAND** PLAYED THEIR FIRST WORLD CUP GAME SINCE 1970. IT TOOK **BRYAN ROBSON** JUST 27 SECONDS TO OPEN THE SCORING AGAINST **FRANCE** -- THE FASTEST **ENGLAND** GOAL IN WORLD CUP HISTORY. **ENGLAND** WENT ON TO WIN 3-1. **HAKAN SUKER** SCORED THE FASTEST GOAL IN WORLD CUP HISTORY IN 2002, WHEN HE SCORED FOR **TURKEY** AFTER JUST 11 SECONDS OF THE GAME AGAINST **SOUTH KOREA**.

ROBSON SCORED TWICE AT THE 1982 WORLD CUP. IDENTIFY THESE OTHER GOALSCORERS FOR **ENGLAND** AT THE TOURNAMENT:

1. **MANCHESTER CITY** STRIKER WHO SCORED TWICE AND WOULD MOVE TO **SAMPDORIA** LATER THAT SUMMER.

2. STRIKER WHO WON THE FA CUP AND THE UEFA CUP WITH **IPSWICH TOWN**, SUBSEQUENT CLUBS INCLUDE **ARSENAL** AND **PORTSMOUTH**.

3. **JOZEF BARMOŠ** SCORED AN OWN GOAL IN WHICH COUNTRY'S 2-0 LOSS TO **ENGLAND?**

JUN
17

ALAN DZAGOEV WAS BORN IN BESLAN, ON JUNE 17, 1990. HAVING DEBUTED FOR LOWER LEAGUE **KRYLIA SOVETOV-SOK** AT THE AGE OF 15, HE WAS VOTED 2008 BEST YOUNG PLAYER IN THE RUSSIAN PREMIER LEAGUE IN HIS DEBUT SEASON FOR **CSKA MOSCOW**. HE MADE HIS INTERNATIONAL DEBUT FOR **RUSSIA** THE SAME YEAR, AT THE AGE OF 18 YEARS AND 116 DAYS.

HIS THREE GOALS AT THE 2012 UEFA EUROPEAN CHAMPIONSHIPS MADE HIM JOINT TOURNAMENT TOP SCORER WITH FIVE OTHER PLAYERS, IDENTIFY THEM:

1. **ITALY**

2. **GERMANY**

3. **CROATIA**

4. **SPAIN**

5. **PORTUGAL**

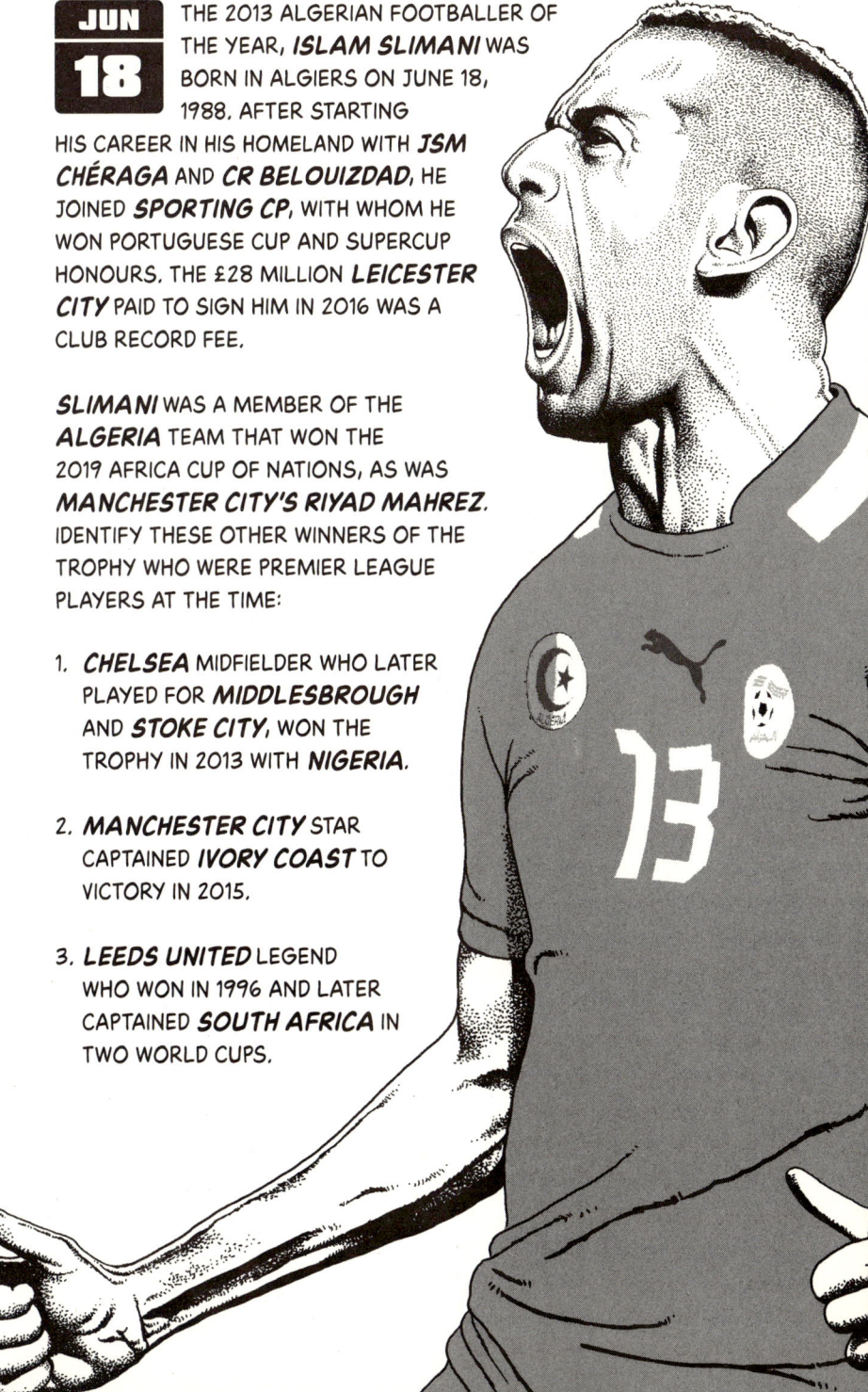

JUN 18

THE 2013 ALGERIAN FOOTBALLER OF THE YEAR, *ISLAM SLIMANI* WAS BORN IN ALGIERS ON JUNE 18, 1988. AFTER STARTING HIS CAREER IN HIS HOMELAND WITH *JSM CHÉRAGA* AND *CR BELOUIZDAD*, HE JOINED *SPORTING CP*, WITH WHOM HE WON PORTUGUESE CUP AND SUPERCUP HONOURS. THE £28 MILLION *LEICESTER CITY* PAID TO SIGN HIM IN 2016 WAS A CLUB RECORD FEE.

SLIMANI WAS A MEMBER OF THE *ALGERIA* TEAM THAT WON THE 2019 AFRICA CUP OF NATIONS, AS WAS *MANCHESTER CITY'S RIYAD MAHREZ*. IDENTIFY THESE OTHER WINNERS OF THE TROPHY WHO WERE PREMIER LEAGUE PLAYERS AT THE TIME:

1. *CHELSEA* MIDFIELDER WHO LATER PLAYED FOR *MIDDLESBROUGH* AND *STOKE CITY*, WON THE TROPHY IN 2013 WITH *NIGERIA*.

2. *MANCHESTER CITY* STAR CAPTAINED *IVORY COAST* TO VICTORY IN 2015.

3. *LEEDS UNITED* LEGEND WHO WON IN 1996 AND LATER CAPTAINED *SOUTH AFRICA* IN TWO WORLD CUPS.

JUN 19 WITH THE SECOND WORLD WAR JUST A MATTER OF MONTHS AWAY, THE THIRD WORLD CUP FINAL WAS STAGED IN PARIS ON JUNE 19, 1938. TWO GOALS EACH FROM *GINO COLAUSSI* AND *SILVIO PIOLA* HELPED *ITALY* BEAT *HUNGARY* 4-2 TO RETAIN THE TITLE THEY HAD WON FOUR YEARS EARLIER. IT WOULD BE 12 YEARS BEFORE THE TOURNAMENT WAS HELD AGAIN.

1. WHO MANAGED *ITALY'S* 1934 AND 1938 WORLD CUP-WINNING TEAMS?

2. HOW MANY TIMES HAS *ITALY* NOW WON THE WORLD CUP?

3. HOME TO *INTERNAZIONALE* AND *AC MILAN*, THE STADIUM COMMONLY KNOWN AS THE *SAN SIRO*, IS OFFICIALLY NAMED AFTER WHICH LEGENDARY CAPTAIN OF *ITALY'S* 1938 TEAM?

COUPE DU MONDE 1938

JUN 20

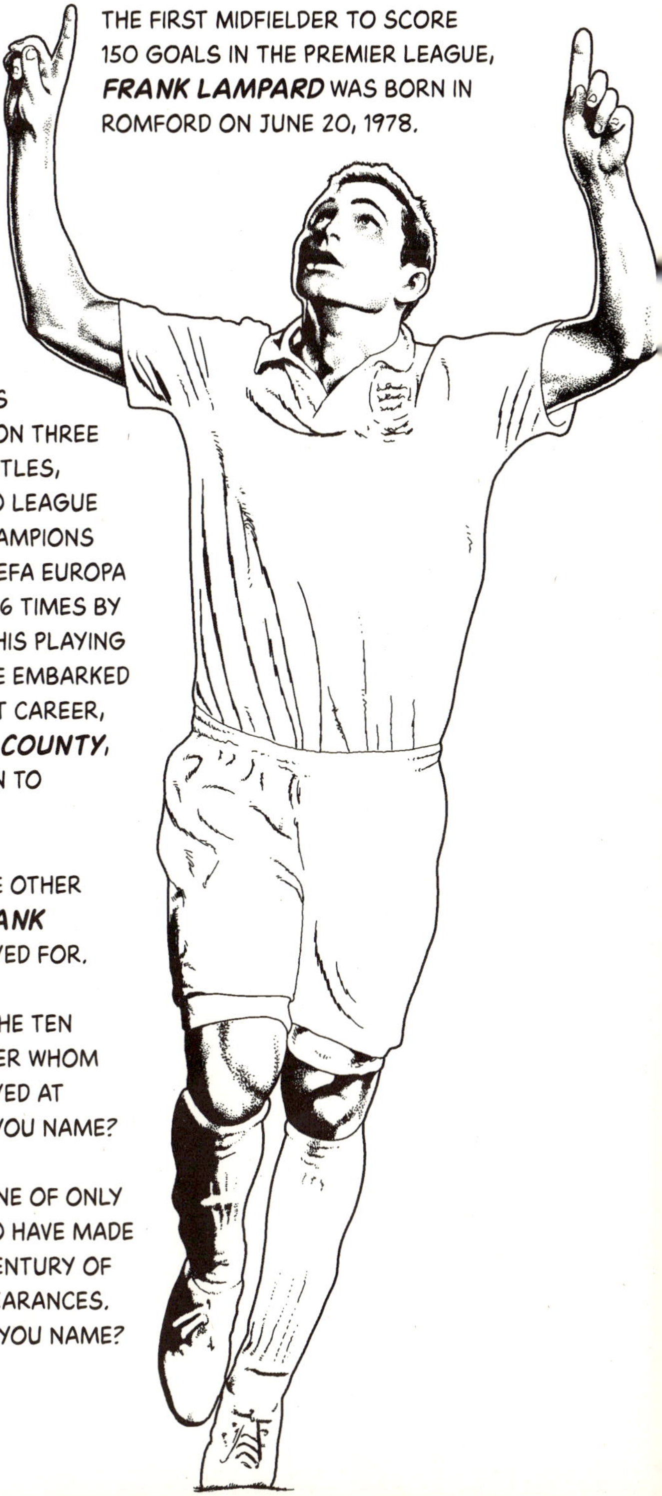

THE FIRST MIDFIELDER TO SCORE 150 GOALS IN THE PREMIER LEAGUE, *FRANK LAMPARD* WAS BORN IN ROMFORD ON JUNE 20, 1978.

HAVING MADE HIS NAME AT *WEST HAM UNITED, FRANK LAMPARD* JOINED *CHELSEA* IN 2001. IN 13 YEARS AT THE CLUB, HE WON THREE PREMIER LEAGUE TITLES, FOUR FA CUPS, TWO LEAGUE CUPS, THE UEFA CHAMPIONS LEAGUE AND THE UEFA EUROPA LEAGUE. CAPPED 106 TIMES BY *ENGLAND*, WHEN HIS PLAYING DAYS WERE OVER HE EMBARKED ON A MANAGEMENT CAREER, FIRST WITH *DERBY COUNTY*, BEFORE MOVING ON TO *CHELSEA*.

1. NAME THE THREE OTHER CLUBS THAT *FRANK LAMPARD* PLAYED FOR.

2. HOW MANY OF THE TEN MANAGERS UNDER WHOM *LAMPARD* PLAYED AT *CHELSEA* CAN YOU NAME?

3. *LAMPARD* IS ONE OF ONLY NINE PLAYERS TO HAVE MADE MORE THAN A CENTURY OF *ENGLAND* APPEARANCES. HOW MANY CAN YOU NAME?

**JUN
21**

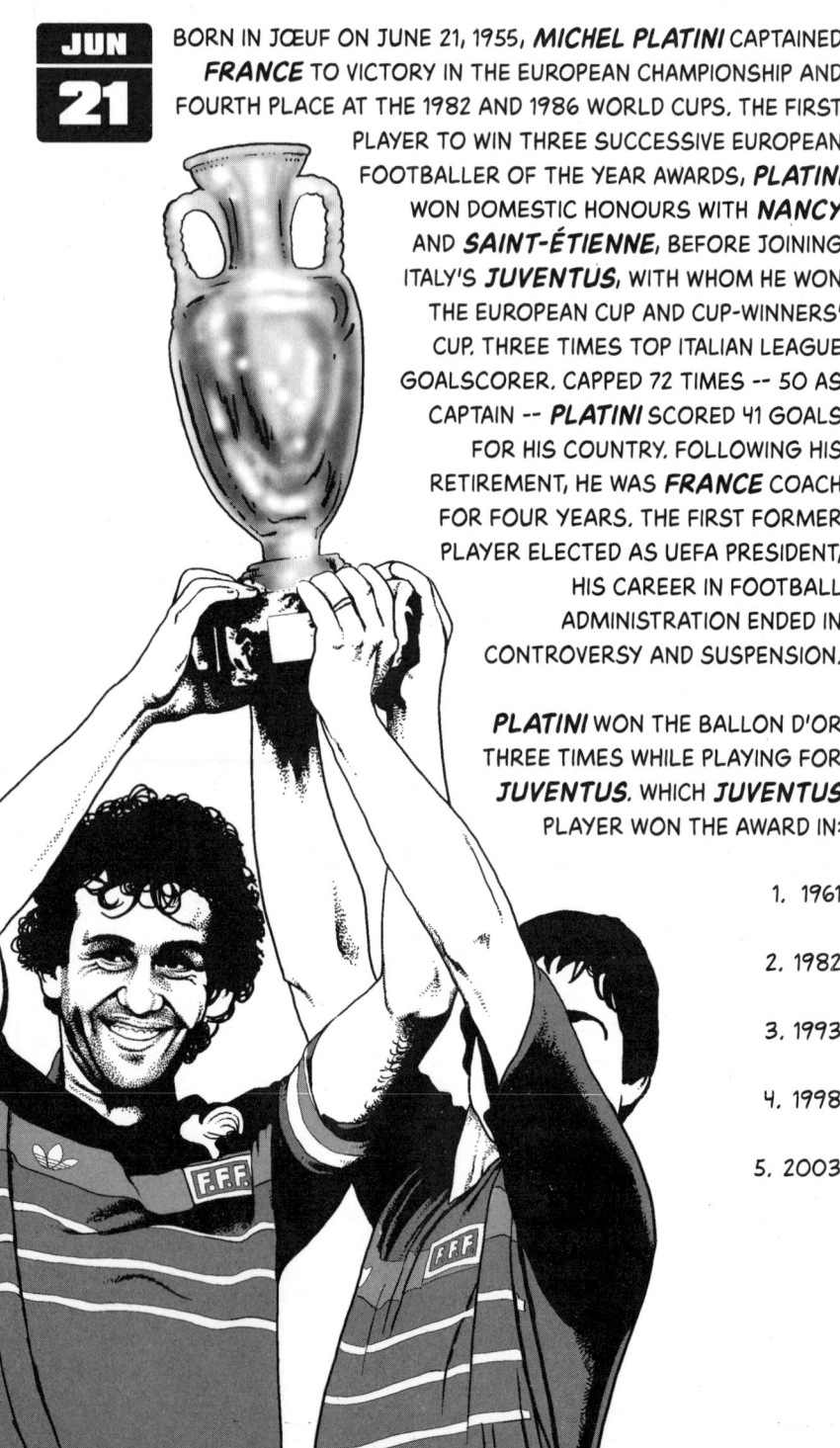

BORN IN JŒUF ON JUNE 21, 1955, *MICHEL PLATINI* CAPTAINED *FRANCE* TO VICTORY IN THE EUROPEAN CHAMPIONSHIP AND FOURTH PLACE AT THE 1982 AND 1986 WORLD CUPS. THE FIRST PLAYER TO WIN THREE SUCCESSIVE EUROPEAN FOOTBALLER OF THE YEAR AWARDS, *PLATINI* WON DOMESTIC HONOURS WITH *NANCY* AND *SAINT-ÉTIENNE*, BEFORE JOINING ITALY'S *JUVENTUS*, WITH WHOM HE WON THE EUROPEAN CUP AND CUP-WINNERS' CUP. THREE TIMES TOP ITALIAN LEAGUE GOALSCORER, CAPPED 72 TIMES -- 50 AS CAPTAIN -- *PLATINI* SCORED 41 GOALS FOR HIS COUNTRY. FOLLOWING HIS RETIREMENT, HE WAS *FRANCE* COACH FOR FOUR YEARS. THE FIRST FORMER PLAYER ELECTED AS UEFA PRESIDENT, HIS CAREER IN FOOTBALL ADMINISTRATION ENDED IN CONTROVERSY AND SUSPENSION.

PLATINI WON THE BALLON D'OR THREE TIMES WHILE PLAYING FOR *JUVENTUS*. WHICH *JUVENTUS* PLAYER WON THE AWARD IN:

1. 1961

2. 1982

3. 1993

4. 1998

5. 2003

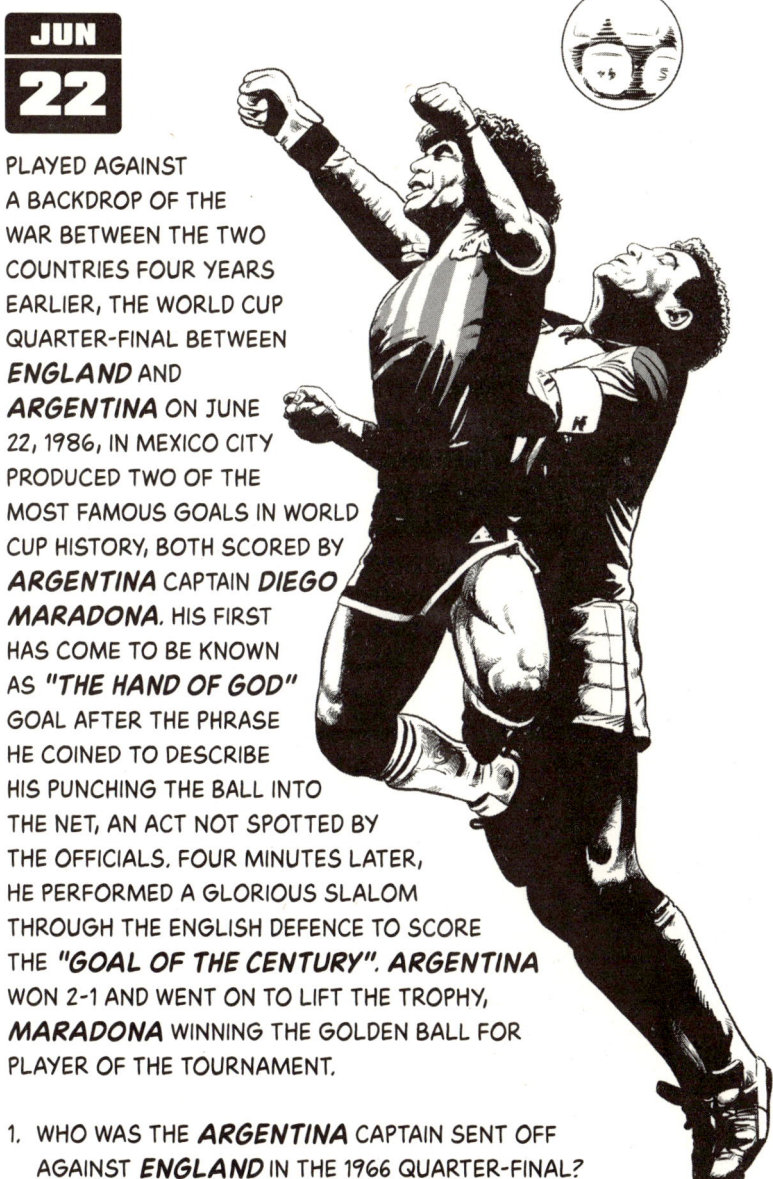

JUN 22

PLAYED AGAINST A BACKDROP OF THE WAR BETWEEN THE TWO COUNTRIES FOUR YEARS EARLIER, THE WORLD CUP QUARTER-FINAL BETWEEN **ENGLAND** AND **ARGENTINA** ON JUNE 22, 1986, IN MEXICO CITY PRODUCED TWO OF THE MOST FAMOUS GOALS IN WORLD CUP HISTORY, BOTH SCORED BY **ARGENTINA** CAPTAIN **DIEGO MARADONA**. HIS FIRST HAS COME TO BE KNOWN AS **"THE HAND OF GOD"** GOAL AFTER THE PHRASE HE COINED TO DESCRIBE HIS PUNCHING THE BALL INTO THE NET, AN ACT NOT SPOTTED BY THE OFFICIALS. FOUR MINUTES LATER, HE PERFORMED A GLORIOUS SLALOM THROUGH THE ENGLISH DEFENCE TO SCORE THE **"GOAL OF THE CENTURY"**. **ARGENTINA** WON 2-1 AND WENT ON TO LIFT THE TROPHY, **MARADONA** WINNING THE GOLDEN BALL FOR PLAYER OF THE TOURNAMENT.

1. WHO WAS THE **ARGENTINA** CAPTAIN SENT OFF AGAINST **ENGLAND** IN THE 1966 QUARTER-FINAL?

2. WHO WAS THE **ENGLAND** PLAYER RED-CARDED AGAINST **ARGENTINA** WHEN THE TWO COUNTRIES MET IN THE ROUND OF 16 AT THE 1998 WORLD CUP?

3. WHO SCORED THE ONLY GOAL OF THE GAME WHEN THE TWO COUNTRIES MET IN THE OPENING ROUND OF THE 2002 WORLD CUP?

JUN 23

ZINEDINE "ZIZOU" ZIDANE WAS BORN IN MARSEILLE, ON JUNE 23, 1972. THE BRILLIANT MIDFIELDER WAS THE INSPIRATIONAL FORCE BEHIND **FRANCE'S** 1998 WORLD CUP AND EURO 2000 WINS. IN 2001, **REAL MADRID** BROKE THE WORLD TRANSFER RECORD TO TAKE HIS TALENTS TO SPAIN -- AND **"LOS BLANCOS"** WERE REWARDED WITH NUMEROUS TROPHIES, INCLUDING LA LIGA AND THE UEFA CHAMPIONS LEAGUE. THREE TIMES FIFA WORLD PLAYER OF THE YEAR AND A BALLON D'OR WINNER, HIS FINAL GAME FOR **FRANCE** WAS THE 2006 WORLD CUP FINAL LOSS AGAINST **ITALY**, A GAME IN WHICH HE NOT ONLY SCORED BUT WAS SENT OFF! HE IS A RECIPIENT OF FRANCE'S HIGHEST DECORATION, THE LÉGION D'HONNEUR. AFTER RETIRING, HE WORKED BEHIND THE SCENES WITH **REAL MADRID**, BEFORE COACHING THE RESERVES, THEN TAKING THE REINS OF THE SENIOR TEAM IN 2016. HIS SUCCESS WAS IMMEDIATE, BECOMING THE FIRST MANAGER TO WIN THREE UEFA CHAMPIONS LEAGUES IN SUCCESSION. FOLLOWING A TEN-MONTH BREAK AWAY FROM THE CLUB, HE RETURNED TO **REAL MADRID** IN 2019 AND ADDED A SECOND LA LIGA TITLE TO HIS TROPHY HAUL.

1. **ZIDANE'S** PARENTS HAILED FROM WHICH NORTH AFRICAN COUNTRY?

2. NAME ONE OF THE TWO FRENCH CLUBS FOR WHOM **ZIDANE** PLAYED.

3. **ZIDANE** WON TWO SERIE A TITLES WITH WHICH ITALIAN CLUB BEFORE JOINING **REAL MADRID?**

JUN 24 THE FIRST PLAYER IN HISTORY TO WIN THE BALLON D'OR SIX TIMES, *LIONEL ANDRÉS MESSI* WAS BORN IN ROSARIO, SANTA FE, ARGENTINA, ON JUNE 24, 1987. HE WAS DIAGNOSED WITH A GROWTH HORMONE DEFICIENCY AT THE AGE OF 10 AND ALTHOUGH HE WAS ON THE BOOKS WITH *NEWELL'S OLD BOYS* AND *RIVER PLATE* WERE INTERESTED IN HIM, NEITHER CLUB COULD AFFORD TO PAY THE $900 A MONTH REQUIRED FOR HIS TREATMENT. *BARCELONA* STEPPED IN AND OFFERED TO UNDERWRITE HIS MEDICAL BILLS, PROVIDED THAT HE MOVED TO SPAIN. THE FAMILY RELOCATED TO BARCELONA AND *MESSI* ENROLLED IN THE CLUB'S YOUTH ACADEMY.

CLUB ATLÉTICO NEWELL'S OLD BOYS WAS FOUNDED IN 1903, AND IS NAMED AFTER ENGLISHMAN *ISAAC NEWELL*, A TEACHER FROM KENT WHO PIONEERED FOOTBALL IN ARGENTINA.

1. THE *NEWELL'S OLD BOYS* STADIUM IS NAMED AFTER WHICH ENGLISH PREMIER LEAGUE MANAGER?

2. WHICH FORMER *NEWELL'S OLD BOYS* PLAYER WON A SERIE A TITLE WITH *ROMA* IN 2001 AND WAS *ARGENTINA'S* ALL-TIME TOP GOALSCORER UNTIL *MESSI* SURPASSED HIS 54-GOAL RECORD?

3. AFTER LEAVING WHICH SPANISH CLUB IN 1993 DID *DIEGO MARADONA* PLAY FOR *NEWELL'S OLD BOYS?*

JUN 25

THE EIGHTH EUROPEAN CHAMPIONSHIP TOURNAMENT WAS STAGED IN **WEST GERMANY** IN 1988. THE FIRST SEMI-FINAL PITTED THE HOSTS AGAINST **NETHERLANDS**, WITH THE DUTCH FULLY AWARE THAT THEY HAD NOT BEATEN THE GERMANS IN THE PREVIOUS 32 YEARS! **MARCO VAN BASTEN'S** LATE WINNER LAID THAT PARTICULAR GHOST TO REST. IN THE OTHER SEMI-FINAL, GOALS FROM **LITOVCHENKO** AND **PROTASOV** DISPOSED OF **ITALY** AND TOOK THE **USSR** THROUGH TO YET ANOTHER FINAL. PLAYED ON JUNE 25, THAT FINAL SHOWCASED THE BRILLIANCE OF THE ORANGEMEN AS CAPTAIN **RUUD GULLIT** GAVE THEM THE LEAD AND **VAN BASTEN** SEALED VICTORY WITH A SUPERB VOLLEY THAT HAS BEEN ACCLAIMED AS THE GREATEST GOAL EVER SEEN IN THE EUROPEAN CHAMPIONSHIPS.

1. WHO WAS THE MANAGER OF THE **NETHERLANDS** TEAM?

2. THE DUTCH SQUAD FEATURED WHICH TWO BROTHERS, ONE OF WHOM WOULD GO ON TO COACH **BARCELONA?**

3. **GULLIT** AND **VAN BASTEN** PLAYED FOR **AC MILAN** AT THE TIME OF THE TOURNAMENT. WHICH MEMBER OF THE DUTCH TEAM WOULD JOIN THEM FROM **REAL ZARAGOZA** AFTER EURO 88?

JUN 26

BORN IN MARSEILLES, ON JUNE 26, 1987, *SAMIR NASRI* WAS NINE YEARS OLD WHEN HE JOINED *MARSEILLE'S* ACADEMY. HE MADE HIS DEBUT FOR THE SENIOR TEAM IN 2004, AND WAS NAMED FRENCH FOOTBALL'S YOUNG PLAYER OF THE YEAR IN 2006-07. AFTER PLAYING FOR *FRANCE* AT EURO 2008, HE SIGNED FOR *ARSENAL*. A BROKEN LEG IN 2009 WAS FOLLOWED BY THE DISAPPOINTMENT OF BEING LEFT OUT OF THE *FRANCE* SQUAD FOR THE 2010 WORLD CUP. HE BOUNCED BACK TO WIN THE FRENCH FOOTBALLER OF THE YEAR AWARD, CAPTAIN HIS COUNTRY AND EARN A BIG-MONEY MOVE TO *MANCHESTER CITY*, WITH WHOM HE WON TWO PREMIER LEAGUE TITLES. HE RETIRED FROM INTERNATIONAL FOOTBALL AFTER BEING LEFT OUT OF FRANCE'S 2014 WORLD CUP SQUAD, SPENT A SEASON ON LOAN AT SEVILLA BEFORE A SHORT-LIVED MOVE TO TURKEY'S *ANTALYASPOR*. HIS CAREER WENT INTO A TAILSPIN FOLLOWING A LENGTHY UEFA BAN AFTER RECEIVING AN AN INTRAVENOUS DRIP OF WATER CONTAINING NUTRIENTS.

1. WHICH PREMIER LEAGUE-WINNING MANAGER RECEIVED A FOUR-MONTH BAN AS A PLAYER WITH *BRESCIA* AFTER TESTING POSITIVE FOR THE STEROID NANDROLONE? (HE WAS SUBSEQUENTLY CLEARED TWICE AFTER INVESTIGATIONS.)

2. WHICH LEGENDARY WORLD CUP WINNER FAILED A DRUG TEST AT THE 1994 WORLD CUP TOURNAMENT?

3. WHICH *MANCHESTER UNITED* AND *ENGLAND* STAR WAS BANNED FOR EIGHT MONTHS IN 2004 AFTER MISSING A DRUGS TEST?

JUN 27 DESPITE HAVING PLAYED AT U-21 LEVEL FOR TURKEY, *GÖKHAN INLER* WENT ON TO BECOME CAPTAIN OF *SWITZERLAND*. BORN IN OLTEN, SWITZERLAND, ON JUNE 27, 1984, HE WON TWO LEAGUE TITLES WITH *FC ZÜRICH* AND SPENT FOUR YEARS AT *UDINESE*, BEFORE JOINING *NAPOLI* IN 2011. AT THE PRESS CONFERENCE TO ANNOUNCE HIS SURPRISE SIGNING, HE WORE A LION MASK BEFORE HIS TRUE IDENTITY WAS REVEALED! HAVING WON CUP HONOURS IN ITALY, HE JOINED *LEICESTER CITY* IN 2015. AS A RESULT OF BEING UNABLE TO WIN A REGULAR PLACE IN THE TEAM, HE MISSED OUT ON A PLACE IN *SWITZERLAND'S* EURO 2016 SQUAD -- BUT HIS FIVE PREMIER LEAGUE APPEARANCES EARNED HIM A TITLE-WINNER'S MEDAL!

1. WHO IS *SWITZERLAND'S* TOP ALL-TIME GOALSCORER?

2. WHICH ENGLISHMAN WAS *SWITZERLAND* COACH IN THE 1990S?

3. BEFORE COACHING THE SWISS NATIONAL TEAM FOR SIX YEARS FROM 2008, WHICH MANAGER HAD WON FIVE BUNDESLIGA TITLES AND THE UEFA CHAMPIONS LEAGUE WITH *BAYERN MUNICH*?

JUN 28

BORN IN KLERKSDORP, SOUTH AFRICA, ON JUNE 28, 1969, *PHIL MASINGA* WAS THE FIRST-EVER *SOUTH AFRICA* PLAYER TO BE RED-CARDED, RECEIVING HIS MARCHING ORDERS IN A 1992 GAME AGAINST *ZAMBIA*. CAPPED 58 TIMES BY THE *"BAFANA BAFANA"*, HIS CAREER TOOK HIM TO CLUBS IN ITALY, SWITZERLAND AND THE UAE AND INCLUDED TWO YEARS IN THE ENGLISH PREMIER LEAGUE WITH *LEEDS UNITED*. SADLY, *PHIL MASINGA* PASSED AWAY IN EARLY 2019 AFTER LOSING HIS BATTLE WITH CANCER.

IDENTIFY THESE OTHER *SOUTH AFRICA* INTERNATIONALS WHO HAVE PLAYED IN THE ENGLISH PREMIER LEAGUE:

1. *SOUTH AFRICA* CAPTAIN WON TWO TITLES WITH *AJAX* AND PLAYED FOR *EVERTON*, *TOTTENHAM HOTSPUR* AND *SUNDERLAND*.

2. A PREMIER LEAGUE WINNER WITH *MANCHESTER UNITED*, HE ALSO PLAYED FOR *BOLTON WANDERERS* AND *DONCASTER ROVERS*.

3. FIRST MAN TO PLAY 100 GAMES FOR *SOUTH AFRICA*, HE PLAYED FOR *BLACKBURN ROVERS* AND *PORTSMOUTH*.

JUN 29

ON JUNE 29, 1950, BELO HORIZONTE IN BRAZIL WAS THE LOCATION FOR ONE OF THE BIGGEST UPSETS IN WORLD CUP HISTORY WHEN THE PART-TIMERS OF THE *USA* BEAT HIGHLY FANCIED *ENGLAND* 1-0 WITH A GOAL FROM HAITIAN STUDENT *JOE GAETJENS.* THE STORY HAD A TRAGIC ENDING. AFTER PLAYING IN FRANCE, *GAETJENS* ULTIMATELY RETURNED TO HAITI, WHERE HIS FAMILY WAS ACTIVE IN POLITICS. WHEN THE BRUTAL DESPOT *"PAPA DOC" DUVALIER* DECLARED HIMSELF *"PRESIDENT FOR LIFE"* IN 1964, THE FAMILY FLED. *JOE* REMAINED -- AND PAID A TERRIBLE PRICE. HE WAS ARRESTED BY THE *"TONTON MACOUTES"* SECRET POLICE, IMPRISONED, TORTURED AND MURDERED.

IN WHICH YEAR DID *HAITI* MAKE ITS ONE AND ONLY APPEARANCE IN A WORLD CUP TOURNAMENT?

JUN 30

THE 17TH WORLD CUP FINAL WAS HELD ON JUNE 30, 2002, IN YOKOHAMA, JAPAN. TWO GOALS FROM *RONALDO* WERE ENOUGH TO TAKE HIS TOURNAMENT TALLY TO EIGHT, EARNING HIM THE GOLDEN SHOE, AND GIVE *BRAZIL* VICTORY OVER *GERMANY* TO SECURE AN UNPRECEDENTED FIFTH WORLD TITLE. *BRAZIL* CAPTAIN *CAFU* PLAYED IN EVERY MINUTE OF THE TEAM'S CAMPAIGN AND BECAME THE FIRST PLAYER TO APPEAR IN THREE WORLD CUP FINALS.

BOTH *RONALDO* AND *CAFU* PLAYED THEIR CLUB FOOTBALL IN EUROPE AT THAT TIME, WITH *INTERNAZIONALE* AND *ROMA* RESPECTIVELY. WHICH EUROPEAN CLUB DID THE FOLLOWING *BRAZIL* STARS PLAY FOR IN 2002?

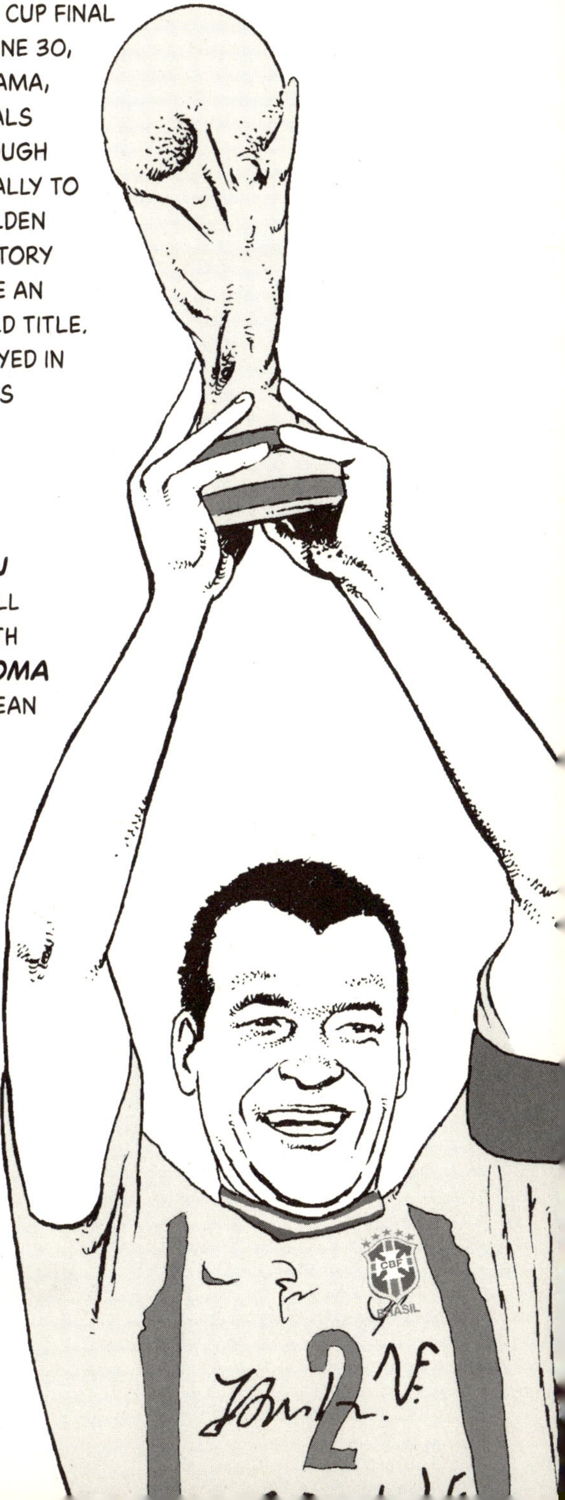

1. *RIVALDO*
   (SPAIN)

2. *RONALDINHO*
   (FRANCE)

3. *ROBERTO CARLOS*
   (SPAIN)

JULY

**JUL
1**

BORN IN OSS, NETHERLANDS, ON JULY 1, 1976, *RUUD VAN NISTELROOY* WON TWO EREDIVISIE TITLES WITH *PSV EINDHOVEN* BEFORE JOINING *MANCHESTER UNITED* IN 2001. THE TRANSFER HAD BEEN DELAYED A YEAR WHILE *RUUD* OVERCAME INJURY PROBLEMS, ALTHOUGH HE WON EVERY DOMESTIC HONOUR WITH *"THE RED DEVILS"* AND BECAME THE CLUB'S ALL-TIME TOP EUROPEAN GOALSCORER HE FELL OUT OF FAVOUR AND WAS TRANSFERRED TO *REAL MADRID* IN 2006, HAVING BEEN TOP SCORER IN THE EREDIVISIE AND THE PREMIER LEAGUE, HE WAS TOP SCORER IN LA LIGA IN HIS DEBUT SEASON. HE SCORED 35 GOALS IN 70 GAMES FOR *NETHERLANDS.*

1. NAME ONE OF THE TWO CLUBS HE PLAYED FOR AFTER LEAVING *REAL MADRID.*

2. HE WON TWO LA LIGA TITLES IN HIS THREE AND A HALF SEASONS WITH *REAL MADRID.* NAME ONE OF THE THREE COACHES HE PLAYED UNDER.

3. HE WAS TOP UEFA CHAMPIONS LEAGUE GOALSCORER IN THREE SEASONS, WHO HOLDS THE RECORD OF SEVEN SEASONS?

JUL 2

ALEX MORGAN WAS BORN IN SAN DIMAS, CALIFORNIA, ON JULY 2, 1989. A GOLD MEDAL WINNER AT THE 2012 OLYMPIC GAMES, SHE WAS A MEMBER OF THE **USA** TEAMS THAT WON THE FIFA WOMEN'S WORLD CUP IN 2015 AND 2019. SHE HAS WON HONOURS WITH **WESTERN NEW YORK FLASH** AND **PORTLAND THORNS FC**, WON A CONTINENTAL EUROPEAN TREBLE WITH **LYON** IN FRANCE, AND PLAYED FOR **TOTTENHAM HOTSPUR. TIME MAGAZINE** NAMED HER THE HIGHEST PAID PLAYER IN AMERICAN WOMEN'S SOCCER THANKS TO HER MANY ENDORSEMENT DEALS.

NAME ONE OF THE ONLY FOUR WOMEN WHO HAVE SCORED MORE GOALS THAN **ALEX MORGAN** FOR THE **USA**.

ON JULY 3, 2012, TWO DAYS BEFORE HIS 36TH BIRTHDAY, **PORTUGAL** STAR **NUNO GOMES** SIGNED A TWO-YEAR DEAL WITH **BLACKBURN ROVERS** IN THE FOOTBALL LEAGUE CHAMPIONSHIP. CAPPED 79 TIMES BY HIS COUNTRY, **GOMES** HAD PREVIOUSLY WON HONOURS WITH **BOAVISTA** AND **FIORENTINA** AND WON TWO LEAGUE TITLES WITH **BENFICA**.

SINCE BEING RELEGATED FROM THE PREMIER LEAGUE IN 2012, IDENTIFY THE FOLLOWING PLAYERS THAT **BLACKBURN ROVERS** HAVE SIGNED:

1. FORMER **EVERTON** AND **MANCHESTER CITY** MIDFIELDER, CAPPED THREE TIMES BY **ENGLAND**, SIGNED ON A FREE TRANSFER FROM **SUNDERLAND** IN 2018-19 SEASON.

2. CAPPED 35 TIMES BY **ENGLAND**, HIS FORMER CLUBS INCLUDED **MIDDLESBROUGH, SUNDERLAND, ASTON VILLA, LIVERPOOL** AND **WEST HAM UNITED** BEFORE SIGNING FOR **ROVERS** IN 2019.

3. CAPPED 35 TIMES BY **ENGLAND**, TWO-TIME UEFA CHAMPIONS LEAGUE AND FIVE TIMES PREMIER LEAGUE WINNER WITH **MANCHESTER UNITED**, SPENT FIVE SEASONS AT **SUNDERLAND** BEFORE JOINING **BLACKBURN ROVERS** IN 2016.

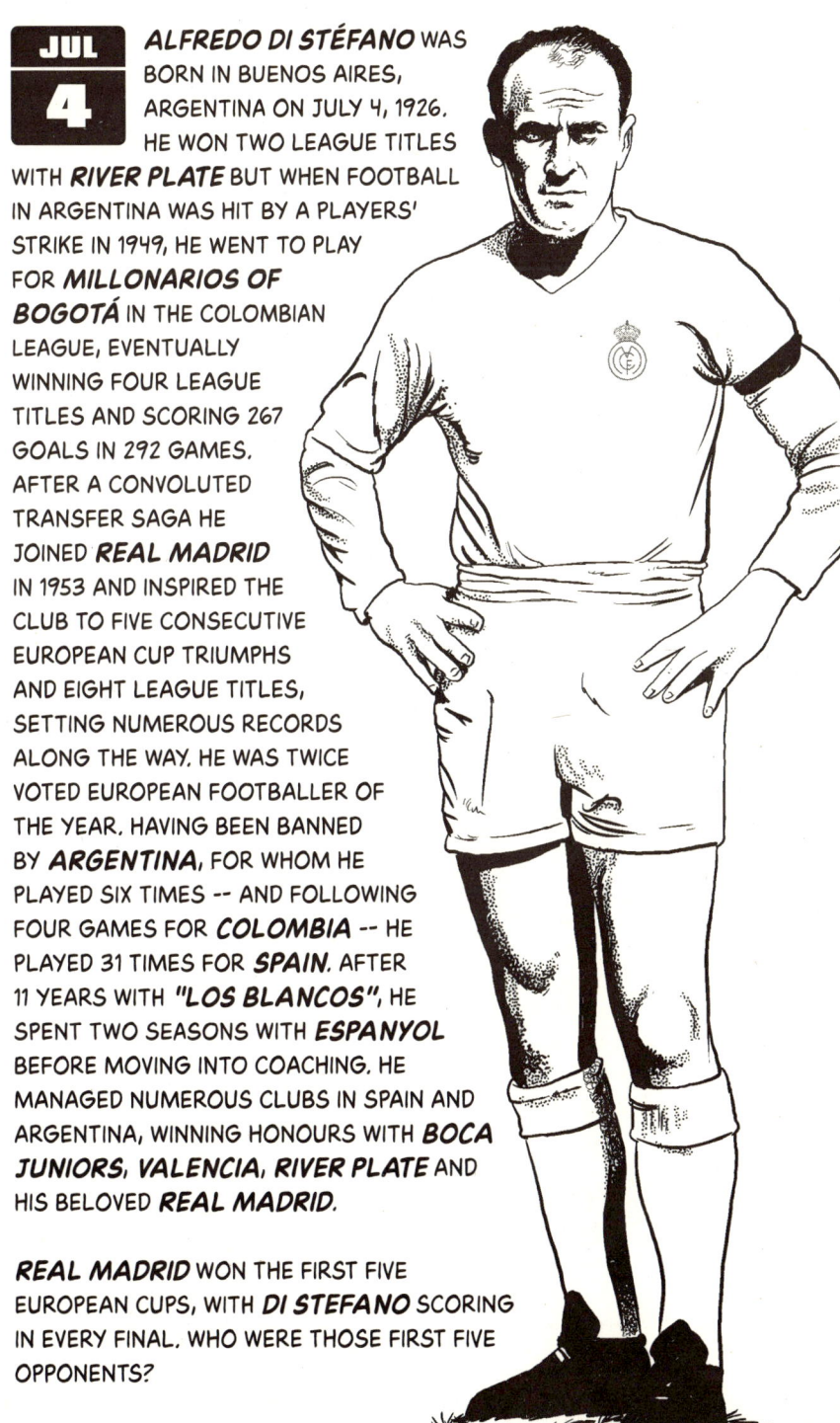

JUL 4

ALFREDO DI STÉFANO WAS BORN IN BUENOS AIRES, ARGENTINA ON JULY 4, 1926. HE WON TWO LEAGUE TITLES WITH **RIVER PLATE** BUT WHEN FOOTBALL IN ARGENTINA WAS HIT BY A PLAYERS' STRIKE IN 1949, HE WENT TO PLAY FOR **MILLONARIOS OF BOGOTÁ** IN THE COLOMBIAN LEAGUE, EVENTUALLY WINNING FOUR LEAGUE TITLES AND SCORING 267 GOALS IN 292 GAMES. AFTER A CONVOLUTED TRANSFER SAGA HE JOINED **REAL MADRID** IN 1953 AND INSPIRED THE CLUB TO FIVE CONSECUTIVE EUROPEAN CUP TRIUMPHS AND EIGHT LEAGUE TITLES, SETTING NUMEROUS RECORDS ALONG THE WAY. HE WAS TWICE VOTED EUROPEAN FOOTBALLER OF THE YEAR. HAVING BEEN BANNED BY **ARGENTINA**, FOR WHOM HE PLAYED SIX TIMES -- AND FOLLOWING FOUR GAMES FOR **COLOMBIA** -- HE PLAYED 31 TIMES FOR **SPAIN**. AFTER 11 YEARS WITH **"LOS BLANCOS"**, HE SPENT TWO SEASONS WITH **ESPANYOL** BEFORE MOVING INTO COACHING. HE MANAGED NUMEROUS CLUBS IN SPAIN AND ARGENTINA, WINNING HONOURS WITH **BOCA JUNIORS**, **VALENCIA**, **RIVER PLATE** AND HIS BELOVED **REAL MADRID**.

REAL MADRID WON THE FIRST FIVE EUROPEAN CUPS, WITH **DI STEFANO** SCORING IN EVERY FINAL. WHO WERE THOSE FIRST FIVE OPPONENTS?

JUL 5

HERNÁN CRESPO WAS BORN IN FLORIDA ESTE, ARGENTINA ON JULY 5, 1975. HAVING ESTABLISHED HIS GOALSCORING REPUTATION WITH **RIVER PLATE**, HE JOINED ITALY'S **PARMA** -- WHERE HE FAILED TO SCORE IN HIS FIRST SIX MONTHS AT THE CLUB! HE WENT ON TO WIN ITALIAN CUP, SUPERCUP AND UEFA CUP HONOURS AND EARN HIMSELF A £35.5 MILLION TRANSFER TO **LAZIO** IN 2000 THAT MADE HIM THE WORLD'S MOST EXPENSIVE PLAYER. TOP SERIE A SCORER IN HIS FIRST SEASON, HE SPENT A SEASON WITH **INTERNAZIONALE** BEFORE HE JOINED **CHELSEA** IN 2003. A YEAR LATER, SURPLUS TO REQUIREMENTS WHEN **JOSÉ MOURINHO** REPLACED **CLAUDIO RANIERI** AS MANAGER, HE WAS LOANED TO **AC MILAN**, WITH WHOM HE REACHED THE 2005 UEFA CHAMPIONS LEAGUE FINAL. RECALLED BY **MOURINHO** THE FOLLOWING SEASON, HE WENT ON TO WIN THE PREMIER LEAGUE TITLE. HIS SECOND SPELL IN ENGLAND WAS BRIEF, AND HE RETURNED TO MILAN, THIS TIME TO JOIN **INTERNAZIONALE** ON LOAN. THE MOVE WAS MADE PERMANENT IN 2008. HE WON THREE CONSECUTIVE SERIE A CHAMPIONSHIPS WITH **INTERNAZIONALE**. CAPPED 64 TIMES BY **ARGENTINA**, FOR WHOM HE SCORED 35 GOALS, HE ENDED HIS PLAYING CAREER WITH SPELLS AT **GENOA** AND **PARMA** BEFORE MOVING INTO COACHING AND MANAGEMENT.

IDENTIFY THESE OTHER TRANSFERS TO ENGLISH FOOTBALL FROM **INTERNAZIONALE:**

1. SIGNED TO **LIVERPOOL** IN 2013, HE JOINED **BARCELONA** IN 2018 FOR AN INITIAL £105 MILLION.

2. SWISS INTERNATIONAL WHO JOINED **STOKE CITY** IN 2015 BEFORE MOVING ON TO **LIVERPOOL** IN 2018.

3. UEFA CUP WINNER WITH BOTH **AJAX** AND **INTERNAZIONALE**, HE JOINED **ARSENAL** IN 1995 AND WON THE PREMIER LEAGUE THREE TIMES.

JUL 6

BORN IN DEDOVSK, MOSCOW, ON JULY 6, 1981, MIDFIELDER ***ROMAN SHIROKOV*** WON A HOST OF HONOURS WITH ***ZENIT SAINT PETERSBURG***, INCLUDING TWO RUSSIAN PREMIER LEAGUE TITLES AND THE UEFA CUP, BEFORE MOVING ON TO ***SPARTAK MOSCOW*** IN 2014. WHEN HE WAS BENCHED DURING THE 2015-16 SEASON, IT IS SAID THAT HE WASN'T SELECTED BECAUSE OF A CLAUSE IN HIS CONTRACT GUARANTEEING AN ADDITIONAL PAYMENT IF HE PLAYED MORE THAN A SPECIFIED NUMBER OF MINUTES! HE ENDED HIS PLAYING DAYS AT ***CSKA MOSCOW***. IN 2020, HE WAS SENTENCED TO 100 HOURS OF COMMUNITY SERVICE AFTER PUNCHING AND KICKING A REFEREE WHILE PLAYING IN AN AMATEUR TOURNAMENT!

SHIROKOV MADE 57 APPEARANCES FOR ***RUSSIA*** BETWEEN 2008 AND 2016. NAME ONE OF THE FOUR COACHES HE PLAYED UNDER.

JUL 7

PLAYED ON JULY 7, 1974, THE TENTH WORLD CUP FINAL PITTED EUROPE'S BEST TWO TEAMS AGAINST EACH OTHER. DIRECT FROM THE KICK-OFF, *NETHERLANDS* PUT TOGETHER A STRING OF 15 PASSES THAT ENDED WITH *JOHAN CRUYFF* BEING BROUGHT DOWN IN THE PENALTY BOX. *JOHAN NEESKENS* STEPPED UP TO TAKE THE PENALTY -- AND HOSTS *WEST GERMANY* WERE A GOAL DOWN BEFORE ANY GERMAN PLAYER HAD EVEN TOUCHED THE BALL! 25 MINUTES LATER THE BALL WAS ON THE PENALTY SPOT AGAIN. THIS TIME *WEST GERMANY'S BERND HÖLZENBEIN* HAD BEEN FLOORED AND *PAUL BREITNER* MADE NO MISTAKE WITH THE KICK. TWO MINUTES BEFORE HALF-TIME, *GERD MÜLLER* MADE IT 2-1 TO *WEST GERMANY* AND, DESPITE SOME FABULOUS PLAY FROM THE DUTCH IN THE SECOND HALF, *"DER BOMBER'S"* GOAL PROVED TO BE ENOUGH TO CROWN *WEST GERMANY* NEW WORLD CHAMPIONS.

FRANZ BECKENBAUER WAS THE WINNING CAPTAIN. WHO CAPTAINED THE VICTORIOUS GERMAN WORLD CUP TEAM IN:

1. 1954

2. 1990

3. 2014

JUL 8

ROBBIE KEANE WAS BORN IN DUBLIN ON JULY 8, 1980. HIS 146 APPEARANCES MAKE HIM THE MOST-CAPPED **REPUBLIC OF IRELAND** PLAYER OF ALL TIME, AND WITH 68 GOALS, HE IS ALSO HIS COUNTRY'S ALL-TIME LEADING GOALSCORER. ALTHOUGH HE PLAYED AT THE HIGHEST LEVEL IN ENGLAND, SCOTLAND AND ITALY, BEFORE JOINING **LOS ANGELES GALAXY** HE HAD ONLY EVER WON ONE CLUB TROPHY -- THE ENGLISH FOOTBALL LEAGUE CUP. HE WON THREE MLS CUPS AND THE SUPPORTERS' SHIELD WITH THE CALIFORNIAN CLUB. HE ENDED HIS PLAYING DAYS WITH A TWO-YEAR STINT IN THE INDIAN SUPER LEAGUE WITH **ATK**, WHOSE HEAD COACH WAS FORMER TEAMMATE **TEDDY SHERINGHAM**. WHEN **SHERINGHAM** WAS SACKED, **KEANE** TOOK OVER AS PLAYER-MANAGER.

NAME FOUR CLUBS BESIDES THE **GALAXY** AND **ATK** THAT **ROBBIE KEANE** PLAYED FOR.

JUL 9

GIANLUCA VIALLI WAS BORN IN CREMONA ON JULY 9, 1964. THE SON OF A MILLIONAIRE, HE WAS RAISED IN A 60-ROOM CASTLE!

IN A GLITTERING CAREER THAT SAW HIM WIN SERIE A TITLES WITH TWO DIFFERENT CLUBS, THE ITALIAN BECAME THE FIRST MAN TO WIN WINNER'S AND RUNNERS-UP MEDALS IN ALL THREE MAJOR EUROPEAN COMPETITIONS. A RENOWNED PRACTICAL JOKER, HE ONCE FAMOUSLY PRANKED HARDMAN **GRAEME SOUNESS** BY SPRINKLING PEPPER IN THE SCOT'S UNDERPANTS, SQUIRTING SHAVING FOAM IN HIS SHOES AND CUTTING THE LEGS OFF HIS TROUSERS! **VIALLI** PLAYED 59 TIMES FOR **ITALY** BUT IT IS RUMOURED THAT HIS INTERNATIONAL CAREER WAS CURTAILED AFTER PLAYING A PRANK ON **ITALY** MANAGER **ARRIGO SACCHI**.

1. NAME TWO OF THE FOUR CLUBS HE PLAYED FOR.

2. NAME TWO OF THE CLUBS HE MANAGED.

JUL 10

BORN IN MIDDLESBROUGH ON JULY 10, 1927, *DON REVIE* TURNED PROFESSIONAL WITH *LEICESTER CITY* AT THE AGE OF 17, WHILE WORKING AS AN APPRENTICE BRICKLAYER. A TRIPLE BREAK OF THE ANKLE MIGHT HAVE DERAILED HIS CAREER, BUT HE FOUGHT BACK TO FITNESS AND LED *"THE FOXES"* TO THE 1949 FA CUP FINAL. A NASAL HAEMORRHAGE RULED HIM OUT OF THE GAME, WHICH *LEICESTER* LOST TO *WOLVERHAMPTON WANDERERS*. THE FOLLOWING TWO SEASONS SAW *REVIE* PLAYING FOR *HULL CITY*, BEFORE SIGNING FOR *MANCHESTER CITY* IN 1951. IT WAS THERE THAT HE MASTERED THE ROLE OF DEEP-LYING CENTRE-FORWARD IN WHAT BECAME KNOWN AS *"THE REVIE PLAN"*. HE WON THE FA CUP WITH *CITY* IN 1956, THE SAME YEAR HE PLAYED THE LAST OF HIS SIX GAMES FOR *ENGLAND*. HE WENT ON TO PLAY FOR *SUNDERLAND*, BEFORE ENDING HIS PLAYING DAYS AS PLAYER-MANAGER WITH *LEEDS UNITED*. A SUPERSTITIOUS MAN, HIS BELIEF THAT BIRDS WERE BAD LUCK RESULTED IN HIM GETTING RID OF THE OWL ON THE CLUB BADGE AND THE DISCONTINUATION OF *"THE PEACOCKS"* NICKNAME IN FAVOUR OF *"THE WHITES"*. AS MANAGER, HE STEERED THE CLUB TO UNPRECEDENTED GLORY, INCLUDING TWO LEAGUE TITLES, BEFORE ACCEPTING THE *ENGLAND* MANAGER JOB IN 1974. HIS ABRUPT DEPARTURE IN 1977 FOR A LUCRATIVE CONTRACT WITH THE *UNITED ARAB EMIRATE*S DREW CONDEMNATION. *REVIE* DIED IN 1989.

1. NAME THE TWO *ENGLAND* MANAGERS SINCE *DON REVIE* WHO HAVE ALSO MANAGED *LEEDS UNITED*.

2. WHO SUCCEEDED *DON REVIE* AS MANAGER OF *LEEDS UNITED?*

3. WHO SUCCEEDED *DON REVIE* AS MANAGER OF *ENGLAND?*

JUL 11

HUGO SÁNCHEZ WAS BORN IN MEXICO CITY, ON JULY 11, 1958. HE REPRESENTED MEXICO IN THE 1976 OLYMPICS AND PLAYED FOR UNAM, A PROFESSIONAL TEAM REPRESENTING MEXICO'S NATIONAL UNIVERSITY, AS WELL AS SPENDING A SUMMER ON LOAN IN THE NASL WITH THE SAN DIEGO SOCKERS. HE ACTUALLY QUALIFIED AS A DENTIST BEFORE DECAMPING TO SPAIN TO JOIN ATLÉTICO MADRID, WITH WHOM HE WON A COPA DEL REY AND FINISHED TOP SCORER IN LA LIGA. HE WAS TRANSFERRED TO RIVALS REAL MADRID IN 1985, GOING ON TO WIN FIVE CONSECUTIVE LEAGUE TITLES, A COPA DEL REY AND THE UEFA CUP, AND HE FINISHED TOP LEAGUE GOALSCORER FOUR SEASONS IN A ROW. EACH OF HIS GOALS WAS FOLLOWED BY A CELEBRATORY BACKFLIP SOMERSAULT, A TRICK HE LEARNED FROM HIS OLYMPIC GYMNAST SISTER. FOLLOWING A CONCACAF CHAMPIONS CUP WIN IN 1992 WITH CLUB AMÉRICA ON HIS RETURN TO MEXICO, HE PLAYED WITH CLUBS IN SPAIN, AUSTRIA AND THE USA BEFORE RETIRING AND GOING INTO TEAM MANAGEMENT. AT INTERNATIONAL LEVEL, HE PLAYED 58 GAMES FOR MEXICO, SCORING 29 GOALS. HE PLAYED IN THREE WORLD CUPS, ALTHOUGH IN ALTERNATE TOURNAMENTS -- IN 1978, 1986 AND 1994.

HUGO SÁNCHEZ SERVED TWO SPELLS AS MANAGER OF THE MEXICO NATIONAL TEAM. IDENTIFY THESE OTHER MANAGERS OF MEXICO:

1. MANAGED ARGENTINA'S 1978 WORLD CUP-WINNING TEAM.

2. ALSO MANAGED ENGLAND, IVORY COAST, PHILIPPINES AND CLUBS IN ENGLAND, ITALY, SWEDEN, PORTUGAL AND CHINA.

3. REPLACED TITO VILANOVA AS MANAGER OF BARCELONA.

JUL 12

BORN IN CÚCUTA, COLOMBIA, ON JULY 12,1991, *JAMES RODRÍGUEZ* WAS ONLY 14 YEARS OLD WHEN HE MADE HIS PROFESSIONAL DEBUT FOR *ENVIGADO* IN THE COLOMBIAN SECOND DIVISION. HE JOINED *BANFIELD* WHERE, AGED 17, HE BECAME THE YOUNGEST FOREIGN PLAYER TO SCORE A GOAL IN ARGENTINA. HIS NEXT STOP WAS EUROPE, WHERE HE WON MULTIPLE HONOURS WITH THREE OF THE CONTINENT'S MOST-STORIED CLUBS, INCLUDING THREE PORTUGUESE LEAGUE TITLES AND THE UEFA EUROPA LEAGUE WITH *PORTO*, TWO LA LIGAS AND TWO UEFA CHAMPIONS LEAGUES WITH *REAL MADRID*, AND TWO BUNDESLIGA TITLES WITH *BAYERN MUNICH*. HE ALSO PLAYED A SEASON WITH *MONACO*. IN 2020, HE WAS REUNITED AT *EVERTON* WITH *CARLO ANCELOTTI* WHO HAD MANAGED HIM AT *REAL MADRID* AND *BAYERN MUNICH*.

IDENTIFY THESE *COLOMBIA* STARS WHO HAVE MADE THEIR MARK IN EUROPE:

1. ALL-TIME *COLOMBIA* TOP SCORER, HIS EUROPEAN CLUBS INCLUDE *PORTO, ATLÉTICO MADRID, MONACO, MANCHESTER UNITED, CHELSEA* AND *GALATASARAY*.

2. DEFENDER WHO WAS A *TOTTENHAM HOTSPUR* RECORD SIGNING FROM *AJAX* IN 2017.

3. *ASTON VILLA* RECORD SIGNING IN 2001, MOVED ON TO *NEW YORK RED BULLS* IN 2007.

BORN IN ASTRAKHAN IN SOUTHERN RUSSIA ON JULY 13, 1957, *RINAT DASAYEV* PLAYED MUCH OF HIS CAREER WITH *SPARTAK MOSCOW*. SOVIET FOOTBALLER OF THE YEAR IN 1982, HE PLAYED IN THREE WORLD CUPS AND WAS A MEMBER OF THE *SOVIET* TEAMS THAT EARNED BRONZE IN THE 1980 OLYMPICS AND FINISHED RUNNERS-UP AT EURO 88. NICKNAMED *"THE IRON WALL"*, *DASAYEV* PLAYED 91 TIMES FOR THE *SOVIET UNION*.

IDENTIFY THESE RUSSIAN GOALKEEPERS:

1. UEFA CUP WINNER WITH *CSKA MOSCOW*, CAPPED 111 TIMES BY *RUSSIA*, HE PLAYED IN TWO WORLD CUPS AND FOUR EUROPEAN CHAMPIONSHIPS.

2. 1963 BALLON D'OR WINNER IN 1963, THE BLACK-CLAD OLYMPICS AND EUROPEAN CHAMPIONSHIP WINNER PLAYED IN FOUR WORLD CUPS.

3. OLYMPIC CHAMPION IN 1988, HE WON HONOURS WITH *CHELSEA* AND *CELTIC*.

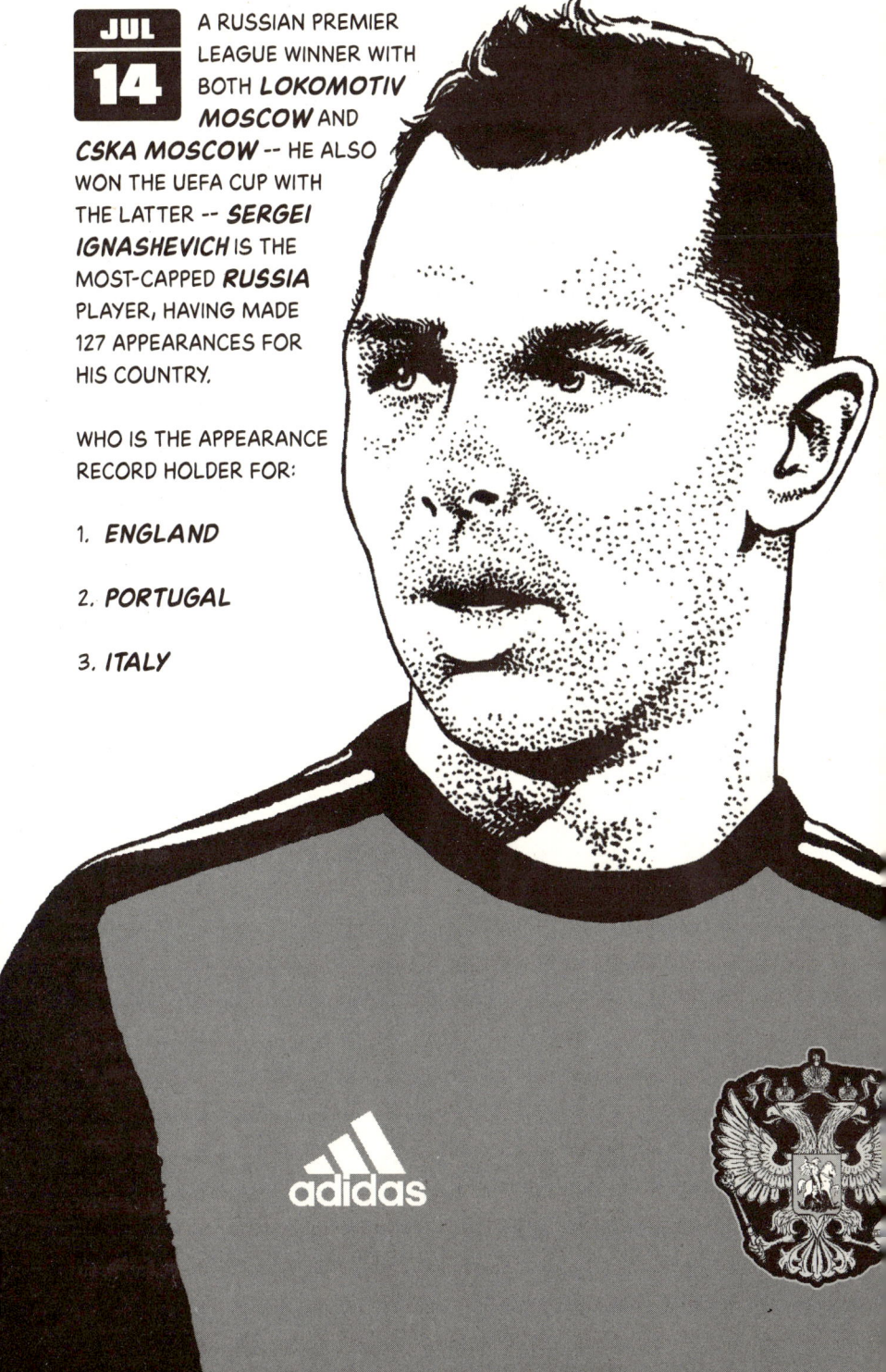

JUL 14

A RUSSIAN PREMIER LEAGUE WINNER WITH BOTH *LOKOMOTIV MOSCOW* AND *CSKA MOSCOW* -- HE ALSO WON THE UEFA CUP WITH THE LATTER -- *SERGEI IGNASHEVICH* IS THE MOST-CAPPED *RUSSIA* PLAYER, HAVING MADE 127 APPEARANCES FOR HIS COUNTRY.

WHO IS THE APPEARANCE RECORD HOLDER FOR:

1. *ENGLAND*

2. *PORTUGAL*

3. *ITALY*

JUL 15

BORN IN BELL VILLE, ARGENTINA, ON JULY 15, 1954, **MARIO KEMPES** WAS THE ONLY EUROPEAN-BASED PLAYER IN **ARGENTINA'S** 1978 WORLD CUP SQUAD. HE SCORED SIX GOALS, INCLUDING TWO IN THE FINAL IN THE VICTORY OVER **NETHERLANDS**. HE GAINED A EUROPEAN CUP-WINNERS' CUP MEDAL WITH **VALENCIA** IN 1980, BEFORE RETURNING TO ARGENTINA WITH **RIVER PLATE** IN 1981. AFTER REJOINING **VALENCIA**, HE MOVED ON TO **HÉRCULES**, BEFORE HE WOUND DOWN HIS CAREER IN AUSTRIA. HE LATER COACHED ALBANIAN SIDE **LUSHNJË**, BUT HAD TO FLEE THE COUNTRY WITH THE OUTBREAK OF CIVIL UNREST IN 1996. HE SUBSEQUENTLY COACHED THROUGHOUT SOUTH AMERICA.

HE WAS TWICE TOP SCORER IN LA LIGA WHILE PLAYING FOR **VALENCIA**. WHO IS THE ONLY PLAYER FROM THE FOLLOWING COUNTRIES TO WIN THAT PICHICHI TROPHY:

1. CAMEROON (2006)

2. ITALY (1998)

3. CHILE (1995)

JUL 16

BORN IN CARDIFF ON JULY 16, 1989, *GARETH BALE* MADE HIS DEBUT FOR *SOUTHAMPTON* AT THE AGE OF 16 YEARS AND 275 DAYS, BECOMING THE CLUB'S SECOND-YOUNGEST PLAYER TO THAT POINT. IN MAY 2006, AGED 16 YEARS AND 315 DAYS, HE BECAME THE YOUNGEST PLAYER TO APPEAR FOR *WALES* AT THAT TIME. *BALE* JOINED *TOTTENHAM HOTSPUR* IN 2007. IN 2013, HE BECAME ONLY THE SECOND PLAYER AFTER *CRISTIANO RONALDO* TO WIN THE PFA YOUNG PLAYER OF THE YEAR, THE PFA PLAYERS' PLAYER OF THE YEAR AND THE FWA FOOTBALLER OF THE YEAR AWARDS IN ONE SEASON. HE JOINED *REAL MADRID* THAT SAME YEAR, WHERE HIS MEDAL TALLY INCLUDES FOUR UEFA CHAMPIONS LEAGUES. HE RETURNED TO *SPURS* ON LOAN IN 2020.

IDENTIFY THESE PLAYERS WHO ALL MADE THEIR *SOUTHAMPTON* DEBUTS AT A YOUNGER AGE THAN *GARETH BALE*:

1. WENT ON TO PLAY FOR *ARSENAL* AND *EVERTON*, BEFORE RETURNING TO *SOUTHAMPTON* ON LOAN IN 2020.

2. HE WON THREE FA CUPS WITH *ARSENAL* AND THE PREMIER LEAGUE AND UEFA CHAMPIONS LEAGUE WITH *LIVERPOOL*.

3. *ENGLAND* INTERNATIONAL DEFENDER WHO JOINED *MANCHESTER UNITED* IN 2014.

JUL 17

BORN IN KAMPEN, NETHERLANDS ON JULY 17, 1972, *JAAP STAM* WON LEAGUE AND CUP HONOURS WITH *PSV EINDHOVEN* BEFORE HIS 1998 TRANSFER TO *MANCHESTER UNITED* MADE HIM THE MOST EXPENSIVE DUTCH PLAYER IN HISTORY TO THAT POINT. IN THREE SEASONS WITH *"THE RED DEVILS"* HE WON THREE LEAGUE TITLES, THE FA CUP, THE INTERCONTINENTAL CUP AND THE UEFA CHAMPIONS LEAGUE. *SIR ALEX FERGUSON* LATER LAMENTED THAT SELLING *STAM* TO *LAZIO* IN 2001 WAS A MISTAKE. *STAM* WON FURTHER HONOURS WITH *LAZIO*, *AC MILAN* AND *AJAX* BEFORE HANGING UP HIS BOOTS IN 2007. AFTER WORKING AS *MANCHESTER UNITED'S* SOUTH AMERICAN SCOUT, HE ENTERED MANAGEMENT.

1. *STAM* WAS APPOINTED MANAGER OF WHICH ENGLISH CHAMPIONSHIP TEAM IN 2016?

2. WHICH 1998 WORLD CUP-WINNING FRENCH DEFENDER WAS SIGNED AS *STAM'S* REPLACEMENT AT *MANCHESTER UNITED?*

3. WHICH WORLD CUP-WINNING GOALKEEPER WAS MANAGING *LAZIO* WHEN *STAM* WAS SIGNED?

JUL 18

IN HIS FOUR YEARS WITH **BOLTON WANDERERS**, **NIGERIA** GREAT **JAY-JAY OKOCHA** BECAME A FAN FAVOURITE, HELPING STEER THE CLUB AWAY FROM THE PREMIER LEAGUE RELEGATION ZONE AND LEADING THEM TO THE LEAGUE CUP FINAL. ON JULY 18, 2006, HE COMPLETED HIS MOVE TO **QATAR SC**. HIS STAY IN THE MIDDLE EAST WAS SHORT-LIVED AND HE RETURNED TO ENGLAND TO PLAY FOR **HULL CITY** IN 2017.

IDENTIFY THESE **NIGERIA** STARS:

1. WITH 101 APPEARANCES FOR THE NATIONAL TEAM, GOALKEEPER **VINCENT ENYEAMA** SHARES THE ALL-TIME **NIGERIA** RECORD WITH WHICH **EVERTON** STAR?

2. OLYMPIC GOLD MEDAL WINNER WHO PLAYED FOR **ARSENAL**, **WEST BROMWICH ALBION** AND **PORTSMOUTH**.

3. FA CUP WINNER WITH **LEICESTER CITY**, FORMERLY OF **MANCHESTER CITY**.

JUL 19

IT HAS BEEN CALLED *"ITALY'S GREATEST HUMILIATION"*. ON JULY 19, 1966, IN A GAME IN WHICH THE *"AZZURRI"* WERE EXPECTED TO COAST TO VICTORY, A GOAL FROM 24-YEAR-OLD *PAK DOO IK* WAS ENOUGH TO KNOCK *ITALY* OUT OF THE WORLD CUP AND SEND *NORTH KOREA* THROUGH TO THE QUARTER-FINALS. IT WAS THE FIRST TIME IN HISTORY THAT A TEAM FROM ASIA HAD ADVANCED BEYOND THE GROUP STAGE.

1. WHICH COUNTRY OVERTURNED A 3-0 DEFICIT TO BEAT *NORTH KORE*A 5-3 IN THE 1966 QUARTER-FINALS?

2. IN WHICH YEAR DID *NORTH KOREA* NEXT APPEAR IN THE WORLD CUP?

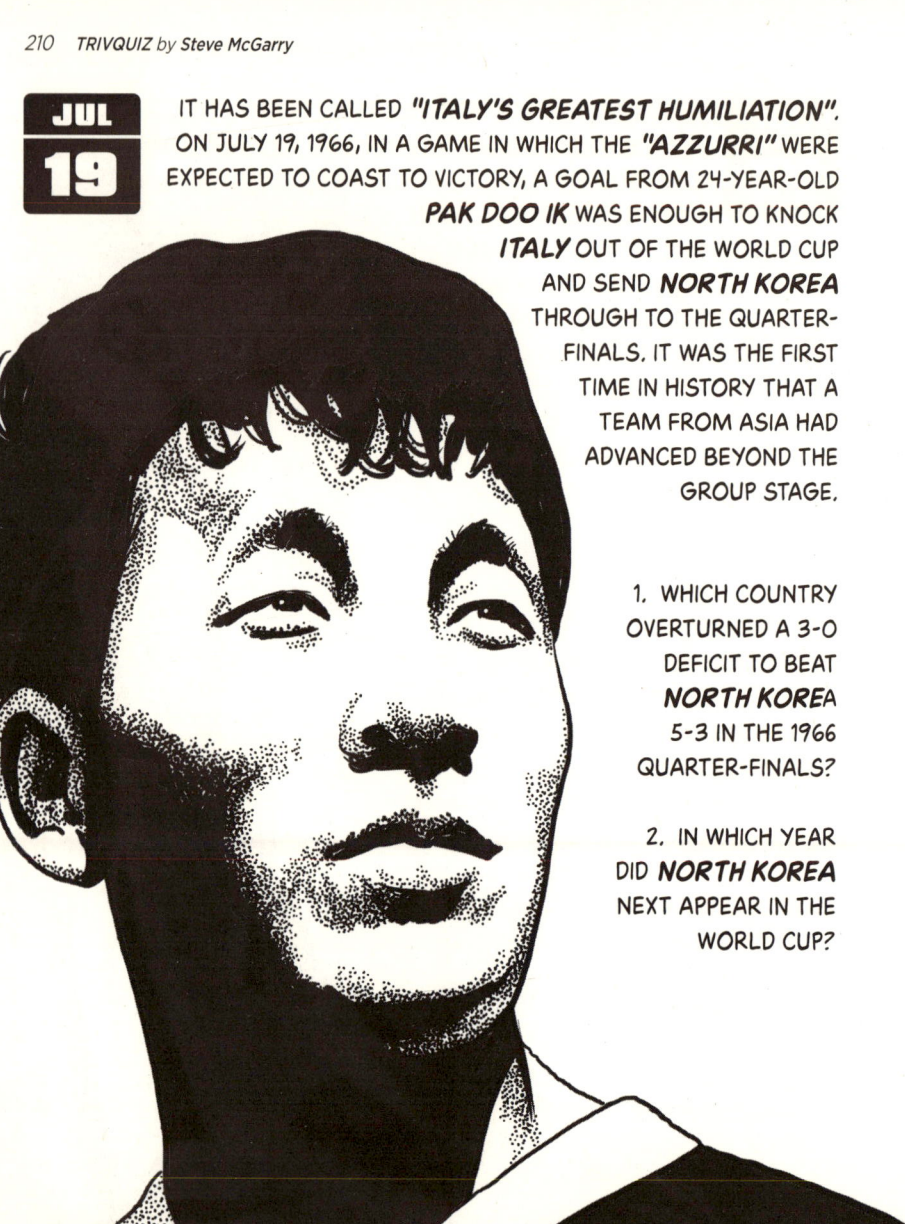

JUL 20

ROGER HUNT'S FIRST GOAL FOR **LIVERPOOL** WAS IN A SECOND DIVISION FIXTURE AGAINST **SCUNTHORPE UNITED** IN 1959. WHEN HE LEFT THE CLUB A DECADE LATER, HE HAD NETTED A CLUB RECORD 286 GOALS, WON TWO FIRST DIVISION TITLES AND THE FA CUP AND PLAYED IN EVERY GAME OF **ENGLAND'S** TRIUMPHANT 1966 WORLD CUP CAMPAIGN, DURING WHICH HE SCORED 3 GOALS. BORN IN GLAZEBURY, LANCASHIRE, ON JULY 20, 1938, HE REMAINS **LIVERPOOL'S** ALL-TIME TOP LEAGUE GOALSCORER.

1. **HUNT'S** OVERALL **LIVERPOOL** GOAL TALLY STOOD FOR 23 YEARS UNTIL OVERTAKEN BY WHICH PLAYER?

2. WHICH **ENGLAND** AND **BOLTON WANDERERS** GREAT WAS MANAGING **BOLTON** WHEN **HUNT** JOINED IN 1969?

3. **HUNT** PLAYED MOST OF HIS **LIVERPOOL** FOOTBALL UNDER **BILL SHANKLY** -- BUT WHO WAS THE EX-**ENGLAND** PLAYER WHO SIGNED HIM TO THE CLUB IN 1958?

JUL 21

BORN IN LEEDS ON JULY 21, 2000, SON OF A **NORWAY** INTERNATIONAL WHO PLAYED FOR **NOTTINGHAM FOREST, LEEDS UNITED** AND **MANCHESTER CITY**, **ERLING HAALAND** PLAYED AT NORWEGIAN CLUB **BRYNE** FROM THE AGE OF FIVE, BEFORE SIGNING FOR **MOLDE** WHEN HE WAS 16. HIS PROGRESS WAS RAPID AND HE WAS SNAPPED UP BY **RED BULL SALZBURG** IN 2016. HAVING WON AN AUSTRIAN LEAGUE AND CUP DOUBLE IN 2019 -- AND BEEN NAMED AUSTRIAN FOOTBALLER OF THE YEAR -- THE NEXT SEASON SAW HIM BECOME BECOME THE FIRST TEENAGER TO SCORE IN FIVE CONSECUTIVE UEFA CHAMPIONS LEAGUE GAMES. HE JOINED **BORUSSIA DORTMUND** MID-SEASON, AND HIT SEVEN GOALS IN HIS FIRST THREE GAMES!

1. **HAALAND** PLAYED UNDER WHICH SUBSEQUENT PREMIER LEAGUE MANAGER AT **MOLDE?**

2. **HAALAND** IS THE SECOND **BORUSSIA DORTMUND** PLAYER TO WIN EUROPE'S PRESTIGIOUS GOLDEN BOY AWARD. WHO WAS THE FIRST, A WINNER IN 2011, WHOSE SUBSEQUENT TRANSFER TO **BAYERN MUNICH** MADE HIM THE SECOND-MOST EXPENSIVE GERMAN PLAYER TO DATE?

3. WHAT IS THE NAME OF **ERLING'S** FATHER?

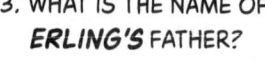

DIRK KUYT WON SILVERWARE WITH **UTRECHT**, **LIVERPOOL**, **FENERBAHÇE** AND **FEYENOORD**, AND WAS A WORLD CUP RUNNER-UP WITH **NETHERLANDS**. BORN IN KATWIJK ON JULY 22, 1980, HE MADE 104 APPEARANCES FOR HIS COUNTRY.

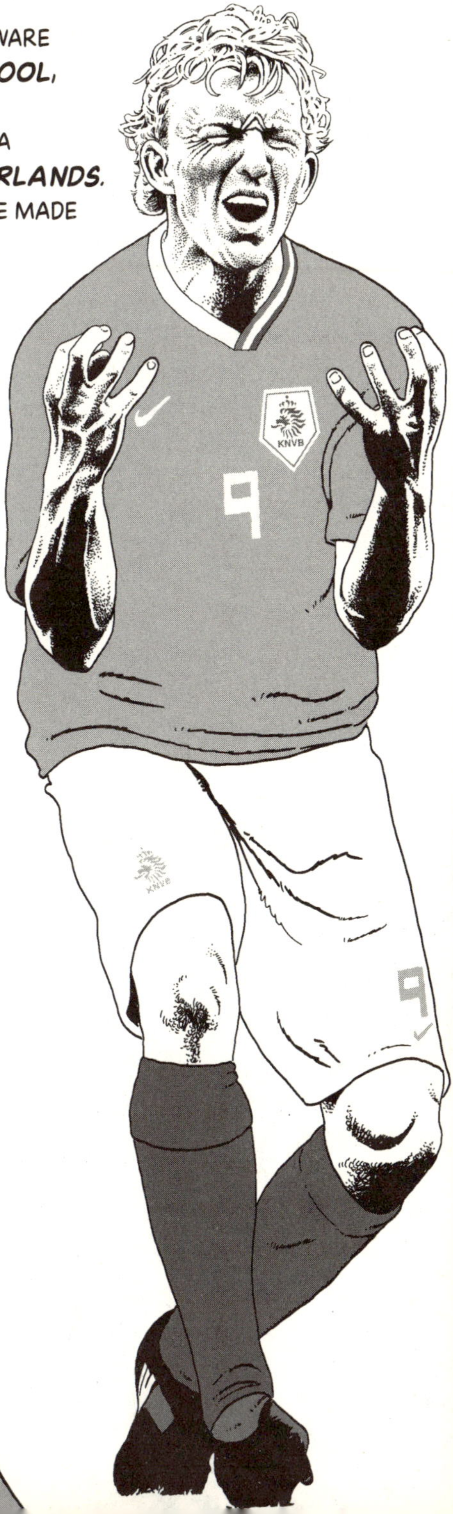

KUYT WAS NAMED DUTCH FOOTBALLER OF THE YEAR IN 2006, THE SAME YEAR HE LEFT **FEYENOORD** FOR **LIVERPOOL**. NAME THESE OTHER WINNERS OF THE AWARD WHO SUBSEQUENTLY PLAYED FOR **LIVERPOOL**:

1. WON IN 2015 WITH **PSV** BEFORE JOINING **NEWCASTLE**.

2. GOALKEEPER WHO WON IN 2000 WITH **FEYENOORD**, WON THE UEFA CHAMPIONS LEAGUE WITH **LIVERPOOL** IN 2005.

3. 2010 WINNER WITH **AJAX**, HIS SUBSEQUENT CLUBS INCLUDE **BARCELONA** AND **ATLÉTICO MADRID**.

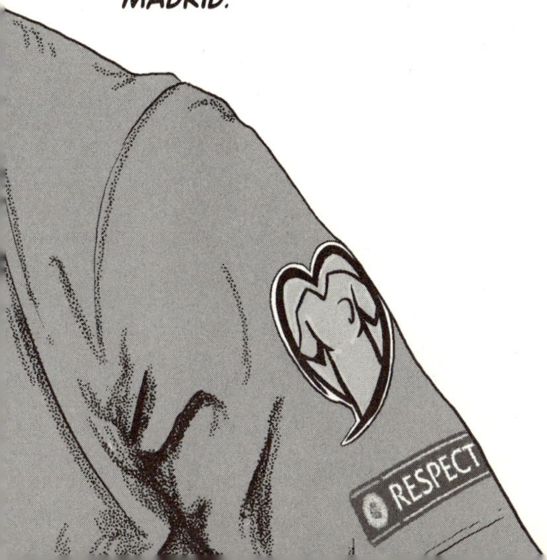

JUL 23

ON JULY 23, 1980, *KEVIN KEEGAN* MADE HIS DEBUT FOR *SOUTHAMPTON* IN A PRE-SEASON FRIENDLY AGAINST *SHAMROCK ROVERS*. THE SIGNING OF THE TWO-TIME EUROPEAN FOOTBALLER OF THE YEAR FROM *HAMBURGER SV* WAS A MAJOR COUP FOR *"SAINTS"* BOSS LAWRIE MCMENEMY. *KEEGAN'S* TWO SEASONS AT *THE DELL* SAW HIM PLAY ALONGSIDE THE LIKES OF *ALAN BALL, MICK CHANNON* AND *CHARLIE GEORGE*, BEFORE HIS EMOTIONAL DEPARTURE FOR *NEWCASTLE UNITED*, THE CLUB HIS FATHER SUPPORTED.

1. WITH WHICH CLUB DID *KEEGAN* BEGIN HIS PROFESSIONAL CAREER?

2. HE ENDED HIS PLAYING CAREER AT *BLACKTOWN CITY* -- A CLUB IN WHICH COUNTRY?

3. NAME THREE OF THE FOUR TEAMS HE SUBSEQUENTLY MANAGED.

JUL 24

BORN IN ROME ON JULY 24, 1983, *DANIELE DE ROSSI* SPENT THE VAST MAJORITY OF HIS CAREER WITH *ROMA*. SERIE A YOUNG FOOTBALLER OF THE YEAR IN 2006 AND ITALIAN FOOTBALLER OF THE YEAR IN 2009, HE WON THE COPPA ITALIA TWICE AND THE SUPERCOPPA ITALIANA. CAPPED 117 TIMES, HE WAS A MEMBER OF THE *ITALY* TEAM THAT WON THE 2004 EUROPEAN UNDER-21 CHAMPIONSHIP, THE SAME YEAR HE WON AN OLYMPIC BRONZE MEDAL, AND HE WAS A WORLD CUP WINNER IN 2006. HE ENDED HIS PLAYING DAYS WITH A SPELL IN ARGENTINA WITH *BOCA JUNIORS*, WHERE HE WAS A PRIMERA DIVISIÓN TITLE-WINNER.

NAME TWO OF THE COACHES THAT *DANIELE DE ROSSI* PLAYED UNDER AT *ROMA* BETWEEN 2001 AND 2019.

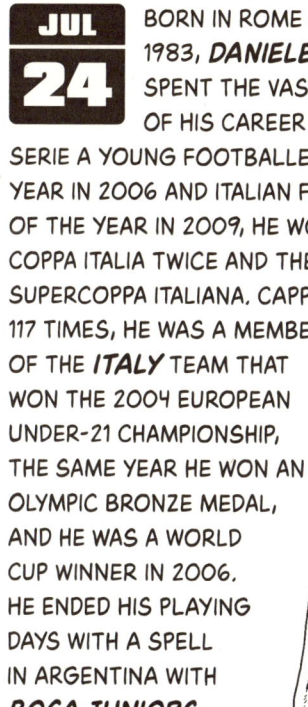

JUL 25

PAULINHO WAS BORN IN SÃO PAULO, BRAZIL ON JULY 25, 1988. HIS ROUTE TO THE TOP TOOK HIM TO LITHUANIA WITH **FC VILNIUS**, ON TO POLAND'S **ŁKS ŁÓDŹ**, THEN BACK TO BRAZIL AND SPELLS IN THE LOWER LEAGUES WITH **PÃO DE AÇÚCAR** AND **BRAGANTINO**. EVENTUALLY, **CORINTHIANS** CAME CALLING AND **PAULINHO** TASTED COPA LIBERTADORES AND WORLD CLUB CUP GLORY. ALTHOUGH HE SUBSEQUENTLY PLAYED FOR **TOTTENHAM HOTSPUR** AND **BARCELONA**, HE FOUND MOST SUCCESS IN TWO SPELLS WITH **GUANGZHOU EVERGRANDE**, WINNING THREE CHINESE SUPER LEAGUES AND THE AFC CHAMPIONS LEAGUE.

NAME THE TWO WORLD CUP-WINNING COACHES AND ONE WORLD CUP-WINNING CAPTAIN WHO HAVE MANAGED **GUANGZHOU EVERGRANDE**.

JUL 26

FOLLOWING THE SHOCK RESIGNATION OF *BILL SHANKLY* AS *LIVERPOOL* MANAGER, HIS ASSISTANT WAS ANNOUNCED AS HIS REPLACEMENT ON JULY 26, 1974. THE RELUCTANT *BOB PAISLEY* BECAME THE MOST SUCCESSFUL BOSS IN THE CLUB'S HISTORY, WINNING 20 HONOURS IN NINE SEASONS, INCLUDING SIX LEAGUE TITLES. HE WAS THE FIRST MANAGER TO WIN THE EUROPEAN CUP THREE TIMES. SIX TIMES MANAGER OF THE YEAR, HE RETIRED IN 1983. HE PASSED AWAY IN 1996, AGED 77.

1. HOW MANY OF THE TEN MEN WHO HAVE MANAGED *LIVERPOOL* SINCE *BOB PAISLEY* CAN YOU NAME?

2. *BOB PAISLEY* WON A LEAGUE TITLE AS A *LIVERPOOL* PLAYER -- BUT WITH WHICH NORTH-EAST AMATEUR CLUB DID HE LAUNCH HIS PLAYING CAREER?

3. A STATUE ERECTED OUTSIDE ANFIELD IN 2020 DEPICTS *BOB PAISLEY* CARRYING WHICH INJURED *LIVERPOOL* PLAYER FROM THE FIELD?

JUL 27

THREE-TIME *IFFHS* WORLD'S BEST GOALKEEPER, *JOSÉ LUIS CHILAVERT* WAS BORN IN LUQUE, PARAGUAY, ON JULY 27, 1965. *PARAGUAY'S* CAPTAIN WAS ALSO A DEAD-BALL EXPERT WHO SCORED 67 GOALS DURING HIS CAREER -- INCLUDING A HAT-TRICK IN ONE GAME! HE WAS ALSO RENOWNED FOR HIS FIERY TEMPER, WHICH FREQUENTLY LANDED HIM IN TROUBLE WITH AUTHORITIES! THE 1996 SOUTH AMERICAN FOOTBALLER OF THE YEAR, HE SPENT THREE SEASONS IN SPAIN WITH *REAL ZARAGOZA* AND WON HONOURS IN PARAGUAY WITH *GUARANI*, IN ARGENTINA WITH *VÉLEZ SÁRSFIELD*, A COUPE DE FRANCE WITH *STRASBOURG*, AND A URUGUAYAN LEAGUE TITLE WITH *PEÑAROL*.

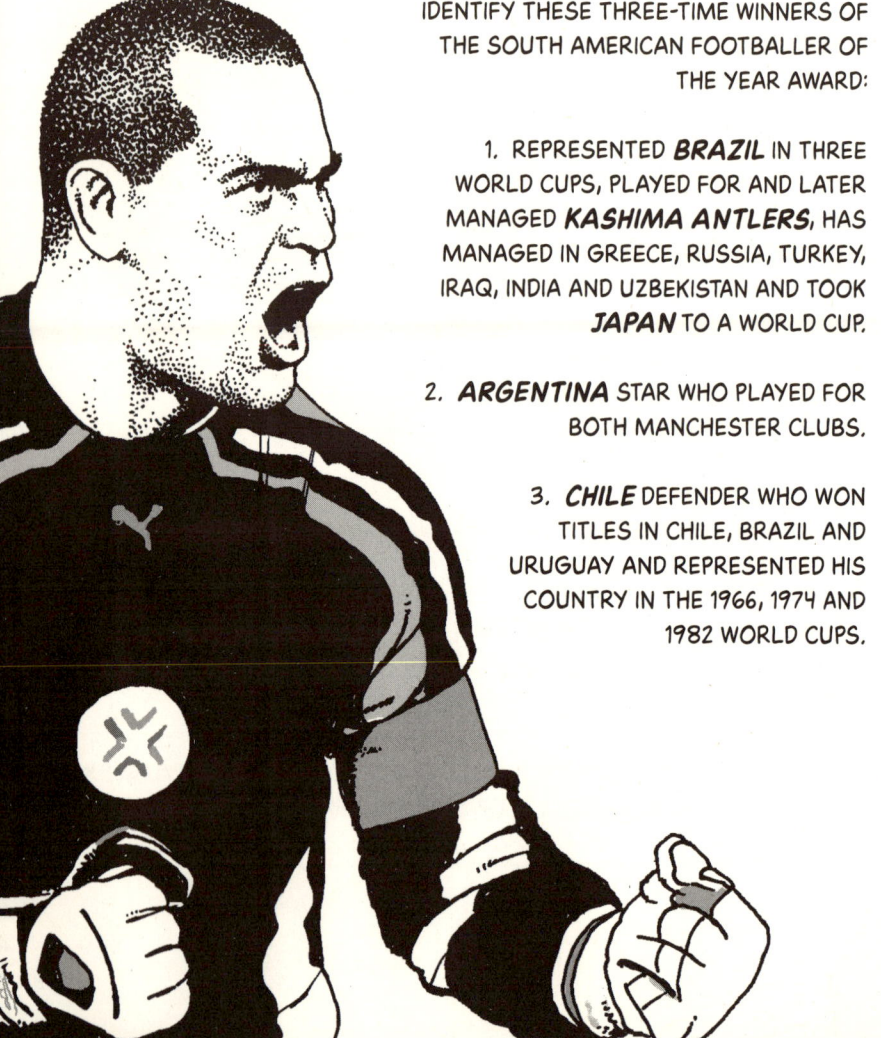

IDENTIFY THESE THREE-TIME WINNERS OF THE SOUTH AMERICAN FOOTBALLER OF THE YEAR AWARD:

1. REPRESENTED *BRAZIL* IN THREE WORLD CUPS, PLAYED FOR AND LATER MANAGED *KASHIMA ANTLERS*, HAS MANAGED IN GREECE, RUSSIA, TURKEY, IRAQ, INDIA AND UZBEKISTAN AND TOOK *JAPAN* TO A WORLD CUP.

2. *ARGENTINA* STAR WHO PLAYED FOR BOTH MANCHESTER CLUBS.

3. *CHILE* DEFENDER WHO WON TITLES IN CHILE, BRAZIL AND URUGUAY AND REPRESENTED HIS COUNTRY IN THE 1966, 1974 AND 1982 WORLD CUPS.

JUL
28

BRAZIL MIDFIELDER **JAIR DA ROSA PINTO** -- KNOWN SIMPLY AS **JAIR** -- DIED ON JULY 28, 2005, AT THE AGE OF 84. THE PRESIDENT OF BRAZIL, **JAIR BOLSONARO**, WAS BORN ON THE LEGENDARY STAR'S 34TH BIRTHDAY AND IS NAMED AFTER HIM. OUTSTANDING IN THE 1950 WORLD CUP, A TOURNAMENT IN WHICH HOSTS **BRAZIL** WERE EXPECTED TO TRIUMPH, **JAIR** COULD DO NOTHING TO PREVENT THE TRAUMATIC 2-1 LOSS TO **URUGUAY** IN THE FINAL GAME THAT PLUNGED HIS COUNTRY INTO DESPAIR AND EFFECTIVELY ENDED HIS INTERNATIONAL CAREER. **"I'LL TAKE THAT LOSS TO MY GRAVE"**, HE LATER REMARKED.

IDENTIFY THESE OTHER 2006 DEATHS:

1. **FULHAM** GREAT WHO BECAME THE FIRST £100 A WEEK PLAYER AFTER THE ABOLITION OF THE MAXIMUM WAGE.

2. **MANCHESTER UNITED** AND **NORTHERN IRELAND** STAR, DEAD AGED 59.

3. ARGENTINE-ITALIAN STAR, EUROPEAN FOOTBALLER OF THE YEAR IN 1961.

JUL 29

THE FIRST BLACK PLAYER TO REPRESENT **ENGLAND** IN A FULL INTERNATIONAL MATCH, **VIV ANDERSON** WAS BORN IN NOTTINGHAM ON JULY 29, 1956. RELEASED AS A SCHOOLBOY BY **MANCHESTER UNITED**, HE BECAME AN INTEGRAL PART OF THE **NOTTINGHAM FOREST** TEAM THAT **BRIAN CLOUGH** CREATED, TAKING THE EAST MIDLANDERS FROM THE SECOND DIVISION TO BECOME CHAMPIONS OF ENGLAND AND WIN TWO EUROPEAN CUPS. CAPPED 30 TIMES BY **ENGLAND, ANDERSON** WON HONOURS WITH A NUMBER OF ENGLISH CLUBS BEFORE RETIRING IN 1994.

NAME THREE OF THE FIVE CLUBS FOR WHOM **VIV ANDERSON** PLAYED AFTER LEAVING **NOTTINGHAM FOREST.**

JUL 30

BORN IN GÖPPINGEN ON JULY 30, 1964, *JÜRGEN KLINSMANN'S* GLITTERING CAREER SAW HIM WIN THE WORLD CUP IN 1990, CAPTAIN THE 1996 EUROPEAN CHAMPIONSHIP VICTORS, AND PLAY AT THE HIGHEST LEVEL IN THE LEAGUES OF GERMANY, ITALY, FRANCE AND ENGLAND. AS A MANAGER, HE STEERED *GERMANY* TO A THIRD-PLACE FINISH IN THE 2006 WORLD CUP AND WAS COACH OF A NUMBER OF OTHER TEAMS INCLUDING *BAYERN MUNICH* AND THE *UNITED STATES*.

1. NAME THREE TEAMS THAT *KLINSMANN* PLAYED FOR.

2. WHO DID *GERMANY* DEFEAT IN THE 1990 WORLD CUP FINAL?

3. WHO DID *GERMANY* DEFEAT IN THE FINAL OF THE 1996 EUROPEAN CHAMPIONSHIP?

A FORMER MEMBER OF THE NATIONAL YOUTH BASKETBALL TEAM, **PAULO WANCHOPE** WAS BORN IN HEREDIA, COSTA RICA, ON JULY 31, 1976. HAVING LAUNCHED HIS FOOTBALL CAREER WITH **CS HEREDIANO**, HE ARRIVED IN ENGLAND AS A 20-YEAR-OLD TO PLAY FOR **DERBY COUNTY**. TWO YEARS LATER, HE SIGNED FOR **WEST HAM UNITED**, AND A SEASON LATER, HE JOINED **MANCHESTER CITY**. THE CLUB WAS RELEGATED TO THE SECOND TIER IN HIS DEBUT SEASON, BUT BOUNCED BACK TO THE PREMIER LEAGUE THE FOLLOWING YEAR. HE WAS DOGGED BY INJURY DURING HIS TIME WITH **CITY**. HE SUBSEQUENTLY PLAYED FOR CLUBS IN SPAIN, QATAR, COSTA RICA, ARGENTINA, JAPAN AND THE UNITED STATES BEFORE RETIRING. MOVING INTO MANAGEMENT, HE TOOK OVER THE REINS OF THE **COSTA RICA** NATIONAL TEAM BUT RESIGNED IN 2015 AFTER A POST-GAME BRAWL.

IDENTIFY THESE **COSTA RICA** INTERNATIONAL PLAYERS:

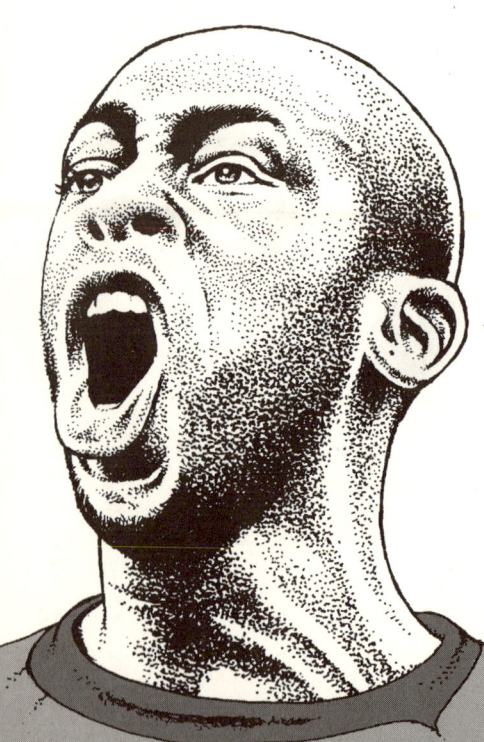

1. FORWARD WHO SIGNED FOR **ARSENAL** IN 2011 BUT WAS UNABLE TO GET A WORK PERMIT, HE WAS LOANED OUT TO CLUBS IN EUROPE, EVENTUALLY DEBUTING FOR **"THE GUNNERS"** IN 2014.

2. WON DUTCH LEAGUE AND CUP HONOURS WITH **TWENTE** BEFORE PLAYING FOUR SEASONS WITH **FULHAM**.

3. **PARIS SAINT-GERMAIN** GOALKEEPER WHO WON THE UEFA CHAMPIONS LEAGUE THREE TIMES WITH **REAL MADRID**.

AUGUST

AUG 1

BORN IN KOLBERMOOR, WEST GERMANY, ON AUGUST 1, 1984, **BASTIAN SCHWEINSTEIGER** ABANDONED THE PROSPECT OF A CAREER IN PROFESSIONAL SKIING TO SIGN FOR **BAYERN MUNICH.** HE WON TITLES WITH THE CLUB'S JUNIOR TEAM, AND AFTER JUST TWO TRAINING SESSIONS WITH THE FIRST TEAM, HE WAS HANDED HIS DEBUT BY COACH **OTTMAR HITZFELD** IN A 2002 UEFA CHAMPIONS LEAGUE GAME. HE WENT ON TO HELP BAYERN TO A LEAGUE AND CUP DOUBLE THAT FIRST TERM, A FEAT HE REPEATED IN SIX OF THE NEXT 12 SEASONS. HIS TALLY WITH THE BAVARIANS EVENTUALLY INCLUDED EIGHT LEAGUE TITLES AND THE UEFA CHAMPIONS LEAGUE. HE SPENT AN UNHAPPY 18 MONTHS WITH **MANCHESTER UNITED** BEFORE ENDING HIS PLAYING CAREER IN THE MSL WITH **CHICAGO FIRE.**

SCHWEINSTEIGER MADE THE FIRST OF HIS 121 APPERANCES FOR **GERMANY** IN 2004. A MEMBER OF THE TEAMS THAT FINISHED THIRD IN THE 2006 AND 2010 WORLD CUPS AND TRIUMPHED IN 2014, HE RETIRED FROM INTERNATIONAL FOOTBALL FOLLOWING HIS FOURTH EUROPEAN CHAMPIONSHIP CAMPAIGN IN 2016.

1. HE PLAYED UNDER WHICH MANAGER AT BOTH **BAYERN MUNICH** AND **MANCHESTER UNITED?**

2. HE PLAYED UNDER WHICH MANAGER AT BOTH **BAYERN MUNICH** AND FOR **GERMANY?**

3. WHO COACHED **SCHWEINSTEIGER** AND **GERMANY** AT:
   A) EURO 2004
   B) WORLD CUP 2006
   C) ALL TOURNAMENTS 2008-2016

AUG 2

THE FIRST TRINIDADIAN TO PLAY IN THE UEFA CHAMPIONS LEAGUE, *RUSSELL LATAPY* WAS BORN IN PORT OF SPAIN ON AUGUST 2, 1968. HE TURNED DOWN THE CHANCE TO ATTEND UNIVERSITY IN FLORIDA TO PURSUE HIS FOOTBALL AMBITIONS, AND PLAYED IN TRINIDAD AND JAMAICA BEFORE MOVING TO PORTUGAL TO PLAY FOR SECOND DIVISION OUTFIT *ACADÉMICA DE COIMBRA*. *BOBBY ROBSON* SIGNED HIM TO *PORTO* AND HE REPAID THE CLUB BY HELPING WIN TWO TITLES. HE WON CUP HONOURS WITH *BOAVISTA FC* BEFORE HEADING TO SCOTLAND, WHERE HE ADDED TO HIS MEDAL HAUL DURING SPELLS WITH *HIBERNIAN, RANGERS* AND *FALKIRK*, ALTHOUGH HIS FONDNESS FOR PARTYING FREQUENTLY LANDED HIM IN TROUBLE. HE MOVED INTO COACHING AND MANAGEMENT, AND HAS HELMED BOTH THE *TRINIDAD AND TOBAGO* AND *BARBADOS* NATIONAL TEAMS.

LATAPY MADE 81 APPEARANCES FOR HIS COUNTRY. IDENTIFY THESE *TRINIDAD AND TOBAGO* INTERNATIONALS:

1. HE LEFT *ASTON VILLA* FOR *MANCHESTER UNITED*, WITH WHOM HE WON THREE LEAGUE TITLES AND THE UEFA CHAMPIONS LEAGUE.

2. HIS COUNTRY'S TOP ALL-TIME GOALSCORER, HIS CLUBS INCLUDED *BRISTOL CITY, NOTTINGHAM FOREST, BIRMINGHAM CITY, SUNDERLAND, SOUTHAMPTON, CRYSTAL PALACE, COVENTRY CITY* AND *DERBY COUNTY*.

3. HE SPENT MUCH OF HIS CAREER WITH *ASTON VILLA* AND *BOLTON WANDERERS* AND WAS KILLED IN A CHESHIRE CAR CRASH IN 2018, AGED 37.

AUG 3

OSVALDO CÉSAR ARDILES WAS BORN IN BELL VILLE, CÓRDOBA, ARGENTINA, ON AUGUST 3, 1952. A LAWYER'S SON, HE JOINED **INSTITUTO DE CÓRDOBA** AT 15 AND MOVED ON TO **CLUB ATLÉTICO BELGRANO**, BUT INSISTED ON PASSING HIS LAW EXAMS BEFORE SIGNING FOR **HURACÁN** AT THE AGE OF 22. FOLLOWING SUPERB DISPLAYS IN THE MIDFIELD OF **ARGENTINA'S** 1978 WORLD CUP-WINNING SIDE, HE WAS SIGNED BY **TOTTENHAM HOTSPUR**, WHERE HE QUICKLY BECAME A FOLK HERO. FOLLOWING THE OUTBREAK OF THE FALKLANDS WAR BETWEEN BRITAIN AND ARGENTINA IN 1982, HE LEFT ENGLAND TO PLAY ON LOAN IN FRANCE, BUT LATER RETURNED TO PLAY FOR A NUMBER OF ENGLISH CLUBS. HE HAS SUBSEQUENTLY COACHED IN ENGLAND, CROATIA, SAUDI ARABIA, MEXICO, JAPAN, ISRAEL, ARGENTINA AND PARAGUAY.

1. WHICH FELLOW WORLD CUP-WINNER SIGNED FOR **TOTTENHAM HOTSPUR** AT THE SAME TIME AS **ARDILES?**

2. NAME ONE OF THE FOUR JAPANESE CLUBS HE COACHED.

3. **ARDILES** HAD A BRIEF SPELL IN THE UNITED STATES IN 1989 PLAYING FOR WHICH FLORIDA ASL CLUB?

AUG 4

BORN IN GLASGOW, SCOTLAND, ON AUGUST 4, 1957, MIDFIELDER *JOHN WARK* HAD THREE SEPARATE SPELLS WITH *IPSWICH TOWN*, WITH WHOM HE WON THE UEFA CUP AND THE FA CUP. HE ALSO SPENT FOUR YEARS WITH *LIVERPOOL*, DURING WHICH TIME THE CLUB WON TWO LEAGUE TITLES, AND HE ALSO PLAYED A SEASON AT *MIDDLESBROUGH*. CAPPED 29 TIMES BY *SCOTLAND*, HE WAS VOTED 1981 PFA PLAYER OF THE YEAR IN ENGLAND, THE SAME YEAR HE WAS NAMED YOUNG EUROPEAN PLAYER OF THE YEAR. HE WAS ONE OF A NUMBER OF PLAYERS, INCLUDING *PELÉ, BOBBY MOORE, MIKE SUMMERBEE, OSSIE ARDILES* AND *PAUL VAN HIMST*, WHO APPEARED OPPOSITE *MICHAEL CAINE* IN THE 1981 PRISONER OF WAR SOCCER MOVIE *"ESCAPE TO VICTORY"*.

1. WHICH AMERICAN ACTOR PLAYED A GOALKEEPER IN *"ESCAPE TO VICTORY"*?

2. *JOHN WARK* SCORED TWICE FOR *SCOTLAND* AS A MEMBER OF THE 1982 WORLD CUP SQUAD - WHO WAS THE MANAGER?

3. WHO COACHED *IPSWICH TOWN* AND *WARK* TO VICTORY IN THE 1981 UEFA CUP FINAL?

AUG 5

BORN IN SKEGNESS ON AUGUST 5, 1948, *RAY CLEMENCE* BEGAN HIS CAREER AT *SCUNTHORPE UNITED*. IN 1967, HE WAS SNAPPED UP BY *LIVERPOOL*, WITH WHOM HE WENT ON TO WIN THREE EUROPEAN CUPS, TWO UEFA CUPS, FIVE CHAMPIONSHIPS, THE FA CUP AND THE LEAGUE CUP, BEFORE JOINING *TOTTENHAM HOTSPUR* IN 1981. HAVING WON THE FA CUP AND THE UEFA CUP WITH *SPURS*, HE JOINED THE CLUB'S COACHING STAFF WHEN HE RETIRED IN 1988, AND WAS APPOINTED JOINT MANAGER IN THE EARLY 1990S. CAPPED 61 TIMES BY *ENGLAND*, HE WAS MANAGING *BARNET* WHEN HE WAS INVITED TO BECOME GOALKEEPING COACH TO THE NATIONAL TEAM IN 1996, A POSITION HE HELD FOR 11 YEARS, UNTIL *FABIO CAPELLO* REPLACED HIM WITH *FRANCO TANCREDI. CLEMENCE* REMAINED ON STAFF AND WAS REINSTATED BY THE INCOMING *ROY HODGSON*. HE DIED IN 2020 AT THE AGE OF 72.

1. *ENGLAND* MANAGER *RON GREENWOOD* USED TO REGULARLY ALTERNATE *CLEMENCE* WITH WHICH OTHER GOALKEEPING GREAT?

2. *CLEMENCE* WAS THE FIRST GOALKEEPER TO CAPTAIN *ENGLAND* SINCE WHICH *MANCHESTER CITY* STAR IN THE LATE 1940S?

3. WHO WAS *TOTTENHAM* CO-MANAGER WITH *CLEMENCE?*

AUG 6

BORN IN ROTTERDAM, ON AUGUST 6, 1983, *ROBIN VAN PERSIE* MADE HIS SENIOR DEBUT FOR *FEYENOORD* AT THE AGE OF 17. DESPITE BEING A MEMBER OF THE SIDE THAT WON THE 2002 UEFA CUP, HIS CLASHES WITH COACH *BERT VAN MARWIJK* SAW HIM INCREASINGLY SIDELINED. HE JOINED *ARSENAL* IN 2004, AND MADE HIS SENIOR *NETHERLANDS* DEBUT IN 2005. ALTHOUGH HIS *"GUNNERS"* CAREER WAS BLIGHTED BY INJURY, HE WAS INVARIABLY THE CLUB'S TOP SCORER EACH SEASON. BUT WITH JUST THE 2005 FA CUP AND A GOLDEN BOOT TO SHOW FOR EIGHT SEASONS IN LONDON, HE MOVED ON TO *MANCHESTER UNITED* IN 2012 ... AND WON A LEAGUE TITLE AND ANOTHER GOLDEN BOOT IN HIS DEBUT SEASON! YET AGAIN, HE WAS PLAGUED BY INJURIES AND IN 2015 HE WAS ALLOWED TO LEAVE FOR *FENERBAHÇE*. INJURIES RESTRICTED HIS PLAYING TIME AND IN EARLY 2018 HE LEFT TURKEY TO REJOIN *FEYENOORD*, WITH WHOM HE WON THE KNVB CUP BEFORE RETIRING IN 2019. HIS 50 GOALS IN 102 APPEARANCES MAKE HIM THE ALL-TIME TOP *NETHERLANDS* GOALSCORER.

1. HE PLAYED UNDER *BERT VAN MARWIJK* AT CLUB AND INTERNATIONAL LEVEL. WHICH MANAGER COACHED HIM FOR BOTH *NETHERLANDS* AND:
   A) *MANCHESTER UNITED*
   B) *FENERBAHÇE*

2. *VAN PERSIE* SIGNED FOR *FENERBAHÇE* IN JULY, 2015, A FEW DAYS AFTER WHICH *MANCHESTER UNITED* TEAMMATE ALSO JOINED THE TURKISH CLUB?

3. NAME THE TWO OTHER DUTCH PLAYERS WHO HAVE WON THE PREMIER LEAGUE GOLDEN BOOT.

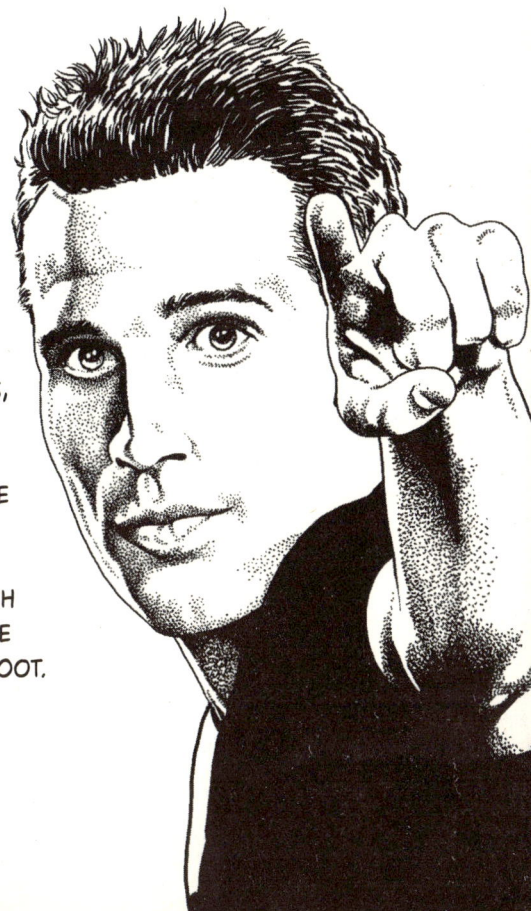

AUG 7

TWO LEGENDARY PLAYERS ANNOUNCED THEIR RETIREMENT FROM THE GAME ON AUGUST 7, 1973 -- BOTH SUFFERING FROM EYE INJURIES. A DETACHED RETINA HAD THREATENED **TOSTÃO'S** CHANCES OF PLAYING FOR **BRAZIL** IN THE 1970 WORLD CUP, BUT THE **CRUZEIRO** STAR HAD RECOVERED SUFFICIENTLY TO HELP HIS COUNTRY WIN THE **JULES RIMET TROPHY** FOR A RECORD THIRD TIME. SOUTH AMERICAN PLAYER OF THE YEAR IN 1971, HE JOINED **VASCO DA GAMA** IN A RECORD DEAL IN 1972, BUT HIS EYE PROBLEMS RESURFACED AND ENDED HIS CAREER AT THE AGE OF 27. **ENGLAND** GOALKEEPER **GORDON BANKS** LOST AN EYE IN A 1972 ROAD ACCIDENT. IT MEANT HIS CAREER IN THE TOP FLIGHT WAS OVER, ALTHOUGH THE 1966 WORLD CUP WINNER RECOVERED SUFFICIENTLY TO PLAY BRIEFLY IN THE US.

1. ON THE WAY TO WINNING THE 1970 WORLD CUP, **BRAZIL** DEFEATED HOLDERS **ENGLAND**, IN A GAME IN WHICH BOTH **BANKS** AND **TOSTÃO** PLAYED. HOW MANY OTHER TIMES HAVE THE TWO COUNTRIES MET IN A WORLD CUP GAME?

2. **BANKS** WAS TAKEN ILL ON THE EVE OF **ENGLAND'S** QUARTER-FINAL GAME IN THAT 1970 WORLD CUP. WHO WAS THE UNDERSTUDY WHO STEPPED IN AND KEPT GOAL IN THE 3-2 LOSS TO **WEST GERMANY?**

3. NAME ONE OF THE THREE ENGLISH CLUBS FOR WHOM **BANKS** PLAYED.

AUG 8

ROBERTO ROJAS WAS BORN IN SANTIAGO, CHILE, ON AUGUST 8, 1957. HAVING WON TITLES WITH **COLO-COLO**, HE WAS SIGNED BY BRAZIL'S **SÃO PAULO**. IT WAS IN BRAZIL THAT **ROJAS** WAS INVOLVED IN ONE OF THE MOST INFAMOUS INCIDENTS IN WORLD CUP HISTORY. IN 1989, WITH **CHILE** LOSING 1-0 AND ON THE VERGE OF MISSING OUT ON QUALIFICATION FOR **ITALIA 90**, A FIREWORK WAS THROWN FROM THE STANDS AND GOALKEEPER **ROJAS** COLLAPSED, WRITHING IN AGONY AND CLUTCHING HIS BLOODIED HEAD, APPARENTLY INJURED BY THE EXPLOSION. HE WAS CARRIED OFF THE FIELD, HIS TEAMMATES REFUSING TO CONTINUE IN SUCH UNSAFE CONDITIONS. THE MATCH WAS UNFINISHED, AND THERE WAS TALK THAT THE GAME MIGHT BE NULLIFIED AND **BRAZIL** FACE SANCTIONS. HOWEVER, VIDEO EVIDENCE PROVED THAT **ROJAS** HAD NOT BEEN HIT BY THE FIREWORK. IT WAS DISCOVERED THAT HE HAD INFLICTED HIS OWN WOUND WITH A RAZORBLADE HIDDEN IN HIS GLOVE. **FIFA** AWARDED **BRAZIL** A 2-0 WIN AND BANNED **CHILE** FROM THE 1994 WORLD CUP. FOR HIS PART, **ROJAS** WAS BANNED FOR LIFE, ALONG WITH THE **CHILE** COACH AND TEAM DOCTOR. HIS BAN WAS EVENTUALLY LIFTED BY **FIFA** IN 2001.

1. WHICH **FRANCE** STRIKER WAS SENT HOME FROM THE 2010 WORLD CUP AFTER INSULTING COACH **RAYMOND DOMENECH**, LEADING THE ENTIRE TEAM TO ABANDON A TRAINING SESSION IN PROTEST?

2. DUBBED THE **"BATTLE OF SANTIAGO"**, WHICH TWO TEAMS WERE INVOLVED IN CLASHES IN A 1962 TOURNAMENT GAME THAT WERE SO VIOLENT THAT TWO PLAYERS WERE SENT OFF AND THE POLICE HAD TO INTERVENE FOUR TIMES?

3. IN 1978, WHICH PEDANTIC WELSH REFEREE BLEW FOR FULL-TIME WHILE THE BALL WAS IN THE AIR FROM A CORNER, THUS DISALLOWING WHAT SHOULD HAVE BEEN **ZICO'S** WINNER FOR **BRAZIL** AGAINST **SWEDEN**?

 **AUG 9** A WORLD CUP WINNER WITH *ITALY* IN 2006, *FILIPPO INZAGHI* WAS BORN IN PLACENZA, ON AUGUST 9, 1973. HE BEGAN HIS TOP-FLIGHT CAREER WITH *PARMA*, BEFORE JOINING *ATALANTA*, WHERE HE FINISHED TOP SERIE A SCORER IN 1997, EARNING HIMSELF A TRANSFER TO *JUVENTUS*, WITH WHOM HE WON A LEAGUE TITLE. *"PIPPO"* JOINED *AC MILAN* IN 2001, GOING ON TO WIN ANOTHER TWO TITLES AND TWO UEFA CHAMPIONS LEAGUE TROPHIES, AS WELL AS A FIFA CLUB WORLD CUP AND TWO UEFA SUPER CUPS. HE WON 57 CAPS, SCORING 25 GOALS. IN HIS COACHING CAREER HE HAS MANAGED A NUMBER OF TEAMS, INCLUDING *AC MILAN*.

INZAGHI IS NOT THE ONLY MEMBER OF *ITALY'S* 2006 WORLD CUP-WINNING SQUAD TO ENTER MANAGEMENT. IDENTIFY THESE OTHERS:

1. LEGENDARY PLAYMAKER WHO WON TITLES WITH *AC MILAN* AND *JUVENTUS*, SACKED AS *JUVENTUS* MANAGER IN 2021 AFTER ONE SEASON, DESPITE WINNING THE COPPA ITALIA AND SUPERCOPPA ITALIANA.

2. COMBATIVE MIDFIELDER WHO ONCE HEADBUTTED *JOE JORDAN*.

3. CAPTAIN OF THE 2006 SIDE, HIS COACHING CAREER HAS SEEN HIM MANAGE TWO CHINESE CLUBS AND THE *CHINA* NATIONAL TEAM.

BORN IN CORK, IRELAND, ON AUGUST 10, 1971, **ROY KEANE** WAS STILL A TEENAGER WHEN **NOTTINGHAM FOREST'S BRIAN CLOUGH** SIGNED HIM FROM **COBH RAMBLERS**. IN 1993, **MANCHESTER UNITED** PAID A RECORD FEE TO TAKE HIM TO **OLD TRAFFORD**, WHERE HE CAPTAINED **ALEX FERGUSON'S** SIDE TO UNPRECEDENTED TRIUMPHS, INCLUDING SEVEN LEAGUE TITLES. HE OVERCAME A SERIOUS KNEE INJURY TO LEAD **UNITED** TO THE 1999 TREBLE OF LEAGUE, FA CUP AND EUROPEAN CHAMPIONS LEAGUE -- ALTHOUGH SUSPENSION ROBBED HIM OF HIS PLACE IN THE EUROPEAN CHAMPIONS LEAGUE FINAL. **UNITED'S** MOST SUCCESSFUL CAPTAIN, HE LEFT THE CLUB IN 2005 AFTER HIS RELATIONSHIP WITH **FERGUSON** DETERIORATED.

1. WITH WHICH OTHER CLUB DID HE WIN A LEAGUE AND CUP DOUBLE?

2. HE WON THE FOOTBALL LEAGUE CHAMPIONSHIP TITLE IN 2007 AS MANAGER OF WHICH CLUB?

3. HE WAS SENT HOME FROM THE **REPUBLIC OF IRELAND'S** 2002 WORLD CUP TRAINING CAMP AFTER A TIRADE AGAINST WHICH MANAGER?

AUG 11

ON AUGUST 11, 2012, *SENEGAL'S* CONTROVERSIAL *EL HADJI DIOUF* COMPLETED HIS MOVE FROM *DONCASTER ROVERS* TO *LEEDS UNITED*. AFTER PLAYING IN FRANCE WITH A NUMBER OF TEAMS, HE JOINED *LIVERPOOL* IN 2002, FOLLOWING HIS IMPRESSIVE FORM IN THAT SUMMER'S WORLD CUP. IN TWO SEASONS HE MANAGED JUST 6 GOALS -- BUT PICKED UP 21 YELLOW CARDS AND CAUSED MAYHEM WHEN HE SPAT AT A *CELTIC* FAN! FARMED OUT TO *BOLTON WANDERERS*, HE SUBSEQUENTLY PLAYED FOR *SUNDERLAND, BLACKBURN ROVERS* AND *RANGERS* BEFORE LANDING IN DONCASTER. FOLLOWING TWO SEASONS WITH *LEEDS* -- ONE OF WHICH HE MISSED COMPLETELY WITH A SHIN INFECTION -- HAVING COMPLETED 12 YEARS OF INCIDENTS, INJURIES AND OUTRAGEOUS ANTICS IN BRITISH FOOTBALL, HE JOINED MALAYSIA'S *SABAH* IN 2014.

EL HADJI DIOUF SCORED 24 GOALS IN 70 APPEARANCES FOR *SENEGAL*. IDENTIFY THESE OTHER *SENEGAL* STARS:

1. DEFENSIVE MIDFIELDER WHO PLAYED FOR *ASTON VILLA* AND *EVERTON* BEFORE JOINING *PARIS SAINT-GERMAIN* IN 2019.

2. JOINED *LIVERPOOL* FROM *SOUTHAMPTON* IN 2016, VOTED AFRICAN FOOTBALLER OF THE YEAR IN 2019.

3. WON MULTIPLE HONOURS WITH *ANDERLECHT* AND SPENT FOUR SEASONS WITH *WEST HAM UNITED* BEFORE JOINING *CRYSTAL PALACE* IN 2018.

AUG 12

BORN TO GHANAIAN IMMIGRANTS IN PALERMO, ITALY, ON AUGUST 12, 1990, *MARIO BARWUAH* WAS VERY SERIOUSLY ILL AS AN INFANT AND WAS HOSPITALISED FOR LONG PERIODS. WHEN THE FAMILY MOVED TO BRESCIA, *MARIO'S* HEALTH PROBLEMS AND THE FAMILY'S CRAMPED LIVING CONDITIONS PERSUADED THE *BARWUAHS* TO PLACE HIM WITH FOSTER PARENTS, AND IN 1993, *MARIO* WENT TO LIVE WITH THE *BALOTELLI* FAMILY. HIS FOOTBALL SKILLS WERE EVIDENT FROM A VERY EARLY AGE AND HE JOINED THE *LUMEZZANE* YOUTH TEAM IN 2001. ALTHOUGH HE WAS NEVER OFFICIALLY ADOPTED, HE HAD TAKEN HIS FOSTER FAMILY'S NAME, AND BY THE AGE OF 15, *MARIO BALOTELLI* HAD BROKEN THROUGH TO THE SENIOR TEAM AND WAS PLAYING IN THE LOWER DIVISIONS OF THE ITALIAN LEAGUE. HE HAD TO WAIT UNTIL HIS 18TH BIRTHDAY TO REQUEST ITALIAN CITIZENSHIP.

NAME FIVE CLUBS THAT *BALOTELLI* HAS SUBSEQUENTLY PLAYED FOR.

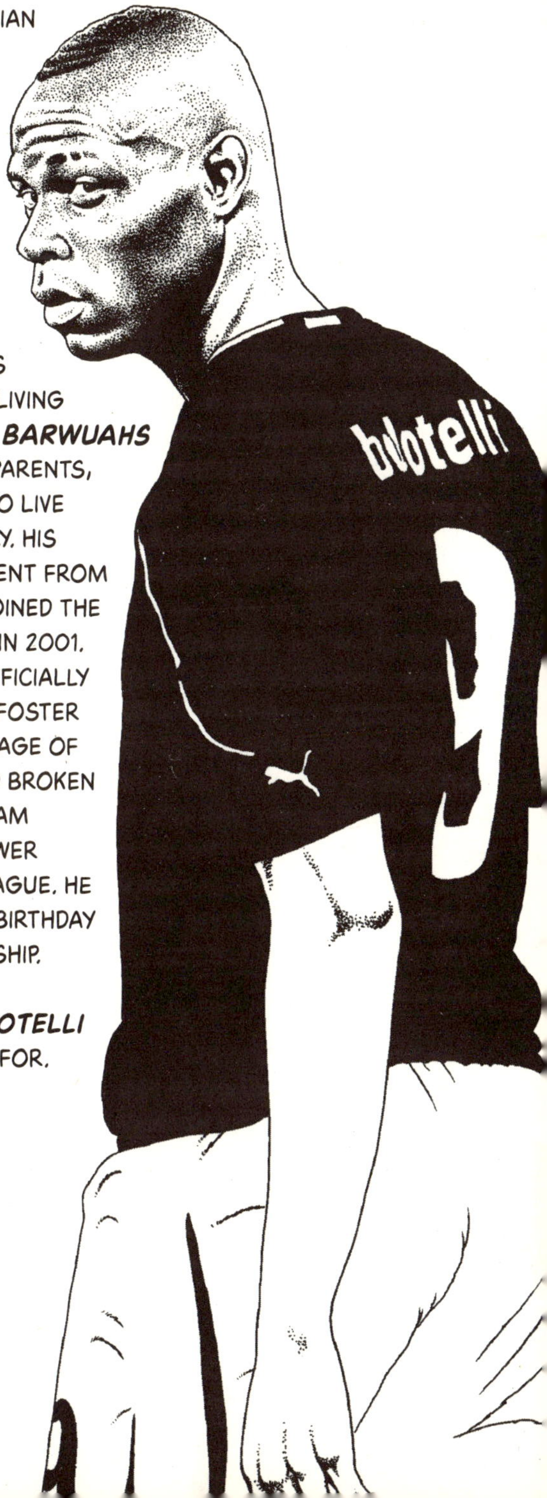

AUG
13

BORN IN NEWCASTLE ON AUGUST 13, 1970, **ALAN SHEARER** WAS 17 YEARS AND 240 DAYS OLD WHEN HE MADE HIS FULL DEBUT FOR **SOUTHAMPTON** AND BECAME THE YOUNGEST PLAYER TO SCORE AN ENGLISH TOP-FLIGHT HAT-TRICK. HE JOINED **BLACKBURN ROVERS** IN 1992, WHERE HE WON A PREMIER LEAGUE TITLE, BEFORE SIGNING FOR **NEWCASTLE UNITED** IN A WORLD RECORD £15 MILLION TRANSFER IN 1996. THREE TIMES TOP SCORER IN THE PREMIER LEAGUE, HE WAS TWICE VOTED PFA PLAYER OF THE YEAR AND IS THE PREMIER LEAGUE RECORD SCORER WITH 260 GOALS. HAVING NOTCHED A RECORD 13 GOALS IN 11 GAMES FOR **ENGLAND** AT U21 LEVEL, HE MADE HIS SENIOR DEBUT IN 1992 AND WON THE GOLDEN BOOT AT EURO 1996 WITH FIVE GOALS. HE WENT ON TO CAPTAIN HIS COUNTRY 34 TIMES, BEFORE RETIRING FROM INTERNATIONAL FOOTBALL AFTER EURO 2000.

1. WHICH MANAGER STEERED **BLACKBURN ROVERS** TO THE PREMIER LEAGUE TITLE IN 1995?

2. **SHEARER** SCORED 206 GOALS FOR **NEWCASTLE UNITED**, BREAKING THE RECORD PREVIOUSLY HELD BY WHICH CLUB LEGEND?

3. WHO SUCCEEDED **ALAN SHEARER** AS **ENGLAND** CAPTAIN?

JARED BORGETTI WAS BORN IN CULIACÁN, SINALOA, ON AUGUST 14, 1973. **MEXICO'S** SECOND ALL-TIME TOP GOALSCORER, HE BECAME THE FIRST MEXICAN TO PLAY FOR AN ENGLISH CLUB WHEN HE SIGNED FOR **BOLTON WANDERERS** IN 2005. IDENTIFY THESE MEXICAN STARS WHO HAVE PLAYED FOR PREMIER LEAGUE CLUBS:

1. **WOLVERHAMPTON WANDERERS** TOP SCORER TWO SEASONS IN A ROW, HE FRACTURED HIS SKULL IN A CLASH WITH **ARSENAL'S DAVID LUIZ** IN 2020.

2. SIGNED FROM **BARCELONA**, HE SPENT FOUR YEARS WITH T**OTTENHAM HOTSPUR**, ALTHOUGH MUCH OF THAT TIME WAS ON LOAN WITH **IPSWICH TOWN**, **GALATASARAY** AND **RACING DE SANTANDER**.

3. GOALSCORER WHO PLAYED FOR **ARSENAL** AND **WEST BROMWICH ALBION**.

AUG 15 SON OF **STOKE CITY, PORTSMOUTH** AND **ENGLAND** STAR **MARK CHAMBERLAIN, ALEX OXLADE-CHAMBERLAIN** WAS BORN IN PORTSMOUTH ON AUGUST 15, 1993. HE PLAYED RUGBY UNION AS A YOUNGSTER -- AND WAS OFFERED A TRIAL BY **LONDON IRISH** -- AND WAS AN ACCOMPLISHED CRICKETER WHO WAS OFFERED TRIALS WITH **HAMPSHIRE**. BUT FOOTBALL WAS HIS OVERRIDING PASSION AND, HAVING BEEN WITH **SOUTHAMPTON'S** ACADEMY FROM THE AGE OF SEVEN, HE ENJOYED A METEORIC RISE THROUGH THE RANKS, MAKING HIS SENIOR DEBUT AT THE AGE OF 16 YEARS AND 199 DAYS. HE JOINED ARSENAL A WEEK BEFORE HIS 18TH BIRTHDAY. IN HIS SEVEN SEASONS WITH **"THE GUNNERS"**, HE WON THREE FA CUPS AND BECAME AN **ENGLAND** REGULAR, BEFORE SIGNING FOR **LIVERPOOL** IN 2017. A SERIOUS KNEE INJURY CURTAILED HIS DEBUT SEASON AND SIDELINED HIM FOR MOST OF THE FOLLOWING SEASON AND THE SUCCESSFUL UEFA CHAMPIONS LEAGUE CAMPAIGN. RETURNING TO FULL FITNESS FOR 2019-20, HE HELPED **LIVERPOOL** TO THE PREMIER LEAGUE TITLE -- BUT A BAD KNEE INJURY THAT SUMMER HAMPERED HIS 2020-21 CONTRIBUTIONS.

IDENTIFY THESE OTHER **LIVERPOOL** SIGNINGS FROM 2017:

1. **ROMA**, £36.9M

2. **HULL CITY**, £8M

3. **SOUTHAMPTON**, £75M

AUG 16

ROQUE SANTA CRUZ WAS BORN IN ASUNCIÓN, ON AUGUST 16, 1981. FOLLOWING OUTSTANDING PERFORMANCES FOR **PARAGUAY** AT THE UNDER-20 WORLD CUP AND IN THE COPA AMÉRICA, THE 17-YEAR-OLD WAS SNAPPED UP BY **BAYERN MUNICH**. HE WON FIVE LEAGUE TITLES AND THE UEFA CHAMPIONS LEAGUE WITH THE GERMANS BEFORE JOINING **BLACKBURN ROVERS** IN 2007. IN 2009, HE FOLLOWED MANAGER **MARK HUGHES** TO **MANCHESTER CITY**. A CHANGE OF MANAGER SAW HIM FALL OUT OF FAVOUR AT **CITY**, AND HE REJOINED **BLACKBURN** ON LOAN IN 2011. HE SUBSEQUENTLY PLAYED IN SPAIN WITH **BETIS** AND **MÁLAGA**, AND IN MEXICO WITH **CRUZ AZUL**, BEFORE RETURNING TO PARAGUAY TO REJOIN HIS FIRST CLUB, **OLIMPIA**.

SANTA CRUZ IS **PARAGUAY'S** ALL-TIME LEADING GOALSCORER. WHICH PREMIER LEAGUE PLAYER HOLDS THE GOALSCORING RECORD FOR:

1. **BOSNIA AND HERZEGOVINA**

2. **IVORY COAST**

3. **CAMEROON**

4. **AUSTRALIA**

5. **BERMUDA**

6. **BELGIUM**

7. **CHILE**

AUG 17

BORN IN LES ULIS, PARIS, ON AUGUST 17, 1977, **THIERRY HENRY** BEGAN HIS CAREER AT **ARSÈNE WENGER'S MONACO**, WITH WHOM HE WON A LEAGUE TITLE IN 1997, BEFORE HE STARRED FOR **FRANCE** IN THE TRIUMPHANT 1998 WORLD CUP AND EURO 2000 CAMPAIGNS. FOLLOWING AN UNHAPPY YEAR IN ITALY, HE WAS REUNITED WITH WENGER AT **ARSENAL** AND HIS GOALS HELPED WIN A LEAGUE AND CUP DOUBLE IN 2002. TWO YEARS LATER, **ARSENAL** ROARED THROUGH THE LEAGUE CAMPAIGN UNDEFEATED, THE FIRST TIME THAT FEAT HAD BEEN ACHIEVED IN MORE THAN A CENTURY. HE JOINED **BARCELONA** IN 2007, AND HELPED THE CATALANS TO THE TREBLE OF LEAGUE, CUP AND EUROPEAN CHAMPIONS LEAGUE IN 2009, BEFORE MOVING ON TO **NEW YORK RED BULLS** IN 2010. HE MADE AN EMOTIONAL RETURN TO **ARSENAL** ON LOAN IN 2012, AND ENDED HIS PLAYING CAREER BACK IN NEW YORK BEFORE MOVING INTO MANAGEMENT.

1. **HENRY** JOINED **ARSENAL** FROM WHICH ITALIAN CLUB?

2. HE SCORED 226 GOALS FOR **ARSENAL**, SURPASSING THE 185 GOAL TALLY OF WHICH **ENGLAND** STRIKER?

3. WITH WHICH **VILLAREAL** STRIKER DID **HENRY** SHARE THE EUROPEAN GOLDEN BOOT IN 2005?

BORN IN MARRAKESH, MOROCCO, ON AUGUST 18, 1933, **JUST FONTAINE** HAD ONLY PLAYED TWICE FOR **FRANCE** BEFORE THE 1958 WORLD CUP AND WAS ONLY INCLUDED IN THE FIRST TEAM BECAUSE OF AN INJURY TO **RENÉ BILIARD.** HE WAS A SENSATION AT THE TOURNAMENT, SCORING A RECORD 13 GOALS IN SIX GAMES. AFTER THE WORLD CUP, HE MOVED FROM **NICE** TO **STADE REIMS** AND APPEARED FOR THEM IN THE 1959 EUROPEAN CUP FINAL. TWICE FRENCH LEAGUE TOP SCORER, HIS CAREER ENDED IN 1961 WHEN HE BROKE HIS LEG FOR A SECOND TIME. HIS GOAL TALLY STOOD AT 30 IN 21 INTERNATIONALS. HE LATER BECAME PRESIDENT OF THE FRENCH PLAYERS' UNION AND COACHED BOTH **FRANCE** AND **MOROCCO.**

1. **FONTAINE** SCORED FOUR GOALS AGAINST WHICH DEFENDING CHAMPIONS AT THE 1958 WORLD CUP?

2. HE WAS THE SECOND PLAYER TO SCORE IN EVERY MATCH OF A WORLD CUP, FOLLOWING **ALCIDES GHIGGIA** FOR WHICH COUNTRY?

3. WHO HOLDS THE RECORD OF 16 CAREER WORLD CUP GOALS?

AUG 19

AN ELEVENTH-HOUR BAN ON *YUGOSLAVIA* ALLOWED *DENMARK* TO COMPETE IN THE 1992 EUROPEAN CHAMPIONSHIPS -- AND THE DANES STUNNED EVERYONE BY WINNING THE TOURNAMENT! *RICHARD MØLLER NIELSEN,* THE COACH WHO STEERED DENMARK TO THAT UNLIKELY TRIUMPH, WAS BORN ON AUGUST 19, 1937. HE HAD PREVIOUSLY WON TWO LEAGUE TITLES AS COACH OF *ODENSE BK,* AND HAD COACHED BOTH THE DANISH UNDER-21 AND OLYMPIC SIDES. HE WENT ON TO COACH *FINLAND* AND *ISRAEL,* AND RETIRED IN 2003, AFTER HELMING THE DANISH SECOND DIVISION TEAM *KOLDING FC.* HE PASSED AWAY IN 2014.

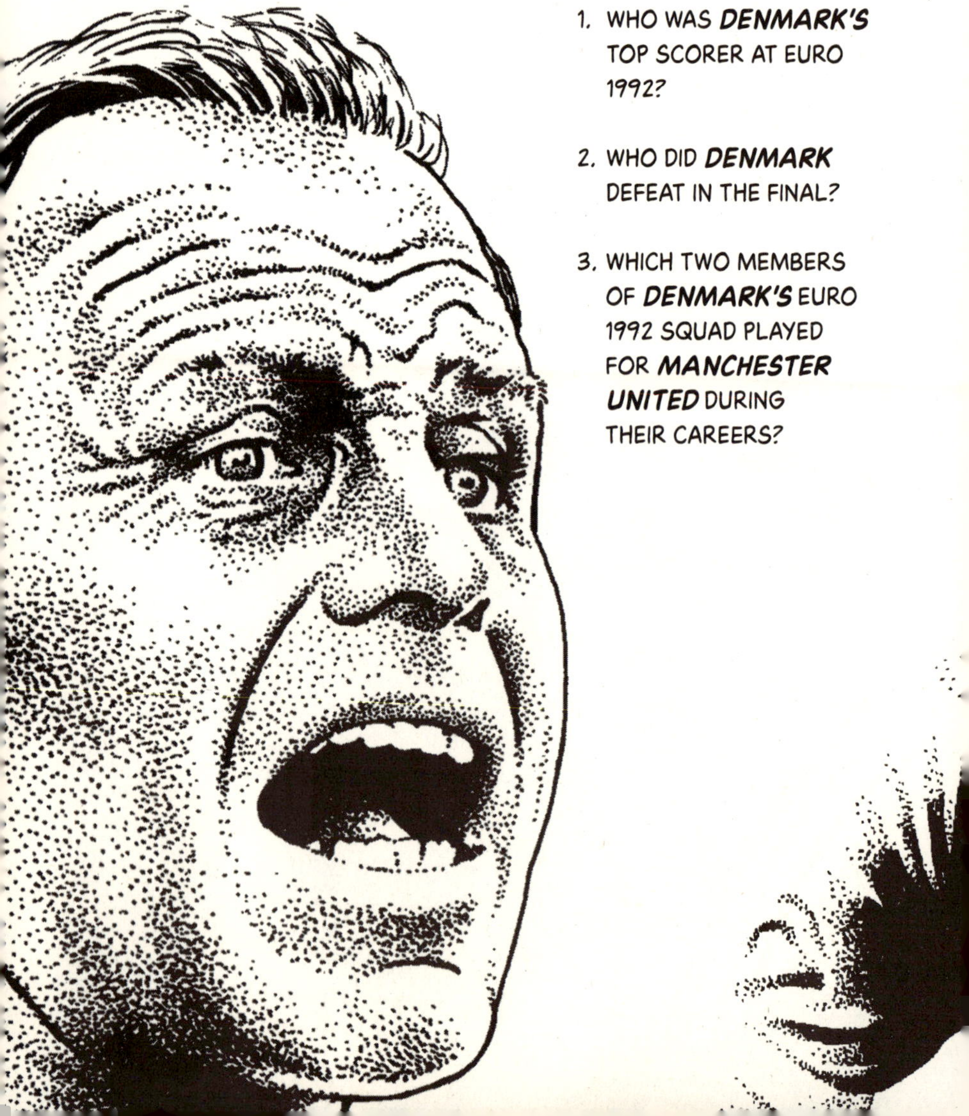

1. WHO WAS *DENMARK'S* TOP SCORER AT EURO 1992?

2. WHO DID *DENMARK* DEFEAT IN THE FINAL?

3. WHICH TWO MEMBERS OF *DENMARK'S* EURO 1992 SQUAD PLAYED FOR *MANCHESTER UNITED* DURING THEIR CAREERS?

ON AUGUST 20, 1966, DURING A TWO-WEEK TRIAL WITH *LIVERPOOL*, 15-YEAR-OLD *KENNY DALGLISH* APPEARED FOR THE CLUB'S "B" TEAM IN A 1-0 LOSS TO *SOUTHPORT*. ELEVEN YEARS TO THE DAY LATER, IN 1977, HE MADE HIS LEAGUE DEBUT FOR *LIVERPOOL*, FOLLOWING HIS £440,000 BRITISH RECORD-BREAKING TRANSFER FROM *CELTIC*. HE BECAME ONE OF THE MOST LEGENDARY FIGURES IN THE CLUB'S HISTORY, WINNING SIX LEAGUE TITLES AND THREE EUROPEAN CUPS AS A PLAYER, BEFORE STEERING THE CLUB TO A LEAGUE AND CUP DOUBLE IN HIS FIRST SEASON AS MANAGER. HE WON TWO MORE LEAGUE TITLES AND THE FA CUP BEFORE RESIGNING FROM THE POST IN 1991. 20 YEARS AFTER HIS FIRST SPELL AT THE HELM, HE RETURNED TO MANAGE *LIVERPOOL* AGAIN IN 2011.

NAME THE THREE CLUBS THAT *DALGLISH* MANAGED IN BETWEEN HIS TWO SPELLS IN CHARGE OF *LIVERPOOL*.

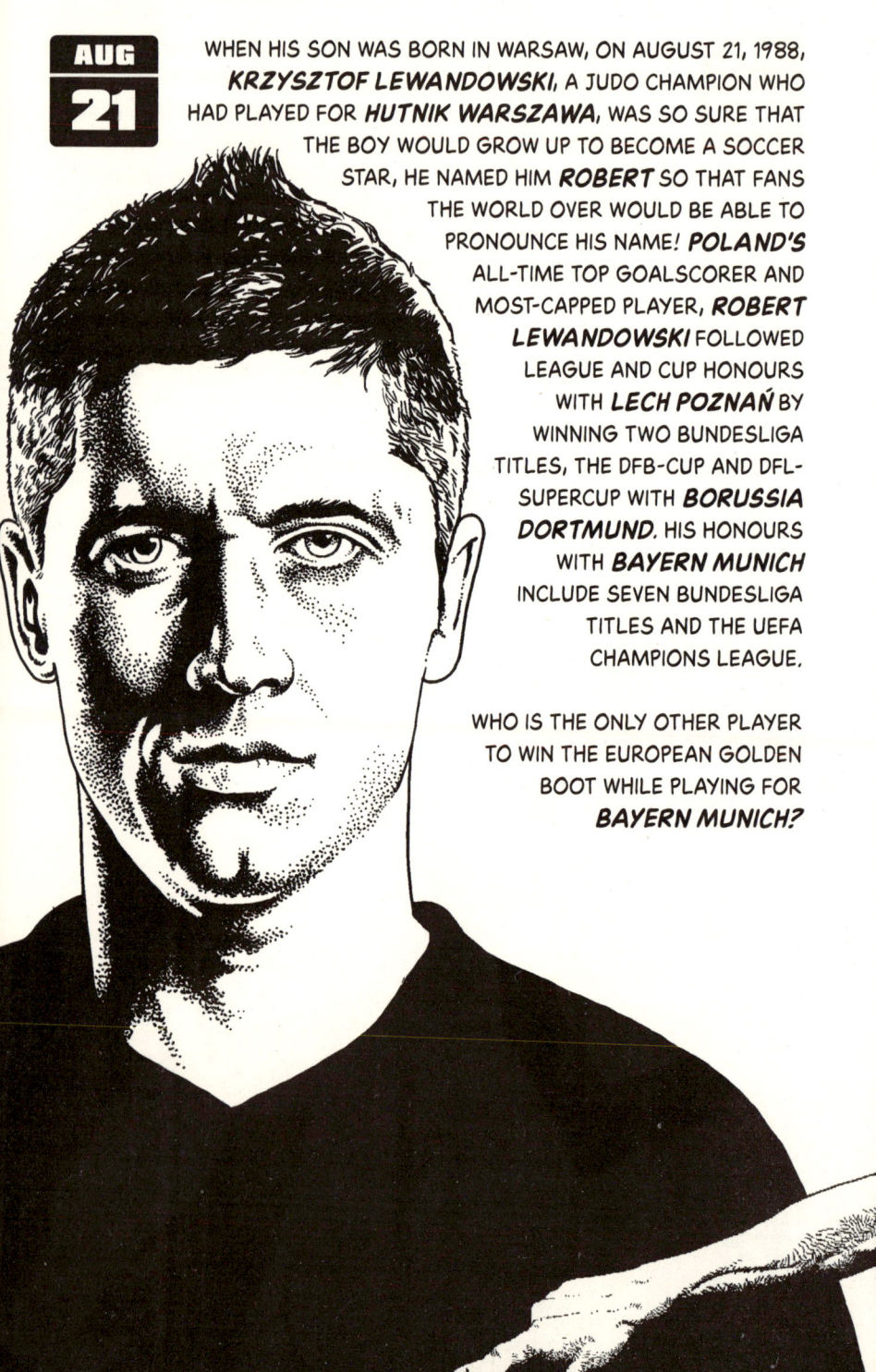

AUG 21

WHEN HIS SON WAS BORN IN WARSAW, ON AUGUST 21, 1988, *KRZYSZTOF LEWANDOWSKI*, A JUDO CHAMPION WHO HAD PLAYED FOR *HUTNIK WARSZAWA*, WAS SO SURE THAT THE BOY WOULD GROW UP TO BECOME A SOCCER STAR, HE NAMED HIM *ROBERT* SO THAT FANS THE WORLD OVER WOULD BE ABLE TO PRONOUNCE HIS NAME! *POLAND'S* ALL-TIME TOP GOALSCORER AND MOST-CAPPED PLAYER, *ROBERT LEWANDOWSKI* FOLLOWED LEAGUE AND CUP HONOURS WITH *LECH POZNAŃ* BY WINNING TWO BUNDESLIGA TITLES, THE DFB-CUP AND DFL-SUPERCUP WITH *BORUSSIA DORTMUND*. HIS HONOURS WITH *BAYERN MUNICH* INCLUDE SEVEN BUNDESLIGA TITLES AND THE UEFA CHAMPIONS LEAGUE.

WHO IS THE ONLY OTHER PLAYER TO WIN THE EUROPEAN GOLDEN BOOT WHILE PLAYING FOR *BAYERN MUNICH?*

AUG 22 BORN IN ROME ON AUGUST 22, 1991, *FEDERICO MACHEDA* BEGAN HIS CAREER AT *LAZIO* BUT WAS SIGNED BY *MANCHESTER UNITED* SHORTLY AFTER HIS 16TH BIRTHDAY. HE MADE HIS FIRST TEAM DEBUT IN A LEAGUE GAME AGAINST *ASTON VILLA* IN APRIL, 2009. COMING ON AS A SUBSTITUTE IN THE SECOND HALF WHEN *UNITED* WERE 2-1 DOWN, HE SCORED THE WINNER IN THE THIRD MINUTE OF INJURY TIME! HE FAILED TO MAKE A BREAKTHROUGH AT *OLD TRAFFORD* AND, FOLLOWING LOAN SPELLS IN ITALY, GERMANY AND ENGLAND, JOINED *CARDIFF CITY* IN 2014. THE MOVE DIDN'T WORK OUT, NOR DID SPELLS WITH *NOTTINGHAM FOREST* AND BACK IN ITALY WITH SERIE B SIDE *NOVARA*, BUT HIS 2018 TRANSFER TO *PANATHINAIKOS* OF GREECE PROVED MORE SUCCESSFUL.

IDENTIFY THESE *MANCHESTER UNITED* ITALIANS:

1. BORN IN CADERZONE, RAISED IN MANCHESTER, HE PLAYED FOR *UNITED* BETWEEN 1965 AND 1973, BEFORE JOINING *BOLOGNA*.

2. BORN IN THE UNITED STATES, HE LEFT UNITED FOR *VILLAREAL* IN 2007, AND MADE HIS DEBUT FOR *ITALY* IN 2008.

3. GOALKEEPER SIGNED FROM *VENEZIA* IN 1999.

AUG 23

BORN ON AUGUST 23, 1961, *GARY MABBUTT* JOINED *TOTTENHAM HOTSPUR* FROM *BRISTOL ROVERS* IN 1982. HE PLAYED 16 YEARS WITH *SPURS*, 11 AS CAPTAIN, DURING WHICH HE WON THE UEFA CUP AND THE FA CUP. FOLLOWING A FRACTURED SKULL AND EYE SOCKET FROM *JUSTIN FASHANU'S* ELBOW IN LATE 1993 -- AFTER WHICH HE BECAME THE FIRST PLAYER TO WEAR A PROTECTIVE MASK DURING A GAME -- A BROKEN LEG KEPT HIM OUT FOR A FULL SEASON IN 1996-97. HE RETIRED AT THE END OF THE NEXT SEASON. HE HAD MANAGED TYPE 1 DIABETES TO ENJOY A TOP-FLIGHT CAREER THAT SAW HIM CAPPED 16 TIMES BY *ENGLAND*. IN 2013, HE REQUIRED SURGERY TO SAVE HIS LEFT LEG, DIABETES HAVING LEFT HIM WITH LITTLE FEELING IN HIS FEET. IN 2018, WHILE ON A SAFARI TRIP IN SOUTH AFRICA, HE WAS FORCED TO FLY BACK TO THE UK FOR SURGERY AFTER A RAT ATE PART OF HIS FOOT WHILE HE WAS SLEEPING!

IDENTIFY THESE OTHER DIABETIC PLAYERS:

1. CAPPED 62 TIMES BY *SCOTLAND*, HE WON SEVEN LEAGUE TITLES WITH *CELTIC* AND LATER SPENT TWO SEASONS AS *ARBROATH* MANAGER.

2. *NORTHERN IRELAND* INTERNATIONAL, WHO SPENT MUCH OF HIS CAREER IN SCOTTISH FOOTBALL AFTER PLAYING FOR *MIDDLESBROUGH* AND *MANCHESTER CITY*, THEN MANAGED CLUBS INCLUDING *DUNDEE* AND *GLENTORAN*.

3. A *SPAIN* INTERNATIONAL WHO HAS WON FOUR UEFA CHAMPIONS LEAGUES WITH *REAL MADRID*.

AUG 24

BORN IN LAMBETH, LONDON, ON AUGUST 24, 1967, *MICHAEL LAURISTON THOMAS* WAS CAPTAIN OF *ENGLAND SCHOOLBOYS* AND JOINED *ARSENAL* AS A 15-YEAR-OLD. THE 1988-89 SEASON SAW HIM MAKE HIS *ENGLAND* DEBUT AND ENDED WITH HIM SCORING A SENSATIONAL LAST-MINUTE GOAL IN A TITLE-DECIDER AT *LIVERPOOL* THAT CLINCHED THE CHAMPIONSHIP. HE WON A SECOND TITLE WITH *ARSENAL* BEFORE JOINING *LIVERPOOL* IN 1991, WHERE HE WENT ON TO WIN THE LEAGUE CUP AND THE FA CUP DURING HIS SEVEN-YEAR STAY. HE ENDED HIS CAREER WITH SPELLS AT *MIDDLESBROUGH*, *BENFICA* AND *WIMBLEDON*.

IDENTIFY THESE OTHER FOOTBALLERS WHO HAVE PLAYED FOR BOTH *ARSENAL* AND *LIVERPOOL*:

1. *ENGLAND* INTERNATIONAL WHO WON THREE EUROPEAN CUPS WITH *LIVERPOOL*, LEAGUE TITLES WITH BOTH CLUBS AND THE WELSH CUP WITH *SWANSEA*.

2. EURO 2000 WINNER WITH *FRANCE*, A STRIKER WHO PLAYED IN FRANCE, ENGLAND, SPAIN, TURKEY, ITALY, CHINA AND INDIA.

3. WINGER WHOSE OTHER CLUBS INCLUDE *NOTTS COUNTY*, *STOKE CITY*, *WOLVES*, *REAL ZARAGOZA*, *WIGAN ATHLETIC*, *BIRMINGHAM CITY*, *WATFORD*, *LEEDS UNITED*, *PORTSMOUTH* AND TEAMS IN INDIA AND SINGAPORE.

ON AUGUST 25, 1990, *SPAIN* GOALKEEPER *ANDONI ZUBIZARRETA* WAS FINED $10,000 BY FIFA FOR EXCEEDING THE REGULATIONS CONCERNING SPONSORSHIP LOGOS ON HIS GLOVES AT THAT SUMMER'S WORLD CUP. THE 1987 SPANISH PLAYER OF THE YEAR MADE 126 APPEARANCES FOR *SPAIN*, REPRESENTING HIS COUNTRY AT FOUR WORLD CUPS AND THREE EUROPEAN CHAMPIONSHIPS. AT CLUB LEVEL, *ZUBIZARRETA* -- WHO BEGAN HIS CAREER AT *ALAVÉS* -- WON TWO LEAGUE TITLES, THE SPANISH CUP AND SUPERCUP WITH *ATHLETIC BILBAO*, AND FOUR LEAGUE TITLES, TWO SPANISH CUPS, TWO SPANISH SUPER CUPS, THE UEFA CHAMPIONS LEAGUE, THE UEFA CUP WINNERS' CUP AND THE UEFA SUPER CUP WITH *BARCELONA*. HIS FINAL CLUB WAS *VALENCIA* AND HE RETIRED AT THE AGE OF 37, HAVING PLAYED MORE THAN 950 GAMES DURING HIS CLUB CAREER. HE LATER SERVED AS *BARCELONA'S* DIRECTOR OF FOOTBALL.

IDENTIFY THESE GOALKEEPERS WHO HAVE EARNED MORE THAN 100 CAPS:

1. *ITALY:* 176

2. *SPAIN:* 167

3. *SWEDEN:* 143

4. *REPUBLIC OF IRELAND:* 134

THE FIRST PLAYER TO APPEAR IN FIVE FA CUP FINALS WAS
ENGLAND WINGER *JOE HULME*. HE WON IN TWO OF THE
FOUR FINALS HE PLAYED IN AS AN *ARSENAL* PLAYER -- WITH
WHOM HE ALSO GAINED THREE LEAGUE CHAMPIONSHIP MEDALS
-- BEFORE PLAYING FOR *HUDDERSFIELD* ON THE LOSING SIDE IN THE 1938
FINAL. BORN IN STAFFORD ON AUGUST 26, 1904, HE BEGAN HIS CAREER
WITH NON-LEAGUE *YORK CITY*, BEFORE JOINING *BLACKBURN ROVERS*
AS A 19-YEAR-OLD. HE SIGNED FOR *ARSENAL* TWO YEARS LATER. HE
WAS ALSO A TOP-CLASS BATSMAN WITH *MIDDLESEX* AND EXCELLED AT
BOTH BILLIARDS AND GOLF. HE LATER MANAGED *TOTTENHAM HOTSPUR*
BEFORE BECOMING A RESPECTED SPORTSWRITER.

1. WHICH *ENGLAND* DEFENDER HOLDS THE RECORD FOR MOST FA CUP
   FINAL WINS -- THREE WITH *ARSENAL* AND FOUR WITH *CHELSEA?*

2. NAME THE ONLY NON-ENGLISH TEAM TO WIN THE FA CUP.

3. NAME THE FIRST TEAM TO WIN THE FA CUP AND BE RELEGATED FROM
   THE TOP FLIGHT IN THE SAME SEASON.

JOSÉ RENÉ HIGUITA ZAPATA, THE FLAMBOYANT, UPFIELD-ROAMING, PENALTY-TAKING GOALKEEPER WHO MADE 68 APPEARANCES FOR **COLOMBIA**, WAS BORN IN MEDELLÍN ON AUGUST 27, 1966. HE WAS RENOWNED FOR HIS FREE-KICK AND PENALTY-TAKING PROWESS -- AND ACTUALLY SCORED 8 GOALS FOR HIS COUNTRY -- AND IS LEGENDARY AMONG FOOTBALL FANS WORLDWIDE FOR HIS EXTRAORDINARY **"SCORPION"** KICK, WHERE HE WOULD LEAP FORWARD, ARCH HIS LEGS OVER HIS HEAD AND KICK THE BALL WITH HIS HEELS! HE PLAYED FOR CLUBS IN COLOMBIA, MEXICO, ECUADOR, SPAIN AND VENEZUELA, AND FINALLY RETIRED IN 2010. HIS PERSONAL LIFE HAS PROVED EXCEPTIONALLY COLOURFUL. HE WAS JAILED IN 1993 AFTER ACTING AS A GO-BETWEEN IN A KIDNAPPING CASE INVOLVING NOTORIOUS CARTEL BOSS **PABLO ESCOBAR**, TESTED POSITIVE FOR COCAINE WHILE PLAYING IN ECUADOR, AND UNDERWENT MAJOR PLASTIC SURGERY, RADICALLY ALTERING HIS APPEARANCE!

HIGUITA'S NICKNAME WAS **"EL LOCO"**. WHICH PLAYERS ARE KNOWN BY THE FOLLOWING NICKNAMES:

1. **"THE GALLOPING MAJOR"**

2. **"THE NON-FLYING DUTCHMAN"**

3. **"EL BUITRE" (THE VULTURE)**

4. **"THE KAISER"**

AUG 28

EMLYN HUGHES WAS BORN IN BARROW-IN-FURNESS ON AUGUST 28, 1947. HE BEGAN HIS CARER AT **BLACKPOOL** AND WAS STILL IN HIS TEENS WHEN **BILL SHANKLY** SIGNED HIM TO **LIVERPOOL**. NICKNAMED **"CRAZY HORSE"**, **HUGHES** MADE 665 APPEARANCES IN HIS 12 YEARS AT THE CLUB, WINNING A HOST OF HONOURS, INCLUDING TWO EUROPEAN CUPS, TWO UEFA CUPS, FOUR LEAGUE TITLES AND AN FA CUP. HE PLAYED 62 TIMES FOR **ENGLAND**, CAPTAINING HIS COUNTRY ON 23 OCCASIONS. IN RETIREMENT, HE WORKED AS A RADIO AND TV PUNDIT AND WAS A CAPTAIN ON THE POPULAR TV QUIZ SHOW **"A QUESTION OF SPORT"**. HE DIED OF A BRAIN TUMOUR IN 2004, AT THE AGE OF 57.

1. WITH WHICH CLUB DID HE WIN THE 1980 LEAGUE CUP?

2. NAME ONE OF THE OTHER CLUBS FOR WHOM **HUGHES** PLAYED.

3. WHICH CARETAKER BOSS MADE **HUGHES ENGLAND** CAPTAIN IN 1974?

AUG 29

NIGERIA'S MOST-CAPPED PLAYER OF ALL TIME, **VINCENT ENYEAMA** WAS BORN IN ABA, ABIA STATE, ON AUGUST 29, 1982. MUCH OF HIS CAREER WAS DIVIDED BETWEEN FRENCH CLUB **LILLE** AND PLAYING FOR TEAMS IN ISRAEL, WHERE HE WAS NAMED FOOTBALLER OF THE YEAR OF ISRAEL IN 2009.

IDENTIFY THESE OTHER PLAYERS NAMED FOOTBALLER OF THE YEAR OF ISRAEL:

1. **ISRAEL'S** MOST-CAPPED PLAYER OF ALL TIME, HIS CLUBS INCLUDED **WEST HAM UNITED, LIVERPOOL, CHELSEA, ARSENAL** AND **QUEENS PARK RANGERS.**

2. HE PLAYED FOR **CELTIC, BLACKBURN ROVERS, MANCHESTER CITY** AND **PORTSMOUTH,** AFTER HIS TIME AT **WEST HAM UNITED** WAS MARKED BY A WELL-PUBLICISED CLASH WITH **JOHN HARTSON.**

3. WINNER OF HONOURS WITH **LIVERPOOL** AND **RANGERS,** HE DIED AFTER A ROAD ACCIDENT IN 2010, FOLLOWING WHICH HIS FOOTBALLER SON CELEBRATED SCORING A WINNER FOR **BOLTON WANDERERS** AGAINST **ARSENAL** BY REVEALING A T-SHIRT SHOWING HIS DAD'S FACE.

BORN IN CHEB, CZECHOSLOVAKIA, ON AUGUST 30, 1972, **PAVEL NEDVĚD** BEGAN HIS CAREER WITH **DUKLA PRAGUE,** MOVING ACROSS THE CAPITAL AFTER JUST ONE SEASON TO **SPARTA PRAGUE.** HE WON THREE TITLES AND A CUP WITH THE CLUB, BEFORE HIS PERFORMANCES FOR THE **CZECH REPUBLIC** TEAM THAT FINISHED RUNNERS-UP AT EURO '96 EARNED HIM A MOVE TO **LAZIO.** HIS HONOURS AT **LAZIO** INCLUDED A SERIE A TITLE AND THE UEFA CUP WINNERS' CUP. HE JOINED **JUVENTUS** IN 2001, AND WON FOUR CONSECUTIVE LEAGUE TITLES *(ALTHOUGH THE LAST TWO WERE REVOKED IN THE WAKE OF A MATCH-RIGGING SCANDAL.)* HIS INDIVIDUAL HONOURS INCLUDED THE SERIE A FOOTBALLER OF THE YEAR AND BALLON D'OR EUROPEAN FOOTBALLER OF THE YEAR AWARD IN 2003. AFTER RETIRING IN 2009, HE WAS APPOINTED TO THE **JUVENTUS** BOARD OF DIRECTORS.

1. HE WAS THE SECOND CZECH TO WIN THE BALLON D'OR -- WHO WAS THE FIRST?

2. NAME THE SUBSEQUENT MANAGER OF **ENGLAND** WHO COACHED **NEDVĚD** AT **LAZIO.**

3. NAME THE MANAGER WHO STEERED **NEDVĚD** AND **JUVENTUS** TO SERIE A TITLES IN 2003 AND 2004.

WAYNE ROONEY BECAME THE WORLD'S MOST EXPENSIVE TEENAGER WHEN HE JOINED **MANCHESTER UNITED** FROM **EVERTON** ON AUGUST 31, 2004, IN A DEAL WORTH AS MUCH AS £27 MILLION. THE TRANSFER HAD BEEN COMPLICATED BY THE INJURY THAT **ROONEY** WAS CARRYING, A BROKEN METATARSAL SUSTAINED AT EURO 2004. HE RECOVERED IN TIME TO MAKE HIS DEBUT ON SEPTEMBER 28 IN A UEFA CHAMPIONS LEAGUE CLASH WITH **FENERBAHÇE**, A GAME THAT **UNITED** WON 6-2 ... AND IN WHICH **ROONEY** SCORED A HAT-TRICK!

FROM WHICH CLUBS DID THESE PLAYERS MOVE IN THE SUMMER OF 2004:

1. **DIDIER DROGBA** TO **CHELSEA**

2. **MARK VIDUKA** TO **MIDDLESBROUGH**

3. **XABI ALONSO** TO **LIVERPOOL**

4. **DJIBRIL CISSÉ** TO **LIVERPOOL**

5. **JONATHAN WOODGATE** TO **REAL MADRID**

6. **ZOLTAN GERA** TO **WEST BROMWICH ALBION**

SEPTEMBER

SEP 1

BORN IN AMSTERDAM ON SEPTEMBER 1, 1962, **RUUD GULLIT** MADE HIS DEBUT FOR **NETHERLANDS** AT THE AGE OF 19, WHILE PLAYING FOR **HAARLEM**. AFTER SPELLS AT **FEYENOORD** AND **PSV EINDHOVEN**, HE JOINED **AC MILAN** FOR A WORLD RECORD US$10 MILLION IN 1987, THE YEAR HE WAS VOTED BOTH WORLD AND EUROPEAN FOOTBALLER OF THE YEAR. IN 1988, HE WON A SERIE A TITLE WITH MILAN AND CAPTAINED HIS COUNTRY TO VICTORY IN THE UEFA EUROPEAN CHAMPIONSHIP. HAVING SPENT TWO SPELLS AT **SAMPDORIA**, HE MOVED TO **CHELSEA**, WHERE HE SOON BECAME PLAYER/MANAGER.

1. WHO DID **RUUD GULLIT** SUCCEED AS **CHELSEA** MANAGER?

2. NAME TWO OTHER CLUBS THAT **GULLIT** MANAGED.

3. **GULLIT** WAS EUROPEAN FOOTBALLER OF THE YEAR IN 1987. THE FOLLOWING YEAR, HE WAS RUNNER-UP TO WHICH **AC MILAN** AND **NETHERLANDS** TEAMMATE ?

SEP 2

NAMED **COLOMBIA'S** PLAYER OF THE CENTURY, **CARLOS ALBERTO VALDERRAMA PALACIO** WAS BORN IN SANTA MARTA ON SEPTEMBER 2, 1961. HE PLAYED IN THREE WORLD CUPS AND FIVE COPA AMÉRICAS, AND WAS TWICE VOTED SOUTH AMERICAN PLAYER OF THE YEAR. **"EL PIBE"** -- WHICH MEANS **"THE KID"** -- BEGAN HIS CAREER WITH **UNION MAGDALENA** AND HIS TRAVELS TOOK HIM TO CLUBS IN EUROPE AND THE US, AS WELL AS NUMEROUS COLOMBIAN TEAMS. HE MADE A RECORD 111 APPEARANCES FOR **COLOMBIA**. IN 2006, A BRONZE STATUE OF **VALDERRAMA** WAS PLACED OUTSIDE A STADIUM IN HIS HOMETOWN OF SANTA MARTA.

VALDERRAMA WON THE INAUGURAL MLS MVP AWARD IN 1996 WITH **TAMPA BAY MUTINY**. IDENTIFY THESE OTHER RECIPIENTS OF THE AWARD:

1. **SPAIN'S** ALL-TIME TOP GOALSCORER, EURO 2008 AND 2010 WORLD CUP WINNER, UEFA CHAMPIONS LEAGUE WINNER WITH **BARCELONA**.

2. **REPUBLIC OF IRELAND** TOP SCORER AND MOST-CAPPED PLAYER.

3. GOALKEEPER WHO WON A CENTURY OF **USA** CAPS AND HAD BRIEF SPELLS WITH **BRIGHTON & HOVE ALBION** AND **WATFORD**.

SEP 3

THE SON OF URUGUAYAN INTERNATIONAL *JULIO MONTERO CASTILLO*, WHO PLAYED AT THE 1970 AND 1974 WORLD CUPS, *PAOLO MONTERO* WAS BORN IN MONTEVIDEO, ON SEPTEMBER 3, 1971. HE BEGAN HIS CAREER AT *PEÑAROL*, BEFORE MOVING TO ITALY WITH *ATALANTA*. HE SPENT FOUR YEARS AT THE CLUB BEFORE JOINING *JUVENTUS*, WHERE HE WON A HOST OF HONOURS, INCLUDING FOUR SERIE A TITLES. AN UNCOMPROMISING HARDMAN, BY THE TIME HE LEFT FOR ARGENTINIAN CLUB *SAN LORENZO* IN 2005, HE HAD SET THE SERIE A RECORD FOR RED CARDS RECEIVED. HE RETURNED TO *PEÑAROL* FOR A SEASON BEFORE RETIRING IN 2007. HIS MANAGEMENT CV INCLUDES A SPELL AS *PEÑAROL* INTERIM MANAGER.

IDENTIFY THE FOLLOWING FORMER *PEÑAROL* PLAYERS:

1. *URUGUAY* INTERNATIONAL WHO PLAYED FOR *SOUTHAMPTON* AND *HULL CITY*, HE EXPERIENCED PROMOTION AND RELEGATION WITH *MIDDLESBROUGH* BEFORE LEAVING FOR *SAMPDORIA*.

2. *DAVID MOYES'S* FIRST SIGNING FOR *MANCHESTER UNITED*, WON A LEAGUE TITLE WITH *COPENHAGEN* IN 2019.

3. GOLDEN BALL WINNER AT THE 2010 WORLD CUP, THE FIRST URUGUAYAN TO WIN 100 CAPS, HE WON A PREMIER LEAGUE WITH *MANCHESTER UNITED*.

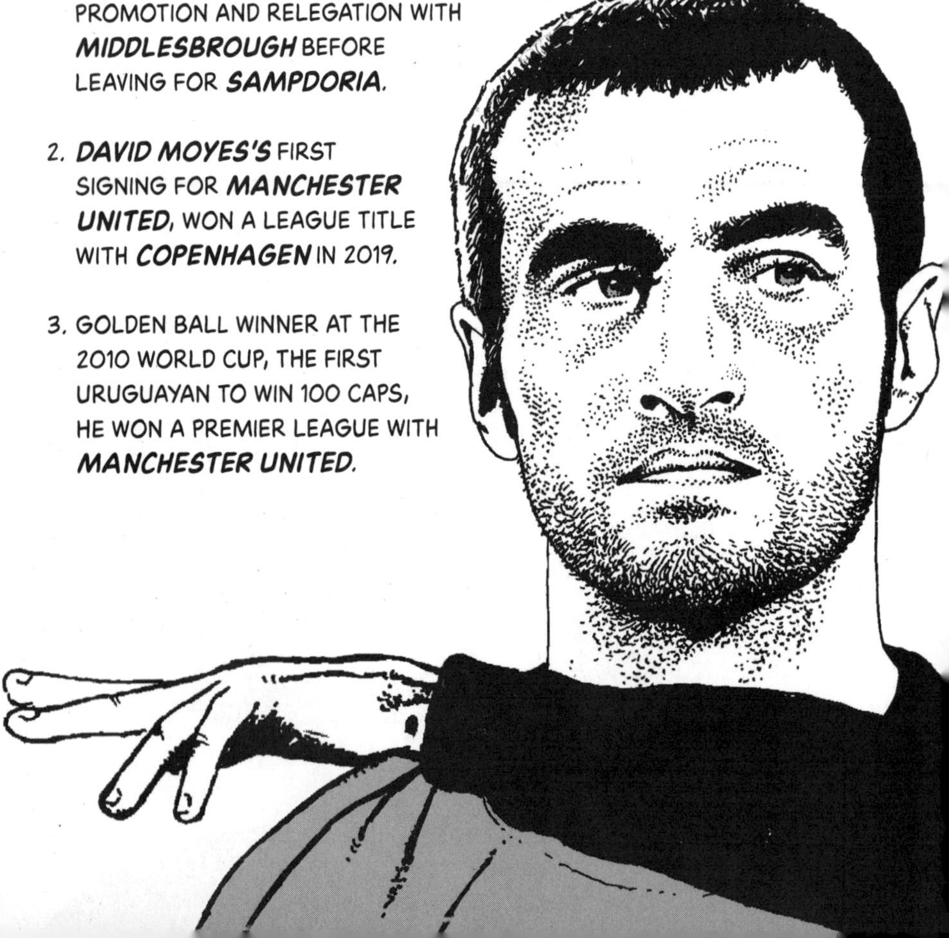

BORN IN ROESELARE ON SEPTEMBER 4, 1965, **MARC DEGRYSE** WON THE FIRST OF HIS 63 **BELGIUM** CAPS AT THE AGE OF 19. PLAYING FOR **CLUB BRUGGE** AND THEN **ANDERLECHT**, HE WON FIVE LEAGUE TITLES BEFORE JOINING **SHEFFIELD WEDNESDAY** IN THE SUMMER OF 1995. DURING HIS TIME WITH THE SOUTH YORKSHIRE CLUB, HE HAD A CAMEO ROLE IN **"THE FULL MONTY"**, ALTHOUGH HIS SCENES DIDN'T MAKE THE FILM'S FINAL CUT. HE MOVED ON TO **PSV**, WHERE HE ADDED A DUTCH LEAGUE TITLE TO HIS HAUL OF SILVERWARE, BEFORE HEADING BACK TO BELGIUM TO PLAY FOR **GENT**, AND THEN **GERMINAL BEERSCHOT**, BEFORE RETIRING IN 2002.

DURING HIS ONE SEASON WITH **SHEFFIELD WEDNESDAY**, **DEGRYSE** BECAME THE FIRST NON-BRITISH PLAYER TO WIN THE CLUB'S PLAYER OF THE YEAR AWARD. IDENTIFY THESE OTHER RECIPIENTS:

1. **ENGLAND** INTERNATIONAL WHO WON IN 1993, HIS PREVIOUS CLUBS WERE **NEWCASTLE UNITED**, **TOTTENHAM HOTSPUR** AND **MARSEILLE**. HE LATER MANAGED **BURNLEY**.

2. **REPUBLIC OF IRELAND** GOALKEEPER WHO HAS WON TWICE, IN 2015 AND 2017.

3. CONTROVERSIAL ITALIAN WHOSE CLUBS INCLUDED **CELTIC**, **WEST HAM UNITED**, **CHARLTON ATHLETIC**, **NAPOLI**, **AC MILAN**, **JUVENTUS** AND **LAZIO**. HE WON IN 1998.

SEP 5 YOUNG **CELTIC** GOALKEEPER **JOHN THOMSON** WAS BADLY INJURED IN A GAME AGAINST **AIRDRIEONIANS** IN EARLY 1930, BREAKING HIS JAW, FRACTURING SEVERAL RIBS, DAMAGING HIS COLLAR BONE, AND LOSING TWO TEETH WHEN MAKING A DIVING SAVE. HE RECOVERED SUFFICIENTLY TO MAKE HIS DEBUT FOR **SCOTLAND** THREE MONTHS LATER. ON SEPTEMBER 5, 1931, FIVE MINUTES INTO THE SECOND HALF OF THE 1931 "AULD FIRM" DERBY BETWEEN **CELTIC** AND **RANGERS**, **THOMSON** COLLIDED WITH **RANGERS** FORWARD **SAM ENGLISH** AND SUFFERED A FRACTURED SKULL. HE WAS RUSHED TO HOSPITAL WHERE A SURGEON BATTLED TO SAVE HIS LIFE, BUT THE 23-YEAR-OLD NEVER REGAINED CONSCIOUSNESS AND DIED LATER THAT EVENING. 30,000 JAMMED THE STREETS FOR HIS FUNERAL, MANY WALKING THE 55 MILES FROM GLASGOW TO HIS RESTING PLACE IN CARDENDEN. TO THIS DAY, HIS GRAVE REMAINS A PLACE OF PILGRIMAGE FOR **CELTIC** SUPPORTERS.

1. NAME THE **MACHESTER UNITED** GOALKEEPER WHOSE CHEEKBONE WAS BROKEN IN A CHALLENGE BY **ASTON VILLA** FORWARD **PETER MCPARLAND** DURING THE 1957 FA CUP FINAL.

2. NAME THE **CHELSEA** GOALKEEPER WHOSE SKULL WAS FRACTURED IN A 2006 GAME AGAINST **READING**, AND WHO SUBSEQUENTLY WORE PROTECTIVE HEADGEAR FOR THE REST OF HIS CAREER.

3. NAME THE **WOLVERHAMPTON WANDERERS** GOALKEEPER STRETCHERED OFF AGAINST **LIVERPOOL** IN 2021 AFTER RECEIVING A HEAD INJURY IN A COLLISION WITH HIS OWN PLAYER.

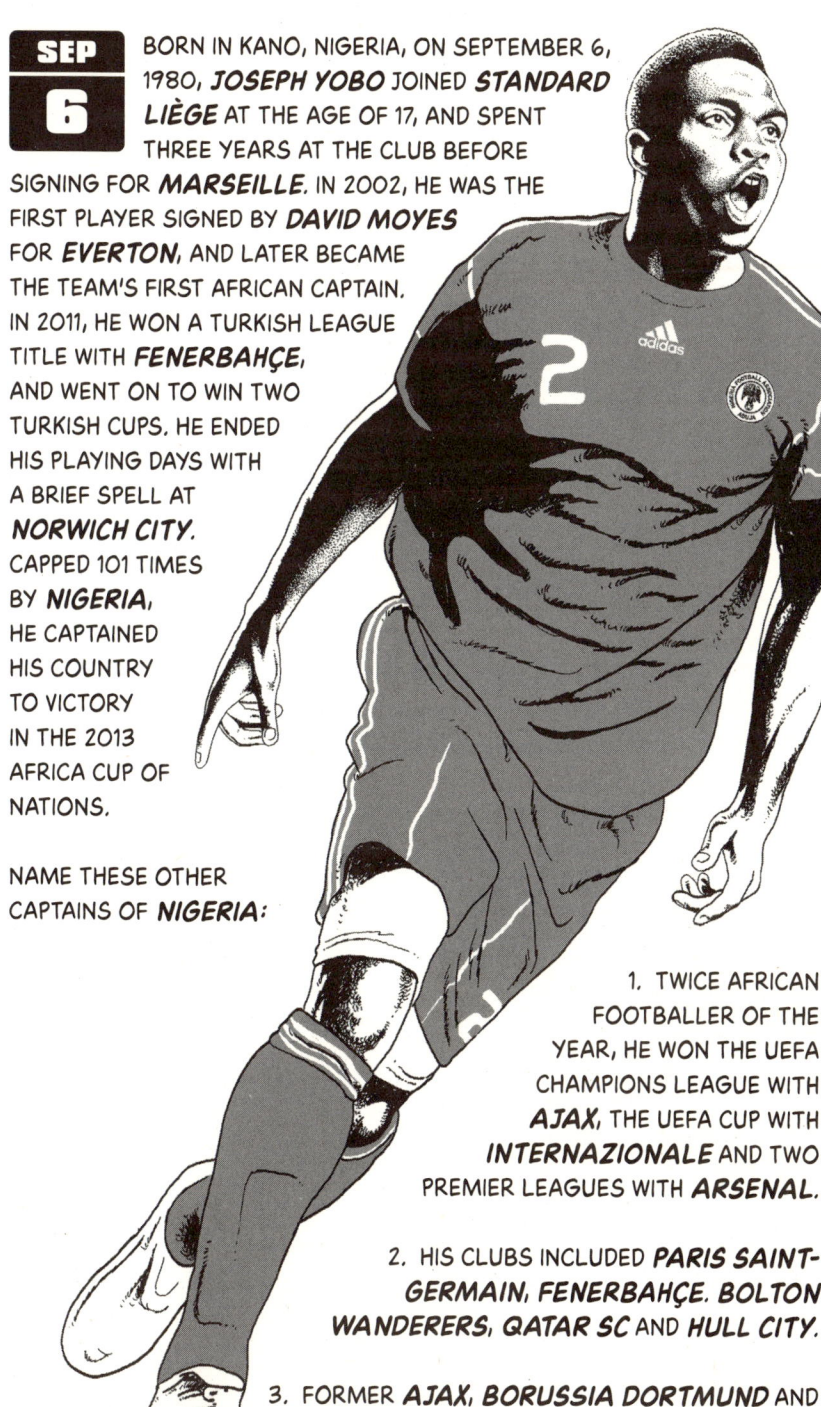

SEP 6

BORN IN KANO, NIGERIA, ON SEPTEMBER 6, 1980, *JOSEPH YOBO* JOINED *STANDARD LIÈGE* AT THE AGE OF 17, AND SPENT THREE YEARS AT THE CLUB BEFORE SIGNING FOR *MARSEILLE*. IN 2002, HE WAS THE FIRST PLAYER SIGNED BY *DAVID MOYES* FOR *EVERTON*, AND LATER BECAME THE TEAM'S FIRST AFRICAN CAPTAIN. IN 2011, HE WON A TURKISH LEAGUE TITLE WITH *FENERBAHÇE*, AND WENT ON TO WIN TWO TURKISH CUPS. HE ENDED HIS PLAYING DAYS WITH A BRIEF SPELL AT *NORWICH CITY*. CAPPED 101 TIMES BY *NIGERIA*, HE CAPTAINED HIS COUNTRY TO VICTORY IN THE 2013 AFRICA CUP OF NATIONS.

NAME THESE OTHER CAPTAINS OF *NIGERIA*:

1. TWICE AFRICAN FOOTBALLER OF THE YEAR, HE WON THE UEFA CHAMPIONS LEAGUE WITH *AJAX*, THE UEFA CUP WITH *INTERNAZIONALE* AND TWO PREMIER LEAGUES WITH *ARSENAL*.

2. HIS CLUBS INCLUDED *PARIS SAINT-GERMAIN*, *FENERBAHÇE*, *BOLTON WANDERERS*, *QATAR SC* AND *HULL CITY*.

3. FORMER *AJAX*, *BORUSSIA DORTMUND* AND *JUVENTUS* STAR WENT ON TO COACH *NIGERIA*.

SEP 7 FOLLOWING CONTROVERSY SURROUNDING A GOALSCORING SPREE IN CYPRUS FOOTBALL, THE EUROPEAN GOLDEN BOOT -- ALSO KNOWN AS THE GOLDEN SHOE -- WAS NOT OFFICIALLY AWARDED FOR A PERIOD OF A FEW YEARS IN THE EARLY '90S. DESPITE FINISHING EUROPE'S TOP SCORER WITH 34 GOALS IN 1990-91, *RED STAR BELGRADE* STRIKER *DARKO PANČEV* WAS DENIED THE AWARD. THE SITUATION WAS REMEDIED IN 2006, WHEN *PANČEV* RECEIVED HIS TROPHY FROM UEFA PRESIDENT *MICHEL PLATINI* IN A SPECIALLY STAGED CEREMONY IN *DARKO'S* HOMETOWN OF SKOPJE, MACEDONIA. BORN ON SEPTEMBER 7, 1965, *DARKO PANČEV* MADE HIS NAME AT *VARDAR SKOPJE*, BEFORE JOINING *RED STAR BELGRADE*, WITH WHOM HE WON THE EUROPEAN CUP. HE SIGNED FOR *INTERNAZIONALE* IN 2002, A TRANSFER THAT HE WOULD LATER DECRY AS HIS *"GREATEST FOOTBALL MISTAKE"*. THE MOVE WAS A DISASTER, LACK OF GAME TIME EFFECTIVELY DERAILING HIS CAREER. FOLLOWING SPELLS AT CLUBS IN POLAND, GERMANY AND SWITZERLAND, HE RETIRED IN 1997.

IDENTIFY THESE FORMER *RED STAR BELGRADE* PLAYERS:

1. *SERBIA* DEFENDER, WON TWO LEAGUE TITLES WITH *MANCHESTER CITY* AFTER JOINING FROM *LAZIO*, MOVED ON TO *ROMA* AND WAS A SERIE A WINNER WITH *INTERNAZIONALE* IN 2021.

2. *SERBIA* DEFENSIVE MIDFIELDER WHO WON LEAGUE TITLES WITH *BENFICA* AND *CHELSEA* BEFORE SIGNING FOR *MANCHESTER UNITED* IN 2017.

3. *SERBIA* CENTRE-BACK WHO WON FIVE PREMIER LEAGUES AND THE UEFA CHAMPIONS LEAGUE WITH *MANCHESTER UNITED* BEFORE JOINING *INTERNAZIONALE* IN 2014.

SEP 8

A PACY STRIKER WHO ESTABLISHED HIS GOALSCORING CREDENTIALS WITH **HALIFAX TOWN, NORTHAMPTON TOWN** AND **PETERBOROUGH UNITED, DAVID LONGHURST** JOINED **YORK CITY** IN 1990. ON SEPTEMBER 8, 1990, IN A GAME AGAINST **LINCOLN CITY**, THE 25-YEAR-OLD SUFFERED A HEART ATTACK ON THE FIELD AND WAS PRONOUNCED DEAD ON ARRIVAL AT HOSPITAL. HE WAS THE FIRST PLAYER TO DIE IN A FOOTBALL LEAGUE GAME IN 63 YEARS, FOLLOWING THE DEATH OF **BURY** DEFENDER **SAM WYNNE** IN 1927. THE INQUEST INTO **DAVID'S** DEATH REVEALED HE SUFFERED FROM A RARE HEART CONDITION.

IDENTIFY THESE OTHER DEATHS IN THE WORLD OF FOOTBALL IN 1990:

1. LEGENDARY **SOVIET UNION** GOALKEEPER WHO APPEARED IN FOUR WORLD CUPS, DEAD AT THE AGE OF 60.

2. WON LEAGUE TITLES WITH **ARSENAL** AND **EVERTON** AS A PLAYER, MANAGED **MANCHESTER CITY** TO MULTIPLE HONOURS AND WAS CARETAKER MANAGER OF **ENGLAND**.

3. A WORLD CUP WINNER WITH ITALY IN 1934, HE IS **BOLOGNA'S** HIGHEST GOALSCORER AND LATER MANAGED BOTH **BOLOGNA** AND THE **ITALY** NATIONAL TEAM.

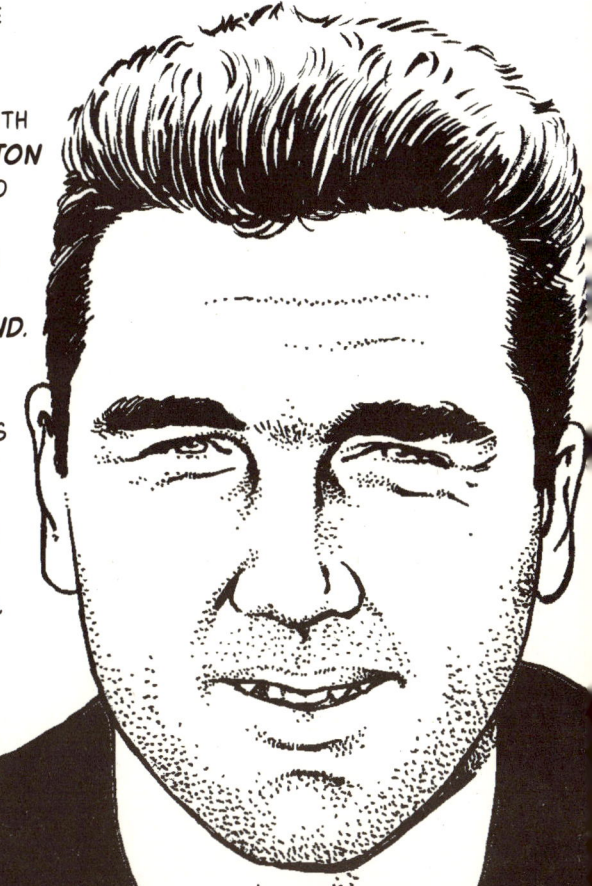

SEP 9

ROBERTO DONADONI WAS BORN IN CISANO BERGAMASCO, ON SEPTEMBER 9, 1963. HE BEGAN HIS CAREER AT **ATALANTA**, BEFORE JOINING **AC MILAN** IN 1986, WHERE HIS HONOURS INCLUDED SIX SERIE A TITLES AND THREE EUROPEAN CUPS/CHAMPIONS LEAGUES. HE LATER PLAYED FOR TWO SEASONS IN THE STATES WITH **NEW YORK/NEW JERSEY METROSTARS**, BEFORE ENDING HIS CAREER WITH A SEASON AT **AL-ITTIHAD**, WITH WHOM HE WON THE SAUDI PREMIER LEAGUE. HIS MANAGEMENT CAREER HAS TAKEN IN SPELLS WITH A NUMBER OF ITALIAN CLUBS AND CHINA'S **SHENZEN**. CAPPED 63 TIMES BY **ITALY**, HE IS ONE OF A NUMBER OF FORMER **ITALY** INTERNATIONALS WHO HAVE COACHED THE NATIONAL TEAM SINCE THE SECOND WORLD WAR. CAN YOU NAME THESE OTHERS?

1. **JUVENTUS** LEGEND AS A PLAYER, AS A MANAGER HE HAS WON LEAGUE TITLES WITH **JUVENTUS, CHELSEA** AND **INTERNAZIONALE**.

2. COACHED **MANCHESTER CITY** TO THE CLUB'S FIRST TOP-FLIGHT TROPHY IN 44 YEARS.

3. WORLD CUP-WINNING GOALKEEPER WHO WON THE UEFA CUP AS MANAGER OF **JUVENTUS**.

SEP 10

ANDREAS HERZOG WAS BORN IN VIENNA, AUSTRIA, ON SEPTEMBER 10, 1968. HE BEGAN HIS CAREER AT **RAPID VIENNA**, WHERE HE WON TWO LEAGUE TITLES, BUT SPENT MANY YEARS IN GERMAN FOOTBALL, WINNING THE BUNDESLIGA WITH **WERDER BREMEN** AND THE UEFA CUP WITH **BAYERN MUNICH**. CAPPED A RECORD 103 TIMES BY **AUSTRIA**, HE ENDED HIS PLAYING DAYS IN THE US WITH **LOS ANGELES GALAXY**. HIS MANAGEMENT CAREER HAS INCLUDED PERIODS AS ASSISTANT COACH TO THE **AUSTRIA** AND **UNITED STATES** NATIONAL TEAMS, AND **ISRAEL** MANAGER, A CONTROVERSIAL APPOINTMENT AS IT WAS HIS LAST-MINUTE GOAL THAT DENIED **ISRAEL** A 2002 WORLD CUP PLAY-OFF BERTH!

IDENTIFY THESE OTHER **AUSTRIA** INTERNATIONALS:

1. FORWARD WHO PLAYED FOR **STOKE CITY** AND **WEST HAM UNITED** BEFORE JOINING CHINA'S **SHANGHAI PORT** IN 2019.

2. LEFT BACK WHO HAS WON THE PREMIER LEAGUE AND THE FA CUP WITH **LEICESTER CITY**, FORMER **AUSTRIA** CAPTAIN.

3. GOALKEEPER WHO DEPUTISED FOR **DAVID SEAMAN** AT **ARSENAL**, WINNING A LEAGUE AND FA CUP DOUBLE IN 1998 BEFORE WINNING A SERIE A TITLE WITH **JUVENTUS** IN 2012.

SEP 11

BORN IN MUNICH ON SEPTEMBER 11, 1945, *FRANZ BECKENBAUER* WON THE FIRST OF HIS 103 CAPS AT THE AGE OF 20, AFTER JUST 27 SENIOR GAMES FOR *BAYERN MUNICH*. A LOSING FINALIST IN 1966, HE CAPTAINED HIS COUNTRY TO WORLD CUP GLORY IN 1974, HAVING PERFECTED THE ROLE OF ATTACKING SWEEPER. TWO YEARS EARLIER, HE HAD LED *WEST GERMANY* TO VICTORY IN THE EUROPEAN CHAMPIONSHIPS. TWICE EUROPEAN FOOTBALLER OF THE YEAR, HE WON FOUR LEAGUE TITLES, FOUR WEST GERMAN CUPS, THREE EUROPEAN CUPS AND THE EUROPEAN CUP-WINNERS' CUP WITH *BAYERN MUNICH*, AND THEN HELPED THE *NEW YORK COSMOS* WIN TWO NASL TITLES, BEFORE RETURNING TO GERMANY TO CAPTURE THE 1982 LEAGUE CROWN WITH *HAMBURG*. APPOINTED NATIONAL COACH IN 1984, *"KAISER FRANZ"* BOWED OUT IN GLORY AFTER STEERING *GERMANY* TO TRIUMPH IN THE 1990 WORLD CUP. HE WENT ON TO COACH *MARSEILLE* TO A TITLE AND *BAYERN MUNICH* TO A BUNDESLIGA TITLE AND THE UEFA CUP.

BECKENBAUER IS ONE OF ONLY THREE MEN TO WIN THE WORLD CUP AS A PLAYER AND A COACH. NAME THE OTHER TWO.

SEP 12

BORN IN MANSFIELD ON SEPTEMBER 12, 1957, *STEVE OGRIZOVIC* LAUNCHED HIS CAREER AT *CHESTERFIELD*, WAS UNABLE TO BREAK INTO THE FIRST TEAM AT *LIVERPOOL* AND SPENT TWO SEASONS WITH *CHESTERFIELD*, WHERE HE ALSO TURNED OUT AS A BOWLER FOR *SHROPSHIRE COUNTY CRICKET CLUB*. HE FINALLY MADE HIS MARK AT *COVENTRY CITY*, WHERE HE ACHIEVED LEGENDARY STATUS, PLAYING IN A RECORD 601 GAMES OVER 16 YEARS, INCLUDING THE 1987 FA CUP FINAL WIN OVER *TOTTENHAM HOTSPUR*.

NAME THREE OF THE MANAGERS UNDER WHOM *OGRIZOVIC* PLAYED AT *COVENTRY CITY*.

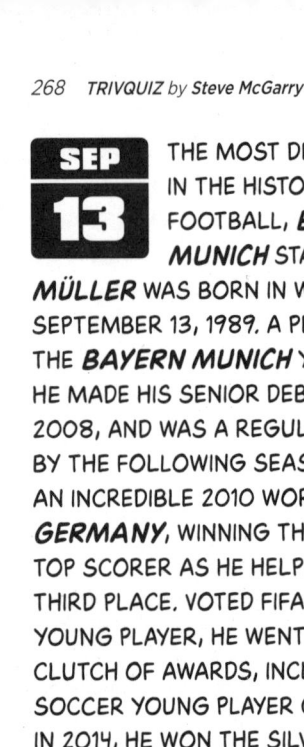

SEP 13

THE MOST DECORATED PLAYER IN THE HISTORY OF GERMAN FOOTBALL, *BAYERN MUNICH* STAR *THOMAS MÜLLER* WAS BORN IN WEILHEIM ON SEPTEMBER 13, 1989. A PRODUCT OF THE *BAYERN MUNICH* YOUTH SYSTEM, HE MADE HIS SENIOR DEBUT IN AUGUST, 2008, AND WAS A REGULAR IN THE TEAM BY THE FOLLOWING SEASON. HE HAD AN INCREDIBLE 2010 WORLD CUP WITH *GERMANY*, WINNING THE GOLDEN BOOT AS TOP SCORER AS HE HELPED HIS COUNTRY TO THIRD PLACE. VOTED FIFA WORLD CUP BEST YOUNG PLAYER, HE WENT ON TO WIN A CLUTCH OF AWARDS, INCLUDING WORLD SOCCER YOUNG PLAYER OF THE YEAR. IN 2014, HE WON THE SILVER BOOT AS *GERMANY* BECAME WORLD CHAMPIONS. HIS CLUB HONOURS TO DATE INCLUDE TEN LEAGUE TITLES, TWO UEFA CHAMPIONS LEAGUES AND TWO FIFA CLUB WORLD CUPS.

1. HE IS THE THIRD GERMAN TO WIN THE WORLD CUP GOLDEN BOOT OR SHOE -- NAME ONE OF THE OTHERS.

2. NAME THE GERMAN PLAYER WHO WAS VOTED FIFA WORLD CUP BEST YOUNG PLAYER IN 2006?

3. THE LAST TWO FIFA WORLD CUP BEST YOUNG PLAYER AWARDS WENT TO WHICH TWO *FRANCE* PLAYERS?

SEP 14

GÜNTER NETZER WAS BORN IN MÖNCHENGLADBACH ON SEPTEMBER 14, 1944. THE MIDFIELD GENERAL WAS SUPERB IN **WEST GERMANY'S** 1972 EUROPEAN CHAMPIONSHIP-WINNING SIDE -- YET PLAYED JUST 21 MINUTES IN THE 1974 WORLD CUP CAMPAIGN. TWICE VOTED GERMAN FOOTBALLER OF THE YEAR, HE WON TWO LEAGUE TITLES WITH **BORUSSIA MÖNCHENGLADBACH**, BEFORE WINNING TWO SPANISH TITLES WITH **REAL MADRID**. FOLLOWING A 1976 MOVE TO **GRASSHOPPER CLUB ZÜRICH**, **NETZER** RETURNED TO GERMANY TO BECOME GENERAL MANAGER OF **HAMBURGER SV**, AND HELPED STEER THE CLUB TO THREE BUNDESLIGA TITLES.

IDENTIFY THESE OTHER **BORUSSIA MÖNCHENGLADBACH** PLAYERS WHO WON THE GERMAN FOOTBALLER OF THE YEAR AWARD:

1. WORLD CUP WINNER WHO WENT ON TO MANAGE **SCOTLAND**, **KUWAIT**, **NIGERIA**, **AZERBAIJAN** AND GUIDED **GERMANY** TO GLORY AT EURO 96.

2. FEATURED COVER PLAYER ON THE **FIFA 17** GAME, HE HAS WON NUMEROUS CUP HONOURS WITH **BORUSSIA DORTMUND**.

THE SON OF A BLACKSMITH, *FLORIAN ALBERT* WAS BORN IN HERCEGSZÁNTÓ, HUNGARY, ON SEPTEMBER 15, 1941. HE SPENT HIS ENTIRE CAREER AT *FERENCVÁROS*, WITH WHOM HE WON FIVE CHAMPIONSHIPS AND THE 1965 INTER-CITIES FAIRS CUP. A PROLIFIC GOALSCORER, HE MADE HIS DEBUT FOR *HUNGARY* AT THE AGE OF 17 -- AFTER JUST TWO APPEARANCES AT CLUB LEVEL -- AND SCORED 31 GOALS IN 75 INTERNATIONALS. VOTED EUROPEAN FOOTBALLER OF THE YEAR IN 1967, HE SUBSEQUENTLY HAD TWO SPELLS AS MANAGER OF LIBYAN TEAM *AL AHLY BENGHAZI*.

WITH FOUR GOALS, *ALBERT* WAS JOINT TOP SCORER AT THE 1962 WORLD WITH FIVE OTHER PLAYERS -- *VAVÁ, GARRINCHA, LEONEL SÁNCHEZ, DRAZAN JERKOVIC* AND *VALENTIN IVANOV*. WHICH COUNTRIES DID THOSE PLAYERS REPRESENT?

BORN IN WEILER IM ALLGÄU ON SEPTEMBER 16, 1965,
KARL-HEINZ RIEDLE ESTABLISHED HIS CREDENTIALS AT
FC AUGSBURG, BEFORE JOINING ***SPVGG BLAU-WEIß
1890 BERLIN*** IN 1986, FOR THE CLUB'S ONLY SEASON IN
THE GERMAN TOP FLIGHT. THEY WERE RELEGATED AT THE END OF THAT
SEASON, BEGINNING A COLLAPSE THAT ENDED IN BANKRUPTCY AND
DISSOLUTION IN 1992. ***RIEDLE*** WENT ON TO BIGGER AND BETTER THINGS,
SCORING 18 GOALS IN 33 GAMES TO HELP ***WERDER BREMEN*** WIN
THE 1988 BUNDESLIGA IN HIS FIRST SEASON. FOLLOWING A SPELL WITH
LAZIO, HE RETURNED HOME TO WIN TWO CHAMPIONSHIPS AND THE UEFA
CHAMPIONS LEAGUE WITH ***BORUSSIA DORTMUND***. CAPPED 42 TIMES,
HE WON THE WORLD CUP WITH ***GERMANY*** IN 1990.

1. NAME THE TWO ENGLISH CLUBS HE PLAYED FOR, ONE OF WHOM HE
   BRIEFLY CO-MANAGED ON A CARETAKER BASIS.

2. HE WAS A MEMBER OF THE ***GERMANY*** TEAM THAT LOST THE EURO
   1992 FINAL TO WHICH COUNTRY?

3. HE SCORED TWICE IN THE 1997 CHAMPIONS LEAGUE FINAL AS
   BORUSSIA DORTMUND BEAT WHICH TEAM 3-1?

SEP 17

LIKE MANY BIG IVORIAN FOOTBALL STARS, *BAKARI KONÉ* -- WHO WAS BORN IN ABIDJAN, CÔTE D'IVOIRE, ON SEPTEMBER 17, 1981 -- WAS A PRODUCT OF THE YOUTH ACADEMY AT *ASEC MIMOSAS*. HE SPENT FIVE YEARS IN THE JUNIOR RANKS, TURNING PROFESSIONAL IN 1999. CAPPED 42 TIMES BY *IVORY COAST*, HE WON A LEAGUE TITLE WITH *NICE* IN A CAREER THAT TOOK HIM TO CLUBS IN FRANCE, QATAR AND THE UAE

IDENTIFY THESE OTHER *ASEC MIMOSAS* GRADUATES:

1. BROTHERS WHO WERE ON THE BOOKS TOGETHER AT *MANCHESTER CITY*.

2. FORMER *FEYENOORD* STAR WHO WON A LEAGUE TITLE AND THE UEFA CHAMPIONS LEAGUE WITH *CHELSEA*.

3. HE WON A LEAGUE TITLE WITH *LILLE*, SPENT TWO YEARS AT *ARSENAL*, AND JOINED *ROMA* IN 2013.

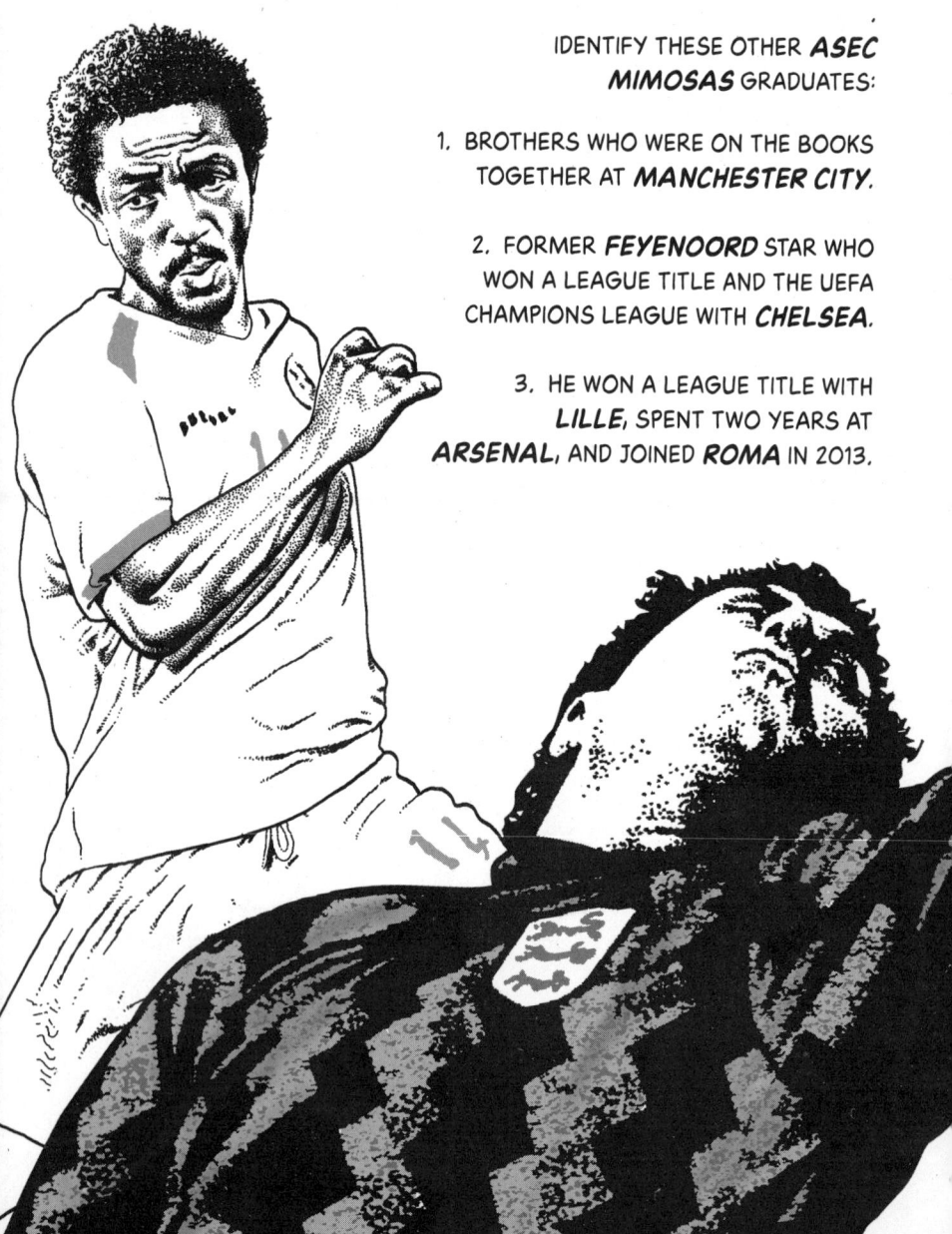

SEP 18

BORN ON SEPTEMBER 18, 1949, *PETER SHILTON* WAS 16 YEARS OLD WHEN HE MADE HIS DEBUT FOR *LEICESTER CITY*. HIS FORM SOON PERSUADED THE CLUB TO SELL WORLD CUP WINNER *GORDON BANKS. SHILTON* WAS STILL A TEEN WHEN HE WAS A MEMBER OF THE TEAM THAT LOST THE 1969 FA CUP FINAL AND WAS RELEGATED IN THE SAME SEASON. A WORLD RECORD FEE OF £325,000 TOOK HIM TO *STOKE CITY* IN 1974 BUT RELEGATION IN 1977 SAW HIM SOLD TO *BRIAN CLOUGH'S NOTTINGHAM FOREST*. HIS HONOURS WITH *FOREST* INCLUDED A LEAGUE TITLE AND TWO EUROPEAN CUPS.

AT INTERNATIONAL LEVEL, HE MADE HIS *ENGLAND* DEBUT IN 1970 AND EARNED THE LAST OF HIS RECORD 125 CAPS TWO DECADES LATER! HE WAS 32 YEARS OLD WHEN HE MADE HIS WORLD CUP FINALS DEBUT BUT WENT ON TO PLAY 17 GAMES OVER THREE TOURNAMENTS, AND SHARES THE RECORD OF TEN CLEAN SHEETS IN WORLD CUP FINALS MATCHES WITH *FRANCE* GOALKEEPER *FABIEN BARTHEZ*. HE RETIRED FROM PLAYING IN 1997, HAVING SET A RECORD OF PLAYING 1,390 COMPETITIVE GAMES IN WORLD FOOTBALL, INCLUDING 1,005 LEAGUE GAMES!

1. NAME THREE OF *SHILTON'S* EIGHT CLUBS AFTER LEAVING *NOTTINGHAM FOREST* IN 1982.

2. AT WHICH CLUB WAS HE PLAYER/MANAGER?

3. IN 1967, HE SCORED A GOAL FOR *LEICESTER CITY* AGAINST WHICH TEAM, HIS LONG PUNT BEATING *CAMPBELL FORSYTH* IN THE OPPOSITION GOAL?

SEP 19

BORN IN ROTHERHAM, SOUTH YORKSHIRE, ON SEPTEMBER 19, 1963, *DAVID SEAMAN* WON THREE LEAGUE TITLES, FOUR FA CUPS, THE LEAGUE CUP AND THE UEFA CUP WINNERS' CUP DURING HIS 13 SEASONS WITH *ARSENAL*. CAPPED 75 TIMES FOR *ENGLAND*, HE WAS AWARDED THE MBE IN 1997 FOR SERVICES TO SPORT.

1. *SEAMAN* WAS PLAYING FOR WHICH LONDON CLUB WHEN HE WON HIS FIRST ENGLAND CAP IN 1988?

2. *SEAMAN* PLAYED FOR WHICH SEVEN ENGLAND COACHES DURING HIS INTERNATIONAL CAREER?

3. WITH WHICH CLUB DID *SEAMAN* END HIS CAREER?

SEP 20

BORN IN HELSINGBORG, ON SEPTEMBER 20, 1971, SWEDISH STRIKER **HENRIK LARSSON** WAS 6 YEARS OLD WHEN HE JOINED **HÖGABORG**, WHERE HE WORKED HIS WAY THROUGH THE RANKS AND LAUNCHED HIS PROFESSIONAL CAREER AT THE AGE OF 17. HE SIGNED FOR **HELSINGBORG** IN 1992, WHERE HIS 50 GOALS IN 56 GAMES EARNED HIM A MOVE TO **FEYENOORD** THE FOLLOWING YEAR. HE JOINED **CELTIC** IN 1997, GOING ON TO WIN FOUR LEAGUE TITLES, TWO SCOTTISH LEAGUE CUPS AND TWO SCOTTISH CUPS. HE WAS TOP SCORER IN THE SPL IN FIVE OF HIS SIX SEASONS IN SCOTLAND, MISSING OUT ON MOST OF THE 1999-2000 SEASON WITH A BROKEN LEG.

HE SIGNED FOR **BARCELONA** IN 2004, AND ALTHOUGH HIS TIME IN SPAIN WAS HAMPERED BY INJURY, HE WON TWO LEAGUE TITLES AND THE UEFA CHAMPIONS LEAGUE, BEFORE REJOINING **HELSINGBORG** IN 2006. IN EARLY 2007, HE SPENT THREE MONTHS ON LOAN AT **MANCHESTER UNITED**, HELPING THE CLUB WIN THE PREMIER LEAGUE TITLE. CAPPED 107 TIMES BY **SWEDEN**, SCORING 37 GOALS, HE RETIRED IN 2009, THEN MOVED INTO MANAGEMENT WITH **LANDSKRONA BOIS**.

NAME TWO OTHER SWEDES WHO HAVE PLAYED IN THE SCOTTISH PREMIER LEAGUE FOR **CELTIC**.

SEP 21

THERE IS A STAND AT **BLACKPOOL'S** BLOOMFIELD ROAD GROUND NAMED IN HIS HONOUR, AND HIS LIFE-SIZE STATUE STANDS AT THE CLUB'S MAIN ENTRANCE. BORN IN DENTON, NEAR MANCHESTER, ON SEPTEMBER 21, 1935, **JIMMY ARMFIELD** PLAYED 627 GAMES FOR **BLACKPOOL** IN A ONE-CLUB CAREER. AN ATTACKING RIGHT-BACK, HE WAS CAPPED 43 TIMES BY **ENGLAND**, CAPTAINING THE TEAM ON 15 OCCASIONS, AND WAS A MEMBER OF THE 1966 WORLD CUP-WINNING SQUAD. HIS MANAGERIAL CAREER SAW HIM GUIDE **BOLTON WANDERERS** TO THE THIRD DIVISION CHAMPIONSHIP IN 1973, AND **LEEDS UNITED** TO THE 1975 EUROPEAN CUP FINAL.

1. WHO TURNED OUT FOR **BLACKPOOL:**
   A) AT THE AGE OF 46 IN 1961?   B) AT THE AGE OF 14 IN 1980?

2. WHICH **BLACKPOOL** LEGEND SCORED 23 GOALS IN 25 GAMES FOR **ENGLAND**?

3. WHICH FORMER **BLACKPOOL** PLAYER WENT ON TO MANAGE:

   A) **PHILADELPHIA FURY, BLACKPOOL, PORTSMOUTH, STOKE CITY, EXETER CITY, SOUTHAMPTON, MANCHESTER CITY**

   B) **BLACKPOOL, NORWICH CITY, LEICESTER CITY, NORTHERN IRELAND**

SEP 22

RONALDO LUÍS NAZÁRIO DE LIMA WAS BORN IN RIO DE JANEIRO ON SEPTEMBER 18, 1976. AFTER SCORING 12 GOALS IN 14 GAMES TO HELP LAND **CRUZEIRO'S** FIRST-EVER COPA DO BRASIL CHAMPIONSHIP, HE BEGAN HIS EUROPEAN ADVENTURE. 30 GOALS IN HIS FIRST SEASON WITH **PSV EINDHOVEN** BROUGHT THE DUTCH CUP. IN HIS ONE SEASON AT **BARCELONA**, HE SCORED 47 GOALS IN 49 GAMES TO HELP LAND THE 2007 COPA DEL REY AND THE UEFA CUP WINNERS' CUP. FIVE SEASONS IN MILAN WITH **INTERNAZIONALE** ADDED THE UEFA CUP TO HIS MEDAL HAUL, BEFORE HE SIGNED FOR **REAL MADRID** IN 2002, GOING ON TO WIN TWO LEAGUE TITLES IN FOUR YEARS. HE SCORED 62 GOALS IN 98 APPEARANCES FOR **BRAZIL**, WINNING TWO WORLD CUPS, TWO COPA AMÉRICAS AND THE FIFA CONFEDERATIONS CUP.

1. NAME THE TWO ENGLISH MANAGERS UNDER WHOM **RONALDO** PLAYED DURING HIS CAREER.

2. HE ENDED HIS CAREER BACK IN BRAZIL WITH WHICH CLUB?

3. IN 2018, **RONALDO** BECAME THE MAJORITY OWNER OF WHICH LA LIGA CLUB?

SEP 23

KNOWN AS *"GOLDEN HEAD"* FOR HIS SUPERB ABILITY IN THE AIR, *SÁNDOR KOCSIS* -- BORN IN BUDAPEST ON SEPTEMBER 23, 1929 -- BEGAN HIS CAREER WITH *FERENCVÁROS*, WITH WHOM HE WON A LEAGUE TITLE, BUT HE WAS SOON POACHED BY *HONVÉD*, THE ARMY TEAM THAT RECRUITED HUNGARY'S BEST PLAYERS. HE WON THREE CHAMPIONSHIPS WITH *HONVÉD*, SHARING TOP-SCORING HONOURS WITH TEAMMATE *FERENC PUSKÁS*. *KOCSIS* WAS CAPPED 68 TIMES BY *HUNGARY*, SCORING AN INCREDIBLE 75 GOALS -- INCLUDING SEVEN HAT-TRICKS! OUTSTANDING IN THE SIDE THAT WON OLYMPIC GOLD IN 1952, HE SPEARHEADED *HUNGARY'S* ATTACK IN THE 1954 WORLD CUP, FINISHING AS THE TOURNAMENT TOP SCORER WITH 11 GOALS. HE WAS THE FIRST PLAYER TO SCORE TWO HAT-TRICKS IN A WORLD CUP. FOLLOWING THE 1956 HUNGARIAN UPRISING, HE PLAYED A SEASON AT *YOUNG FELLOWS ZÜRICH*, BEFORE SETTLING IN SPAIN WITH *BARCELONA* -- WITH WHOM HE WON TWO LEAGUE TITLES, TWO SPANISH CUPS AND THE INTER-CITIES FAIRS CUP. HE DIED IN 1979, AT THE AGE OF 49.

1. NAME THE TWO OTHER PLAYERS, A FRENCHMAN AND A GERMAN, WHO HAVE SCORED TWO HAT-TRICKS IN ONE WORLD CUP TOURNAMENT.

2. WHIO WAS THE *ARGENTINA* STAR WHO BECAME THE FIRST PLAYER TO SCORE HAT-TRICKS IN TWO WORLD CUP TOURNAMENTS?

3. WHICH *ENGLAND* PLAYER HIT A HAT-TRICK IN A WORLD CUP FINAL?

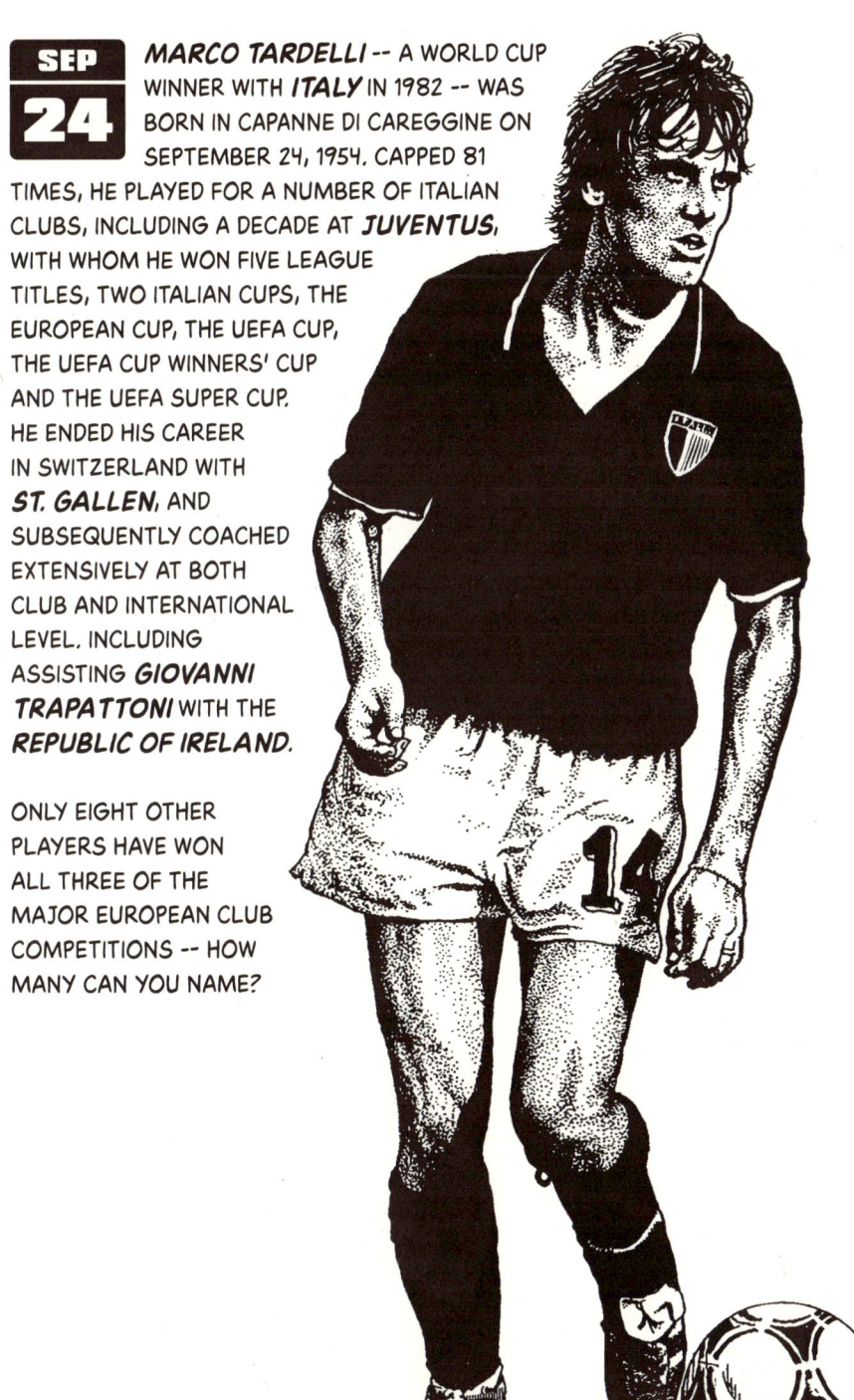

SEP 24

MARCO TARDELLI -- A WORLD CUP WINNER WITH *ITALY* IN 1982 -- WAS BORN IN CAPANNE DI CAREGGINE ON SEPTEMBER 24, 1954. CAPPED 81 TIMES, HE PLAYED FOR A NUMBER OF ITALIAN CLUBS, INCLUDING A DECADE AT *JUVENTUS*, WITH WHOM HE WON FIVE LEAGUE TITLES, TWO ITALIAN CUPS, THE EUROPEAN CUP, THE UEFA CUP, THE UEFA CUP WINNERS' CUP AND THE UEFA SUPER CUP. HE ENDED HIS CAREER IN SWITZERLAND WITH *ST. GALLEN*, AND SUBSEQUENTLY COACHED EXTENSIVELY AT BOTH CLUB AND INTERNATIONAL LEVEL, INCLUDING ASSISTING *GIOVANNI TRAPATTONI* WITH THE *REPUBLIC OF IRELAND*.

ONLY EIGHT OTHER PLAYERS HAVE WON ALL THREE OF THE MAJOR EUROPEAN CLUB COMPETITIONS -- HOW MANY CAN YOU NAME?

BORN IN WESTPHALIA, ON SEPTEMBER 25, 1955, *KARL-HEINZ RUMMENIGGE* LEFT SCHOOL TO BECOME A BANK CLERK, PLAYING PART-TIME FOR LOCAL CLUB *BORUSSIA LIPPSTADT.* IN 1974, HE SIGNED FOR *BAYERN MUNICH.* IN TEN SEASONS HE SCORED 162 LEAGUE GOALS AND WON TWO CHAMPIONSHIPS, TWO GERMAN CUPS AND TWO EUROPEAN CUPS. HE PLAYED 95 TIMES FOR *WEST GERMANY* AND SCORED 45 GOALS, STARRING IN THREE WORLD CUPS AND WINNING THE EUROPEAN CHAMPIONSHIPS IN 1980. TWICE VOTED EUROPEAN FOOTBALLER OF THE YEAR, *"KALLE"* JOINED *INTERNAZIONALE* IN 1984, BUT HIS TIME THERE WAS PLAGUED BY INJURY. HE RETIRED AT THE AGE OF 34, WHILE PLAYING IN SWITZERLAND WITH *SERVETTE.*

1. *RUMMENIGGE* CAPTAINED HIS COUNTRY 51 TIMES -- NAME ONE OF THE THREE GERMAN PLAYERS TO BETTER THAT RECORD.

2. HE WAS ON THE LOSING SIDE IN BOTH THE 1982 AND 1986 WORLD CUP FINALS -- AGAINST WHICH COUNTRIES?

3. HE WON EUROPEAN CUPS WITH *BAYERN MUNICH* IN 1975 AND 1976 -- WHO WERE THE OPPONENTS?

SEP 26

BORN IN GÖRLITZ, EAST GERMANY, ON SEPTEMBER 26, 1976, THREE TIMES GERMAN FOOTBALLER OF THE YEAR *MICHAEL BALLACK* WAS TWICE ON THE LOSING SIDE IN A UEFA CHAMPIONS LEAGUE FINAL, AND WAS A WORLD CUP AND EUROPEAN CHAMPIONSHIPS RUNNER-UP WITH THE NATIONAL TEAM. HE DID, HOWEVER, WIN FIVE LEAGUE TITLES WITH THREE DIFFERENT CLUBS, INCLUDING THE 2010 PREMIER LEAGUE WITH *CHELSEA*. CAPPED 98 TIMES BY *GERMANY*, HE REFUSED THE OFFER TO PLAY IN TWO FRIENDLIES TO COMPLETE A CENTURY OF APPEARANCES BEFORE HIS 2012 RETIREMENT.

1. NAME THE TWO GERMAN TEAMS WITH WHOM HE WON LEAGUE TITLES.

2. HOW MANY TIMES DID HE WIN THE FA CUP WITH *CHELSEA*?

3. HE WORE WHICH SHIRT NUMBER THROUGHOUT MOST OF HIS CAREER?

SEP
27

FIVE TIMES ITALIAN FOOTBALLER OF THE YEAR, AND WINNER OF TWO SERIE A FOOTBALLER OF THE YEAR AWARDS, *FRANCESCO TOTTI* SPENT HIS ENTIRE CAREER WITH *ROMA*, AND IS UNIVERSALLY ACKNOWLEDGED AS THE GREATEST PLAYER IN THE CLUB'S HISTORY. BORN IN ROME, ON SEPTEMBER 27, 1976, HE MADE HIS SENIOR DEBUT AT THE AGE OF 16 AND HOLDS THE CLUB'S APPEARANCE AND GOALSCORING RECORDS. A WORLD CUP WINNER WITH *ITALY*, HE HAS WON A LEAGUE TITLE, TWO ITALIAN CUPS AND TWO ITALIAN SUPERCUPS AT CLUB LEVEL. HE RETIRED IN 2017.

NAME THE CLUBS WITH WHICH THE FOLLOWING PLAYERS SPENT THEIR ENTIRE SENIOR CAREERS:

1. *JACK CHARLTON*

2. *LEV YASHIN*

3. *ANTONIO RATTIN*

4. *PAOLO MALDINI*

5. *NAT LOFTHOUSE*

6. *GERRY BYRNE*

7. *RONNIE CLAYTON*

8. *TONY HIBBERT*

9. *PACKIE BONNER*

SEP 28

LEEDS UNITED SACKED CLUB LEGEND **BILLY BREMNER** AS MANAGER ON SEPTEMBER 28, 1988. **BREMNER** HAD SPENT THREE YEARS AT THE HELM, BUT HAD FAILED TO STEER THE CLUB BACK TO THE TOP FLIGHT OF ENGLISH FOOTBALL. HE WAS REPLACED BY **HOWARD WILKINSON**, WHO NOT ONLY TOOK **LEEDS** BACK TO THE FIRST DIVISION, BUT DELIVERED THE LEAGUE TITLE IN 1992. **BREMNER** RETURNED TO MANAGEMENT WITH **DONCASTER ROVERS**, A CLUB HE HAD TWICE PREVIOUSLY MANAGED.

SCOTTISH INTERNATIONAL **BREMNER**, WHO CAPTAINED **LEEDS** TO TWO LEAGUE TITLES, DIED IN 1997, AT THE AGE OF 54. A STATUE OF **BREMNER** NOW STANDS OUTSIDE **LEEDS UNITED'S ELLAND ROAD** GROUND.

IDENTIFY THESE OTHER **SCOTLAND** INTERNATIONALS WHO BECAME MANAGERS OF **LEEDS UNITED**:

1. WINGER WHO SPENT HIS ENTIRE CAREER AT THE CLUB BEFORE BECOMING PLAYER-MANAGER IN 1982, HE RETURNED AS CARETAKER MANAGER IN 2003.

2. WON LEAGUE TITLES AS BOTH PLAYER AND MANAGER WITH **ARSENAL**, HE ALSO MANAGED **MILLWALL** AND TOTTENHAM HOTSPUR.

3. PLAYED FOR **LEEDS UNITED**, **COVENTRY CITY**, **LEICESTER CITY AND LIVERPOOL**, AND STARTED HIS MANAGERIAL CAREER AT **COVENTRY CITY**.

SEP 29

A STAR OF THREE WORLD CUPS, *WOLFGANG OVERATH* WAS CAPPED AS A SCHOOLBOY, YOUTH, UNDER-23 AND FULL INTERNATIONAL -- AND FACED *ENGLAND'S MARTIN PETERS* AT EVERY LEVEL. HE WAS A WORLD CUP RUNNER-UP IN 1966, SCORED THE GOAL THAT CLINCHED THIRD PLACE FOR *WEST GERMANY* IN 1970, AND THEN BEAT OUT *GÜNTER NETZER* FOR THE MIDFIELD GENERAL'S ROLE IN THE TRIUMPHANT 1974 SIDE, FOLLOWING WHICH HE RETIRED FROM INTERNATIONAL FOOTBALL. BORN IN SIEGBURG, ON SEPTEMBER 29, 1943, HE WAS CAPPED 81 TIMES BY HIS COUNTRY.

OVERATH SPENT HIS ENTIRE SENIOR CAREER WITH *1. FC KÖLN.* IDENTIFY THESE FORMER *1. FC KÖLN.* PLAYERS:

1. GOALKEEPER WHOSE INFAMOUS 1982 WORLD CUP CHALLENGE ON *PATRICK BATTISTON* LEFT THE *FRANCE* DEFENDER IN A COMA, WITH THREE CRACKED RIBS AND MISSING TWO TEETH.

2. *NOTTINGHAM FOREST, ARSENAL* AND *ENGLAND* STRIKER.

3. 1990 WORLD CUP-WINNING WINGER WHO SUCCEEDED *STEVE MCCLAREN* AS COACH OF *VFL WOLFSBURG.*

SEP 30

BORN IN AMSTERDAM, ON SEPTEMBER 30, 1962, *FRANK RIJKAARD* MADE HIS DEBUT FOR *AJAX* AT THE AGE OF 17. HE WENT ON TO WIN THREE LEAGUE TITLES, THREE DUTCH CUPS AND THE UEFA CUP WINNERS' CUP IN AN EIGHT-SEASON SPELL THAT SAW HIM TWICE NAMED DUTCH FOOTBALLER OF THE YEAR. HE LEFT THE CLUB FOLLOWING A DISAGREEMENT WITH COACH *JOHAN CRUYFF*, AND WAS BRIEFLY ON THE BOOKS AT *SPORTING CP* AND *REAL ZARAGOZA*, BEFORE JOINING *AC MILAN* IN 1988. THE DUTCH TRIO OF *RIJKAARD*, *VAN BASTEN* AND *GULLIT* HELPED THE ITALIANS WIN TWO LEAGUE TITLES AND TWO EUROPEAN CUPS, AS WELL AS INSPIRING *NETHERLANDS* TO VICTORY IN THE 1988 EUROPEAN CHAMPIONSHIPS. *RIJKAARD* RETURNED TO *AJAX* IN 1993, ADDING TWO MORE LEAGUE TITLES TO HIS TALLY, BEFORE WINNING THE 1995 EUROPEAN CUP FINAL IN THE FINAL GAME OF HIS PLAYING CAREER.

NAME THREE OF THE TEAMS *FRANK RIJKAARD* MANAGED IN HIS SUBSEQUENT COACHING CAREER.

OCTOBER

**OCT
1**

HAILED BY PEERS AND FANS ALIKE AS THE GREATEST FOOTBALLER THAT BRITAIN HAS EVER PRODUCED, *DUNCAN EDWARDS* WAS BORN IN DUDLEY, ON OCTOBER 1, 1936. HE MADE HIS *MANCHESTER UNITED* DEBUT AT THE AGE OF 16 YEARS AND 185 DAYS IN 1953, BECOMING THE YOUNGEST PLAYER TO APPEAR IN THE TOP FLIGHT OF ENGLISH FOOTBALL. HE WON HIS FIRST *ENGLAND* CAP TWO YEARS LATER, AGAINST *SCOTLAND* IN 1955, AGED 18 YEARS AND 183 DAYS. HE INSPIRED *UNITED* TO CONSECUTIVE LEAGUE TITLES IN 1956 AND 1957, AND WAS IN THE SIDE THAT LOST THE 1957 FA CUP FINAL TO *ASTON VILLA. EDWARDS* WAS ONLY 21 YEARS OLD WHEN, HAVING WAGED A COURAGEOUS TWO-WEEK BATTLE FOR LIFE IN A GERMAN HOSPITAL, HE DIED OF INJURIES SUSTAINED IN THE 1958 MUNICH AIR DISASTER THAT DECIMATED THE YOUNG *MANCHESTER UNITED* TEAM.

1. *DUNCAN* WAS ONE OF FIVE *ENGLAND* INTERNATIONALS WHO PERISHED IN THE AIR DISASTER -- NAME THE OTHER FOUR.

2. WHO BECAME THE YOUNGEST PLAYER IN THE ENGLISH FOOTBALL LEAGUE, PLAYING FOR *FULHAM* IN 2008?

3. WHO BECAME THE YOUNGEST PREMIER LEAGUE PLAYER, DEBUTING FOR *FULHAM* IN 2007?

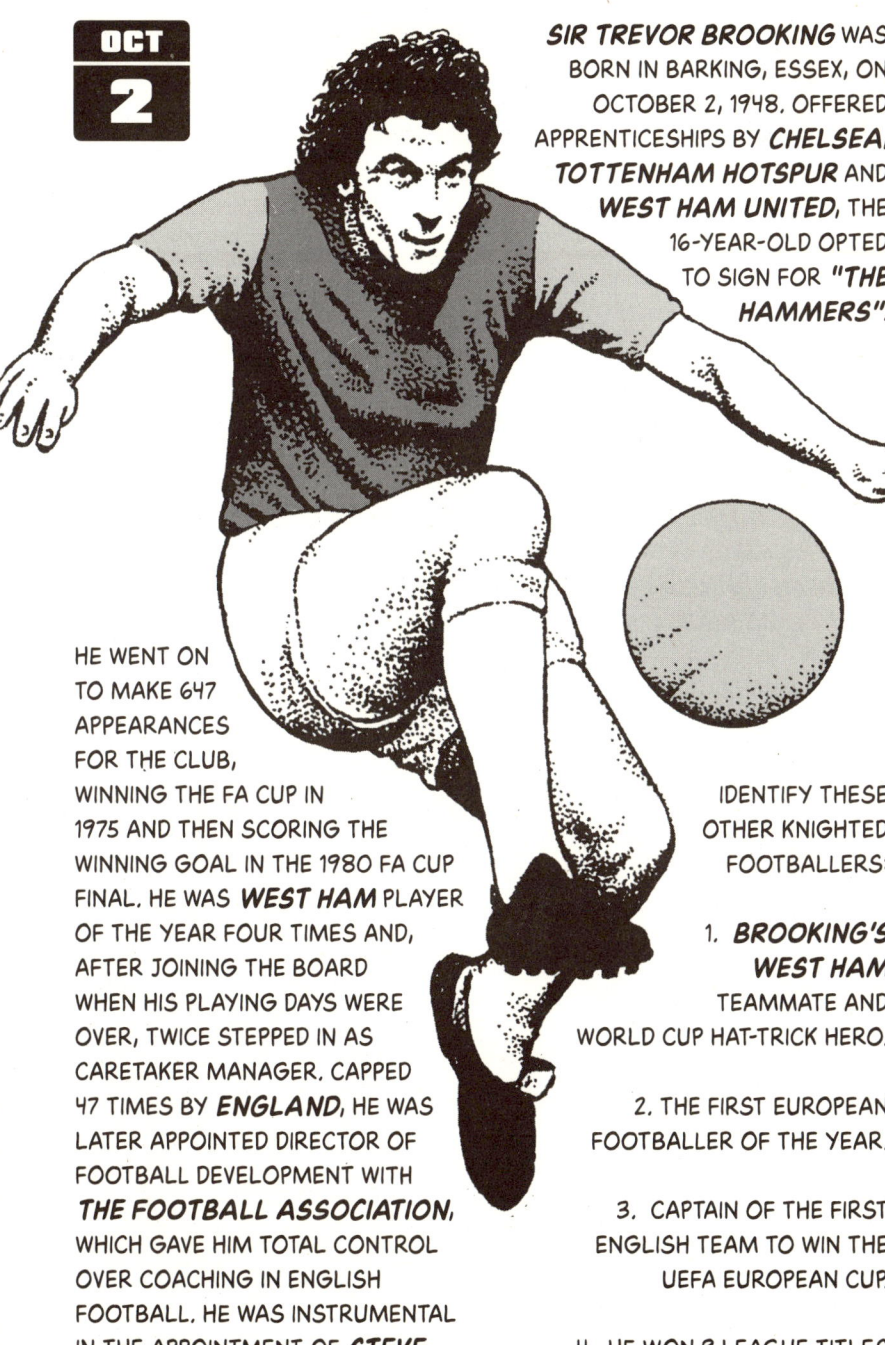

OCT 2

SIR TREVOR BROOKING WAS BORN IN BARKING, ESSEX, ON OCTOBER 2, 1948. OFFERED APPRENTICESHIPS BY *CHELSEA*, *TOTTENHAM HOTSPUR* AND *WEST HAM UNITED*, THE 16-YEAR-OLD OPTED TO SIGN FOR *"THE HAMMERS"*.

HE WENT ON TO MAKE 647 APPEARANCES FOR THE CLUB, WINNING THE FA CUP IN 1975 AND THEN SCORING THE WINNING GOAL IN THE 1980 FA CUP FINAL. HE WAS *WEST HAM* PLAYER OF THE YEAR FOUR TIMES AND, AFTER JOINING THE BOARD WHEN HIS PLAYING DAYS WERE OVER, TWICE STEPPED IN AS CARETAKER MANAGER. CAPPED 47 TIMES BY *ENGLAND*, HE WAS LATER APPOINTED DIRECTOR OF FOOTBALL DEVELOPMENT WITH *THE FOOTBALL ASSOCIATION*, WHICH GAVE HIM TOTAL CONTROL OVER COACHING IN ENGLISH FOOTBALL. HE WAS INSTRUMENTAL IN THE APPOINTMENT OF *STEVE MCCLAREN* AS *ENGLAND* MANAGER IN 2006.

IDENTIFY THESE OTHER KNIGHTED FOOTBALLERS:

1. *BROOKING'S WEST HAM* TEAMMATE AND WORLD CUP HAT-TRICK HERO.

2. THE FIRST EUROPEAN FOOTBALLER OF THE YEAR.

3. CAPTAIN OF THE FIRST ENGLISH TEAM TO WIN THE UEFA EUROPEAN CUP.

4. HE WON 9 LEAGUE TITLES WITH *LIVERPOOL* -- 6 AS A PLAYER AND 3 AS MANAGER.

BORN ON OCTOBER 3, 1981, IN MALMÖ, SWEDEN, TO A BOSNIAN FATHER AND CROATIAN MOTHER, **ZLATAN IBRAHIMOVIĆ** STARTED PLAYING FOOTBALL AT THE AGE OF 6. HE ONCE CAME ON AS A SECOND-HALF SUBSTITUTE WITH HIS **FBK BALKAN** YOUTH TEAM TRAILING 4-0, AND SCORED 8 GOALS! AS A TEEN, HE WAS A REGULAR FOR **MALMÖ FF**, BUT CAME CLOSE TO QUITTING SO HE COULD WORK AS A DOCKER! HE WAS PERSUADED TO CONTINUE HIS **MALMÖ** CAREER AND BY 1999 WAS A FIRST-TEAM REGULAR. A POWERFUL STRIKER -- HE WAS A TAE KWAN DO BLACK BELT BY THE AGE OF 17 -- HE HAS WON THE GULDBOLLEN, THE AWARD GIVEN TO THE SWEDISH FOOTBALLER OF THE YEAR, 12 TIMES, AND HAS WON LEAGUE TITLES IN FOUR DIFFERENT COUNTRIES. HE MADE HIS FIRST APPEARANCE FOR **SWEDEN** IN 1991, AT THE AGE OF 19 AND WENT ON TO SCORE A RECORD 62 GOALS IN 116 APPEARANCES, RETIRING FROM INTERNATIONAL FOOTBALL IN 2016. HE MADE A SENSATIONAL RETURN TO THE NATIONAL TEAM FIVE YEARS LATER AFTER ANNOUNCING HE WOULD PLAY IN THE EUROPEAN CHAMPIONSHIP. ALTHOUGH HE ADDED TWO MORE CAPS TO HIS TALLY, INJURY RULED HIM OUT OF THE TOURNAMENT.

1. WITH WHICH DUTCH CLUB DID **IBRAHIMOVIĆ** WIN TWO LEAGUE TITLES AND THE KNVB CUP?

2. NAME THE THREE ITALIAN CLUBS HE HAS PLAYED FOR.

3. **IBRAHIMOVIĆ** SPENT TWO SEASONS IN THE STATES PLAYING FOR WHICH MLS TEAM?

BORN IN PRAGUE, IN THE CZECH REPUBLIC, ON OCTOBER 4, 1980, **TOMÁŠ ROSICKÝ** CAME THROUGH THE RANKS AT **SPARTA PRAGUE,** HELPING HIS HOMETOWN CLUB WIN THREE LEAGUE TITLES. A FULL INTERNATIONAL BY THE AGE OF 19, HE JOINED **BORUSSIA DORTMUND** IN 2001. NICKNAMED **"THE LITTLE MOZART"** FOR HIS ABILITY TO ORCHESTRATE PLAY, HE WON A LEAGUE TITLE IN HIS FIRST SEASON IN THE BUNDESLIGA, HIS DISPLAYS EARNING HIM THE FIRST OF HIS THREE CZECH PLAYER OF THE YEAR AWARDS. HE SIGNED FOR **ARSENAL** IN 2006 AND WON TWO FA CUPS IN HIS TEN YEARS AT THE CLUB, BEFORE RETURNING TO **SPARTA PRAGUE.** CAPPED 106 TIMES, HIS 23 GOALS MAKE HIM HIS COUNTRY'S FOURTH-HIGHEST GOALSCORER OF ALL TIME. HE RETIRED IN 2017.

IDENTIFY THESE OTHER **CZECH REPUBLIC** STARS:

1. WON THE UEFA CUP, FA CUP AND LEAGUE CUP WITH **LIVERPOOL** AND PLAYED FOR **PORTSMOUTH, ASTON VILLA** AND **STOKE CITY.**

2. EURO 2004 GOLDEN BOOT WINNER, HIS CLUBS INCLUDE **LIVERPOOL, ASTON VILLA, LYON, PORTSMOUTH** AND **GALATASARAY.**

3. A PREMIER LEAGUE CHAMPION WITH **MANCHESTER UNITED** IN 1997, HE WAS CAPPED 118 TIMES BY HIS COUNTRY.

BORN **ANTÔNIO DE OLIVEIRA FILHO** IN ARARAQUARA, ON OCTOBER 5, 1960, **CARECA** WON THE BRAZILIAN CHAMPIONSHIP WITH BOTH **GUARANI** AND **SÃO PAULO**. FOLLOWING THE 1986 WORLD CUP, IN WHICH HIS FIVE GOALS PLACED HIM SECOND IN THE GOLDEN BOOT RANKINGS, HE JOINED **NAPOLI**, WITH WHOM HE WON A LEAGUE TITLE AND THE UEFA CUP. HE SCORED TWICE AT THE 1990 WORLD CUP, AND EVENTUALLY AMASSED A TOTAL OF 29 GOALS IN 60 GAMES FOR **BRAZIL**. AFTER A SPELL IN JAPAN WITH **KASHIWA REYSOL**, HE RETURNED TO BRAZIL TO JOIN **SANTOS**.

NAME THESE OTHER BRAZILIANS WHO WON A SERIE A TITLE IN ITALY:

1. GOALKEEPER WHO WON FIVE CONSECUTIVE TITLES WITH **INTERNAZIONALE** BETWEEN 2006 AND 2010.

2. FORMER **SANTOS**, **REAL MADRID** AND **MANCHESTER CITY** STAR, HE WON THE TITLE WITH **AC MILAN** IN 2010.

3. WON THE BALLON D'OR, FIFA WORLD PLAYER OF THE YEAR AWARD AND THE 2004 TITLE WITH **AC MILAN**, BEFORE JOINING **REAL MADRID**.

OCT 6

TOMMY LAWTON WAS BORN IN FARNWORTH, ON OCTOBER 6, 1919. HE BEGAN HIS CAREER AT **BURNLEY**, BEFORE JOINING **EVERTON** IN 1936 FOR £6,500 -- A WORLD RECORD FEE FOR A TEENAGER. TWO YEARS LATER, AGED 19 YEARS AND 16 DAYS, HE SCORED ON HIS **ENGLAND** DEBUT, AND THEN SCORED IN HIS NEXT FIVE INTERNATIONALS. BUT FOR THE INTERRUPTION OF THE SECOND WORLD WAR, **LAWTON** WOULD PROBABLY HAVE BECOME **ENGLAND'S** ALL-TIME LEADING MARKSMAN -- HIS TALLY WAS 22 GOALS IN 23 APPEARANCES -- BUT HE ALSO SCORED 25 GOALS IN WARTIME MATCHES. POSTWAR, HE PLAYED FOR **CHELSEA**, **NOTTS COUNTY**, **BRENTFORD** AND **ARSENAL**, BEFORE MOVING INTO MANAGEMENT, INCLUDING TWO SPELLS AT **KETTERING TOWN**. **LAWTON** APPEARED IN THE 1953 FILM **"THE GREAT GAME"**, ALONG WITH **THORA HIRD** AND **DIANA DORS**.

WHICH FOOTBALL-THEMED MOVIE STARRED:

1. **VINNIE JONES, JASON STATHAM, DAVID HEMMINGS** (2001)

2. **MICHAEL SHEEN, TIMOTHY SPALL, COLM MEANEY** (2009)

3. **SEAN BEAN, EMILY LLOYD, PETE POSTLETHWAITE** (1996)

4. **SYLVESTER STALLONE, MICHAEL CAINE, MAX VON SYDOW, PELÉ** (1981)

OCT 7

BORN IN LAGARTO, BRAZIL, ON OCTOBER 7, 1988, *DIEGO COSTA* LEFT SÃO PAULO'S *BARCELONA EC* AT THE AGE OF 16 TO SIGN FOR PORTUGAL'S *BRAGA*, BEGINNING A PERIOD OF TRANSFERS AND LOANS THAT TOOK HIM TO *PENAFIEL*, *ATLÉTICO MADRID*, *CELTA*, *ALBACETE* AND *VALLADOLID*. DURING A SECOND SPELL WITH *ATLÉTICO MADRID*, HE FOLLOWED A SERIOUS KNEE INJURY WITH A SUCCESSFUL LOAN SPELL WITH *RAYO VALLECANO*, BEFORE RETURNING AND CEMENTING HIS PLACE IN THE TEAM THAT WON THE 2013 COPA DEL REY. THE FOLLOWING SEASON, HIS 36 GOALS PROPELLED *"THE COLCHONEROS"* TO A LEAGUE TITLE AND THE UEFA CHAMPIONS LEAGUE FINAL. HAVING PLAYED TWICE FOR *BRAZIL* IN 2013, HE TOOK SPANISH NATIONALITY AND TURNED HIS BACK ON HIS HOMELAND TO PLAY FOR HIS ADOPTIVE COUNTRY. IN 2014, *CHELSEA* MET THE £32 MILLION BUY-OUT CLAUSE IN HIS CONTRACT, AND HE WENT ON TO WIN TWO LEAGUE TITLES AND A LEAGUE CUP, BEFORE AN ACRIMONIOUS PARTING OF THE WAYS IN 2017 RESULTED IN HIS RETURN TO *ATLÉTICO MADRID*. HE BECAME A FREE AGENT IN LATE 2020.

1. NAME THE FOUR *CHELSEA* MANAGERS UNDER WHOM HE PLAYED.

2. *COSTA* PLAYED FOR *SPAIN* AT THE 2014 AND 2018 WORLD CUP FINALS -- WHO WERE THE TWO COACHES?

3. WHICH MANAGER STEERED *DIEGO COSTA* AND *ATLÉTICO MADRID* TO LA LIGA TITLE IN 2014?

OCT 8 CAPPED 73 TIMES BY *ITALY*, *ANTONIO CABRINI* STARRED IN THREE WORLD CUPS, INCLUDING THE TRIUMPHANT 1982 CAMPAIGN. BORN IN CREMONA, LOMBARDY, ON OCTOBER 7, 1957, HE BEGAN HIS CAREER AS A TEENAGER IN SERIE C WITH LOCAL CLUB *CREMONESE*, MOVED UP TO SERIE B WITH *ATALANTA*, AND THEN JOINED SERIE A GIANTS *JUVENTUS* IN 1976. IN 13 SEASONS WITH *"THE BIANCONERI"* HE WON SIX LEAGUE TITLES AND TWO ITALIAN CUPS, AND BECAME ONE OF THE FEW PLAYERS IN HISTORY TO WIN ALL UEFA CLUB COMPETITIONS! HE SPENT TWO YEARS AT *BOLOGNA* BEFORE BEGINNING A MANAGEMENT CAREER THAT INCLUDED TWO YEARS IN CHARGE OF THE *ITALY WOMEN'S* NATIONAL TEAM.

1. NAME TWO OTHER MEMBERS OF *ITALY'S* 1982 WORLD CUP-WINNING TEAM WHO WERE *JUVENTUS* PLAYERS AT THAT TIME.

2. WHO DID *JUVENTUS* BEAT IN THE 1985 EUROPEAN CUP FINAL?

3. WHO WAS THE MANAGER OF *ITALY'S* 1982 WORLD CUP-WINNING TEAM?

**OCT
9**

JORGE LUIS BURRUCHAGA, THE MIDFIELD GENERAL WHO SCORED THE WINNING GOAL FOR *ARGENTINA* IN THE 3-2 VICTORY OVER *WEST GERMANY* IN THE 1986 WORLD CUP FINAL, WAS BORN IN GUALEGUAY, ENTRE RÍOS, ON OCTOBER 9, 1962.

HAVING WON A LEAGUE TITLE, A COPA LIBERTADORES AND AN INTERCONTINENTAL CUP WITH *INDEPENDIENTE*, HE HEADED TO FRANCE TO JOIN *NANTES*, AND LATER PLAYED FOR *VALENCIENNES*. HE ENDED HIS PLAYING CAREER BACK AT *INDEPENDIENTE*, BEFORE MOVING INTO MANAGEMENT WITH A NUMBER OF ARGENTINIAN CLUBS.

IDENTIFY THESE OTHER EUROPE-BASED MEMBERS OF THE 1986 WORLD CUP-WINNING *ARGENTINA* TEAM:

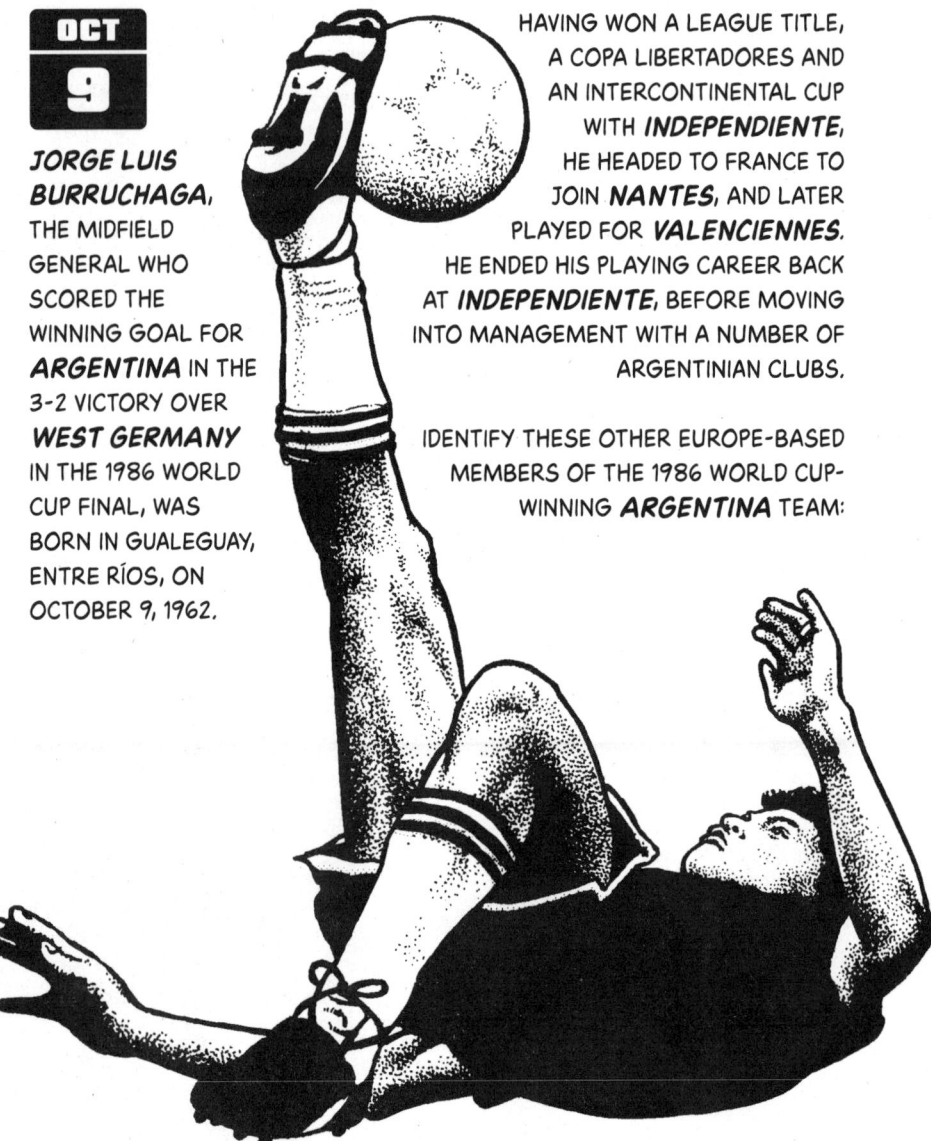

1. TEAM CAPTAIN WHO PLAYED FOR *FIORENTINA*, AND WENT ON TO COACH *ARGENTINA* AND *URUGUAY*.

2. A GOALSCORER IN THE FINAL, HE PLAYED FOR -- AND SUBSEQUENTLY COACHED -- *REAL MADRID*.

3. HE WON TWO SERIE A TITLES WITH *NAPOLI*.

OCT
10

XHERDAN SHAQIRI WAS BORN ON OCTOBER 10, 1991, IN GJILAN, SFR YUGOSLAVIA, TO KOSOVAR ALBANIAN PARENTS,THE FAMILY EMIGRATING TO SWITZERLAND THE FOLLOWING YEAR. SCOUTED BY **FC BASEL** AT THE AGE OF EIGHT, HE PROGRESSED THROUGH THE RANKS AND WENT ON TO WIN THREE LEAGUE TITLES, INCLUDING TWO SWISS CUP DOUBLES. HE JOINED **BAYERN MUNICH** IN 2012 AND WON A HOST OF HONOURS WITH THE BAVARIANS, INCLUDING A 2013 HAUL OF A DOMESTIC TREBLE, A UEFA CHAMPIONS LEAGUE, UEFA SUPER CUP AND FIFA CLUB CUP. A SPELL IN ITALY IN EARLY 2015 WAS FOLLOWED BY THREE SEASONS WITH **STOKE CITY**, BEFORE HE SIGNED FOR **LIVERPOOL** IN 2018, THE SAME YEAR THAT HE WAS NAMED THE MOST-GOOGLED PERSON IN SWITZERLAND. A FULL INTERNATIONAL SINCE 2010, **SHAQIRI** HAS REPRESENTED **SWITZERLAND** AT THREE WORLD CUPS TO DATE.

1. WHO WAS THE **STOKE CITY** MANAGER WHO SIGNED **SHAQIRI**?

2. FROM WHICH ITALIAN SERIE A CLUB WAS HE SIGNED?

3. WHO WAS THE COACH WHO:
   A) SIGNED **SHAQIRI** TO **BAYERN MUNICH** IN 2012
   B) SOLD HIM THREE YEARS LATER?

OCT 11

BORN IN ASHINGTON, NORTHUMBERLAND, ON OCTOBER 11, 1937, **BOBBY CHARLTON** MADE HIS DEBUT FOR **MANCHESTER UNITED** IN 1956, ONE WEEK BEFORE HIS 19TH BIRTHDAY, AND SCORED TWICE IN A 4-2 VICTORY OVER **CHARLTON ATHLETIC**. HE WON A LEAGUE CHAMPIONSHIP MEDAL THAT SEASON, THE FIRST HONOUR IN A GLORIOUS CAREER THAT INCLUDED TWO FURTHER LEAGUE TITLES, THE FA CUP, THE EUROPEAN CUP AND THE WORLD CUP WITH ENGLAND. ENGLISH AND EUROPEAN FOOTBALLER OF THE YEAR, HE SCORED 249 GOALS IN 758 GAMES FOR **UNITED**. HE SCORED 49 GOALS IN A RECORD 106 APPEARANCES FOR **ENGLAND**. HIS CAPS RECORD STOOD FOR THREE YEARS AND HIS GOALS RECORDS FOR CLUB AND COUNTRY WERE EVENTUALLY SURPASSED BY **WAYNE ROONEY**.

1. HE SCORED 8 GOALS IN 38 APPEARANCES AS PLAYER/ MANAGER OF WHICH CLUB?

2. HE MADE THREE APPEARANCES, SCORING ONCE, FOR WHICH IRISH CLUB?

3. WHO SURPASSED HIS **ENGLAND** APPEARANCE RECORD IN 1973, BEFORE RETIRING ON 108 CAPS?

OCT 12

BORN IN WOLVERHAMPTON, ON OCTOBER 12, 1935, *DON HOWE* JOINED *WEST BROMWICH ALBION* AS A YOUTH PLAYER IN 1950 AND WENT ON TO PLAY 342 GAMES FOR *"THE BAGGIES"*, WHILE WINNING 23 CAPS FOR *ENGLAND*. HE WAS SIGNED BY *ARSENAL* IN 1964 AND SOON APPOINTED CLUB CAPTAIN, BUT A BROKEN LEG ENDED HIS PLAYING CAREER. HE MOVED INTO A COACHING ROLE WITH THE CLUB, BEFORE ACCEPTING THE JOB OF MANAGER AT *WEST BROMWICH ALBION* IN 1971. HIS TENURE ENDED IN RELEGATION, AFTER WHICH HE ASSISTED *JIMMY ARMFIELD* AT *LEEDS UNITED* BEFORE TAKING THE HELM AT *GALATASARAY SK*. HE SUBSEQUENTLY MANAGED *ARSENAL, QUEENS PARK RANGERS* AND *COVENTRY CITY*. HE DIED IN 2015.

1. FOLLOWING *HOWE'S* 1986 RESIGNATION, WHO SUCCEEDED HIM AS *ARSENAL* MANAGER?

2. *HOWE* COACHED *ENGLAND* UNDER WHICH THREE MANAGERS BETWEEN 1981 AND 1996??

3. HE ASSISTED *BOBBY GOULD* AT WHICH CLUB IN THE LATE 1980S, EARNING CREDIT FOR HIS PART IN THE CLUB'S FA CUP FINAL SUCCESS OVER *LIVERPOOL?*

OCT 13

ALTHOUGH *JUST FONTAINE* WAS *FRANCE'S* 13-GOAL HERO IN THE 1958 WORLD CUP FINALS, IT WAS DEEP-LYING CENTRE-FORWARD *RAYMOND KOPA* WHO WAS THE INSPIRATIONAL ARCHITECT. BORN *RAYMOND KOPACZEWSKI*, IN NOUEX-LES-MINES, ON OCTOBER 13, 1931, HE FOLLOWED HIS FATHER DOWN THE MINES, BEFORE AN ACCIDENT -- IN WHICH HE LOST A FINGER -- CONVINCED HIM HE MUST ESCAPE PIT LIFE AT ALL COSTS. HE JOINED LOCAL CLUB *ANGERS*, BEFORE MOVING TO *REIMS* IN 1951. HE PLAYED IN THE FIRST-EVER EUROPEAN CUP FINAL IN 1956 AGAINST *REAL MADRID* -- AND IMPRESSED THE SPANIARDS SO MUCH THAT THEY SIGNED HIM THE FOLLOWING YEAR. PLAYING AS A WINGER, *KOPA* HELPED THEM TO THREE SUCCESSIVE EUROPEAN CUP FINAL WINS BEFORE REJOINING *REIMS* IN 1959 AND RENEWING HIS WORLD CUP PARTNERSHIP WITH *FONTAINE*. *KOPA* WON 45 CAPS FOR *FRANCE*, SCORING 18 GOALS. IN 1970, HE BECAME THE FIRST FOOTBALLER TO RECEIVE THE LÉGION D'HONNEUR.

KOPA WAS EUROPEAN FOOTBALLER OF THE YEAR IN 1958 -- NAME THE THREE OTHER FRENCHMEN WHO HAVE WON THE BALLON D'OR.

CAPPED 16 TIMES BY **SCOTLAND**, **CHARLIE COOKE** WAS EQUALLY AT HOME ON THE WING OR IN MIDFIELD. BORN IN ST. MONANS, ON OCTOBER 14, 1942, HE BEGAN HIS CAREER AT **ABERDEEN**, BEFORE SIGNING FOR **DUNDEE** IN 1964. TWO YEARS LATER, **TOMMY DOCHERTY** TOOK HIM TO **CHELSEA**, AND HE HELPED THE CLUB TO FA CUP AND EUROPEAN CUP WINNERS' CUP GLORY. FOLLOWING A TWO-YEAR SPELL AT **CRYSTAL PALACE**, HE RETURNED TO **CHELSEA**, WHERE HE EXPERIENCED RELEGATION AND PROMOTION. HE ENDED HIS CAREER IN NORTH AMERICA, PLAYING FOR A NUMBER OF TEAMS BEFORE MOVING INTO MANAGEMENT AS THE HEAD COACH OF THE **MEMPHIS ROGUES** IN 1980. IDENTIFY THESE OTHER MEMBERS OF THE 1970 **CHELSEA** FA CUP-WINNING SIDE WHO ALSO PLAYED IN THE STATES:

1. SCOTTISH INTERNATIONAL FULL-BACK WHO WENT ON TO MANAGE **CHELSEA**, AND WAS LATER SUCCEEDED BY **CHARLIE COOKE** AS MANAGER OF THE **MEMPHIS ROGUES**.

2. PLAYED FOR **SOUTHAMPTON** AND **PHILADELPHIA FURY** BEFORE ENDING HIS CAREER BACK AT **CHELSEA**.

3. **ENGLAND** GOALKEEPER WHO SPENT A SEASON WITH **ST. LOUIS STARS**.

MESUT ÖZIL WAS BORN IN GELSENKIRCHEN, ON OCTOBER 15, 1988. HAVING PLAYED JUST 37 GAMES FOR **FC SCHALKE 04**, HELPING THE CLUB TO A SECOND PLACE FINISH IN THE BUNDESLIGA, HE BECAME THE MOST EXPENSIVE TEENAGER IN GERMAN FOOTBALL HISTORY WHEN HE SIGNED FOR **WERDER BREMEN** IN 2008. THE NEXT SEASON, **BREMEN** WON THE DFB-POKAL AND REACHED THE UEFA CUP FINAL, AFTER WHICH **ÖZIL** WON THE UEFA EUROPEAN UNDER-21 CHAMPIONSHIP WITH **GERMANY**. HE WAS OUTSTANDING AT THE 2010 WORLD CUP AS **GERMANY** FINISHED THIRD, EARNING HIMSELF A TRANSFER TO **REAL MADRID**. HE WON LEAGUE AND CUP HONOURS WITH **"LOS MERENGUES"**, BEFORE BECOMING THE MOST EXPENSIVE GERMAN FOOTBALL PLAYER OF ALL TIME WHEN HE JOINED **ARSENAL** IN 2013 FOR A REPORTED TRANSFER FEE OF £42.5 MILLION.

1. **ÖZIL** WON THREE FA CUPS WITH **ARSENAL** -- IN 2014, 2015 AND 2017. NAME THE OPPONENTS.

2. **ÖZIL** WAS A WORLD CUP WINNER WITH **GERMANY** IN 2014 -- WHO WERE THE OPPONENTS AND WHAT WAS THE SCORE?

3. **ÖZIL** JOINED WHICH CLUB IN 2021?

OCT 16

BORN IN THE BAVARIAN TOWN OF DINKELSBÜHL, ON OCTOBER 16, 1966, *STEFAN REUTER* FIRST GAINED ATTENTION WHEN HE HELPED *1. FC NUREMBERG* BOUNCE STRAIGHT BACK INTO THE BUNDESLIGA AFTER RELEGATION. HE JOINED *BAYERN MUNICH* IN 1988, AND WON BACK-TO-BACK LEAGUE TITLES IN 1989 AND 1990. NICKNAMED *"TURBO"* FOR HIS SPEED AND STAMINA, HE WAS A WORLD CUP WINNER WITH *WEST GERMANY* IN 1990. HE SPENT A YEAR IN ITALY WITH *JUVENTUS*, BEFORE RETURNING TO GERMANY TO WIN THREE LEAGUE TITLES AND THE UEFA CHAMPIONS LEAGUE WITH *BORUSSIA DORTMUND*. A EUROPEAN CHAMPIONSHIP WINNER WITH *GERMANY* IN 1996, HE RETIRED IN 2004, AND LATER MANAGED *TSV 1860 MÜNCHEN*.

IDENTIFY THESE OTHER PLAYERS WHO WON BOTH THE 1990 WORLD CUP AND 1996 UEFA EUROPEAN CHAMPIONSHIPS:

1. UEFA CUP WINNER WITH *INTERNAZIONALE* AND *BAYERN MUNICH*, HIS OTHER CLUBS INCLUDE *TOTTENHAM HOTSPUR* AND *MONACO*.

2. CAPPED 101 TIMES, HE LATER COACHED *NIGERIA* AND *1. FC KÖLN*.

3. CAPPED 105 TIMES, CENTRAL DEFENDER WHO WON TITLES WITH *BAYERN MUNICH*, *JUVENTUS* AND *BORUSSIA DORTMUND*.

OCT 17

FOLLOWING THE ABOLITION OF THE £20 MAXIMUM WEEKLY WAGE IN 1961, *JOHNNY HAYNES* BECAME BRITAIN'S FIRST £100-A-WEEK PLAYER. BORN IN LONDON, ON OCTOBER 17, 1934, HE SPENT HIS ENTIRE FOOTBALL LEAGUE CAREER WITH *FULHAM*, PLAYING ALONGSIDE THE LIKES OF *BOBBY ROBSON* AND *JIMMY HILL*, SCORING 158 GOALS IN A CLUB RECORD 658 GAMES. CAPPED 56 TIMES BY *ENGLAND*, HE FIRST CAPTAINED HIS COUNTRY IN 1960 AND WAS SELECTED IN THREE WORLD CUP FINAL SQUADS, PLAYING IN TWO TOURNAMENTS. TOWARDS THE END OF HIS CAREER, HE HAD A SPELL IN CANADA WITH *TORONTO CITY* BEFORE PLAYING IN SOUTH AFRICA FOR A SEASON WITH *DURBAN CITY*, WHERE A LEAGUE TITLE GAVE HIM THE ONLY WINNERS MEDAL OF HIS CAREER. AN INAUGURAL INDUCTEE TO THE ENGLISH FOOTBALL HALL OF FAME, HE DIED IN 2005.

1. *HAYNES* IS *FULHAM'S* SECOND ALL-TIME TOP SCORER -- WHO HOLDS THE CLUB'S GOALSCORING RECORD?

2. *HAYNES* TOOK OVER AS TEMPORARY MANAGER IN 1968 AFTER WHICH SUBSEQUENT KNIGHT WAS FIRED?

3. WHICH COMEDIAN WAS *FULHAM* CHAIRMAN WHEN *JOHNNY HAYNES* WAS IN HIS HEYDAY?

OCT 18

ON OCTOBER 18, 2005, 21 MINUTES INTO THE UEFA CHAMPIONS LEAGUE GAME AWAY TO *SPARTA PRAGUE*, *THIERRY HENRY* SCORED FOR *"THE GUNNERS"*, AND EQUALLED *IAN WRIGHT'S* RECORD OF 185 GOALS FOR *ARSENAL*. LATE IN THE SECOND HALF, *HENRY* SCORED HIS RECORD-BREAKING 186TH GOAL. BY THE TIME HE LEFT *ARSENAL* IN 2007 TO JOIN *BARCELONA*, HIS TALLY STOOD AT 228 GOALS, WHICH REMAINS THE CLUB RECORD TO THIS DAY.

WHO HOLDS THE RECORD FOR THESE CLUBS:

1. *CHELSEA:* 211 GOALS BETWEEN 2001 AND 2014

2. *REAL MADRID:* 450 GOALS BETWEEN 2009 AND 2018

3. *AC MILAN:* 221 GOALS BETWEEN 1949 AND 1956

4. *TOTTENHAM HOTSPUR:* 266 GOALS BETWEEN 1961 AND 1970

GUNNAR NORDAHL SCORED 43 GOALS IN HIS 33 APPEARANCES FOR **SWEDEN**. BORN IN HÖRNEFORS, SWEDEN, ON OCTOBER 19, 1931, HE WAS ONE OF FIVE BROTHERS WHO GREW UP TO PLAY IN THE SWEDISH TOP FLIGHT! **GUNNAR**, **BERTIL** AND **KNUT NORDAHL** ALL WON OLYMPIC GOLD IN 1948 AND ALL THREE WENT ON TO PLAY PROFESSIONALLY IN ITALY. IN 1949, HE AND HIS FELLOW OLYMPIC CHAMPIONS, **GUNNAR GREN** AND **NILS LEIDHOLM**, JOINED **AC MILAN**, BECOMING THE FABLED **"GRE-NO-LI"** TRIO THAT INSPIRED THE CLUB TO TWO LEAGUE TITLES. HE SCORED A RECORD 210 LEAGUE GOALS IN HIS EIGHT SEASONS WITH **AC MILAN**, BEFORE ENDING HIS CAREER AS PLAYER/MANAGER WITH **ROMA**.

1. WHICH SWEDISH INTERNATIONAL HAS WON SERIE A TITLES WITH THREE DIFFERENT ITALIAN CLUBS?

2. WHICH SWEDISH INTERNATIONAL WON THE COPPA ITALIA, UEFA CUP WINNERS' CUP AND UEFA CUP WITH **PARMA**, BEFORE JOINING **LEEDS UNITED?**

3. WHICH SWEDE SPENT EIGHT SEASONS WITH **ATALANTA** AFTER WINNING LEAGUE TITLES WITH **IFK GÖTEBORG** AND **BENFICA?**

BORN IN ST. ASAPH, WALES, ON OCTOBER 20, 1971, *IAN RUSH* LAUNCHED HIS CAREER AT *CHESTER CITY*, BEFORE JOINING *LIVERPOOL* AS AN 18-YEAR-OLD, BY WHICH TIME HE HAD ALSO MADE HIS DEBUT FOR *WALES*. IN TWO SPELLS WITH THE CLUB -- INTERRUPTED BY A SEASON IN ITALY -- HE WON FIVE LEAGUE TITLES, THREE FA CUPS, FIVE LEAGUE CUPS AND THE 1984 EUROPEAN CUP. HE IS *LIVERPOOL'S* ALL-TIME LEADING SCORER WITH 346 GOALS.

1. HIS 28 INTERNATIONAL GOALS MADE HIM THE ALL-TIME LEADING GOALSCORER FOR *WALES*, A RECORD HE HELD FOR 24 YEARS UNTIL HE WAS OVERTAKEN BY WHICH PLAYER IN 2018?

2. NAME TWO OF THE SIX OTHER CLUBS, IN ADDITION TO *CHESTER CITY* AND *LIVERPOOL*, FOR WHOM *RUSH* PLAYED DURING HIS CAREER.

3. WHICH CLUB DID *IAN RUSH* BRIEFLY MANAGE IN 2004-05?

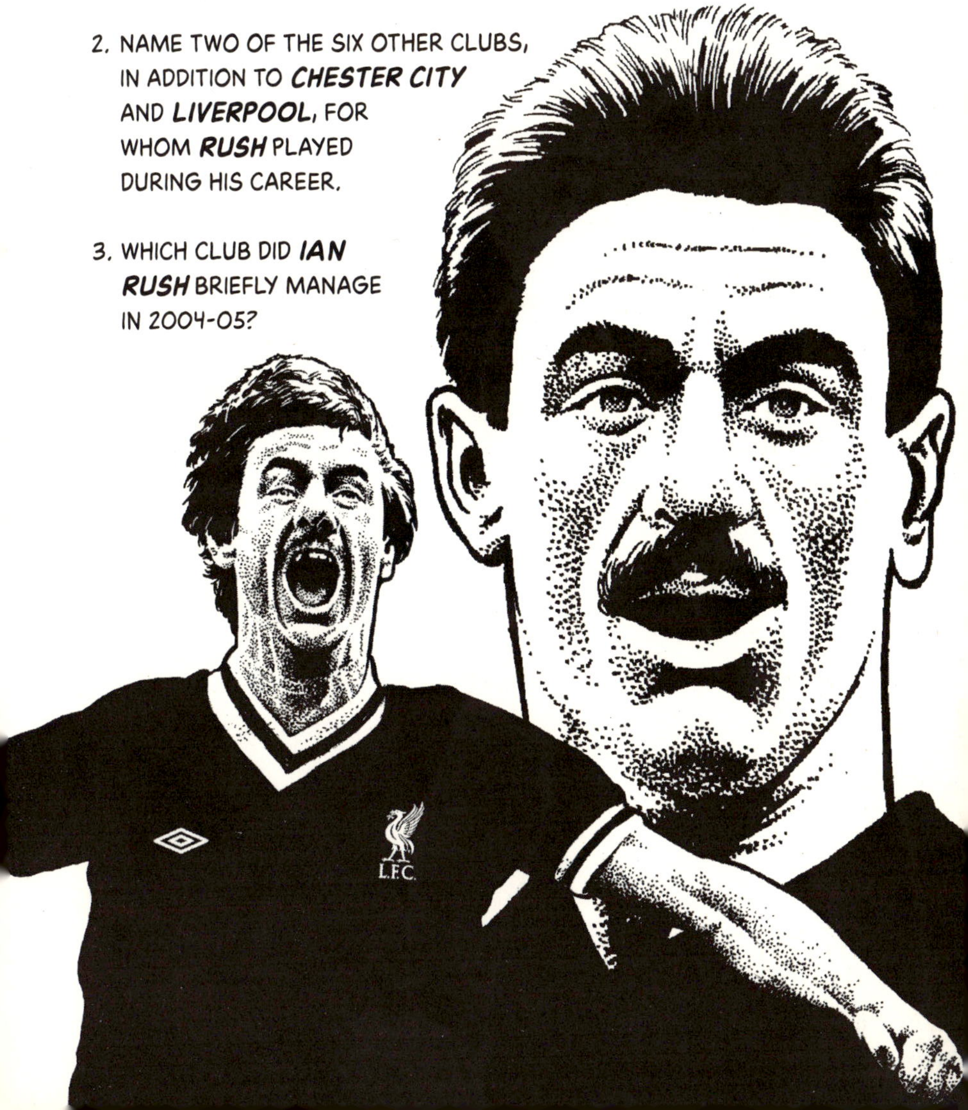

OCT
21

THE FIRST BLACK PLAYER TO CAPTAIN **ENGLAND**, **PAUL INCE** WAS BORN IN ILFORD, ESSEX, ON OCTOBER 21, 1967. HE BEGAN HIS CAREER AT **WEST HAM UNITED**, THEN JOINED **MANCHESTER UNITED** IN 1989, WHERE HE WON EVERY DOMESTIC HONOUR AND A EUROPEAN CUP WINNERS' CUP MEDAL BEFORE HEADING TO ITALY'S **INTERNAZIONALE** IN 1995.

1. NAME TWO OF THE CLUBS **INCE** SUBSEQUENTLY PLAYED FOR.

2. NAME TWO OF THE CLUBS HE MANAGED.

3. NAME **PAUL'S ENGLAND** YOUTH INTERNATIONAL SON, WHOSE CLUBS INCLUDE **BLACKPOOL** AND **DERBY COUNTY**.

OCT 22

STANDING 6'2" AND INVARIABLY CLAD IN BLACK, LEGENDARY GOALKEEPER **LEV YASHIN** WAS A COMMANDING LAST LINE OF DEFENCE FOR THE OLD **USSR** IN 78 INTERNATIONALS, INCLUDING THE 1958, 1962 AND 1966 WORLD CUP TOURNAMENTS *(AND WAS ALSO A MEMBER OF THE 1970 SQUAD)*. BORN IN MOSCOW ON OCTOBER 22, 1929, THE FORMER ICE HOCKEY PLAYER SPENT HIS ENTIRE CAREER WITH **DYNAMO MOSCOW**, WINNING FIVE LEAGUE TITLES AND THREE CUPS. AN OLYMPIC GOLD MEDAL WINNER IN 1956, HE WAS VOTED EUROPEAN FOOTBALLER OF THE YEAR IN 1963. HE WAS AWARDED HIS COUNTRY'S HIGHEST HONOUR -- THE ORDER OF LENIN -- FOR HIS CONTRIBUTION TO SPORT. **YASHIN** DIED IN 1990.

1. NAME THE TWO OTHER **SOVIET UNION** PLAYERS TO WIN THE EUROPEAN FOOTBALLER OF THE YEAR AWARD.

2. BETWEEN 1994 AND 2006, THE BEST GOALKEEPER AT THE WORLD CUP RECEIVED THE **YASHIN AWARD**, SUBSEQUENTLY RENAMED THE GOLDEN GLOVE. NAME ONE OF THOSE FOUR RECIPIENTS.

3. **YASHIN** WAS A MEMBER OF THE **SOVIET UNION** TEAM THAT WON THE 1960 EUROPEAN CHAMPIONSHIP *(KNOWN THEN AS THE EUROPEAN NATIONS' CUP)*. WHO DID THEY DEFEAT IN THE FINAL?

OCT 23

EDSON ARANTES DO NASCIMENTO WAS BORN IN TRES CORAÇÕES, MINAS GERAIS, BRAZIL, ON OCTOBER 23, 1940. KNOWN TO THE WORLD AS **PELÉ**, BY THE TIME HE FINALLY RETIRED IN 1977, HE HAD BECOME THE MOST FAMOUS SOCCER PLAYER ON EARTH! HE MADE HIS INTERNATIONAL DEBUT AT 16 AND WENT ON TO SCORE 97 GOALS IN 111 GAMES FOR **BRAZIL**, INCLUDING A DOZEN IN THE FOUR WORLD CUP TOURNAMENTS THAT EARNED HIM THREE WINNER'S MEDALS. **PELÉ** WAS 15 WHEN HE SCORED ON HIS DEBUT FOR **SANTOS** -- 14 YEARS AND 1,254 GAMES LATER HE RETIRED FOR THE FIRST TIME, HAVING SCORED 1,216 GOALS. IN 1975, THE **NEW YORK COSMOS** TEMPTED HIM BACK INTO THE SPORT WITH A $4.5 MILLION CONTRACT. HE TOOK HIS CAREER TALLY TO A TOTAL OF 1,283 GOALS AS HE ALMOST SINGLE-HANDEDLY LAUNCHED SOCCER IN THE UNITED STATES.

IDENTIFY THESE **NEW YORK COSMOS** STARS:

1. TWICE EUROPEAN FOOTBALLER OF THE YEAR, HE WON THE WORLD CUP AS A PLAYER AND AS A MANAGER.

2. CAPTAINED THE 1970 WORLD CUP WINNERS.

3. WON THE FA CUP WITH **SUNDERLAND**, AND THE LEAGUE CUP WITH **MANCHESTER CITY**.

OCT 24

WAYNE MARK ROONEY WAS BORN IN LIVERPOOL, ON OCTOBER 24, 1985. BEFORE HE CELEBRATED HIS 17TH BIRTHDAY, HE BECAME THE SECOND-YOUNGEST PLAYER IN **EVERTON** HISTORY BEHIND **JOE ROYLE**, AND THE YOUNGEST-EVER ENGLISH PREMIER LEAGUE GOALSCORER AT THAT TIME. IN 2003, THE 17-YEAR-OLD BECAME **ENGLAND'S** YOUNGEST PLAYER, AND THEN YOUNGEST GOALSCORER. HE WAS A SENSATION AT EURO 2004 UNTIL INJURY ENDED HIS TOURNAMENT AND **ENGLAND'S** PROGRESS, AFTER WHICH HE JOINED **MANCHESTER UNITED** IN A £25.6 MILLION TRANSFER. **ENGLAND'S** MOST-CAPPED OUTFIELD PLAYER, HE IS ALSO HIS COUNTRY'S ALL-TIME LEADING GOALSCORER.

1. NAME THE SIX **ENGLAND** MANAGERS UNDER WHOM **ROONEY** PLAYED.

2. **ROONEY'S ENGLAND** CAREER SPANNED 15 YEARS, 276 DAYS. NAME ONE OF THE TWO PLAYERS WITH LONGER CAREER SPANS.

3. WHO DID **ROONEY** SUCCEED AS **ENGLAND** CAPTAIN FOLLOWING THE 2014 WORLD CUP?

HARRY GREGG WAS BORN IN TOBERMORE, NORTHERN IRELAND, ON OCTOBER 25, 1932. HE MOVED TO ENGLAND AS A TEENAGER TO SIGN FOR **DONCASTER ROVERS**, AND MADE HIS DEBUT FOR **NORTHERN IRELAND** IN 1954. HE JOINED **MANCHESTER UNITED** IN 1957, AND A FEW MONTHS LATER, HE WAS THE HERO OF THE MUNICH AIR DISASTER THAT DECIMATED THE TEAM, BRAVELY RUNNING BACK INTO THE WRECKAGE TO RESCUE INJURED PASSENGERS. HE STAYED AT **OLD TRAFFORD** UNTIL 1966, AND FOLLOWING A YEAR AT **STOKE CITY**, MOVED INTO MANAGEMENT WITH **SHREWSBURY TOWN**, **SWANSEA CITY**, **CREWE ALEXANDRIA** AND **CARLISLE UNITED**. HE PASSED AWAY IN 2020.

GREGG KEPT GOAL FOR **MANCHESTER UNITED** IN THE 1958 FA CUP FINAL. HOW MANY OF THE TEN GOALKEEPERS WHO HAVE REPRESENTED **UNITED** IN THE 16 FA CUP FINALS (AND TWO REPLAYS) THE CLUB HAS SINCE CONTESTED UP TO 2018 CAN YOU NAME?

ON OCTOBER 26, 1863, THE FIRST MEETING OF **ENGLAND'S** FOOTBALL GOVERNING BODY WAS HELD, MAKING **THE FOOTBALL ASSOCIATION** THE OLDEST NATIONAL FOOTBALL ASSOCIATION IN THE WORLD. ELEVEN LONDON FOOTBALL CLUBS AND SCHOOLS WERE REPRESENTED AT THE MEETING, WHICH WAS HELD IN A PUB IN LONDON'S COVENT GARDEN, TO AGREE ON A COMMON SET OF RULES -- **BARNES, CIVIL SERVICE, CRUSADERS, FOREST OF LEYTONSTONE N.N. (NO NAMES) CLUB KILBURN, CRYSTAL PALACE, BLACKHEATH, KENSINGTON SCHOOL, PERCEVAL HOUSE, AND SURBITON** AND **BLACKHEATH PROPRIETARY SCHOOL. CHARTERHOUSE** SENT A REPRESENTATIVE BUT DECLINED THE OFFER TO JOIN. THE RULES WERE DRAWN UP OVER SIX SUBSEQUENT MEETINGS, WHICH RESULTED IN A SPLIT BETWEEN **THE FOOTBALL ASSOCIATION** AND WHAT WOULD BECOME THE **RUGBY FOOTBALL UNION** IN 1871.

THE FOOTBALL ASSOCIATION IS KNOWN AS **THE FA** -- WHICH COUNTRY'S FOOTBALL ASSOCIATION IS REPRESENTED BY THE INITIALS:

1. **AFA**

2. **FFF**

3. **KNVB**

4. **CBF**

5. **DFB**

6. **FIGC**

7. **FAI**

OCT 27

GLENN HODDLE WAS BORN IN HAYES, MIDDLESEX, ON OCTOBER 27, 1957. IN EIGHT SEASONS WITH **TOTTENHAM HOTSPUR** HE WON THE UEFA CUP AND TWO FA CUPS BEFORE HEADING TO FRANCE, WHERE HE WON A LEAGUE TITLE WITH **AS MONACO**. CAPPED 53 TIMES BY **ENGLAND**, HE CONTINUED PLAYING AFTER LAUNCHING HIS MANAGEMENT CAREER AT **SWINDON TOWN** AND **CHELSEA**. IN 1996, HE SUCCEEDED **TERRY VENABLES** AS **ENGLAND** MANAGER, AND STEERED THE NATIONAL SIDE TO THE 1998 WORLD CUP. DISMISSED IN 1999 FOLLOWING A MEDIA OUTCRY OVER HIS RELIGIOUS VIEWS, HE LATER TOOK THE REINS AT **SOUTHAMPTON, TOTTENHAM HOTSPUR** AND **WOLVERHAMPTON WANDERERS**. IN 2018, ON HIS 61ST BIRTHDAY, HE SUFFERED A HEART ATTACK IN A TV STUDIO AND WAS ONLY SAVED BY THE ACTIONS OF A QUICK-THINKING EMPLOYEE WHO KNEW HOW TO USE A DEFIBRILLATOR.

HODDLE IS ONE OF TEN FORMER **TOTTENHAM HOTSPUR** PLAYERS WHO HAVE MANAGED THE CLUB, INCLUDING CARETAKER MANAGERS, SINCE THE SECOND WORLD WAR. NAME THREE OTHERS.

OCT 28

BORN IN PAU GRANDE, BRAZIL, ON OCTOBER 28, 1933, **MANOEL FRANCISCO DOS SANTOS** CONTRACTED POLIO AS A CHILD ... YET, DESPITE A DEFORMED LEG, HE LEARNED TO RUN AT BLISTERING SPEEDS. KNOWN AS **GARRINCHA** -- WHICH MEANS **"LITTLE BIRD"** -- HE WAS CATAPULTED TO INTERNATIONAL STARDOM WITH HIS MAGNIFICENT DISPLAYS IN THE **BRAZIL** SIDES THAT WON THE 1958 AND 1962 WORLD CUPS. A CAR CRASH AND A SERIOUS KNEE INJURY TOOK A HEAVY TOLL, AND BY THE 1966 WORLD CUP THE LITTLE WINGER WAS A SPENT FORCE -- YET HE STILL MANAGED TO SCORE A SUPERB GOAL AGAINST **BULGARIA**. HIS CHAOTIC PERSONAL LIFE TOOK A HEAVY TOLL, AND HE DIED OF ALCOHOL POISONING AT THE AGE OF 49.

WHICH **BRAZIL** STAR'S REAL NAME IS:

1. **MARCOS EVANGELISTA DE MORAES**

2. **RICARDO IZECSON DOS SANTOS LEITE**

3. **ROBSON DE SOUZA**

BORN IN VERHOOT, ON OCTOBER 29, 1970, LEGENDARY **NETHERLANDS** GOALKEEPER **EDWIN VAN DER SAR** BEGAN HIS CAREER AT **AJAX**, WITH WHOM HE WON FOUR LEAGUE TITLES, THREE DUTCH CUPS, THE UEFA CHAMPIONS LEAGUE, THE UEFA CUP AND THE UEFA SUPER CUP. HE ENDED HIS CAREER AT **MANCHESTER UNITED**, WITH A MEDAL HAUL INCLUDING FOUR LEAGUE TITLES, A FOOTBALL LEAGUE CUP, THE UEFA CHAMPIONS LEAGUE AND THE FIFA CLUB WORLD CUP. HE MADE A RECORD 130 APPEARANCES FOR HIS COUNTRY AND WAS VOTED BEST EUROPEAN GOALKEEPER FOUR TIMES.

1. NAME THE TWO OTHER CLUBS THAT **VAN DER SAR** PLAYED FOR.

2. **VAN DER SAR** WON THE UEFA CHAMPIONS LEAGUE WITH TWO DIFFERENT TEAMS -- WHO WAS THE FIRST PLAYER TO WIN THE TOURNAMENT WITH THREE DIFFERENT TEAMS?

3. HE WON THE PREMIER LEAGUE GOLDEN GLOVE IN 2009. WHO WAS THE NEXT **MANCHESTER UNITED** PLAYER TO WIN THAT HONOUR?

BORN IN BUENOS AIRES, ON OCTOBER 30, 1960, *DIEGO MARADONA* MADE HIS LEAGUE DEBUT AT THE AGE OF 5 FOR *ARGENTINOS JUNIORS*, AND WON HIS FIRST INTERNATIONAL CAP A YEAR LATER. HE JOINED *BOCA JUNIORS* IN 1980, BEFORE MOVING TO *BARCELONA* FOR A WORLD RECORD FEE IN 1982. IN 1984, HE SIGNED FOR *NAPOLI* AND INSPIRED THEM TO THE ITALIAN LEAGUE AND CUP DOUBLE, ONE YEAR AFTER LEADING *ARGENTINA* TO WORLD CUP GLORY IN MEXICO IN 1986. A UEFA CUP IN 1989 WAS FOLLOWED IN 1990 BY A SECOND SERIE A TITLE, THE SAME YEAR HE LED HIS COUNTRY TO A WORLD CUP FINAL AGAINST *GERMANY*. HE WAS EXPELLED FROM THE 1994 WORLD CUP AFTER FAILING A DRUG TEST, AND RETIRED IN 1997. HE PASSED AWAY IN NOVEMBER, 2020.

HIS 34 GOALS FOR HIS COUNTRY PLACE HIM FIFTH ON *ARGENTINA'S* ALL-TIME GOALSCORER LIST. IDENTIFY THE PLAYERS AHEAD OF HIM:

1. WON FIVE PREMIER LEAGUES WITH *MANCHESTER CITY*.

2. PREMIER LEAGUE WINNER WITH *CHELSEA*.

3. SIX TIMES BALLON D'OR WINNER.

4. NICKNAMED *"BATIGOL"*.

BORN *CARLOS CAETANO BLEDORN VERRI* IN IJUÍ, BRAZIL, ON OCTOBER 31, 1963, HE WAS NICKNAMED *DUNGA* -- THE PORTUGUESE TRANSLATION OF THE NAME *DOPEY* FROM *"SNOW WHITE AND THE SEVEN DWARFS"* -- AS A CHILD. A FIFA U-20 WORLD CUP WINNER IN 1983, *DUNGA* WAS CAPPED 91 TIMES BY *BRAZIL*, AND REPRESENTED HIS COUNTRY AT THREE WORLD CUPS, INCLUDING CAPTAINING THE TRIUMPHANT 1994 TEAM. FOLLOWING A CAREER THAT SAW HIM PLAY FOR CLUBS IN BRAZIL, ITALY, GERMANY AND JAPAN, HE COACHED *BRAZIL'S U-23* TEAM, BEFORE COACHING THE SENIOR SIDE FOR FOUR YEARS. HE WAS DISMISSED FOLLOWING *BRAZIL'S* QUARTER-FINAL EXIT FROM THE 2010 WORLD CUP. HE RETURNED TO THE POST IN 2014, BUT WAS DISMISSED ONCE MORE IN 2016.

1. *BRAZIL* HAS WON THE WORLD CUP FIVE TIMES -- IN WHICH YEARS?

2. NAME TWO OF THE FIVE WORLD CUP-WINNING *BRAZIL* COACHES.

3. NAME ONE OF *BRAZIL'S* OTHER WORLD CUP-WINNING CAPTAINS.

NOVEMBER

NOV 1

MARK HUGHES WAS BORN IN WREXHAM, WALES, ON NOVEMBER 1, 1963. HE LAUNCHED HIS CAREER AT **MANCHESTER UNITED**, WINNING THE FA CUP IN 1986, BEFORE **TERRY VENABLES** SIGNED HIM AND **GARY LINEKER** FOR **BARCELONA**. **HUGHES** FAILED TO SETTLE IN SPAIN AND WAS SOON LOANED OUT TO **BAYERN MUNICH**. HE RETURNED TO **MANCHESTER UNITED** IN 1988, AND WENT ON TO WIN TWO LEAGUE TITLES, TWO FA CUPS, THE LEAGUE CUP, THE UEFA CUP WINNERS' CUP AND THE UEFA SUPER CUP WITH THE CLUB. HE JOINED **CHELSEA** IN 1995, WHERE HE WON ANOTHER FA CUP, LEAGUE CUP AND UEFA CUP WINNERS' CUP. HE WAS CAPPED 72 TIMES BY **WALES**, SCORING 16 GOALS, AND WAS APPOINTED COACH OF THE NATIONAL TEAM IN 1999. HE SPENT FIVE YEARS IN CHARGE BEFORE EMBARKING ON A CAREER IN CLUB MANAGEMENT.

1. HE WAS INITIALLY APPOINTED TEMPORARY COACH OF **WALES** IN TANDEM WITH WHICH WELSH GOALKEEPING LEGEND?

2. NAME ONE OF THE OTHER CLUBS **MARK HUGHES** PLAYED FOR.

3. NAME THREE OF THE CLUBS HE HAS SUBSEQUENTLY MANAGED.

NOV 2

CAPTAIN OF **URUGUAY** AT TWO WORLD CUPS, **DIEGO LUGANO** MADE 95 APPEARANCES FOR HIS COUNTRY. BORN IN CANELONES ON NOVEMBER 3, 1980, HE ESTABLISHED HIS REPUTATION AS TOP-CLASS DEFENDER WITH **SÃO PAULO**, HAVING MOVED TO BRAZIL AFTER LAUNCHING HIS CAREER WITH **NACIONAL**. HAVING WON LEAGUE, COPA LIBERTADORES AND FIFA WORLD CLUB HONOURS, HE TOOK HIS SKILLS TO EUROPE, WHERE HE WON TWO LEAGUE TITLES WITH **FENERBAHÇE** AND PLAYED FOR **PARIS SAINT-GERMAIN, MÁLAGA, WEST BROMWICH ALBION** AND SWEDEN'S **BK HÄCKEN**. FOLLOWING A BRIEF SOJOURN IN PARAGUAY WITH **CERRO PORTEÑO**, HE RETURNED TO **SÃO PAULO** AND A HERO'S WELCOME. AFTER RETIRING, HE ACCEPTED AN ADMINISTRATIVE ROLE WITH THE CLUB.

WHICH COUNTRIES DID THE FOLLOWING **WEST BROMWICH ALBION** PLAYERS REPRESENT?

1. **SALOMÓN RONDÓN**

2. **ROBERT SNODGRASS**

3. **DIOMANSY KAMARA**

4. **BRANISLAV IVANOVIĆ**

5. **NACER CHADLI**

NOV 3

GERHARD MÜLLER'S STRIKE RECORD OF 68 GOALS IN 62 GAMES FOR **WEST GERMANY** RANKS HIM AS ONE OF THE DEADLIEST STRIKERS IN INTERNATIONAL FOOTBALL HISTORY. BORN IN NÖRDLINGEN, ON NOVEMBER 3, 1945, AND RAISED IN THE BAVARIAN TOWN OF ZINSEN, THE SQUAT, POWERFUL **MÜLLER** BEGAN HIS CAREER WITH **TSV NÖRDLINGEN**, BEFORE JOINING **BAYERN MUNICH** IN 1963. HIS GOALS BLASTED **BAYERN** TO UNPRECEDENTED GLORY -- THREE EUROPEAN CUPS, THE EUROPEAN CUP WINNERS' CUP, FOUR LEAGUE TITLES AND FOUR GERMAN CUPS. EUROPEAN FOOTBALLER OF THE YEAR IN 1970 -- THE SAME YEAR HE SCORED 10 GOALS IN **WEST GERMANY'S** WORLD CUP CAMPAIGN -- **GERD MÜLLER** WAS OUTSTANDING FOR HIS COUNTRY IN THE 1972 EUROPEAN CHAMPIONSHIP TRIUMPH. HE RETIRED FROM INTERNATIONAL FOOTBALL AFTER SCORING THE WINNING GOAL IN THE 1974 WORLD CUP FINAL. BY THE TIME HE LEFT GERMANY IN 1979 TO JOIN THE **FORT LAUDERDALE STRIKERS**, "**DER BOMBER**" HAD SCORED 600 GOALS, INCLUDING 398 IN 453 GAMES IN THE BUNDESLIGA.

NAME ANOTHER PLAYER WHO SCORED THE WINNING GOAL IN A WORLD CUP FINAL.

NOV 4 2000 EUROPEAN FOOTBALLER OF THE YEAR AND 2001 FIFA WORLD PLAYER OF THE YEAR, *LUÍS FIGO* WAS BORN IN ALMADA, ON NOVEMBER 4, 1972. HAVING LAUNCHED HIS CAREER WITH *SPORTING CP*, HE SIGNED FOR *BARCELONA* IN 1995 AND WENT ON TO WIN A NUMBER OF HONOURS, INCLUDING TWO LEAGUE TITLES AND THE UEFA CUP WINNERS' CUP. IN 2000, HE MADE THE SENSATIONAL SWITCH TO *BARCELONA'S* GREAT RIVALS *REAL MADRID* AND GAINED EVEN MORE HONOURS, INCLUDING TWO LEAGUE TITLES AND THE UEFA CHAMPIONS LEAGUE. HE ENDED HIS CAREER IN ITALY PLAYING FOR *INTERNAZIONALE*, ADDING FOUR SERIE A TITLES, ONE ITALIAN CUP AND THREE ITALIAN SUPERCUPS TO HIS MEDAL TALLY.

IDENTIFY THESE OTHERS WHO ALSO PLAYED FOR BOTH *REAL MADRID* AND *BARCELONA:*

1. EURO 1980 WINNER WITH *WEST GERMANY*, NICKNAMED *"THE BLONDE ANGEL"*, HE WON LA LIGA WITH BOTH CLUBS AND LATER MANAGED *REAL MADRID.*

2. WON LA LIGA AND THE UEFA CHAMPIONS LEAGUE AS *BARCELONA* MANAGER BEFORE COACHING *SPAIN.*

3. NICKNAMED *"THE MARADONA OF THE CARPATHIANS"*, HE WAS CAPPED 124 TIMES BY *ROMANIA.*

NOV 5

BORN ON NOVEMBER 5, 1974, IN ZADAR, IN WHAT WAS THEN YUGOSLAVIA, **MILADIN "DADO" PRŠO** WAS CAPPED 32 TIMES BY **CROATIA**. RELEASED BY **HAJDUK SPLIT** AS A YOUNGSTER WHEN A MEDICAL REVEALED AN IRREGULAR HEARTBEAT, HE PLAYED FOR **PAZINKA** WHEN THE CROATIAN LEAGUE WAS FORMED. HE PLAYED FOR A COUPLE OF CLUBS IN FRANCE, SUPPLEMENTING HIS INCOME BY WORKING AS A CAR MECHANIC, BEFORE **JEAN TIGANA** TOOK HIM TO **AS MONACO**. AFTER HELPING THE CLUB TO A LEAGUE TITLE AND THE FINAL OF THE UEFA CHAMPIONS LEAGUE, HE JOINED **RANGERS** IN 2004, WHERE HE ACHIEVED CULT HERO STATUS. KNEE PROBLEMS FORCED HIS EARLY RETIREMENT FROM THE GAME IN 2007. IDENTIFY THESE OTHER **CROATIA** STRIKERS:

1. A UEFA CHAMPIONS LEAGUE WINNER WITH **REAL MADRID**, TOP SCORER AT THE 1998 WORLD CUP, **CROATIA'S** MOST PROLIFIC GOALSCORER HAD SPELLS WITH **ARSENAL** AND **WEST HAM UNITED**.

2. BORN IN BRAZIL, HE SPENT THREE SEASONS AT **ARSENAL** BEFORE JOINING **SHAKTAR DONETSK** IN 2010.

3. UEFA CHAMPIONS LEAGUE WINNER WITH **BAYERN MUNICH**, HE WON FOUR SERIE A TITLES WITH **JUVENTUS** AND PLAYED BRIEFLY WITH **AC MILAN** IN 2021.

44-YEAR-OLD **ALEX FERGUSON** WAS APPOINTED MANAGER OF **MANCHESTER UNITED** ON NOVEMBER 6, 1986. THREE YEARS LATER, IN THE WAKE OF A 5-1 THRASHING BY **MANCHESTER CITY**, HIS POSITION LOOKED TO BE IN JEOPARDY, BUT VICTORY IN THE 1990 FA CUP FINAL BROUGHT HIM A TROPHY AND JOB SECURITY. KNIGHTED IN 1999, THE FORMER SCOTTISH INTERNATIONAL, WHOSE MANAGEMENT CAREER INCLUDED SPELLS IN CHARGE OF **ABERDEEN** AND **SCOTLAND**, WAS THE LONGEST-SERVING MANAGER IN **MANCHESTER UNITED** HISTORY. HIS TROPHY HAUL AT THE CLUB INCLUDED 13 LEAGUE TITLES, FIVE FA CUPS, TWO UEFA CHAMPIONS LEAGUES AND THE UEFA CUP WINNERS' CUP.

NAME FIVE OTHER MEN WHO HAVE MANAGED **MANCHESTER UNITED** SINCE **MATT BUSBY** WON THE EUROPEAN CUP IN 1968.

NOV 7

RIO GAVIN FERDINAND WAS BORN IN PECKHAM, LONDON, ON NOVEMBER 7, 1978. AT THE AGE OF 11, HE WON A SCHOLARSHIP TO ATTEND LONDON'S CENTRAL SCHOOL OF BALLET, ATTENDING WEEKLY CLASSES FOR THE NEXT FOUR YEARS. CRUCIALLY, HE WAS ALSO INVITED TO TRAIN WITH **QUEENS PARK RANGERS**, A CLUB THAT FIGURES PROMINENTLY IN HIS FAMILY'S LIFE -- HIS COUSIN, **ENGLAND** INTERNATIONAL **LES FERDINAND**, IS A GOALSCORING LEGEND AT THE CLUB, AND **RIO'S** YOUNGER BROTHER, **ANTON**, SIGNED FOR **QPR** IN 2011. **RIO** JOINED THE **WEST HAM UNITED** YOUTH SCHEME IN 1992. HE PROGRESSED THROUGH THE RANKS AND WENT ON TO BECOME THE WORLD'S MOST EXPENSIVE DEFENDER WHEN HE SIGNED FOR **LEEDS UNITED** IN 2000. TWO YEARS LATER, HE BECAME BRITAIN'S MOST EXPENSIVE PLAYER WHEN HE SIGNED FOR **MANCHESTER UNITED**.

NAME THE PROFESSIONAL FOOTBALLING BROTHERS OF THE FOLLOWING **ENGLAND** INTERNATIONAL STARS:

1. **JOHN FASHANU**

2. **GLENN HODDLE**

3. **SHAUN WRIGHT-PHILLIPS**

4. **JOLEON LESCOTT**

5. **RON SPRINGETT**

NOV 8

BORN IN LONDON, ON NOVEMBER 8, 1981, *JOE COLE* ONCE SCORED SEVEN GOALS FOR THE *ENGLAND* YOUTH TEAM IN A GAME AGAINST *SPAIN*. HE MADE HIS SENIOR DEBUT FOR *WEST HAM UNITED* AT THE AGE OF 17, AND WAS GIVEN THE CAPTAIN'S ARMBAND AT THE AGE OF 21. HE JOINED *CHELSEA* IN 2003, WITH WHOM HE WON WIN THREE LEAGUE TITLES, THREE FA CUPS AND TWO LEAGUE CUPS. HE JOINED *LIVERPOOL* ON A FREE TRANSFER IN 2010, BUT WAS LOANED TO *LILLE* IN 2011. FOLLOWING A RETURN TO *WEST HAM*, HE PLAYED FOR *ASTON VILLA* AND *COVENTRY CITY* BEFORE ENDING HIS CAREER WITH TWO SEASONS WITH THE *TAMPA BAY ROWDIES*. HE WAS CAPPED 56 TIMES BY *ENGLAND*.

IDENTIFY THESE *ENGLAND* INTERNATIONALS WHO PLAYED IN FRANCE:

1. FA CUP FINALIST WITH *TOTTENHAM HOTSPUR* AND *SHEFFIELD WEDNESDAY*, HE WON THREE LEAGUE TITLES WITH *MARSEILLE*.

2. SPENT A SEASON WITH *PSG* AND IS THE FIRST PLAYER TO WIN LEAGUE TITLES IN ENGLAND, SPAIN, ITALY AND FRANCE.

3. WON A LEAGUE TITLE WITH *ARSÈNE WENGER'S MONACO* IN BETWEEN SPELLS AT *AC MILAN* AND *RANGERS*.

 **NOV 9**

BORN IN CONEGLIANO, ON NOVEMBER 9, 1974, *ALESSANDRO DEL PIERO* IS ONE OF THE GREAT FIGURES IN *JUVENTUS* HISTORY, HAVING WON EIGHT SERIE A TITLES *(TWO OF WHICH WERE STRIPPED IN THE CALCIOPOLI SCANDAL)*, FOUR ITALIAN SUPERCUPS AND THE UEFA CHAMPIONS LEAGUE. HE HOLDS THE CLUB SCORING AND APPEARANCES RECORD. HE WAS CAPPED 91 TIMES BY *ITALY*, WINNING THE WORLD CUP IN 2006. HE SPENT TWO SEASONS IN AUSTRALIA WITH *SYDNEY FC* AND RETIRED FROM PLAYING AFTER A BRIEF SWANSONG WITH *DELHI DYNAMOS FC* IN THE INDIAN SUPER LEAGUE.

NAME THESE INTERNATIONAL STARS WHO ALSO PLAYED IN AUSTRALIA :

1. *ENGLAND* STRIKER WHOSE CLUBS INCLUDE *LIVERPOOL*, *LEEDS UNITED* AND *MANCHESTER CITY*.

2. IRISH WINGER WHO WON TWO PREMIER LEAGUES WITH *CHELSEA* AND PLAYED FOR *BLACKBURN ROVERS*, *NEWCASTLE UNITED* AND *FULHAM*.

3. WON THE WORLD CUP AND GOLDEN BALL WITH *BRAZIL* IN 1994.

NOV 10

TWICE UEFA CLUB GOALKEEPER OF THE YEAR, *JENS LEHMANN* WAS BORN IN ESSEN ON NOVEMBER 10, 1969. HE BEGAN HIS CAREER AT *FC SCHALKE 04*, WITH WHOM HE WON A UEFA CUP IN 1997. AN UNHAPPY SEASON WITH *AC MILAN* -- HE WON A LEAGUE TITLE BUT MADE JUST FIVE FIRST TEAM APPEARANCES -- WAS FOLLOWED BY A MOVE TO *BORUSSIA DORTMUND*, WHERE HE WON ANOTHER LEAGUE TITLE. HE JOINED *ARSENAL* IN 2003, PLAYED IN EVERY MATCH OF THE TEAM'S UNBEATEN, TITLE-WINNING 2003-04 SEASON, AND WAS AN FA CUP WINNER IN 2005. HE WENT ON TO END HIS CAREER AT *VFB STUTTGART*. HE EMERGED BRIEFLY FROM RETIREMENT TO HELP *ARSENAL* OVERCOME A GOALKEEPING INJURY CRISIS IN 2011.

WHICH GERMAN GOALKEEPER:

1. JOINED *BARCELONA* FROM *BORUSSIA MÖNCHENGLADBACH* IN 2012 AND WON A TREBLE OF LEAGUE, CUP AND UEFA CHAMPIONS LEAGUE IN HIS DEBUT SEASON.

2. GOLDEN GLOVE RECIPIENT WHEN *GERMANY* WON THE 2014 WORLD CUP.

3. EURO 1996 WINNER WHO WON EIGHT LEAGUE TITLES AND THE UEFA CHAMPIONS LEAGUE WITH *BAYERN MUNICH*.

BORN IN WORSTHORNE, LANCASHIRE, ON NOVEMBER 11, 1921, **RON GREENWOOD** PLAYED FOR **BRADFORD PARK AVENUE** AND **BRENTFORD**, BEFORE WINNING A LEAGUE TITLE WITH **CHELSEA** IN 1955. HE PLAYED A SEASON WITH **FULHAM** BEFORE RETIRING AND MOVING INTO COACHING. HE COACHED **EASTBOURNE UNITED**, **OXFORD UNIVERSITY** AND THE **ENGLAND** YOUTH AND UNDER-23 TEAMS, AND WAS ASSISTANT MANAGER AT **ARSENAL**, BEFORE HE WAS APPOINTED MANAGER OF **WEST HAM UNITED** IN 1961. IN 13 YEARS AT THE HELM, HIS TROPHY HAUL INCLUDED THE FA CUP AND EUROPEAN CUP WINNERS' CUP. IN THE MID-1970S, HE BECAME GENERAL MANAGER OF THE CLUB, BEFORE SUCCEEDING **DON REVIE** AS **ENGLAND** MANAGER IN 1977, A POSITION HE HELD UNTIL AFTER THE 1982 WORLD CUP. HE DIED IN 2006, AGED 84.

NAME THE TEN MEN WHO HAVE SUBSEQUENTLY MANAGED **ENGLAND** SINCE **RON GREENWOOD**, INCLUDING THOSE WHO TOOK THE ROLE IN A CARETAKER CAPACITY.

NOV 12

ENZO FRANCESCOLI WAS BORN IN MONTEVIDEO, URUGUAY, ON NOVEMBER 12, 1961. HE MADE HIS FIRST DIVISION DEBUT AT 17 AND GAINED THE FIRST OF HIS 73 CAPS IN 1982. THE INSPIRATION BEHIND ***URUGUAY'S*** 1983, 1987 AND 1995 COPA AMÉRICA TRIUMPHS, HE WAS VOTED SOUTH AMERICAN FOOTBALLER OF THE YEAR IN 1984 AND 1995. HE LAUNCHED HIS CAREER IN URUGUAY WITH ***WANDERERS***, BEFORE JOINING ARGENTINA'S ***RIVER PLATE*** IN 1983. TWO YEARS LATER, HE WAS THE LEAGUE'S TOP SCORER AS ***RIVER PLATE*** WON THE CHAMPIONSHIP. AFTER EIGHT YEARS IN EUROPE, HE RETURNED TO THE CLUB IN 1994.

NAME ONE OF THE FOUR EUROPEAN CLUBS HE PLAYED FOR.

NOV 13

BORN IN CEJKOV, ON NOVEMBER 13, 1947, *JÁN PIVARNÍK* PLAYED MOST OF HIS CLUB FOOTBALL WITH *SLOVAN BRATISLAVA*. CAPTAIN OF THE *CZECHOSLOVAKIA* SIDE THAT BEAT *WEST GERMANY* IN THE FINAL TO WIN THE 1976 EUROPEAN CHAMPIONSHIP, HE REPRESENTED HIS COUNTRY 39 TIMES. FOLLOWING A BRIEF SPELL IN SPAIN WITH *CÁDIZ CF*, HE TOOK UP A COACHING CAREER THAT TOOK HIM TO CLUBS IN AUSTRIA, PORTUGAL, CZECHOSLOVAKIA, OMAN, UAE, SAUDI ARABIA AND KUWAIT.

NAME THE NINE OTHER NATIONAL TEAMS WHO HAVE WON A EUROPEAN CHAMPIONSHIP.

NOV 14

BOBBY MOORE PLAYED THE LAST OF HIS 108 GAMES FOR **ENGLAND** -- AT THAT TIME A RECORD -- ON NOVEMBER 14, 1973, IN A 1-0 LOSS TO ITALY AT WEMBLEY STADIUM. THE ONLY GOAL OF THE GAME WAS SCORED BY FUTURE **ENGLAND** MANAGER **FABIO CAPELLO**. THE GAME ALSO SAW **MOORE** EQUAL **BILLY WRIGHT'S** RECORD OF CAPTAINING **ENGLAND** 90 TIMES.

BILLY WRIGHT CAPTAINED **ENGLAND** AT THREE WORLD CUPS -- 1950, 1954 AND 1958. **BOBBY MOORE** WAS CAPTAIN FOR THE 1966 AND 1970 TOURNAMENTS. NAME THESE OTHER **ENGLAND** WORLD CUP CAPTAINS:

1. 1962   2. 1982   3. 1986 AND 1990   4. 1998
5. 2002 AND 2006   6. 2010 AND 2014   5. 2018

NOV
15

THE FORMER ALL-TIME TOP GOALSCORER FOR THE **CAMEROON** NATIONAL TEAM AND 2000 AFRICAN FOOTBALLER OF THE YEAR, **PATRICK M'BOMA** WAS BORN IN DOUALA, ON NOVEMBER 15, 1970. HE REPRESENTED **CAMEROON** IN TWO WORLD CUP TOURNAMENTS, LED HIS COUNTRY TO THE GOLD MEDAL AT THE 2000 OLYMPICS, AND HELPED **CAMEROON** TRIUMPH AT THE AFRICAN NATIONS CUP IN 2000 AND 2002. HE SCORED 33 GOALS IN 57 INTERNATIONAL APPEARANCES. HIS CLUB CAREER SAW HIM PLAY IN FRANCE, ITALY, JAPAN, ENGLAND -- AS WELL AS A BRIEF SPELL IN LIBYA -- BEFORE RETIRING IN 2005. WHILE PLAYING FOR JAPAN'S **GAMBA OSAKA**, HE WAS THE 1997 J. LEAGUE TOP SCORER.

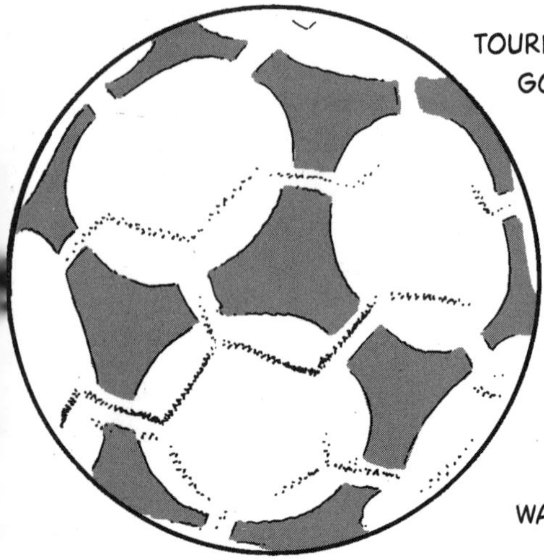

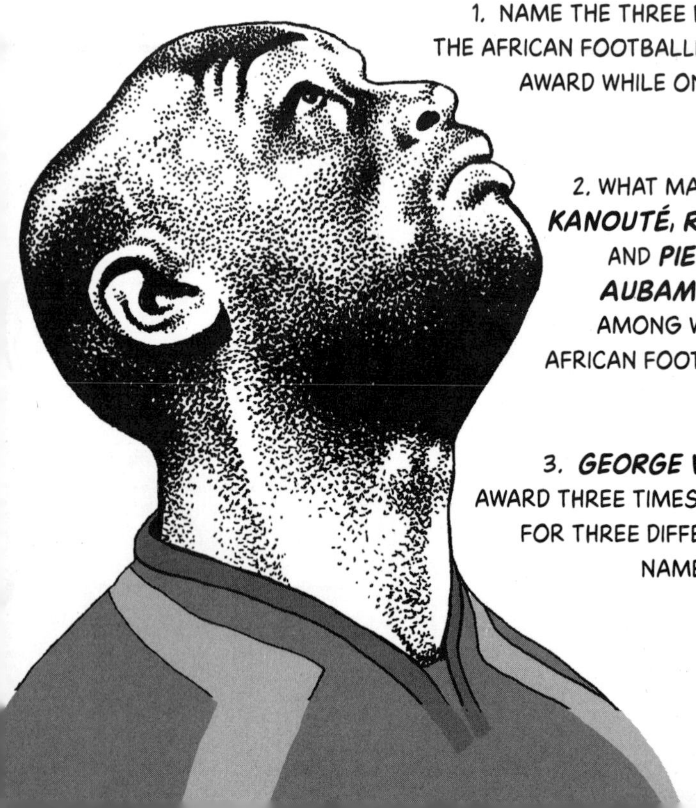

1. NAME THE THREE PLAYERS TO WIN THE AFRICAN FOOTBALLER OF THE YEAR AWARD WHILE ON THE BOOKS AT **LIVERPOOL**.

2. WHAT MAKES **FRÉDÉRIC KANOUTÉ, RIYAD MAHREZ** AND **PIERRE-EMERICK AUBAMEYANG** UNIQUE AMONG WINNERS OF THE AFRICAN FOOTBALLER OF THE YEAR AWARD?

3. **GEORGE WEAH** WON THE AWARD THREE TIMES WHILE PLAYING FOR THREE DIFFERENT TEAMS -- NAME THOSE CLUBS.

NOV 16

IN THE 7-0 THRASHING OF **NORTHERN IRELAND** ON NOVEMBER 16, 1938, **TOTTENHAM'S WILLIE HALL** SCORED FIVE OF ENGLAND'S GOALS -- THREE OF THEM IN JUST OVER THREE MINUTES, THE FASTEST HAT-TRICK IN INTERNATIONAL FOOTBALL HISTORY TO THAT POINT! THIRTY-SEVEN YEARS LATER, **MALCOLM MACDONALD** PUT FIVE PAST **CYPRUS** AT WEMBLEY TO EQUAL **HALL'S** RECORD. IN FEBRUARY, 1993, **ENGLAND** SKIPPER **DAVID PLATT** NOTCHED FOUR AGAINST **SAN MARINO** AT WEMBLEY -- BUT MISSED A PENALTY AND A SHARE IN THE RECORD!

IN 1944, AN ANKLE INJURY FORCED **HALL'S** RETIREMENT FROM PLAYING. HIS HEALTH DETERIORATED RAPIDLY AND WITHIN TWO YEARS BOTH LEGS HAD BEEN AMPUTATED BELOW THE KNEE AFTER A SERIES OF FAILED OPERATIONS AND THROMBOSIS. HE DIED IN 1967.

1. NAME THE **SHEFFIELD WEDNESDAY** STAR, SCORER OF 62 GOALS IN 61 GAMES, WHOSE CAREER WAS CUT SHORT WHEN AN INFECTED LEG HAD TO BE AMPUTATED FOLLOWING A SERIOUS FRACTURE IN HIS LAST MATCH FOR THE CLUB IN 1953.

2. NAME THE **URUGUAY** INTERNATIONAL WHO, SOON AFTER LEAVING **PORTSMOUTH**, WAS SERIOUSLY INJURED IN A CAR CRASH, NECESSITATING THE AMPUTATION OF ONE OF HIS LEGS.

3. NAME THE **COVENTRY CITY** PLAYER WHOSE CAREER WAS ENDED IN 1996 BY AN INJURY, SUSTAINED IN A GAME AGAINST **MANCHESTER UNITED**, THAT WAS SO SEVERE HE REQUIRED 22 OPERATIONS TO SAVE HIS LEG.

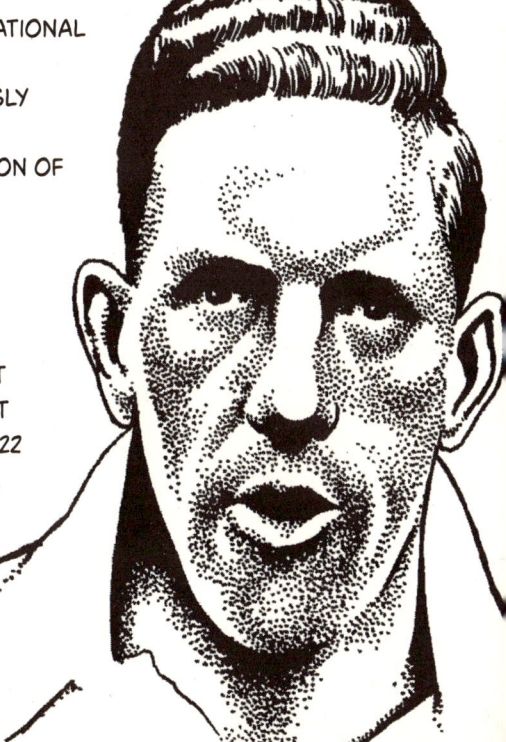

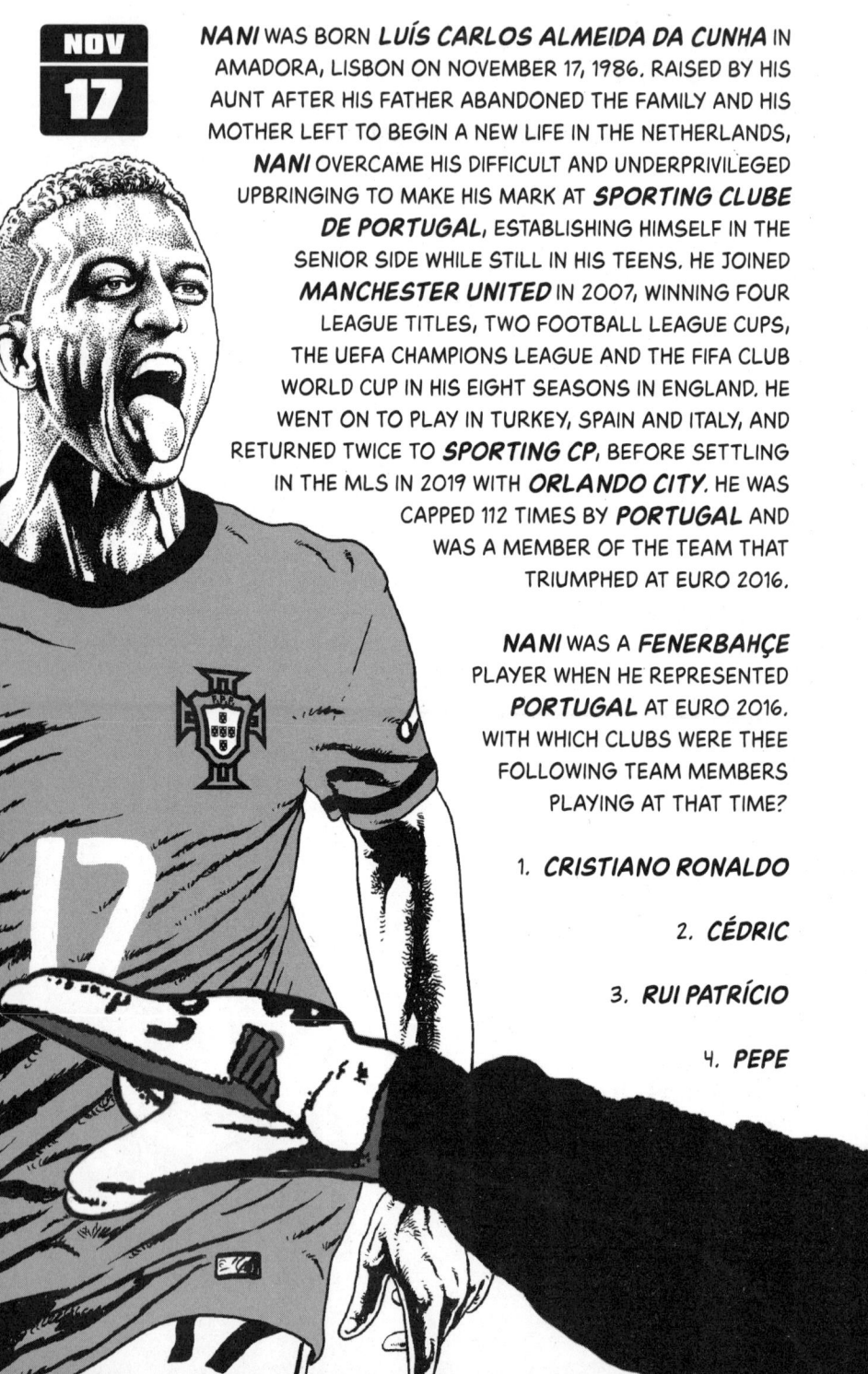

NOV 17

NANI WAS BORN *LUÍS CARLOS ALMEIDA DA CUNHA* IN AMADORA, LISBON ON NOVEMBER 17, 1986. RAISED BY HIS AUNT AFTER HIS FATHER ABANDONED THE FAMILY AND HIS MOTHER LEFT TO BEGIN A NEW LIFE IN THE NETHERLANDS, *NANI* OVERCAME HIS DIFFICULT AND UNDERPRIVILEGED UPBRINGING TO MAKE HIS MARK AT *SPORTING CLUBE DE PORTUGAL*, ESTABLISHING HIMSELF IN THE SENIOR SIDE WHILE STILL IN HIS TEENS. HE JOINED *MANCHESTER UNITED* IN 2007, WINNING FOUR LEAGUE TITLES, TWO FOOTBALL LEAGUE CUPS, THE UEFA CHAMPIONS LEAGUE AND THE FIFA CLUB WORLD CUP IN HIS EIGHT SEASONS IN ENGLAND. HE WENT ON TO PLAY IN TURKEY, SPAIN AND ITALY, AND RETURNED TWICE TO *SPORTING CP*, BEFORE SETTLING IN THE MLS IN 2019 WITH *ORLANDO CITY*. HE WAS CAPPED 112 TIMES BY *PORTUGAL* AND WAS A MEMBER OF THE TEAM THAT TRIUMPHED AT EURO 2016.

NANI WAS A *FENERBAHÇE* PLAYER WHEN HE REPRESENTED *PORTUGAL* AT EURO 2016. WITH WHICH CLUBS WERE THEE FOLLOWING TEAM MEMBERS PLAYING AT THAT TIME?

1. *CRISTIANO RONALDO*

2. *CÉDRIC*

3. *RUI PATRÍCIO*

4. *PEPE*

NOV 18

PETER SCHMEICHEL WAS BORN IN GLADSAXE, ON NOVEMBER 18, 1963. THREE TIMES DANISH FOOTBALL PLAYER OF THE YEAR, HE WON THREE LEAGUE TITLES WITH **BRØNDBY**, BEFORE JOINING **MANCHESTER UNITED** IN 1991. HE WON FIVE LEAGUE TITLES WITH **"THE RED DEVILS"**, INCLUDING LEAGUE AND FA CUP DOUBLES IN 1994 AND 1996, AND A UNIQUE TREBLE OF ENGLISH LEAGUE, FA CUP AND UEFA CHAMPIONS LEAGUE IN 1999. HE MOVED ON TO **SPORTING CP** AND WON A LEAGUE TITLE IN HIS DEBUT SEASON, BEFORE RETURNING TO ENGLISH FOOTBALL WITH **ASTON VILLA** AND **MANCHESTER CITY**. THREE TIMES VOTED IFFHS WORLD'S BEST GOALKEEPER, **DENMARK'S** MOST-CAPPED PLAYER REPRESENTED HIS COUNTRY 129 TIMES AND WAS A MEMBER OF THE TEAM THAT DEFIED THE ODDS TO WIN THE 1992 EUROPEAN CHAMPIONSHIP. HIS GOALKEEPER SON, **KASPER SCHMEICHEL**, HAS FOLLOWED IN HIS FOOTSTEPS, WINNING PREMIER LEAGUE AND FA CUP HONOURS, REPRESENTING **DENMARK** AT INTERNATIONAL LEVEL, AND WINNING MULTIPLE DANISH FOOTBALL PLAYER OF THE YEAR AWARDS.

IDENTIFY THESE DANISH FOOTBALL PLAYER OF THE YEAR AWARD WINNERS:
1. **INTERNAZIONALE** STAR WHO WON THE AWARD A RECORD FIVE TIMES WHILE PLAYING FOR **AJAX** AND **TOTTENHAM HOTSPUR**.

2. WHICH **TOTTENHAM HOTSPUR** PLAYER WON THE 2021 AWARD FOLLOWING HIS TRANSFER FROM **SOUTHAMPTON?**

3. CENTRAL DEFENDER, CAPTAIN OF **DENMARK**, WHO WON THE AWARD TWICE -- IN 2007 AND 2012 -- DURING HIS NINE SEASONS WITH **LIVERPOOL**.

NOV 19

ON NOVEMBER 19, 1969, MORE THAN 80,000 FANS BRAVED THE RAIN AND PACKED THE **MARACANÃ** STADIUM IN RIO DE JANEIRO FOR THE **SANTOS** AGAINST **VASCA DA GAMA** GAME, IN THE HOPE OF SEEING THE GREAT **PELÉ** SCORE HIS 1,000TH GOAL. THE MAESTRO OBLIGED WITH A CALMLY-STRUCK PENALTY AND THE STADIUM ERUPTED. THE MATCH WAS HALTED AS FANS AND REPORTERS STREAMED ONTO THE PITCH AND BALLOONS WERE RELEASED INTO THE NIGHT SKY. FOLLOWING A LAP OF HONOUR, **PELÉ** HAD TO BE SUBSTITUTED BEFORE THE MATCH COULD CONTINUE AND AFTER THE GAME HE WAS PRESENTED WITH A COMMEMORATIVE PLAQUE.

THE **MARACANÃ** IS ONE OF THE MOST FAMOUS STADIUMS IN WORLD FOOTBALL. IN WHICH COUNTRIES ARE THESE STADIUMS LOCATED?

1. **WANDA METROPOLITANO**

2. **ESTADIO CENTENARIO**

3. **SIGNAL IDUNA PARK**

NOV 20

PLAYING FOR **BOURNEMOUTH** IN AN FA CUP FIRST ROUND TIE AGAINST **MARGATE** ON NOVEMBER 20, 1971, **SCOTLAND** INTERNATIONAL STRIKER **TED MACDOUGALL** SCORED 9 GOALS IN AN 11-0 VICTORY! AFTER FAILING TO MAKE THE GRADE AT HIS FIRST CLUB, **LIVERPOOL**, **MACDOUGALL** -- WHO WAS BORN IN INVERNESS ON JANUARY 8, 1947 -- WENT ON TO BECOME A PROLIFIC GOALSCORER IN A CAREER THAT INCLUDED SPELLS AT **MANCHESTER UNITED**, **WEST HAM UNITED**, **SOUTHAMPTON** AND **BLACKPOOL**, AS WELL AS CLUBS IN SOUTH AFRICA AND AUSTRALIA.

MACDOUGALL'S 9-GOAL SPREE IS STILL THE RECORD FOR MOST GOALS SCORED IN AN FA CUP GAME:

1. IN 1946, **BERT TURNER** BECAME THE FIRST PLAYER TO SCORE FOR BOTH TEAMS IN AN FA CUP FINAL. WHO WAS HE PLAYING FOR?

2. IN 1983, AGED 18 YEARS AND 18 DAYS, WHICH **MANCHESTER UNITED** PLAYER BECAME THE YOUNGEST GOALSCORER IN AN FA CUP FINAL?

3. WITH HIS GOAL IN 2012, WHICH **CHELSEA** STAR BECAME THE FIRST PLAYER TO SCORE IN FOUR FA CUP FINALS?

BORN IN HOLLYWOOD, WORCESTERSHIRE, ON NOVEMBER 21, 1962, **ALAN SMITH** STARTED HIS CAREER AT NON-LEAGUE SIDE **ALVECHURCH**, BEFORE TURNING PRO WITH **LEICESTER CITY** IN 1982. HIS STRIKE PARTNERSHIP WITH **GARY LINEKER** EARNED **"THE FOXES"** PROMOTION TO THE TOP FLIGHT. HE WENT ON TO SCORE 84 GOALS IN 206 GAMES, BEFORE SIGNING FOR **ARSENAL** IN 1987. IN EIGHT SEASONS WITH **"THE GUNNERS"**, **SMITH** WON TWO LEAGUE TITLES, THE FA CUP, AND THE LEAGUE CUP, AND SCORED THE GOAL AGAINST **PARMA** THAT DELIVERED VICTORY IN THE 1994 UEFA CUP WINNERS' CUP FINAL. **ARSENAL'S** TOP SCORER FOR FOUR CONSECUTIVE SEASONS AND A TWO-TIME ENGLISH GOLDEN BOOT WINNER, HE WAS CAPPED 13 TIMES BY **ENGLAND** BEFORE INJURY HASTENED HIS RETIREMENT IN 1995.

ALAN SMITH IS ONE OF 19 PLAYERS WHO SCORED 100 GOALS OR MORE FOR **ARSENAL** -- NAME SEVEN OTHERS.

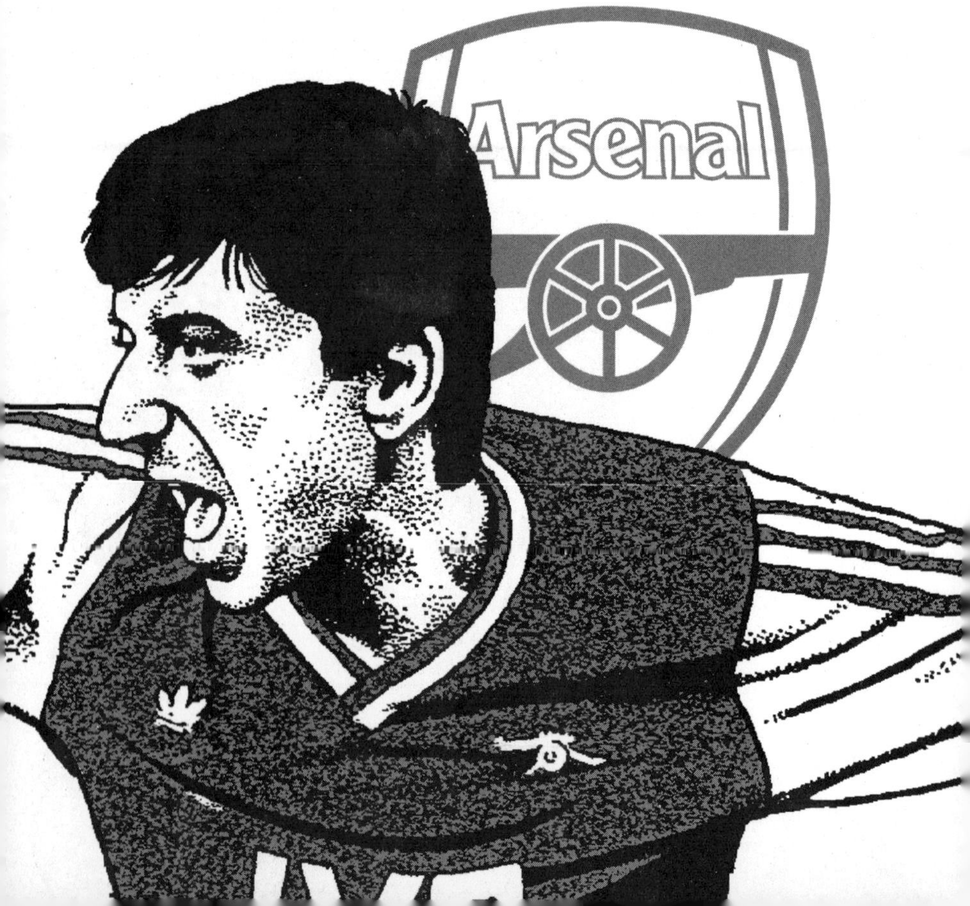

NOV 22

BORN IN ACCRA, ON NOVEMBER 22, 1985, *ASAMOAH "BABY JET" GYAN* JOINED *UDINESE* FROM GHANA'S *LIBERTY PROFESSIONALS* IN 2003, AND WAS LOANED OUT TO *MODENA* TO GAIN EXPERIENCE. HE SCORED ON HIS INTERNATIONAL DEBUT FOR *GHANA* AT THE AGE OF 17, AND SCORED THE FASTEST GOAL OF THE 2006 WORLD CUP, AFTER 68 SECONDS OF THE GAME AGAINST THE *CZECH REPUBLIC*. IT WAS ALSO *GHANA'S* FIRST-EVER GOAL AT THE WORLD CUP. HAVING SIGNED FOR *RENNES* IN 2008, HE WAS OUTSTANDING FOR *GHANA* IN THE 2010 AFRICA CUP OF NATIONS, BEFORE EMERGING AS ONE OF THE STARS OF THE 2010 WORLD CUP. A FEW WEEKS LATER, HE JOINED *SUNDERLAND* AS THE CLUB'S RECORD SIGNING TO THAT POINT -- BUT DESPITE AN IMPRESSIVE FIRST SEASON, HE OPTED TO MOVE ON TO *AL AIN* IN 2011. IN FOUR SEASONS WITH THE UAE TEAM, HE WON THREE LEAGUE TITLES AND WAS THE LEAGUE'S TOP SCORER THREE TIMES. SUBSEQUENT TRAVELS TOOK HIM TO CLUBS IN CHINA, TURKEY, INDIA AND BACK TO GHANA. HIS 51 GOALS IN 109 APPEARANCES MAKE HIM *GHANA'S* ALL-TIME LEADING MARKSMAN.

THE FOLLOWING PLAYERS SCORED WHICH NATION'S FIRST-EVER WORLD CUP GOAL:

1. *JIMMY MURRAY*, 1958

2. *JOSÉ AUGUSTO*, 1966

3. *TIM CAHILL*, 2006

BORN IN BOSTON, LINCOLNSHIRE, ON NOVEMBER 23, 1959, **SIMON GARNER** BEGAN HIS CAREER PLAYING FOR **HOWARD WILKINSON'S BOSTON UNITED**, BEFORE JOINING **BLACKBURN ROVERS** AS A 16-YEAR-OLD TRAINEE. HIS SMOKING HABIT NEARLY DERAILED HIS CAREER BEFORE IT HAD STARTED, BUT HE WENT ON TO SPEND 14 YEARS AT EWOOD PARK, SETTING THE CLUB RECORD OF 192 GOALS. SURPLUS TO REQUIREMENTS AFTER **BLACKBURN'S** ELEVATION TO THE TOP FLIGHT, HE JOINED **WEST BROMWICH ALBION** BEFORE ENDING HIS CAREER AT **WYCOMBE WANDERERS** AND **TORQUAY UNITED**.

WHO HOLDS THE GOALSCORING RECORD FOR THE FOLLOWING CLUBS?

1. **WEST BROMWICH ALBION** -- 279 GOALS BETWEEN 1963 AND 1981

2. **EVERTON** -- 383 GOALS BETWEEN 1925 AND 1937

3. **SOUTHAMPTON** -- 228 GOALS BETWEEN 1966-1977 AND 1979-1982

NOV 24

ROY AITKEN WAS BORN IN IRVINE, SCOTLAND, ON NOVEMBER 24, 1958. HE GRADUATED FROM **CELTIC BOYS CLUB** TO BECOME AN OUTSTANDING SERVANT OF THE CLUB, MAKING 669 APPEARANCES OVER 14 YEARS. CAPPED 57 TIMES BY HIS COUNTRY, HE JOINED **NEWCASTLE UNITED** IN 1990, BUT WITHIN A YEAR, A CHANGE IN MANAGEMENT SAW HIM STRIPPED OF THE CAPTAINCY BY NEW BOSS **OSSIE ARDILES** AND DUMPED IN THE RESERVES. HIS TYNESIDE MISERY ENDED WITH A TRANSFER TO **ST. MIRREN**, BEFORE HE ENDED HIS PLAYING DAYS AT **ABERDEEN**, WHERE HE SUBSEQUENTLY LAUNCHED HIS MANAGEMENT CAREER. HE WENT ON TO COACH UNDER **DAVID O'LEARY** AT **LEEDS UNITED** AND **ASTON VILLA** -- BRIEFLY SERVING AS **VILLA'S** CARETAKER MANAGER AFTER **O'LEARY'S** DEPARTURE -- AND WORKED UNDER **ALEX MCLEISH** WITH **SCOTLAND** AND **BIRMINGHAM CITY**. IN 2010, HE TEAMED UP WITH **O'LEARY** ONCE MORE, TAKING UP A COACHING POSITION IN DUBAI WITH **AL-AHLI**, BEFORE BECOMING THE CLUB'S DIRECTOR OF FOOTBALL.

NAME TWO OF THE THREE **ABERDEEN** MANAGERS SINCE THE SECOND WORLD WAR WHO HAVE ALSO MANAGED **SCOTLAND**.

NOV 25

IN 2010, WHEN **AARON MOKOENA**, THE MOST-CAPPED PLAYER IN **SOUTH AFRICA'S** HISTORY, BECAME THE FIRST PLAYER TO MAKE 100 APPEARANCES FOR THE **"BAFANA BAFANA"**, HE CELEBRATED THE MILESTONE BY TAKING TO THE FIELD WEARING THE NUMBER 100 ON HIS SHIRT. BORN IN BOIPATONG, ON NOVEMBER 25, 1980, HE BECAME THE YOUNGEST PLAYER TO APPEAR FOR **SOUTH AFRICA** WHEN HE MADE HIS INTERNATIONAL DEBUT IN 1999. HAVING GRADUATED FROM YOUTH FOOTBALL WITH **JOMO COSMOS**, HE MOVED TO EUROPE AS A TEENAGER TO PLAY FOR GERMANY'S **BAYER LEVERKUSEN**. SUBSEQUENT CLUBS INCLUDED BELGIUM'S **GERMINAL BEERSCHOT**, DUTCH GIANTS **AJAX**, BELGIUM'S **KRC GENK**, AND **BLACKBURN ROVERS** AND **PORTSMOUTH** IN ENGLAND, BEFORE HE RETURNED HOME TO JOIN **BIDVEST WITS**.

IDENTIFY THESE OTHER **SOUTH AFRICA** RECORD-SETTERS:

1. WHICH FORMER **BLACKBURN ROVERS** STAR IS **SOUTH AFRICA'S** ALL-TIME TOP GOALSCORER?

2. WHICH **SOUTH AFRICA** PLAYER SCORED THE FIRST-EVER WORLD CUP GOAL ON AFRICAN SOIL IN 2010?

3. IN 1988, WHICH SUBSEQUENT **CHARLTON ATHLETIC** STRIKER WAS **SOUTH AFRICA'S** TOP SCORER IN THE COUNTRY'S WORLD CUP DEBUT?

adidas

SOUTH AFRICAN
FOOTBALL ASSOCIATION

4

BORN IN HACKNEY, LONDON, ON NOVEMBER 26, 1965, ***DES WALKER*** MADE HIS DEBUT FOR ***BRIAN CLOUGH'S NOTTINGHAM FOREST*** AT THE AGE OF 18, AND WENT ON TO WIN 59 ***ENGLAND*** CAPS. HE SPENT A SEASON IN ITALY WITH ***SAMPDORIA***, BEFORE HE RETURNED TO ***ENGLAND*** IN 1993 TO JOIN ***SHEFFIELD WEDNESDAY***. HE MADE MORE THAN 300 APPEARANCES FOR THE YORKSHIRE CLUB, PLAYING UNDER EIGHT DIFFERENT MANAGERS IN EIGHT YEARS. HE ENDED HIS CAREER BACK AT ***NOTTINGHAM FOREST***, BEFORE RETIRING AT THE AGE OF 38.

IDENTIFY THESE OTHER BRITISH PLAYERS WHO PLAYED FOR ***SAMPDORIA***:

1. WON THE EUROPEAN CUP WITH ***NOTTINGHAM FOREST*** IN 1979, BUT MISSED THE 1980 FINAL THROUGH INJURY.

2. WON THE UEFA CUP WITH ***JUVENTUS*** AND A LEAGUE AND CUP DOUBLE WITH ***ARSENAL***.

3. LEFT ***SAMPDORIA*** TO BECOME PLAYER/MANAGER AT ***RANGERS***.

NOV 27

ROBERTO MANCINI WAS BORN IN IESI, ITALY ON NOVEMBER 27, 1964. HE BEGAN HIS CAREER AT **BOLOGNA**, BEFORE SPENDING 15 YEARS AT **SAMPDORIA**, WHERE HE WON A SERIE A TITLE, FOUR COPPA ITALIAS, THE UEFA CUP WINNERS' CUP AND A SUPERCOPPA ITALIANA. HE EARNED THE LAST OF HIS 34 ITALY CAPS IN 1994. THREE YEARS LATER, HAVING WON THE SERIE A FOOTBALLER OF THE YEAR AWARD, HE SIGNED FOR **LAZIO**, WHERE HE ADDED ANOTHER SERIE A TITLE, TWO COPPA ITALIAS, A SUPERCOPPA ITALIANA, THE UEFA CUP WINNERS' CUP AND THE UEFA SUPER CUP TO HIS SILVERWARE HAUL. HE JOINED **LEICESTER CITY** ON LOAN IN 2001 BUT FAILED TO COMPLETE 90 MINUTES IN HIS FIVE GAMES FOR THE CLUB, AND CUT THE LOAN DEAL SHORT TO ACCEPT THE JOB OF MANAGER WITH **FIORENTINA**. A LITTLE OVER A YEAR LATER, HE TOOK THE REINS AT **LAZIO**. AT BOTH CLUBS, FINANCES WERE DIRE AND HE HAD TO SELL MAJOR PLAYERS -- BUT HE STILL MANAGED TO WIN THE COPPA ITALIA WITH BOTH TEAMS. HIS EFFORTS WERE REWARDED WITH THE **INTERNAZIONALE** JOB, AND IN FOUR SEASONS HE WON A MULTITUDE OF HONOURS, INCLUDING THREE SERIE A TITLES. HIS NEXT PORT OF CALL WAS **MANCHESTER CITY**, WHERE HE ENDED THE CLUB'S 44-YEAR WAIT FOR A LEAGUE TITLE.

NAME THREE OF THE FOUR TEAMS HE HAS MANAGED SINCE PARTING WAYS WITH **MANCHESTER CITY** IN 2013.

NOV 28

ALESSANDRO ALTOBELLI WAS BORN IN SONNINO, ITALY, ON NOVEMBER 28, 1955. AFTER ESTABLISHING HIS REPUTATION WITH TEAMS IN THE LOWER REACHES OF ITALIAN FOOTBALL, HE JOINED **INTERNAZIONALE** IN 1977, WHERE HE WON A SERIE A TITLE AND TWO ITALIAN CUPS. HE WAS CAPPED 61 TIMES BY **ITALY**, SCORING 25 GOALS, INCLUDING THE GOAL HE SCORED AFTER COMING ON AS A SUBSTITUTE IN THE 1982 WORLD CUP FINAL VICTORY. HE WAS **ITALY'S** TOP SCORER IN THE 1986 WORLD CUP TOURNAMENT, AND CAPTAINED HIS COUNTRY AT EURO 88. HE ENDED HIS PLAYING CAREER WITH A SPELL AT **JUVENTUS**, BEFORE RETURNING TO **BRESCIA**, ONE OF HIS FIRST CLUBS, FOR ONE SEASON IN 1989.

1. WHO, IN 1978, WAS THE FIRST SUBSTITUTE TO SCORE IN A WORLD CUP FINAL ?

2. WHICH SUBSTITUTE SCORED IN THE 1986 WORLD CUP FINAL?

3. NAME THE SUBSTITUTE WHO SCORED THE ONLY GOAL OF THE 2014 WORLD CUP FINAL?

NOV 29

SON OF A PROFESSIONAL RUGBY PLAYER, **RYAN GIGGS** WAS BORN IN CARDIFF, ON NOVEMBER 29, 1973. HE WAS SIGNED TO THE **MANCHESTER CITY** SCHOOL OF EXCELLENCE -- BUT ON **RYAN'S** 14TH BIRTHDAY, **ALEX FERGUSON** TURNED UP AT HIS HOUSE AND PERSUADED HIM TO SIGN FOR **MANCHESTER UNITED**. HE TURNED PROFESSIONAL ON HIS 17TH BIRTHDAY, AND MADE HIS FIRST TEAM DEBUT IN MARCH, 1991. HE PLAYED HIS ENTIRE CAREER WITH THE CLUB, AMASSING A TROPHY HAUL THAT INCLUDES TWO UEFA CHAMPIONS LEAGUES, 13 LEAGUE TITLES, FOUR FA CUPS, THREE LEAGUE CUPS AND THE FIFA WORLD CLUB CUP. HAVING SERVED AS INTERIM AND ASSISTANT MANAGER OF **UNITED**, HE WAS APPOINTED MANAGER OF **WALES** IN 2018.

GIGGS WAS THE FIRST PLAYER IN HISTORY TO WIN TWO CONSECUTIVE PFA YOUNG PLAYER OF THE YEAR AWARDS. HOW MANY OF THE FIVE OTHER **MANCHESTER UNITED** PLAYERS TO WIN THE AWARD CAN YOU NAME?

NOV 30

BORN ON NOVEMBER 30, 1960, *GARY LINEKER* BEGAN HIS CAREER WITH HIS LOCAL CLUB, *LEICESTER CITY*, SCORING 26 GOALS IN THE 1982-83 SEASON, IN WHICH THEY WON PROMOTION TO THE TOP FLIGHT. HE JOINED LEAGUE CHAMPIONS *EVERTON* IN 1985 AND HIT 30 GOALS TO TOP THE LEAGUE'S GOALSCORING CHARTS. HE MADE HISTORY IN THE 1986 WORLD CUP IN MEXICO, WHEN HE BECAME THE FIRST BRITISH PLAYER TO FINISH TOP SCORER IN THE TOURNAMENT, HIS SIX GOALS CATAPULTING HIM TO WORLD SUPERSTARDOM AND EARNING HIM A TRANSFER TO *BARCELONA*. HE WON THE EUROPEAN CUP WINNERS' CUP IN 1989, BEFORE RETURNING TO ENGLAND TO JOIN *TOTTENHAM HOTSPUR*. HE SCORED FOUR OF *ENGLAND'S* GOALS AT ITALIA '90. HAVING NARROWLY MISSED *BOBBY CHARLTON'S ENGLAND* SCORING RECORD, *LINEKER* RETIRED FROM INTERNATIONAL SOCCER IN 1992 AND SIGNED A LUCRATIVE CONTRACT TO PLAY IN JAPAN WITH *NAGOYA GRAMPUS EIGHT*. HE RETIRED IN 1984 AND HAS BECOME A HUGELY SUCCESSFUL SPORTS BROADCASTER.

LINEKER IS THE ONLY PLAYER TO HAVE FINISHED TOP GOALSCORER IN ENGLAND WITH THREE DIFFERENT CLUBS -- *LEICESTER CITY*, *EVERTON* AND *TOTTENHAM HOTSPUR*. NAME ONE OF THE SIX PLAYERS WHO HAVE ACHIEVED THE FEAT WITH TWO DIFFERENT ENGLISH CLUBS.

DECEMBER

DEC 1

SALVATORE "TOTO" SCHILLACI WAS BORN IN PALERMO, SICILY, ON DECEMBER 1, 1964. WITHIN A ONE-YEAR PERIOD HE WENT FROM SECOND DIVISION OBSCURITY WITH **MESSINA** TO SUPERSTARDOM WITH **JUVENTUS** AND THE NATIONAL TEAM. THE FINAL NAME ADDED TO THE ROSTER OF **ITALY'S** 1990 WORLD CUP SQUAD, HE MADE HIS INTERNATIONAL DEBUT AT THE TOURNAMENT, BEFORE EMERGING AS THE TOP SCORER, HIS SIX GOALS IN SEVEN GAMES HELPING THE HOSTS TAKE THIRD PLACE. HIS STAR NEVER SHONE AS BRIGHTLY AFTER ITALIA '90 -- HE SCORED JUST ONE MORE GOAL ON INTERNATIONAL DUTY -- AND A TRANSFER TO **INTERNAZIONALE** WAS FOLLOWED BY A MOVE TO JAPANESE CLUB **JÚBILO IWATA**, WHERE HE BECAME THE FIRST ITALIAN PLAYER TO APPEAR IN THE J. LEAGUE.

IDENTIFY THESE OTHER INTERNATIONALS WHO MOVED TO THE J. LEAGUE:

1. WINNER OF A WORLD CUP AND TWO EUROS WITH **SPAIN**, AND FOUR UEFA CHAMPIONS LEAGUES WITH **BARCELONA**.

2. CAPTAIN OF THE 1994 WORLD CUP WINNERS.

3. **SWEDEN** STAR WHOSE FORMER CLUBS INCLUDE **HALMSTAD**, **ARSENAL**, **WEST HAM UNITED**, **SEATTLE SOUNDERS**, **CHICAGO FIRE** AND **CELTIC**.

DEC 2

RAIMUNDO ORSI WAS BORN IN AVELLANEDA, ARGENTINA, ON DECEMBER 2, 1901. HE BEGAN HIS CAREER AT **INDEPENDIENTE** AND MADE HIS DEBUT FOR **ARGENTINA** IN 1924. HE WAS CAPPED 12 TIMES, WINNING A COPA AMÉRICA AND AN OLYMPIC SILVER MEDAL, BEFORE MOVING TO ITALY IN 1928 TO PLAY FOR **JUVENTUS**, WITH WHOM HE WON FIVE CONSECUTIVE LEAGUE TITLES. BETWEEN 1929 AND 1935 HE MADE 35 APPEARANCES FOR **ITALY**, SCORING 13 GOALS FOR HIS NEW COUNTRY -- INCLUDING A GOAL IN THE 1934 WORLD CUP FINAL VICTORY. HE RETURNED TO SOUTH AMERICA IN 1936 AND PLAYED FOR CLUBS IN ARGENTINA, URUGUAY, BRAZIL AND CHILE, AS WELL AS MAKING ONE MORE APPEARANCE FOR **ARGENTINA**.

1. WHICH **REAL MADRID** STAR REPRESENTED **ARGENTINA** AND **COLOMBIA** AND THEN PLAYED FOR **SPAIN** AT THE 1962 WORLD CUP?

2. **BARCELONA'S LÁSZLÓ KUBALA** -- VOTED THE CLUB'S GREATEST-EVER PLAYER -- REPRESENTED WHICH THREE COUNTRIES?

3. WHICH **REAL MADRID** STAR PLAYED IN WORLD CUPS FOR BOTH **SPAIN** AND **HUNGARY?**

DEC 3

MICHAEL KOJO ESSIEN WAS BORN IN ACCRA, GHANA, ON DECEMBER 3, 1982. HE BEGAN HIS CAREER WITH **LIBERTY PROFESSIONALS**, BEFORE MOVING TO FRANCE AS A 17-YEAR-OLD TO JOIN **SC BASTIA**, WHERE HE SPENT THREE SEASONS. HE JOINED **LYON** IN 2003 AND WON CONSECUTIVE LEAGUE TITLES IN HIS TWO SEASONS AT THE CLUB. HE SIGNED FOR **CHELSEA** IN 2005, BECOMING THE MOST EXPENSIVE AFRICAN PLAYER OF ALL TIME AT THAT POINT. HIS MEDAL HAUL IN LONDON INCLUDED TWO LEAGUE TITLES, FOUR FA CUPS AND THE UEFA CHAMPIONS LEAGUE. AFTER REUNITING WITH FORMER **CHELSEA** MANAGER **JOSÉ MOURINHO** AT **REAL MADRID**, **ESSIEN** PLAYED FOR **AC MILAN**, **PANATHINAIKOS** AND CLUBS IN INDONESIA AND AZERBAIJAN. HE WAS CAPPED 58 TIMES BY **GHANA**.

1. WHAT IS THE NICKNAME GIVEN TO THE **GHANA** NATIONAL TEAM?

2. WHICH FORMER **CHELSEA** MANAGER WAS IN CHARGE OF THE **GHANA** TEAM BETWEEN 2014 AND 2017?

3. IN WHICH YEAR DID **GHANA** MAKE ITS WORLD CUP DEBUT?

DEC 4

GIVEN UP FOR ADOPTION SOON AFTER HE WAS BORN IN LONDON, ON DECEMBER 4, 1959, **PAUL MCGRATH** WAS RAISED IN A NUMBER OF ORPHANAGES IN DUBLIN, IRELAND. HE PLAYED JUNIOR FOOTBALL WITH **PEARSE ROVERS** AND **DALKEY UNITED**, AND WORKED AS A SECURITY GUARD AND AS AN APPRENTICE METAL WORKER BEFORE TURNING PROFESSIONAL WITH **ST. PATRICK'S ATHLETIC**. HE SPENT SEVEN YEARS WITH MANCHESTER UNITED, WINNING THE FA CUP IN 1985, BEFORE JOINING **ASTON VILLA**, WITH WHOM HE WON TWO LEAGUE CUPS. CAPPED 83 TIMES BY THE **REPUBLIC OF IRELAND**, HE PLAYED BRIEFLY FOR BOTH **DERBY COUNTY** AND **SHEFFIELD UNITED**, BEFORE RETIRING IN 1998.

HE WAS INDUCTED INTO THE ENGLISH FOOTBALL HALL OF FAME, AS WERE THE FOLLOWING PLAYERS:

1. **"THE GOLDEN BOY OF WELSH FOOTBALL"**, HE PLAYED FOR **SWANSEA TOWN**, **CARDIFF CITY** AND **NEWCASTLE UNITED** AND SET GOALSCORING AND APPEARANCE RECORDS FOR **WALES** THAT STOOD FOR MANY YEARS.

2. **LEEDS UNITED** LEGEND NICKNAMED **"BITES YER LEGS"** AFTER A FAMOUS CROWD BANNER.

3. MANAGER OF THE 2012 **GREAT BRITAIN** OLYMPIC FOOTBALL TEAM.

DEC 5

BORN IN DÜSSELDORF, ON DECEMBER 5, 1956, *KLAUS ALLOFS* BEGAN HIS CAREER AS AN ATTACKING MIDFIELDER AND WENT ON TO BECOME ONE OF THE MOST PROLIFIC GOALSCORING STRIKERS IN GERMAN FOOTBALL. HE WON TWO GERMAN CUPS AND WAS A UEFA CUP WINNERS' CUP RUNNER-UP WITH *FORTUNA DÜSSELDORF*, AND WAS THE BUNDESLIGA'S TOP SCORER IN 1978-79. IN 1981, HE SIGNED FOR *1. FC KÖLN*, WITH WHOM HE WON ANOTHER GERMAN CUP, REACHED THE UEFA CUP FINAL, AND TOPPED THE LEAGUE GOALSCORING CHARTS ONCE MORE. HE SPENT THREE YEARS IN FRANCE, WINNING A LEAGUE AND CUP DOUBLE WITH *MARSEILLE*, BEFORE JOINING *BORDEAUX*. HE RETURNED TO GERMANY TO JOIN *WERDER BREMEN* IN 1990, AND ADDED LEAGUE, GERMAN CUP, GERMAN SUPERCUP AND A UEFA CUP WINNERS' CUP TO HIS TROPHY HAUL. HE RETIRED IN 1993, HAVING REPRESENTED *WEST GERMANY* ON 56 OCCASIONS, DURING WHICH HE SCORED 17 GOALS, WON THE 1980 UEFA EUROPEAN CHAMPIONSHIPS AND WAS A RUNNER-UP IN THE 1986 WORLD CUP.

ALLOFS WAS TOP SCORER AT EURO 1980. NAME THREE OTHER GERMAN PLAYERS WHO HAVE FINISHED TOP SCORER AT THE EUROPEAN CHAMPIONSHIPS.

DEC 6

SON OF AN ENGLISH FATHER AND A SAMOAN MOTHER, **TIM CAHILL** WAS BORN IN SYDNEY ON DECEMBER 6, 1979. HE PLAYED FOR **WESTERN SAMOA** IN AN UNDER-20 TOURNAMENT IN FIJI WHEN HE WAS 14 -- A DECISION THAT WOULD COME BACK TO HAUNT HIM. FIFA RULES MEANT THAT HE WAS SUBSEQUENTLY INELIGIBLE TO PLAY FOR **AUSTRALIA!** EVENTUALLY, A CHANGE IN THOSE RULES ALLOWED PLAYERS CAPPED AT JUNIOR LEVEL TO SWITCH THEIR INTERNATIONAL ALLEGIANCE, AND **TIM** WAS FREE TO PLAY FOR THE COUNTRY OF HIS BIRTH. HE EARNED HIS FIRST CAP FOR **AUSTRALIA** IN 2004 AND WENT ON TO BECOME HIS COUNTRY'S ALL-TIME LEADING GOALSCORER.

1. WHICH **MIDDLESBROUGH, FULHAM, CHELSEA** AND **LEICESTER CITY** GOALKEEPER HOLDS THE **AUSTRALIA** APPEARANCE RECORD?

2. WHICH FORMER **ENGLAND** MANAGER COACHED **"THE SOCCEROOS"** BETWEEN 1997 AND 1998.

3. WHICH **AUSTRALIA** INTERNATIONAL WON THE UEFA CHAMPIONS LEAGUE WITH **LIVERPOOL** IN 2005 BEFORE JOINING **GALATASARAY?**

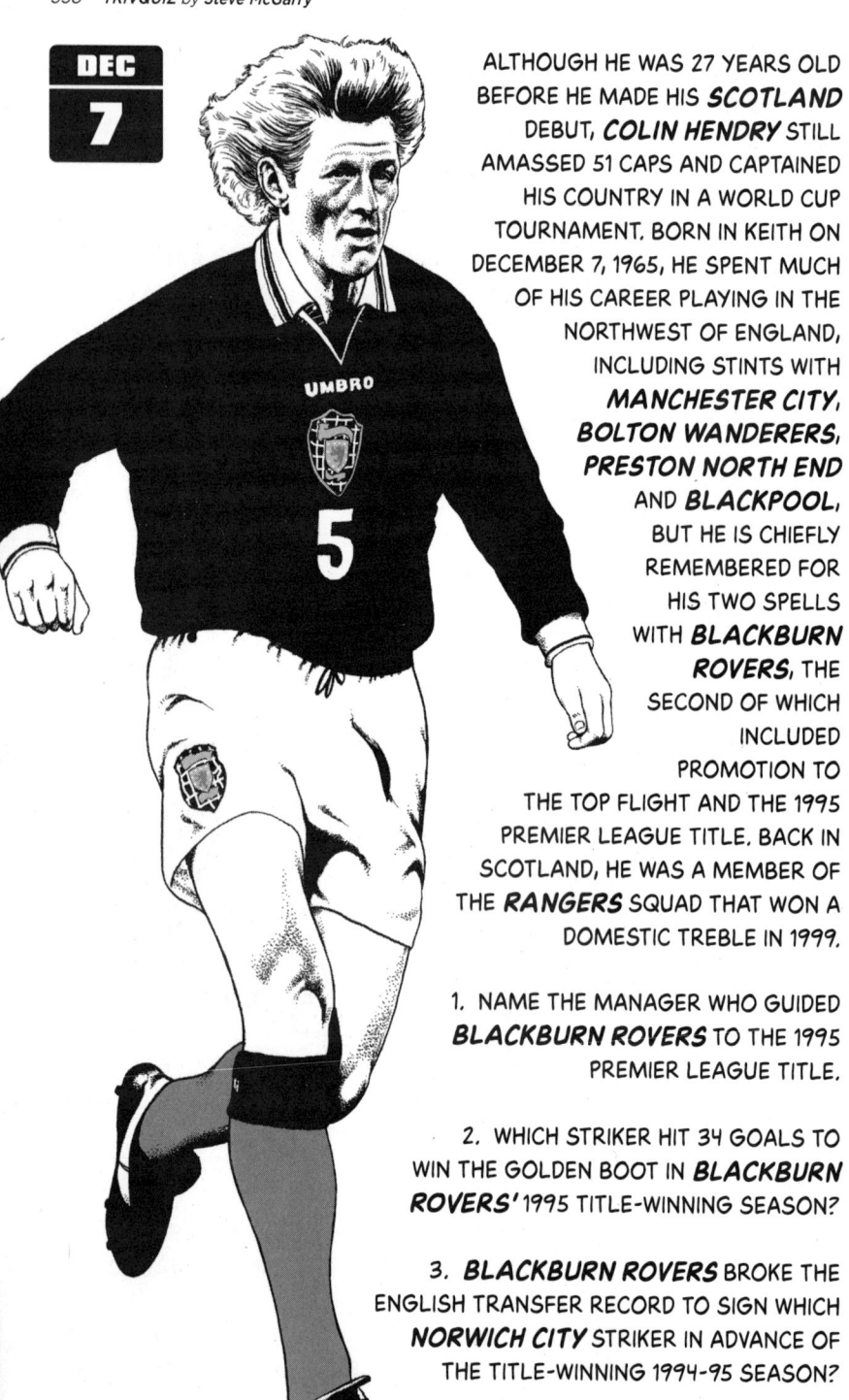

DEC 7

ALTHOUGH HE WAS 27 YEARS OLD BEFORE HE MADE HIS **SCOTLAND** DEBUT, *COLIN HENDRY* STILL AMASSED 51 CAPS AND CAPTAINED HIS COUNTRY IN A WORLD CUP TOURNAMENT. BORN IN KEITH ON DECEMBER 7, 1965, HE SPENT MUCH OF HIS CAREER PLAYING IN THE NORTHWEST OF ENGLAND, INCLUDING STINTS WITH *MANCHESTER CITY*, *BOLTON WANDERERS*, *PRESTON NORTH END* AND *BLACKPOOL*, BUT HE IS CHIEFLY REMEMBERED FOR HIS TWO SPELLS WITH *BLACKBURN ROVERS*, THE SECOND OF WHICH INCLUDED PROMOTION TO THE TOP FLIGHT AND THE 1995 PREMIER LEAGUE TITLE. BACK IN SCOTLAND, HE WAS A MEMBER OF THE *RANGERS* SQUAD THAT WON A DOMESTIC TREBLE IN 1999.

1. NAME THE MANAGER WHO GUIDED *BLACKBURN ROVERS* TO THE 1995 PREMIER LEAGUE TITLE.

2. WHICH STRIKER HIT 34 GOALS TO WIN THE GOLDEN BOOT IN *BLACKBURN ROVERS'* 1995 TITLE-WINNING SEASON?

3. *BLACKBURN ROVERS* BROKE THE ENGLISH TRANSFER RECORD TO SIGN WHICH *NORWICH CITY* STRIKER IN ADVANCE OF THE TITLE-WINNING 1994-95 SEASON?

DEC 8

BORN IN KINGSTON, JAMAICA, ON DECEMBER 8, 1994, *RAHEEM STERLING* -- WHOSE FATHER WAS MURDERED WHEN *RAHEEM* WAS TWO YEARS OLD -- WAS RAISED IN LONDON FROM THE AGE OF FIVE. HE WON THE PRESTIGIOUS GOLDEN BOY AWARD WHILE PLAYING FOR *LIVERPOOL*, AFTER SIGNING FOR THE MERSEYSIDERS FROM THE *QUEENS PARK RANGERS* ACADEMY. HIS RECORD-BREAKING TRANSFER TO *MANCHESTER CITY* IN 2015 EARNED VITRIOL AND CONDEMNATION FROM ALL QUARTERS, INCLUDING FROM A NUMBER OF *LIVERPOOL* PLAYERS-TURNED-PUNDITS. HAVING REPRESENTED *ENGLAND* AT JUNIOR LEVELS, HE MADE HIS SENIOR DEBUT IN 2012, WAS RED-CARDED IN HIS FOURTH GAME AND SCORED HIS FIRST *ENGLAND* GOAL IN EARLY 2015.

NAME THE BIRTH COUNTRY OF THESE *ENGLAND* PLAYERS:

1. *CYRILLE REGIS*

2. *TONY DORIGO*

3. *JOHN BARNES*

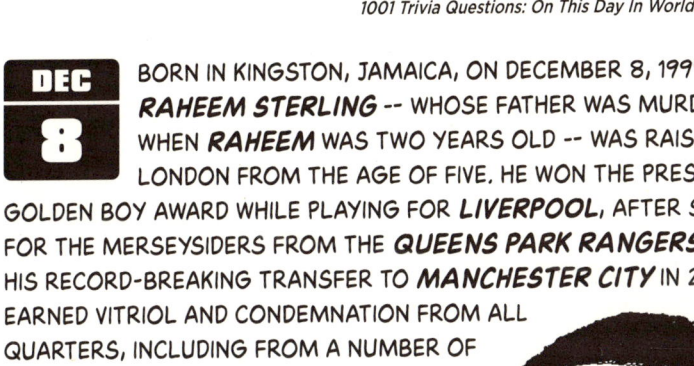

DEC 9

WILLIAM JOHN "BILLY" BREMNER WAS BORN IN STIRLING, SCOTLAND, ON DECEMBER 9, 1942. HE SIGNED FOR **LEEDS UNITED** IN 1959, THE DAY AFTER HIS 17TH BIRTHDAY. HE MADE HIS SENIOR DEBUT THE FOLLOWING MONTH AND BECAME THE HEART OF THE TEAM FOR THE NEXT 16 YEARS. PROMOTED FROM THE SECOND TIER IN 1964, **LEEDS UNITED** AND **BREMNER** WENT ON TO WIN TWO LEAGUE TITLES, THE FA CUP, THE LEAGUE CUP, AND TWO INTER-CITIES FAIRS CUPS, AS WELL AS REACHING THE FINALS OF THE EUROPEAN CUP AND THE EUROPEAN CUP WINNERS' CUP.

CAPPED 54 TIMES BY **SCOTLAND**, HE MADE 772 APPEARANCES FOR **LEEDS UNITED** BEFORE SIGNING FOR **HULL CITY** IN 1976. THREE YEARS LATER, HE MOVED ON TO **DONCASTER ROVERS**, WHERE HE SUBSEQUENTLY BEGAN HIS MANAGEMENT CAREER. HE LATER WENT ON TO MANAGE HIS BELOVED **LEEDS**, BEFORE RETURNING TO **DONCASTER** IN 1989. HE RETIRED FROM THE GAME IN 1991, AND DIED TWO DAYS BEFORE HIS 55TH BIRTHDAY IN 1997.

NAME THREE OF THE FIVE FORMER **LEEDS UNITED** PLAYERS WHO HAVE MANAGED THE CLUB SINCE **BILLY BREMNER**.

DEC 10

GONZALO HIGUAÍN WAS BORN IN BREST, FRANCE, ON DECEMBER 10, 1987, THE SON OF AN ARGENTINIAN FOOTBALLER WHO WAS PLAYING FOR **STADE BRESTOIS 29** AT THAT TIME. THE FAMILY LEFT FOR ARGENTINA WHEN **GONZALO** WAS 10 MONTHS OLD. HE JOINED **REAL MADRID** FROM **RIVER PLATE** IN EARLY 2007 AND DURING HIS SIX YEARS IN SPAIN, HIS HONOURS INCLUDED THREE LA LIGA TITLES. HE WON THE COPPA ITALIA WITH **NAPOLI**, BEFORE SCORING 36 GOALS IN 2015-16, EQUALLING **GINO ROSSETTI'S** 87-YEAR-OLD RECORD FOR GOALS IN AN ITALIAN TOP-FLIGHT SEASON. **JUVENTUS** BROKE THE ITALIAN TRANSFER RECORD TO ACQUIRE HIS SERVICES. HE WON LEAGUE AND CUP DOUBLES IN HIS FIRST TWO SEASONS, WENT OUT ON LOAN TO **AC MILAN** AND **CHELSEA** -- WITH WHOM HE WON THE UEFA EUROPA LEAGUE -- BEFORE RETURNING TO MILAN AND SECURING HIS THIRD SERIE A TITLE. HE RETIRED FROM INTERNATIONAL FOOTBALL IN 2019, HAVING SCORED 31 GOALS IN 75 GAMES, AND JOINED **DAVID BECKHAM'S INTER MIAMI** IN 2020.

NAME THREE OF THE FOUR OTHER **ARGENTINA** INTERNATIONALS WHO HAVE PLAYED IN THE PREMIER LEAGUE FOR **CHELSEA**.

DEC 11

BORN IN BUENOS AIRES ON DECEMBER 11, 1981, *JAVIER SAVIOLA* WAS ONLY 19 YEARS OLD WHEN HE LEFT *RIVER PLATE* TO JOIN *BARCELONA* IN A £15 MILLION TRANSFER IN 2001. THAT SAME YEAR, HE WAS OUTSTANDING IN THE *ARGENTINA* TEAM THAT WON THE FIFA U-20 WORLD CUP, SCORING A RECORD 11 GOALS IN 7 GAMES AND EARNING THE PLAYER OF THE TOURNAMENT AWARD. IT WAS A MAJOR SURPRISE WHEN HE WAS OMITTED FROM HIS COUNTRY'S WORLD CUP 2002 SQUAD, BUT TWO YEARS LATER, HE WON AN OLYMPIC GOLD MEDAL, AND WENT ON TO PLAY AND SCORE AT THE 2006 WORLD CUP. HE PLAYED ON LOAN AT *MONACO* AND *SEVILLA*, WINNING THE UEFA CUP IN 2006 WITH THE LATTER, AND WON THE 2006 SPANISH SUPERCUP WITH *BARCELONA*, BEFORE JOINING *REAL MADRID* IN 2007. HE WON A LEAGUE TITLE AND ANOTHER SPANISH SUPERCUP, BEFORE SIGNING FOR *BENFICA* IN 2009, WHERE HE ADDED A CHAMPIONSHIP AND TWO PORTUGUESE LEAGUE CUPS TO HIS MEDAL HAUL. HE WENT ON TO PLAY FOR *MÁLAGA*, WON A LEAGUE TITLE WITH *OLYMPIACOS*, SPENT A SEASON IN ITALY WITH *VERONA* AND RETURNED TO *RIVER PLATE*, WHERE HE RETIRED IN 2016.

ARGENTINA HAS WON GOLD TWICE IN FOOTBALL AT THE OLYMPICS. WHICH TWO NATIONS HAVE EARNED GOLD THREE TIMES EACH?

DEC 12

DANIEL AGGER WAS BORN IN HVIDOVRE, DENMARK, ON DECEMBER 12, 1984. HE BEGAN HIS CAREER AT **ROSENHØJ BK**, BEFORE JOINING **BRØNDBY** AS A 12-YEAR-OLD. HE ESTABLISHED HIMSELF IN THE SENIOR TEAM IN 2004, AND WON THE DANISH SUPERLIGA CHAMPIONSHIP AND DANISH CUP IN 2005, THE SAME YEAR HE WON THE FIRST OF HIS 75 **DENMARK** CAPS. HE JOINED **LIVERPOOL** IN EARLY 2006, AND WAS VOTED DANISH FOOTBALLER OF THE YEAR IN 2007. AFTER NINE SEASONS ON MERSEYSIDE, HE RETURNED TO **BRØNDBY** AND RETIRED IN 2016. **AGGER** IS A QUALIFIED TATTOO ARTIST!

NAME THE FOUR MANAGERS UNDER WHOM HE PLAYED AT **LIVERPOOL** BETWEEN 2006 AND 2014.

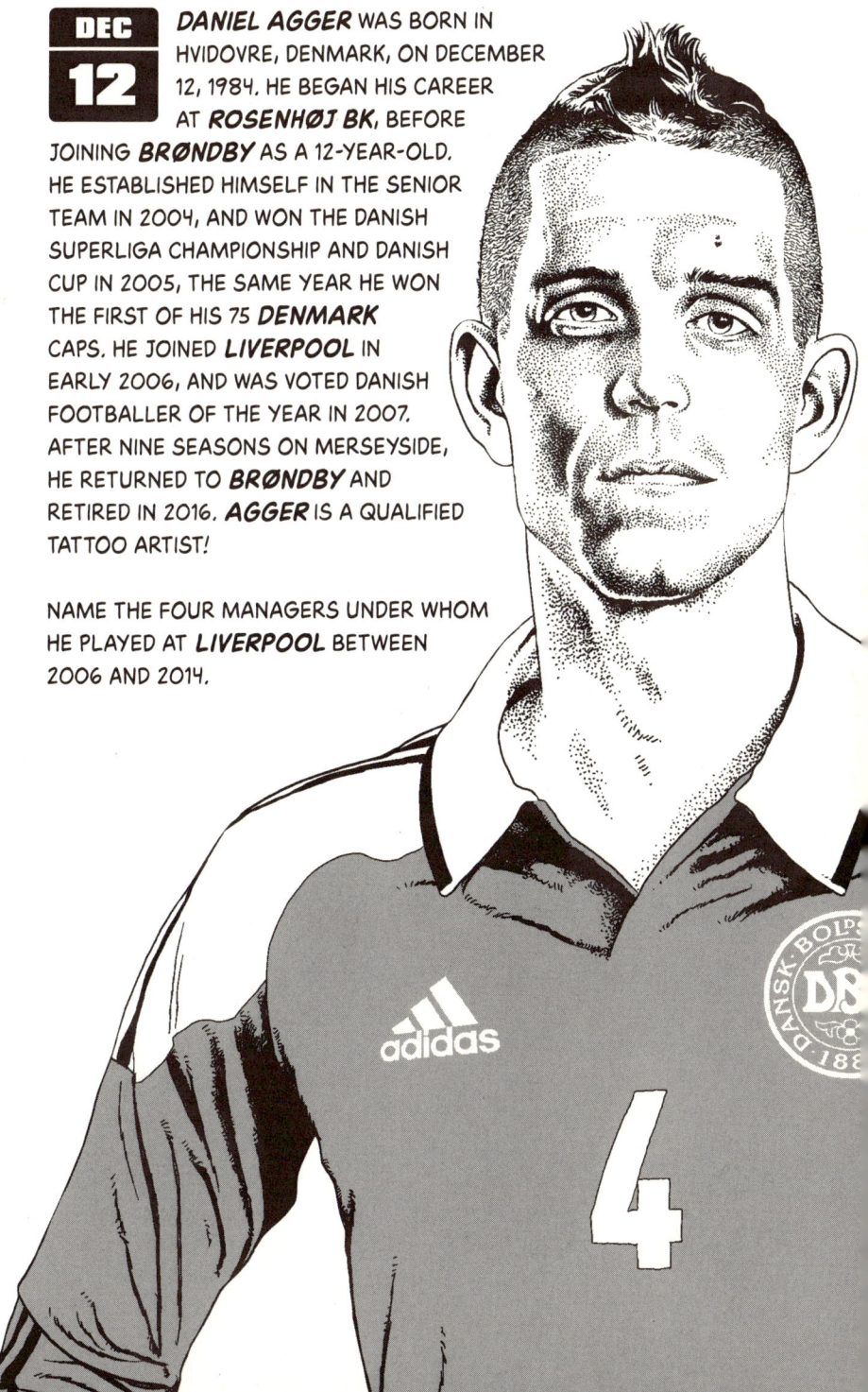

DEC 13

38 SECONDS INTO THE INTERNATIONAL FRIENDLY AGAINST *YUGOSLAVIA* ON DECEMBER 13, 1989, *ENGLAND* CAPTAIN *BRYAN ROBSON* SCORED THE FASTEST GOAL EVER RECORDED IN A PROFESSIONAL GAME AT THE OLD WEMBLEY STADIUM. IT SET UP *ENGLAND* FOR A 2-1 WIN, THE NATIONAL TEAM'S 100TH VICTORY AT THE STADIUM. IT WAS THE THIRD TIME THAT *ROBSON* HAD SCORED WITHIN THE FIRST MINUTE OF A GAME'S KICK-OFF WHILE PLAYING FOR HIS COUNTRY.

1. *ROBSON* TOOK JUST 27 SECONDS TO SCORE IN *ENGLAND'S* OPENING GAME OF THE 1982 WORLD CUP TOURNAMENT AGAINST *FRANCE*. WHO WERE THE OPPONENTS WHEN HE SCORED AFTER 44 SECONDS OF A GAME AT WEMBLEY IN 1982?

2. WHO SCORED THE FASTEST-EVER *ENGLAND* GOAL, AFTER 12 SECONDS OF A GAME AWAY TO *BELGIUM* IN 1947?

3. WHICH COUNTRY SCORED IN JUST 8.3 SECONDS OF A WORLD CUP QUALIFIER GAME AGAINST *ENGLAND* IN 1993?

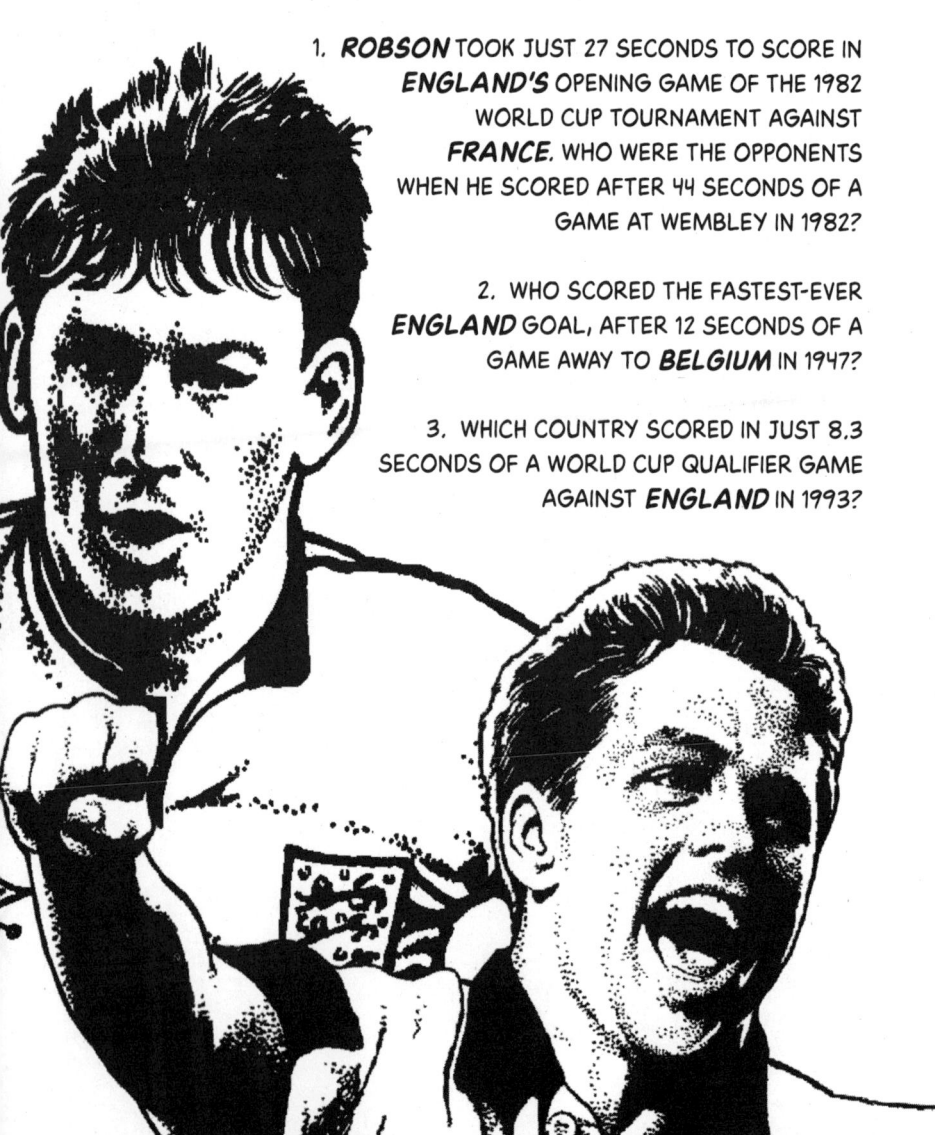

MICHAEL OWEN WAS BORN IN CHESTER, ON DECEMBER 14, 1979. HE JOINED **LIVERPOOL** AS A SCHOOLBOY, AND SCORED ON HIS SENIOR DEBUT IN 1997. HE MADE HIS **ENGLAND** DEBUT IN EARLY 1998, AND FINISHED THAT SEASON AS PFA YOUNG PLAYER OF THE YEAR AND JOINT TOP SCORER IN THE PREMIER LEAGUE, BEFORE ANNOUNCING HIS ARRIVAL ON THE WORLD STAGE WITH TWO GOALS AT THE 1998 WORLD CUP FINALS. HE WON HIS SECOND PREMIER LEAGUE GOLDEN BOOT THE FOLLOWING SEASON.

1. HE WAS 2001 EUROPEAN FOOTBALLER OF THE YEAR -- NAME THE THREE OTHER ENGLISHMEN TO WIN THE BALLON D'OR.

2. ONLY SEVEN PLAYERS HAVE BETTERED **OWEN'S** RECORD OF 158 GOALS FOR **LIVERPOOL** -- HOW MANY CAN YOU NAME?

3. NAME THE FOUR CLUBS THAT **MICHAEL OWEN** PLAYED FOR AFTER LEAVING **LIVERPOOL** IN 2004.

DEC 15

JOE JORDAN WAS BORN IN CLELAND, SCOTLAND, ON DECEMBER 15, 1951. HE TRAINED AS AN APPRENTICE DRAUGHTSMAN AFTER LEAVING SCHOOL AND PLAYED JUNIOR FOOTBALL WITH *BLANTYRE VICTORIA*, BEFORE BECOMING A PART-TIME PLAYER WITH *MORTON*. HE WENT ON TO PLAY AT THE HIGHEST LEVELS IN ENGLAND AND ITALY, AND MADE 52 APPEARANCES FOR *SCOTLAND*. HE IS THE ONLY *SCOTLAND* PLAYER TO SCORE IN THREE CONSECUTIVE WORLD CUP TOURNAMENTS, IN 1974, 1978 AND 1982. HE MOVED INTO COACHING AND MANAGEMENT WHEN HIS PLAYING DAYS WERE OVER IN 1988. *JORDAN* WAS INDUCTED IN THE SCOTTISH FOOTBALL HALL OF FAME IN 2005.

1. NAME THREE CLUBS THAT *JOE JORDAN* PLAYED FOR AFTER LEAVING *MORTON* IN 1970.

2. HE WAS ASSISTANT COACH TO WHICH FORMER *MANCHESTER UNITED* AND *SCOTLAND* STAR AT *STOKE CITY* AND *HUDDERSFIELD TOWN*?

3. HE WORKED AS ASSISTANT MANAGER OR FIRST TEAM COACH WITH WHICH MANAGER AT *PORTSMOUTH*, *TOTTENHAM HOTSPUR* AND *QUEENS PARK RANGERS*?

DEC 16 BORN IN BERGEN, NETHERLANDS, ON DECEMBER 16, 1992, *LIEKE MARTENS* WAS OBSESSED WITH FOOTBALL FROM AN EARLY AGE. AS THERE WEREN'T ANY GIRLS TEAMS IN HER AREA, SHE HAD TO PLAY ON BOYS TEAMS UNTIL SHE WAS INTO HER TEENS! HER PROFESSIONAL CAREER HAS SEEN HER PLAY FOR CLUBS IN NETHERLANDS, GERMANY, BELGIUM AND SWEDEN. *LIEKE* WAS OUTSTANDING IN HER COUNTRY'S VICTORIOUS UEFA WOMEN'S EURO 2017 CAMPAIGN, WINNING THE GOLDEN BALL AS BEST PLAYER IN THE TOURNAMENT AND THE BRONZE BOOT AS THIRD-TOP SCORER. THAT SUMMER, SHE JOINED *FC BARCELONA*, THE CLUB OF HER CHILDHOOD IDOL, *RONALDINHO*. LATER THAT YEAR, SHE WAS NAMED UEFA WOMEN'S PLAYER OF THE YEAR AND FIFA WOMEN'S PLAYER OF THE YEAR! IN 2021, SHE HELPED *FC BARCELONA FEMENÍ* WIN A CONTINENTAL TREBLE OF THE UEFA WOMEN'S CHAMPIONS LEAGUE, THE PRIMERA DIVISION, AND THE COPA DE LA REINA.

IN WHICH YEAR WAS THE UEFA WOMEN'S CHAMPIONSHIP FIRST STAGED?

DEC 17

BORN IN SECLIN, FRANCE, ON DECEMBER 17, 1989, ONE OF THREE SONS OF THREE-TIME AFRICAN FOOTBALLER OF THE YEAR *ABEDI "PELE" AYEW* WHO WOULD ALL FOLLOW IN THEIR DAD'S FOOTSTEPS AND BECOME PROFESSIONAL FOOTBALLERS, *ANDRÉ AYEW* PLAYED FOR GERMANY'S *1860 MUNICH* AS A YOUNG BOY WHILE HIS FATHER WAS AT THE CLUB. HE PLAYED IN THE YOUTH ACADEMY OF HIS FATHER'S GHANAIAN CLUB, *NANIA*, BEFORE RETURNING TO FRANCE TO PLAY FOR HIS DAD'S OLD CLUB, *MARSEILLE.* HE WON TWO LEAGUE TITLES BEFORE JOINING *SWANSEA CITY* IN 2015. A YEAR LATER, *WEST HAM UNITED* PAID A CLUB RECORD £20.5 MILLION TO SIGN HIM -- BUT BY EARLY 2018, HE WAS BACK WITH *SWANSEA CITY.* HE RETURNED FROM A LOAN SPELL WITH *FENERBAHÇE* TO TOP *SWANSEA'S* GOALSCORING LISTS TWO SEASONS IN A ROW, BUT LEFT THE CLUB IN 2021 WHEN HIS CONTRACT EXPIRED. IN 2017, HE SURPASSED HIS FATHER'S TOTAL OF 73 *GHANA* CAPS AND HAS GONE ON TO CAPTAIN *"THE BLACK STARS".*

ANDRE'S £18 MILLION TRANSFER FROM *WEST HAM UNITED* WAS A CLUB RECORD FOR A FEE PAID. WHOSE £45 MILLION TRANSFER TO *EVERTON* IN 2017 SET THE CLUB RECORD FOR TRANSFER FEE RECEIVED?

DEC 18

GEORGE HARDWICK BEGAN HIS LEAGUE CAREER IN DISASTROUS FASHION WHEN HE MADE HIS LEAGUE DEBUT FOR **MIDDLESBROUGH** ON DECEMBER 18, 1937. JUST 60 SECONDS INTO THE GAME AGAINST **BOLTON WANDERERS**, THE 17-YEAR-OLD FULL-BACK SCORED AN OWN GOAL. HIS **ENGLAND** DEBUT, SIX YEARS LATER, WAS A MUCH HAPPIER AFFAIR -- HE CAPTAINED THE SIDE THAT THRASHED **NORTHERN IRELAND** 7-2. REGARDED AS ONE OF THE BEST DEFENDERS IN **MIDDLESBROUGH'S** HISTORY -- A **GEORGE HARDWICK** STATUE STANDS OUTSIDE THE CLUB'S RIVERSIDE STADIUM -- HE FINISHED HIS PLAYING CAREER AT **OLDHAM ATHLETIC** AS PLAYER/ MANAGER, BEFORE EMBARKING ON A CAREER IN MANAGEMENT THAT TOOK HIM TO **PSV EINDHOVEN**, THE **NETHERLANDS** NATIONAL TEAM, **SUNDERLAND** AND **GATESHEAD**.

WHICH **MIDDLESBROUGH** PLAYER:

1. HAD BEEN A WORLD CUP WINNER WITH **ENGLAND** IN 1966?

2. WAS THE FIRST £1,000 TRANSFER PLAYER?

3. WAS A MEMBER OF **BRAZIL'S** 2002 WORLD CUP-WINNING SQUAD?

**DEC
19**

BORN IN LYON, ON DECEMBER 19, 1987, *KARIM BENZEMA* JOINED THE *OLYMPIQUE LYONNAISE* ACADEMY AT THE AGE OF NINE AND BLAZED HIS WAY THROUGH THE RANKS, SCORING 38 GOALS IN ONE SEASON FOR THE UNDER-16 TEAM! IN 2004, HE WAS A MEMBER OF THE *FRANCE* SQUAD THAT WON THE UEFA EUROPEAN UNDER-17 CHAMPIONSHIP. HE WON FOUR CONSECUTIVE LIGUE 1 TITLES WITH *LYON*, INCLUDING A LEAGUE AND CUP DOUBLE IN 2008, A SEASON IN WHICH HE FINISHED TOP LEAGUE GOALSCORER AND WAS VOTED LIGUE 1 PLAYER OF THE YEAR, BEFORE JOINING *REAL MADRID* IN 2009. HE HAS WON A MULTITUDE OF HONOURS WITH *"LOS MERENGUES"*, INCLUDING FOUR UEFA CHAMPIONS LEAGUES.

NAME FIVE OF THE MANAGERS UNDER WHOM *KARIM BENZEMA* HAS PLAYED AT *REAL MADRID*.

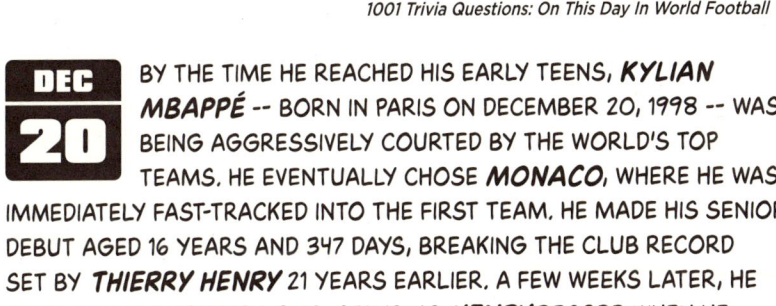

DEC 20

BY THE TIME HE REACHED HIS EARLY TEENS, *KYLIAN MBAPPÉ* -- BORN IN PARIS ON DECEMBER 20, 1998 -- WAS BEING AGGRESSIVELY COURTED BY THE WORLD'S TOP TEAMS. HE EVENTUALLY CHOSE *MONACO*, WHERE HE WAS IMMEDIATELY FAST-TRACKED INTO THE FIRST TEAM. HE MADE HIS SENIOR DEBUT AGED 16 YEARS AND 347 DAYS, BREAKING THE CLUB RECORD SET BY *THIERRY HENRY* 21 YEARS EARLIER. A FEW WEEKS LATER, HE SUPPLANTED ANOTHER LONG-STANDING *HENRY* RECORD WHEN HE BECAME THE CLUB'S YOUNGEST-EVER GOALSCORER. HAVING INITIALLY JOINED *PARIS SAINT-GERMAIN* ON LOAN IN 2017, HIS SUBSEQUENT TRANSFER MADE HIM THE MOST EXPENSIVE TEENAGER IN HISTORY. AT INTERNATIONAL LEVEL, HIS GOALS HAVING FIRED *FRANCE* TO VICTORY IN THE 2016 UEFA EUROPEAN UNDER-19 CHAMPIONSHIP, HE MADE HIS SENIOR DEBUT IN 2017 AND WAS A WORLD CUP WINNER THE FOLLOWING YEAR.

NAME THE THREE MANAGERS UNDER WHOM *MBAPPÉ* HAS PLAYED AT *PSG*.

ON DECEMBER 21, 1990, HAVING BEEN OUT OF ACTION FOR 16 MONTHS WITH KNEE TROUBLE, *GLENN HODDLE* BOUGHT HIS RELEASE FROM HIS CONTRACT WITH *MONACO*. WITHIN MONTHS, HE WAS INSTALLED AS PLAYER/MANAGER AT *SWINDON TOWN*, AND HE WENT ON TO STEER THEM TO PROMOTION TO THE PREMIER LEAGUE FOR THE FIRST TIME IN THE CLUB'S HISTORY. IT WAS THE START OF A CAREER IN MANAGEMENT THAT INCLUDED A THREE-YEAR SPELL AS MANAGER OF THE *ENGLAND* TEAM FOR THE FORMER *ENGLAND* INTERNATIONAL.

HODDLE IS ONE OF TEN PLAYERS WHO WON FULL INTERNATIONAL CAPS FOR *ENGLAND* AND WENT ON TO MANAGE THE *ENGLAND* TEAM -- NAME THREE OTHERS.

DEC 22

DAN PETRESCU WAS BORN IN BUCHAREST ON DECEMBER 22, 1967. HE WON THREE ROMANIAN TITLES WITH **STEAUA BUCHAREST** BEFORE PLAYING IN ITALY WITH **FOGGIA** AND **GENOA**. HIS IMPRESSIVE PERFORMANCES AT THE 1994 WORLD CUP EARNED HIM A MOVE TO **SHEFFIELD WEDNESDAY**, BEFORE HE WAS SIGNED BY **CHELSEA** IN 1995. HE WON THE FA CUP IN 1997 AND THE FOLLOWING YEAR WON THE LEAGUE CUP AND THE UEFA CUP WINNERS' CUP, BEFORE PLAYING IN THE WORLD CUP, WHERE THE ENTIRE **ROMANIA** TEAM FAMOUSLY ALL DYED THEIR HAIR BLONDE! HE LATER PLAYED FOR **BRADFORD CITY** AND **SOUTHAMPTON**, BEFORE ENDING HIS PLAYING DAYS WITH A SEASON AT **NAȚIONAL BUCHAREST. PETRESCU'S** MANAGEMENT CAREER HAS SEEN HIM COACH IN ROMANIA, RUSSIA, THE UAE, QATAR AND TURKEY.

WHO WAS THE **SHEFFIELD WEDNESDAY** MANAGER WHO BROUGHT **PETRESCU** INTO ENGLISH FOOTBALL IN 1994?

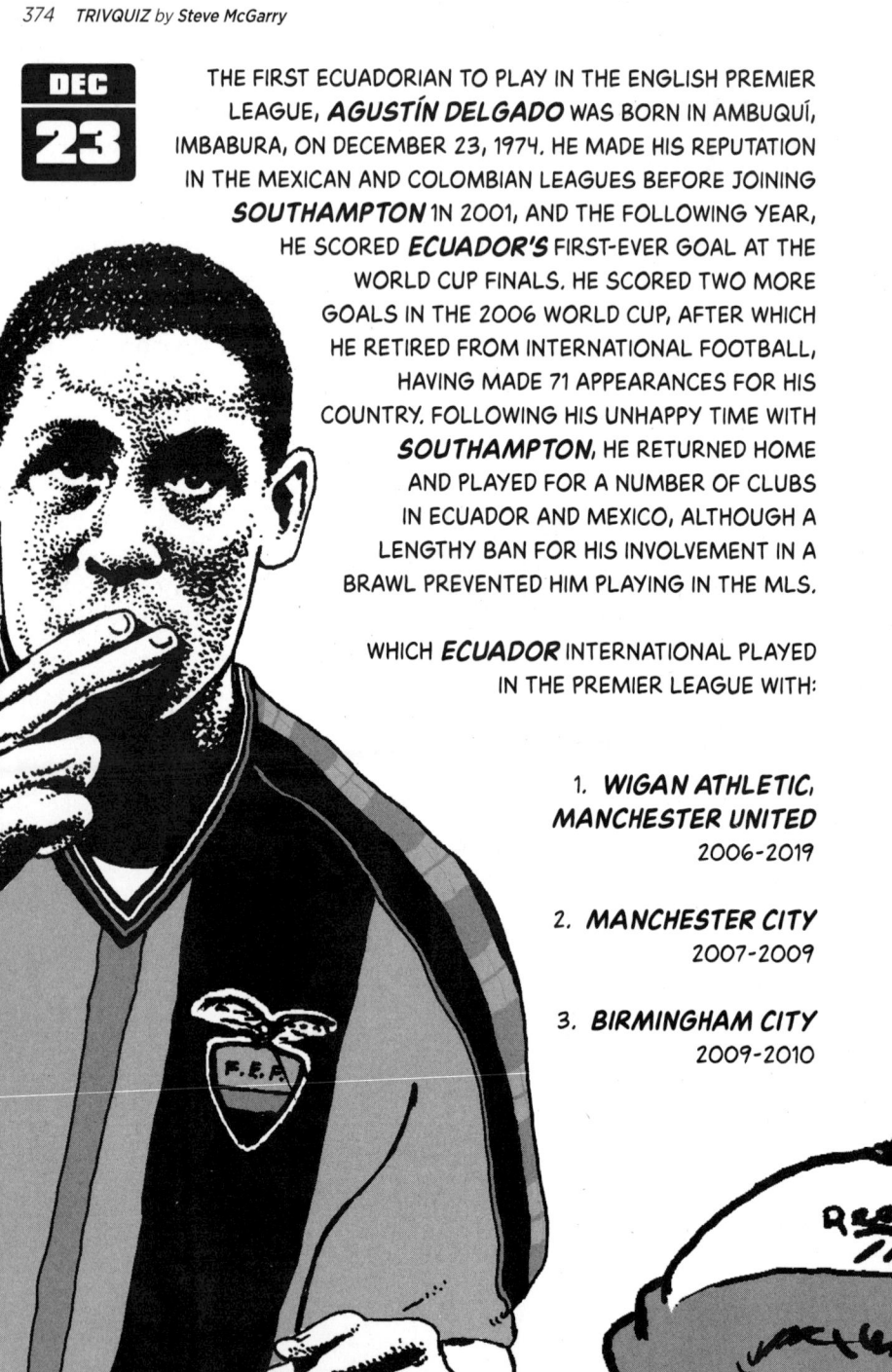

DEC 23

THE FIRST ECUADORIAN TO PLAY IN THE ENGLISH PREMIER LEAGUE, *AGUSTÍN DELGADO* WAS BORN IN AMBUQUÍ, IMBABURA, ON DECEMBER 23, 1974. HE MADE HIS REPUTATION IN THE MEXICAN AND COLOMBIAN LEAGUES BEFORE JOINING *SOUTHAMPTON* IN 2001, AND THE FOLLOWING YEAR, HE SCORED *ECUADOR'S* FIRST-EVER GOAL AT THE WORLD CUP FINALS. HE SCORED TWO MORE GOALS IN THE 2006 WORLD CUP, AFTER WHICH HE RETIRED FROM INTERNATIONAL FOOTBALL, HAVING MADE 71 APPEARANCES FOR HIS COUNTRY. FOLLOWING HIS UNHAPPY TIME WITH *SOUTHAMPTON*, HE RETURNED HOME AND PLAYED FOR A NUMBER OF CLUBS IN ECUADOR AND MEXICO, ALTHOUGH A LENGTHY BAN FOR HIS INVOLVEMENT IN A BRAWL PREVENTED HIM PLAYING IN THE MLS.

WHICH *ECUADOR* INTERNATIONAL PLAYED IN THE PREMIER LEAGUE WITH:

1. *WIGAN ATHLETIC, MANCHESTER UNITED* 2006-2019

2. *MANCHESTER CITY* 2007-2009

3. *BIRMINGHAM CITY* 2009-2010

DEC 24

MARCELO SALAS WAS BORN IN TEMUCO, CHILE, ON DECEMBER 24, 1974. HE BEGAN HIS CAREER AT **UNIVERSIDAD DE CHILE**, SCORING 99 GOALS FOR THE SANTIAGO CLUB, BEFORE JOINING ARGENTINA'S **RIVER PLATE**. HE HELPED THEM WIN THREE LEAGUE TITLES AND WAS VOTED THE 1997 SOUTH AMERICAN PLAYER OF THE YEAR. **SALAS** SCORED 11 GOALS IN HELPING **CHILE** QUALIFY FOR THE 1998 WORLD CUP, EARNING HIMSELF AN $18 MILLION TRANSFER TO ITALY'S **LAZIO** IN THE PROCESS. HE WON A SERIE A TITLE WITH **LAZIO** AND THEN TWO MORE TITLES WITH **JUVENTUS**, BEFORE RETURNING TO **RIVER PLATE** ON LOAN. HE ENDED HIS CAREER IN 2008, HAVING MOVED BACK TO **UNIVERSIDAD DE CHILE**.

NAME ONE OF THE ONLY TWO PLAYERS TO HAVE BETTERED THE TOTAL OF 37 GOALS THAT **SALAS** SCORED FOR **CHILE**.

DEC 25

BORN *JAIR VENTURA FILHO* IN RIO DE JANEIRO, ON DECEMBER 25, 1944, *JAIRZINHO* JOINED *BOTAFOGO* AS A 14-YEAR-OLD, SIGNING PROFESSIONALLY FOR THE CLUB SHORTLY AFTER WINNING A GOLD MEDAL AT THE 1963 PAN AMERICAN GAMES. A BLAZING RIGHT-WINGER, HE MADE THE FIRST OF HIS 81 APPEARANCES FOR *BRAZIL* THE FOLLOWING YEAR -- A CAREER TOTAL THAT WOULD HAVE BEEN CONSIDERABLY HIGHER HAD HE NOT TWICE BROKEN A LEG. HE PLAYED IN ALL THREE OF *BRAZIL'S* GAMES IN THE 1966 WORLD CUP, BUT THE PRESENCE OF *GARRINCHA* IN THE SIDE MEANT THAT HE WAS SWITCHED TO THE LEFT FLANK. FOUR YEARS LATER, HE MADE WORLD CUP HISTORY WHEN HE SCORED IN EVERY GAME OF *BRAZIL'S* MARCH TO GLORY, HIS SEVEN GOALS MAKING HIM THE TOURNAMENT'S SECOND-HIGHEST SCORER. IN THE 1974 FINALS HE PLAYED ON A MUCH-GRITTIER *BRAZIL* TEAM, ADDING TWO MORE GOALS TO HIS TALLY.

WITH 33 GOALS FOR HIS COUNTRY, *JAIRZINHO* IS TIED WITH *RONALDINHO* ON THE ALL-TIME TOP GOALSCORER LIST FOR *BRAZIL*. NAME FIVE OF THE SEVEN PLAYERS WHO SCORED MORE GOALS FOR THE *"SELEÇÃO"*.

DEC 26

THE FIRST GOALKEEPER TO CAPTAIN *ENGLAND* SINCE THE 19TH CENTURY, *FRANK SWIFT* WAS BORN IN BLACKPOOL, ON BOXING DAY, 1914. HE MADE HIS SENIOR DEBUT FOR *MANCHESTER CITY* ON CHRISTMAS DAY, 1933, THE DAY BEFORE HIS 19TH BIRTHDAY. *CITY* WENT ON TO WIN THE FA CUP THAT SEASON, AND *"BIG FRANK"* FAINTED ON HIS WAY UP TO RECEIVE HIS WINNER'S MEDAL! HE CONTINUED TO BE *CITY'S* FIRST-CHOICE GOALKEEPER UNTIL HIS RETIREMENT IN 1949. CAPPED 19 TIMES BY *ENGLAND*, HE BECAME A JOURNALIST WHEN HIS PLAYING DAYS WERE OVER. HE WAS COVERING *MANCHESTER UNITED'S* EUROPEAN CUP CAMPAIGN FOR A SUNDAY PAPER WHEN HE WAS KILLED -- ALONG WITH MANY OF THE *UNITED* TEAM -- IN THE 1958 MUNICH AIR DISASTER.

1. WHO WAS *MANCHESTER CITY'S* GOALKEEPER WHEN THEY WON THE FA CUP IN:
   A) 1956 B) 1969
   C) 2011 D) 2019

2. FOLLOWING *SWIFT*, WHO WAS THE NEXT GOALKEEPER TO CAPTAIN *ENGLAND?*

3. WHO DID *MANCHESTER CITY* BEAT IN THE 1934 FA CUP FINAL?

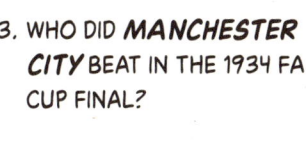

DEC 27

JOHN CHARLES, THE WELSHMAN WHO CONQUERED ITALIAN FOOTBALL IN THE LATE 1950S, WAS BORN IN SWANSEA, ON DECEMBER 27, 1931. HE STARTED HIS CAREER AS A 17-YEAR-OLD CENTRE-HALF WITH **LEEDS UNITED** BEFORE SWITCHING TO CENTRE-FORWARD AND BECOMING A GOALSCORING SENSATION -- HE HIT 42 GOALS IN THE 1953-54 SEASON ALONE. HE JOINED **JUVENTUS** IN 1957 FOR A FEE OF £65,000 -- A BRITISH RECORD AT THE TIME. NICKNAMED **"IL GIGANTE BUONO"**, WHICH MEANS **"THE GENTLE GIANT"**, HE WAS SERIE A TOP SCORER IN HIS FIRST SEASON. HE WENT ON TO WIN THREE LEAGUE TITLES AND TWO ITALIAN CUPS IN HIS FIVE SEASONS AT THE CLUB, BEFORE REJOINING **LEEDS UNITED** IN 1962. HIS RETURN WAS SHORT-LIVED AND HE WAS SOON BACK IN ITALY WITH **ROMA**. HE JOINED **CARDIFF CITY** IN 1963 AND ENDED HIS CAREER WITH SPELLS AS PLAYER/MANAGER AT **HEREFORD UNITED** AND **MERTHYR TYDFIL**. HE WAS CAPPED 38 TIMES BY **WALES**, AND PLAYED IN THE 1958 WORLD CUP TOURNAMENT, THE ONLY TIME **WALES** HAVE QUALIFIED.

NAME THE TWO OTHER **WALES** INTERNATIONALS WHO PLAYED FOR **JUVENTUS**.

DEC 28

TERRY BUTCHER WAS BORN ON DECEMBER 28, 1958, IN SINGAPORE, WHERE HIS FATHER WAS STATIONED IN THE BRITISH ARMED SERVICES. RAISED IN LOWESTOFT, SUFFOLK, HE TURNED DOWN THE CHANCE TO PLAY FOR **NORWICH CITY** AND SIGNED FOR HIS BELOVED **IPSWICH TOWN**. HE MADE HIS DEBUT IN 1978, AND WITHIN TWO YEARS WAS AN **ENGLAND** INTERNATIONAL. A UEFA CUP WINNER WITH **IPSWICH**, HE JOINED **RANGERS** IN 1986 AND CAPTAINED THEM TO THREE LEAGUE TITLES IN HIS FOUR SEASONS AT THE CLUB. CAPPED 77 TIMES BY **ENGLAND**, HE RETIRED FROM INTERNATIONAL FOOTBALL AFTER CAPTAINING HIS COUNTRY TO THE SEMI-FINALS OF THE 1990 WORLD CUP, AND LAUNCHED HIS MANAGEMENT CAREER BY TAKING THE PLAYER/MANAGER JOB AT **COVENTRY CITY**.

1. NAME THREE TEAMS THAT **BUTCHER** SUBSEQUENTLY MANAGED.

2. WITH WHICH SCOTTISH CLUB DID **BUTCHER** END HIS PLAYING CAREER, MAKING THREE APPEARANCES IN 1993?

3. WHICH MANAGER GAVE **BUTCHER** HIS **ENGLAND** DEBUT IN 1980?

DEC 29

NICLAS ALEXANDERSSON WAS BORN IN HALMSTAD, SWEDEN, ON DECEMBER 29, 1971. HE LAUNCHED HIS CAREER AT **VESSIGEBRO BK**, MOVING ON TO **HALMSTADS BK** AND IFK GÖTEBORG, BEFORE JOINING **SHEFFIELD WEDNESDAY** IN 1997.

THE SWEDISH INTERNATIONAL MIDFIELDER -- HE MADE 109 APPEARANCES FOR HIS COUNTRY -- JOINED **EVERTON** IN THE SUMMER OF 2000. A BRIEF LOAN PERIOD AT **WEST HAM UNITED** IN 2003 WAS FOLLOWED BY A RETURN TO **IFK GÖTEBORG**, WHERE HE PLAYED FOR FIVE SEASONS BEFORE RETIRING IN 2009.

WHO WAS THE MANAGER, WHO HAD PREVIOUSLY HELMED **WEST BROMWICH ALBION** AND **MANCHESTER UNITED**, WHO SIGNED **ALEXANDERSSON** TO **SHEFFIELD WEDNESDAY?**

DEC 30

BORN IN CHESTERFIELD, ON DECEMBER 30, 1937, *GORDON BANKS* PLAYED ONE SEASON IN THE ENGLISH THIRD DIVISION WITH *CHESTERFIELD* BEFORE MOVING INTO THE TOP FLIGHT WITH *LEICESTER CITY* IN 1959. HE WON THE FIRST OF HIS 73 CAPS IN 1963 AND WAS OUTSTANDING IN *ENGLAND'S* VICTORIOUS 1966 WORLD CUP CAMPAIGN -- HE DIDN'T CONCEDE A GOAL UNTIL THE SEMI-FINAL! A MYSTERY STOMACH AILMENT RULED BANKS OUT OF THE QUARTER-FINAL OF THE 1970 WORLD CUP, AND IN HIS ABSENCE *ENGLAND* SQUANDERED A 2-0 LEAD TO ALLOW *WEST GERMANY* A FAMOUS COMEBACK VICTORY.

HE JOINED *STOKE CITY* IN 1967 AND HELPED THEM WIN THE 1972 LEAGUE CUP -- THE FIRST TROPHY IN THE CLUB'S HISTORY -- AND WAS VOTED FOOTBALLER OF THE YEAR. LATER THAT SAME YEAR, TRAGEDY STRUCK WHEN *BANKS* LOST AN EYE IN A CAR CRASH AND HIS CAREER AT THE HIGHEST LEVEL WAS OVER.

NAME 10 OF THE GOALKEEPERS WHO HAVE PLAYED FOR *ENGLAND* SINCE *BANKS* WAS FORCED TO RETIRE IN 1972.

DEC
31

DESPITE WINNING MEDALS WITH **NORWICH CITY** AND WINNING EVERY DOMESTIC HONOUR, THE EUROPEAN CUP WINNERS' CUP AND EUROPEAN SUPER CUP, WITH **MANCHESTER UNITED, STEVE BRUCE** NEVER EARNED A FULL **ENGLAND** CAP. BORN IN CORBRIDGE, NORTHUMBERLAND, ON DECEMBER 31, 1960, HE WAS TURNED DOWN BY NUMEROUS PROFESSIONAL CLUBS -- INCLUDING HIS BELOVED **NEWCASTLE UNITED** -- AND WAS ON THE VERGE OF STARTING AS AN APPRENTICE PLUMBER ON THE **SWAN HUNTER** DOCKYARD WHEN HE WAS OFFERED A TRIAL AT **GILLINGHAM**. HE TRAVELLED DOWN TO KENT WITH ANOTHER **WALLSEND BOYS CLUB** YOUNGSTER -- **BRUCE** WAS OFFERED A PLACE BUT THE CLUB TURNED DOWN **PETER BEARDSLEY!** AS HIS PLAYING DAYS NEARED AN END, HE LEFT OLD TRAFFORD FOR **BIRMINGHAM CITY**, BEFORE TAKING A PLAYER/MANAGER JOB WITH **SHEFFIELD UNITED**. IT WAS THE START OF A MANAGEMENT CAREER THAT CULMINATED IN HIS 2019 APPOINTMENT AT **NEWCASTLE UNITED**.

NAME FIVE OTHER TEAMS THAT **STEVE BRUCE** HAS MANAGED.

ANSWERS

JANUARY

Jan 1: 1a) Mário Zagallo b) Cláudio Coutinho 2) Carlos José Castilho, Nílton Santos, Djalma Santos, Pelé, Émerson Leão, Cafu, Ronaldo

Jan 2: 1) AC Milan 2) Chris Waddle 3) Walter Smith

Jan 3: Walter Winterbottom, Alf Ramsey, Joe Mercer, Don Revie, Ron Greenwood, Bobby Robson, Graham Taylor, Terry Venables, Glenn Hoddle, Howard Wilkinson, Kevin Keegan, Peter Taylor, Sven-Göran Eriksson, Steve McClaren, Fabio Capello, Stuart Pearce, Roy Hodgson, Sam Allardyce, Gareth Southgate

Jan 4: 1) David O'Leary 2) Swindon Town 3) Terry Venables

Jan 5: 1) Leeds United, Sheffield United, Chelsea, Queens Park Rangers 2) Stuart Pearce 3) "Lock, Stock and Two Smoking Barrels"

Jan 6: 1) Tottenham Hotspur 2) Australia 3) Barcelona

Jan 7: 1) Rafa Benítez, Roberto Di Matteo, José Mourinho, Guus Hiddink, Antonio Conte, Maurizio Sarri 2) Thibaut Courtois 3) René Vandereycken, Franky Vercauteren, Dick Advocaat, Georges Leekens, Marc Wilmots, Roberto Martínez

Jan 8: 1) Chicago Fire 2) Antonio Carbajal 3a) Algeria b) South Africa c) Ghana d) Nigeria

Jan 9: River Plate, Hellas Verona, Atalanta, Roma, Benfica, Boca Juniors, Atalanta, Dundee, Rangers, Qatar SC, Wembley

Jan 10: 1) Eric Cantona 2) Zinedine Zidane 3) Jean Tigana

Jan 11: 1) Bradford City, West Bromwich Albion, Sheffield United, Thailand, Thailand U23 2) Terry Venables 3) Don Howe, Brian Whitehouse, Johnny Giles, Ronnie Allen, John Wile, Ron Atkinson

Jan 12: 1) Jerzy Dudek 2) Tomasz Kuszczak 3) Kazimierz Deyna

Jan 13: 1) Emmanuel Petit 2) Gilles Grimandi 3) Emmanuel Adebayor

Jan 14: Walter Winterbottom, Alf Ramsey, Bobby Robson

Jan 15: 1) Sócrates 2) Florian Albert 3) Gary Speed

Jan 16: 1) Fulham, England, Manchester City 2) Scunthorpe United, Liverpool, Hamburger SV, Southampton 3) Terry McDermott, Kenny Dalglish, Ruud Gullit, Steve Clarke, Bobby Robson, John Carver, Graeme Souness, Glenn Roeder, Nigel Pearson, Sam Allardyce

Jan 17: 1) George Weah 2) Marc Wilmots 3) Gianni Rivera

Jan 18: 1) Hugo Sánchez 2) Mario Kempes 3) Ronaldo 4) Diego Forlán

Jan 19: 1) Bayer Leverkusen, San Jose Eathquakes, Los Angeles Galaxy, Bayern Munich, Everton, León, San Diego Sockers 2) Brian McBride and Clint Dempsey 3) Swansea City

Jan 20: 1) Alex Oxlade-Chamberlain 2) Alan Ball 3) Ted Drake

Jan 21: 1) Newcastle United, Birmingham City, South China 2) Everton 3) Salford City

Jan 22: 1) Fan Zhiyi 2) Ali Daei 3) Shinji Ono

Jan 23: Wesley Sneijder, Edwin van der Sar, Frank de Boer, Rafael van der Vaart, Giovanni van Bronckhorst, Dirk Kuyt, Robin van Persie, Phillip Cocu

Jan 24: 1) Ghana 2) Groningen, Ajax, Liverpool, Barcelona, Atlético Madrid 3) Paraguay

Jan 25: 1) Neymar 2) Danilo 3) Elano

Jan 26: 1) Claudio Ranieri 2) Roberto Mancini 3) Manuel Pellegrini 4) Rafa Benítez 5) Louis van Gaal 6) Mauricio Pochettino

Jan 27: 1) Park Ji-Sung 2) Son Heung-min 3) Lee Young-Pyo

Jan 28: 1) Gianpiero Combi (1934), Aldo Oliviera (1938), Dino Zoff (1982) 2) Paris Saint-Germain 3) Rafael Márquez (Mexico), Lothar Matthäus (Germnay), Antonio Carbajal (Mexico)

Jan 29: 1) PSV Eindhoven 2) Barcelona 3) Valencia

Jan 30: 1) Carlos Tevez 2) Hristo Stoichkov 3) Bayer Leverkusen, Tottenham Hotspur, Fulham, Monaco, PAOK, Kerala Blasters

Jan 31: 1) Wayne Bridge 2) John Carew 3) Sulley Muntari

FEBRUARY

Feb 1: 1) Mario Kempes 2) Lionel Messi 3) Diego Maradona, Javier Mascherano, Lionel Messi

Feb 2: 1) Real Zaragoza 2) Catalonia 3) Shakira

Feb 3: 1) Andrés Escobar 2) Sir Matt Busby 3) Billy Wright

Feb 4: 1) Oleg Blokhin 2) Rinat Dasayev 3) Igor Netto

Feb 5: 1) Luis Suárez with Liverpool and Barcelona 2) Hugo Sánchez 3) Gareth Bale

Feb 6: 1) Essam El-Hadary 2) John 'Budgie' Burridge 3) Roger Milla

Feb 7: 1) Denis Law 2) Joe Payne 3) Oleg Salenko

Feb 8: 1) Chicago Fire and D.C. United 2) Celta Vigo 3) Sampdoria

Feb 9: 1) Portugal 2) Portugal 3) Soviet Union

Feb 10: Atlético Madrid, Monaco, Manchester United, Chelsea, Galatasaray

Feb 11: 1) Theo Walcott 2) Wayne Rooney 3) Bobby Moore

Feb 12: 1) Paraguay 2) Oman 3) Senegal 4) Ivory Coast 5) Grenada

Feb 13: 1) Claudio Reyna 2) Juan Pablo Ángel 3) Thierry Henry

Feb 14: 1) Luis Suárez 2) Diego Godín 3) Paraguay

Feb 15: 1) Javier Hernández 2) Brian McBride and Landon Donovan 3) Clint Dempsey

Feb 16: 1) Fabien Barthez 2) Oliver Giroud 3) Jérôme Boateng

Feb 17: Vladislao Cap, César Luis Menotti, Carlos Bilardo, Alfio Basile, Daniel Passarella, Diego Maradona, Sergio Batista, Alejandro Sabella, Gerardo Martino, Edgardo Bauza, Lionel Scaloni

Feb 18: 1) Phil Neal 2) Jack and Bobby Charlton 3) Netball

Feb 19: 1) Japan 2) United States 3) England 4) Denmark 5) Norway

Feb 20: Gordon Banks, George Cohen, Jack Charlton, Bobby Moore, Ray Wilson, Nobby Stiles, Alan Ball, Bobby Charlton, Martin Peters, Geoff Hurst, Roger Hunt

Feb 21: 1) Stelios Giannakopoulos 2) Sotirios Kyrgiakos 3) José Holebas

Feb 22: 1) John Jensen 2) Peter Schmeichel 3) Henrik Andersen

Feb 23: 1) James Milner 2) Peter Schmeichel 3) Darius Vassell

Feb 24: 1) Paulo Wanchope 2) Marcel Desailly 3) Pep Guardiola 4) Wesley Sneijder

Feb 25: 1) Queens Park Rangers, PSV Eindhoven 2) Guus Hiddink 3) Barcelona

Feb 26: 1) Monaco 2) Arsenal 3) Crystal Palace

Feb 27: 1) Franz Beckenbauer 2) Gerd Müller, Franz Beckenbauer, Karl-Heinz Rummenigge 3) Jean-Marie Pfaff, Oliver Kahn, Manuel Neuer

Feb 28: 1) Roberto Mancini 2) Antonio Conte 3) Marcello Lippi

Feb 29: 1) Clint Dempsey 2) John Harkes 3) Steve Howey

MARCH

Mar 1: 1934: Italy 1938: France 1950: Brazil 1954: Switzerland 1958: Sweden 1962: Chile 1966: England 1970: Mexico 1974: West Germany 1978: Argentina 1982: Spain 1986: Mexico 1990: Italy 1994: USA 1998: France 2002: South Korea & Japan 2006: Germany 2010: South Africa 2014: Brazil 2018: Russia

Mar 2: 1) Pepe 2) Eduardo da Silva 3) Diego Costa

Mar 3: 1) Arsène Wenger 2) Gary Lineker 3) Gordon Milne

Mar 4: 1) Ray Wilkins (1986), David Beckham (1998), Wayne Rooney (2006) 2) 1990 – Pedro Monzón, Gustavo Dezotti (Argentina), 1998 – Marcel Desailly (France), 2006 – Zinedine Zidane (France), 2010 – John Heitinga (Netherlands) 3) Peru

Mar 5: 1) Phil Jagielka 2) Alan Hodgkinson 3) Brian Deane

Mar 6: 1) Raúl 2) Martin Ødegaard 3) Günter Netzer

Mar 7: 1) Gordon Banks 2) Peter Shilton 3) Bert Williams

Mar 8: Kasey Keller, Roy Wegerle, Cobi Jones, Brad Friedel, Claudia Reyna, Bruce Murray, Joe-Max Moore, Mike Lapper, Tony Meola

Mar 9: Chris Coleman, Lawrie Sanchez, Roy Hodgson, Billy McKinlay, Mark Hughes, Martin Jol, René Meulensteen, Felix Magath

Mar 10: 1) Rigobert Song (138 caps) 2) Marcel Desailly: Marseille, AC Milan; Paulo Sousa: Juventus, Borussia Dortmund; Gerard Piqué: Manchester United, Barcelona 3) 2000

Mar 11: José Mourinho, Avram Grant, Ray Wilkins, Luiz Felipe Scolari, Guus Hiddink, Carlo Ancelotti, Roberto Di Matteo, André Villas-Boas

Mar 12: 1a) Italy b) France 2a) Enzo Bearzot b) Marcello Lippi 3) Brazil - 5, Germany - 4, Argentina - 2, Uruguay -2, France - 2

Mar 13: 1) Clarence Seedorf 2) Aron Winter 3) Jimmy Floyd Hasselbaink

Mar 14: 1) Benni McCarthy 2) Lucas Radebe 3) Quinton Fortune

Mar 15: 1) 19 2) 7 3) 13: 6 European Cups/Champions Leagues, 3 UEFA Cups, 4 UEFA Super Cups

Mar 16: 1) Jermain Defoe, Harry Kane, Raheem Sterling 2) Malcolm MacDonald 3) Wayne Rooney

Mar 17: Norway, Germany and Japan

Mar 18: 1) Marc-Vivien Foé 2) Bobby Moore 3) Paolo Maldini 4) Roberto Baggio

Mar 19: 1) Ruud van Nistelrooy 2) Dennis Violett 3) Wayne Rooney

Mar 20: 1) Bayern Munich 2) Benfica 3) Marseille

Mar 21: Paris Saint-Germain, Barcelona and AC Milan

Mar 22: Sporting CP, Real Sociedad (3 times), Real Madrid (2 times), Deportivo, Besiktas, Saint-Étienne, Catania, Real Murcia, Macedonia, Khazar Lankaran, Wydad Casablanca, Tractor

Mar 23: 1) Xavi 2) Frank Lebouef 3) Wesley Sneijder

Mar 24: Bernard Lama, Vincent Candela, Bixente Lizarazu, Patrick Vieira, Laurent Blanc, Youri Djorkaeff, Didier Deschamps, Marcel Desailly, Zinedine Zidane, Robert Pirès, Thierry Henry, Lilian Thuram, Fabien Barthez, Emmanuel Petit, Frank Lebouef, Christian Karembeu, David Trezeguet

Mar 25: 1) Owen Hargreaves 2) Kevin Keegan 3) Tony Woodcock

Mar 26: 1) Steve McLaren 2) Walter Zenga 3) Luis Enrique

Mar 27: 1) Toni Turek 2) Sepp Maier 3) Bodo Illgner

Mar 28: Hugo Lloris (Tottenham Hotspur), Paul Pogba (Manchester United), Oliver Giroud (Chelsea), N'Golo Kanté (Chelsea), Benjamin Mendy (Manchester City)

Mar 29: Cristiano Ronaldo, Pauleta, Eusébio, Luís Figo, Nuno Gomes, Hélder Postiga

Mar 30: Fernando Torres, Pepe Reina (Liverpool), Cesc Fàbregas (Arsenal)

Mar 31: 1) Diego Maradona 2) Ruud Gullit 3) Lothar Matthäus 4) Mick McCarthy

APRIL

Apr 1: Wesley Sneijder (134), Edwin van der Sar (130), Frank de Boer (112), Rafael van der Vaart (109), Giovanni van Bronckhorst (106), Dirk Kuyt (104), Robin van Persie (102), Phillip Cocu (101), Arjen Robben (96)

Apr 2: 1) Panathinaikos 2) Sándor Kocsis 3) Eintracht Frankfurt

Apr 3: 1) Maicon 2) Sylvinho 3) Robinho

Apr 4: 1) Diego Forlán 2) Jorge Valdano and Zinedine Zidane 3) Argentina

Apr 5: Wayne Rooney, Bobby Charlton, Gary Lineker, Jimmy Greaves, Michael Owen, Harry Kane, Nat Lofthouse, Alan Shearer

Apr 6: 1) Nedum Onuoha 2) Victor Moses 3) Shola Ameobi

Apr 7: 1) Aílton, Grafite, Arjen Robben, Kevin De Bruyne, Robert Lewandowski 2) Jupp Heynckes, Pep Guardiola, Louis van Gaal, Ottmar Hitzfeld, Carlo Ancelotti, Niko Kovac, Jürgen Klinsmann, Andries Jonker, Peter Hermann, Willy Sagnol 3) Fiorentina

Apr 8: 1978 - Mario Kempes (Argentina) 1982 - Paolo Rossi (Italy) 1986 - Gary Lineker (England) 1990 - Salvatore Schillaci (Italy) 1994 - Hristo Stoichkov (Bulgaria) and Oleg Saleko (Russia) 1998 - Davor Šuker (Croatia) 2002 - Ronaldo (Brazil) 2006 - Miroslav Klose (Germany) 2010 - Thomas Müller (Germany) 2014 - James Rodríguez (Colombia) 2018 - Harry Kane (England)

Apr 9: 1) Leeds United, Manchester City, Cardiff City and Blackburn Rovers 2) Ryan Giggs, Wayne Rooney, Dele Alli 3) Sergio Agüero

Apr 10: 1) Christopher Samba 2) Yuri Zhirkov 3) Samuel Eto'o

Apr 11: 1) Alan Smith 2) Dietmar Hamann 3) Tore André Flo

Apr 12: Bryan Robson, David Beckham, Steven Gerrard, Alan Shearer, John Terry, Kevin Keegan, Harry Kane

Apr 13: 1) Bayer Leverkusen, Roma 2) Dick Nanninga (1978), Alessandro Altobelli (1982), Mario Götze (2014) 3) Argentina

Apr 14: 1) Celtic 2) Ajax 3) PSV 4) Barcelona 5) Internazionale 6) Bayern Munich 7) Barcelona 8) Bayern Munich

Apr 15: 1) Danny and Daley Blind 2) Cesare and Paolo Maldini 3) Peter and Kasper Schmeichel

Apr 16: Preston North End, Aston Villa, Tottenham Hotspur, Liverpool, Manchester United, Chelsea, Manchester City

Apr 17: 1960: Soviet Union 1964: Spain 1968: Italy 1972: West Germany 1976: Czechoslovakia 1980: West Germany 1984: France 1988: Netherlands 1992: Denmark, 1996: Germany 2000: France 2004: Greece 2008: Spain 2012: Spain 2016: Portugal 2020: Italy

Apr 18: 1) Artur Borac 2) Hull City 3) Swansea City

Apr 19: 1) Barcelona 2) AC Milan 3) Olympiacos

Apr 20: 1) Kenny Dalglish 2) Arsenal 3) Arsenal

Apr 21: 1) Kylian Mbappé 2) Paul Pogba 3) Raheem Sterling

Apr 22: 1) Robinho 2) David Beckham 3) Gonzalo Higuaín

Apr 23: 1) Guus Hiddink 2) Martin Jol 3) Borussia Dortmund

Apr 24: 1) Nottingham Forest, Newcastle United, West Ham United, Manchester City, Longford 2) Nottingham Forest, Manchester City 3) Psycho

Apr 25: 1) Barcelona, LA Aztecs, Washington Diplomats, Levante, Ajax, Feyenoord 2) Ruud Gullit, Marco van Basten 3) Rinus Michels, Louis van Gaal, Frank Rijkaard, Ronald Koeman

Apr 26: 1) Birmingham City 2) Everton 3) Bournemouth 4) Arsenal

Apr 27: 1) Southampton 2) Bill Nicholson 3) Jermain Defoe

Apr 28: 1) Zlatan Ibrahimović 2) Edinson Cavani 3) Carlos Bianchi, Delio Onnis

Apr 29: 1) Ray Clemence 2) Johnny Giles 3) Ian Callaghan

Apr 30: 1) Jim Holton 2) Bobby Moore 3) Danny Blanchflower

MAY

May 1: 1a) Edin Džeko b) John Charles 2) Sweden 3) Marco van Basten

May 2: Billy Wright, Tom Finney, Bobby Charlton, Bobby Moore, Peter Shilton, Terry Butcher, Bryan Robson, Sol Campbell, Ashley Cole, Joe Cole, Frank Lampard, Wayne Rooney (Charlton, Gerrard and Ferdinand were named in four squads but only played in three)

May 3: 1) Maynor Figueroa 2) Emilio Izaguirre 3) Wilson Palacios

May 4: 1) Leroy Sané 2) Cristiano Ronaldo 3) Harry Kewell

May 5: 1) Wally Barnes – Arsenal 2) Eric Bell – Bolton Wanderers 3) Jimmy Meadows – Manchester City 4) Ray Wood – Manchester United 5) Roy Dwight – Nottingham Forest 6) Dave Whelan – Blackburn Rovers

May 6: Everton, Newcastle United, Bolton Wanderers, Sheffield United

May 7: 1) Bob Paisley 2) Tommy Lawton 3) Helmut Schön

May 8: 1a) Fabio Capello b) Arrigo Sacchi 2) Giuseppe Baresi 3) Paolo Maldini

May 9: 1) West Germany 2) Antonín Panenka 3) Ivo Viktor

May 10: 1) Mario Balotelli 2) Edgar Davids 3) Xherdan Shaqiri

May 11: 1) Vissel Kobe 2) Lionel Messi 3) Arsenal, Manchester United (twice) and Juventus

May 12: 1) Freddie Ljungberg 2) Arsène Wenger (Arsenal) and Gérard Houllier (Liverpool) 3a) Chelsea b) Southampton c) Millwall d) Manchester United e) West Ham United

May 13: 1) Marco van Basten, Ruud Gullit 2) Los Angeles Aztecs, Washington Diplomats 3) Jordi Cruyff

May 14: 1) El Salvador and Honduras 2) Austria 3) 1998

May 15: 1) Galatasaray 2) Ajax, Internazionale, Crystal Palace, Atlanta United 3) Rene and Willy van de Kerkhof

May 16: 1) Portsmouth 2) Everton and Manchester United 3) Ashley Cole

May 17: 1) Guus Hiddink, Louis van Gaal 2) Rafael Benítez, Roberto Martínez, Pep Guardiola, Mikel Arteta 3) Gianluca Vialli

May 18: 1) Ian Callaghan 2) Johnny Giles

May 19: 1) New York City 2) Fabio Cannavaro 3) Gianluigi Buffon, Fabio Cannavaro, Paolo Maldini, Daniele De Rossi

May 20: 1) Michel Preud'homme 2) Fabien Barthez 3) Oliver Kahn 4) Gianluigi Buffon 5) Manuel Neuer 6) Thibaut Courtois

May 21: 1) Rigobert Song 2) Geremi 3) Samuel Eto'o

May 22: 1) Alexis Sánchez 2) Claudio Bravo 3) Marcelo Bielsa

May 23: 1) Tottenham Hotspur, West Bromwich Albion, Chesterfield, Brighton & Hove Albion, Millwall, Crawley Town, Bromley, Worthing, Whitehawk 2) Billy Bingham 3) Bryan Hamilton, Lawrie Sanchez

May 24: 1) Trevor Francis 2) Crystal Palace 3) Howard Wilkinson

May 25: 1) Osvaldo Ardiles 2) Mario Kempes 3) Ricardo Villa

May 26: 1) Ally McCoist 2) Diego Forlán 3) Kevin Phillips

May 27: 1) Yaya Touré 2) Thierry Henry 3) Cristiano Ronaldo

May 28: 1) Terry Venables 2) Lazio 3) Rangers

May 29: 1) Andrei Kanchelskis 2) Alexey Smertin 3) Dmitri Kharine

May 30: 1) Los Angeles Galaxy 2) Gérard Houllier, Rafa Benítez, Roy Hodgson, Kenny Dalglish, Brendan Rodgers, Phil Thompson 3) Kevin Keegan, Sven-Göran Eriksson, Steve McClaren, Fabio Capello, Stuart Pearce, Roy Hodgson

May 31: 1) Oleg Blokhin and Igor Belanov 2) Dynamo Kyiv 3) Anatoliy Tymoshchuk

JUNE

Jun 1: 1) Manchester United, Real Madrid, Bayer Leverkusen, West Ham United, Sevilla, LA Galaxy 2) Jared Borgetti

Jun 2: 1) James Rodríguez 2) Daniel Passarella 3) José Luis Chilavert

Jun 3: 1) Steve Bloomer 2) Tom Finney 3) Wayne Rooney

Jun 4: 1) Wolfgang Weber 2) Miroslav Klose 3) Sepp Piontek

Jun 5: 1) Emilio Butragueño (Spain, 1986), Eusébio (Portugal, 1966), Just Fontaine (France, 1958), Sándor Kocsis (Hungary, 1954), Ademir (Brazil, 1950) 2) Oleg Salenko (Russia, 1994)

Jun 6: 1) Steve Bruce 2) Manchester City 3) Stockholm

Jun 7: 1) Alf Ramsey and Mário Zagallo 2) Carlos Alberto 3) West Germany

Jun 8: 1) Alan Mullery 2) Giacinto Facchetti 3) 1980

Jun 9: 1) Edwin van der Sar 2) Thomas Müller - Germany, David Villa - Spain, Diego Forlán - Uruguay

Jun 10: 1) Bari, Juventus, Sampdoria 2) Bruce Rioch 3) Nottingham Forest

Jun 11: 1) Dimitar Berbatov 2) Emre Can 3) Son Heung-min

Jun 12: 1) Aston Villa 2) Peter Schmeichel 3) Melbourne City

Jun 13: 1) CSKA Moscow 2) AC Milan 3) Cameroon and Denmark

Jun 14: 1) Vavá (Brazil 1958, 1962), Pelé (Brazil 1958, 1970), Zinedine Zidane (France 1998, 2006) 2) 1974 3) Bayern Munich

Jun 15: Hans Tilkowski, Sepp Maier, Harald Schumacher, Andreas Köpke, Manuel Neuer

Jun 16: 1) Trevor Francis 2) Paul Mariner 3) Czechoslovakia

Jun 17: 1) Mario Balotelli 2) Mario Gómez 3) Mario Mandžukic 4) Fernando Torres 5) Cristiano Ronaldo

Jun 18: 1) John Obi Mikel 2) Yaya Touré 3) Lucas Radebe

Jun 19: 1) Vittorio Pozzo 2) Four - 1934, 1938, 1982 and 2006 3) Giuseppe Meazza

Jun 20: 1) Swansea City, New York City, Manchester City 2) Claudio Ranieri, José Mourinho, Avram Grant, Luiz Felipe Scolari, Ray Wilkins, Guus Hiddink, Carlo Ancelotti, Roberto Di Matteo, André Villas-Boas, Rafa Benítez 3) Peter Shilton, Wayne Rooney, David Beckham, Steven Gerrard, Bobby Moore, Ashley Cole, Bobby Charlton, Billy Wright

Jun 21: 1) Omar Sívori 2) Paolo Rossi 3) Roberto Baggio 4) Zinedine Zidane 5) Pavel Nedved

Jun 22: 1) Antonio Rattin 2) David Beckham 3) David Beckham

Jun 23: 1) Algeria 2) Cannes, Bordeaux 3) Juventus

Jun 24: 1) Marcelo Bielsa 2) Gabriel Batistuta 3) Sevilla

Jun 25: 1) Rinus Michels 2) Ronald and Erwin Koeman 3) Frank Rijkaard

Jun 26: 1) Pep Guardiola 2) Diego Maradona 3) Rio Ferdinand

Jun 27: 1) Alexander Frei 2) Roy Hodgson 3) Ottmar Hitzfeld

Jun 28: 1) Steven Pienaar 2) Quinton Fortune 3) Aaron Mokoena

Jun 29: 1974

Jun 30: 1) Barcelona 2) Paris Saint-Germain 3) Real Madrid

JULY

Jul 1: 1) Hamburger SV, Málaga 2) Fabio Capello, Bernd Schuster, Manuel Pellegrini 3) Cristiano Ronaldo

Jul 2: Abby Wambach, Mia Hamm, Kristine Lilly, Carli Lloyd

Jul 3: 1) Jack Rodwell 2) Stewart Downing 3) Wes Brown

Jul 4: Reims, Fiorentina, AC Milan, Reims, Eintracht Frankfurt

Jul 5: 1) Philippe Coutinho 2) Xherdan Shaqiri 3) Dennis Bergkamp

Jul 6: Guus Hiddink, Dick Advocaat, Fabio Capello, Leonid Slutsky

Jul 7: 1) Fritz Walter 2) Lothar Matthäus 3) Philipp Lahm

Jul 8: Wolverhampton Wanderers, Coventry City, Internazionale, Leeds United, Tottenham Hotspur, Liverpool, Celtic, West Ham United, Aston Villa

Jul 9: 1) Cremonese, Sampdoria, Juventus, Chelsea 2) Chelsea, Watford

Jul 10: 1) Howard Wilkinson, Terry Venables 2) Brian Clough 3) Ron Greenwood

Jul 11: 1) César Luis Menotti 2) Sven-Göran Eriksson 3) Gerardo Martino

Jul 12: 1) Radamel Falcao 2) Davinson Sánchez 3) Juan Pablo Ángel

Jul 13: 1) Igor Akinfeev 2) Lev Yashin 3) Dmitri Kharine

Jul 14: 1) Peter Shilton 2) Cristiano Ronaldo 3) Gianluigi Buffon

Jul 15: 1) Samuel Eto'o 2) Christian Vieri 3) Iván Zamorano

Jul 16: 1) Theo Walcott 2) Alex Oxlade-Chamberlain 3) Luke Shaw

Jul 17: 1) Reading 2) Laurent Blanc 3) Dino Zoff

Jul 18: 1) Joseph Yobo 2) Nwankwo Kanu 3) Kelechi Iheanacho

Jul 19: 1) Portugal 2) 2010

Jul 20: 1) Ian Rush 2) Nat Lofthouse 3) Phil Taylor

Jul 21: 1) Ole Gunnar Solskjær 2) Mario Götze 3) Alf-Inge Haaland

Jul 22: 1) Georginio Wijnaldum 2) Jerzy Dudek 3) Luis Suárez

Jul 23: 1) Scunthorpe United 2) Australia 3) Newcastle United, Fulham, England, Manchester City

Jul 24: Fabio Capello, Bruno Conti, Luigi Delneri, Ezio Sella, Luciano Spalletti, Rudi Völler, Claudio Ranieri, Vincenzo Montella, Luis Enrique, Aurelio Andreazzoli, Zdenek Zeman, Rudi Garcia, Eusebio Di Francesco

Jul 25: Marcello Lippi, Luiz Felipe Scolari, Fabio Cannavaro

Jul 26: 1) Joe Fagan, Kenny Dalglish, Ronnie Moran, Graeme Souness, Roy Evans, Gérard Houllier, Rafael Benítez, Roy Hodgson, Brendan Rodgers, Jürgen Klopp 2) Bishop Auckland 3) Emlyn Hughes

Jul 27: 1) Zico 2) Carlos Tevez 3) Elías Figueroa

Jul 28: 1) Johnny Haynes 2) George Best 3) Omar Sívori

Jul 29: Arsenal, Manchester United, Sheffield Wednesday, Barnsley, Middlesbrough

Jul 30: 1) Stuttgarter Kickers, VfB Stuttgart, Internazionale, AS Monaco, Tottenham Hotspur, Bayern Munich, Sampdoria, Orange County Blue Star 2) Argentina 3) Czech Republic

Jul 31: 1) Joel Campbell 2) Bryan Ruiz 3) Keylor Navas

AUGUST

Aug 1: 1) Louis van Gaal 2) Jürgen Klinsmann 3a) Rudi Völler b) Jürgen Klinsmann
c) Joachim Löw

Aug 2: 1) Dwight Yorke 2) Stern John 3) Jlloyd Samuel

Aug 3: 1) Ricardo Villa 2) Shimizu S-Pulse, Yokohama F. Marinos, Tokyo Verdy, FC Machida
Zelvia 3) Fort Lauderdale Strikers

Aug 4: 1) Sylvester Stallone 2) Jock Stein 3) Bobby Robson

Aug 5: 1) Peter Shilton 2) Frank Swift 3) Doug Livermore

Aug 6: 1a) Louis van Gaal b) Dick Advocaat 2) Nani 3) Jimmy Floyd Hasselbaink and
Ruud van Nistelrooy

Aug 7: 1) Three (1958, 1962, 2002) 2) Peter Bonetti 3) Chesterfield, Leicester City, Stoke City

Aug 8: 1) Nicolas Anelka 2) Italy and Chile 3) Clive Thomas

Aug 9: 1) Andrea Pirlo 2) Gennaro Gattuso 3) Fabio Cannavaro

Aug 10: 1) Celtic 2) Sunderland 3) Mick McCarthy

Aug 11: 1) Idrissa Gueye 2) Sadio Mané 3) Cheikhou Kouyaté

Aug 12: Internazionale, Manchester City, AC Milan, Liverpool, Nice, Marseille, Brescia, Monza

Aug 13: 1) Kenny Dalglish 2) Jackie Milburn 3) David Beckham

Aug 14: 1) Raúl Jiménez 2) Giovani dos Santos 3) Carlos Vela

Aug 15: 1) Mohamed Salah 2) Andrew Robertson 3) Virgil van Dijk

Aug 16: 1) Edin Džeko 2) Didier Drogba 3) Samuel Eto'o 4) Tim Cahill 5) Shaun Goater
6) Romelu Lukaku 7) Alexis Sánchez

Aug 17: 1) Juventus 2) Ian Wright 3) Diego Forlán

Aug 18: 1) West Germany 2) Uruguay 3) Miroslav Klose

Aug 19: 1) Henrik Larsen 2) Germany 3) Peter Schmeichel, John Sivebæk

Aug 20: Blackburn Rovers, Newcastle United, Celtic

Aug 21: Gerd Müller

Aug 22: 1) Carlo Sartori 2) Giuseppe Rossi 3) Massimo Taibbi

Aug 23: 1) Danny McGrain 2) Alan Kernaghan 3) Nacho

Aug 24: 1) Ray Kennedy 2) Nicolas Anelka 3) Jermaine Pennant

Aug 25: 1) Gianluigi Buffon 2) Iker Casillas 3)Thomas Ravelli 4) Shay Given

Aug 26: 1) Ashley Cole 2) Cardiff City 3) Wigan Athletic

Aug 27: 1) Ferenc Puskás 2) Dennis Bergkamp 3) Emilio Butragueño 4) Franz Beckenbauer

Aug 28: 1) Wolverhampton Wanderers 2) Rotherham United, Hull City, Mansfield Town,
Swansea City 3) Joe Mercer

Aug 29: 1) Yossi Benayoun 2) Eyal Berkovic 3) Avi Cohen

Aug 30: 1) Josef Masopust in 1962 2) Sven-Göran Eriksson 3) Marcello Lippi

Aug 31: 1) Olympique Marseille 2) Leeds United 3) Real Sociedad 4) Auxerre 5) Newcastle
United 6) Ferencváros

SEPTEMBER

Sep 1: 1) Glenn Hoddle 2) Newcastle United, Feyenoord, Los Angeles Galaxy, Terek Grozny 3) Marco van Basten

Sep 2: 1) David Villa 2) Robbie Keane 3) Tony Meola

Sep 3: 1) Gastón Ramírez 2) Guillermo Varela 3) Diego Forlán

Sep 4: 1) Chis Waddle 2) Keiren Westwood 3) Paolo Di Canio

Sep 5: 1) Ray Wood 2) Petr Cech 3) Rui Patricio

Sep 6: 1) Nwankwo Kanu 2) Jay-Jay Okocha 3) Sunday Oliseh

Sep 7: 1) Aleksandar Kolarov 2) Nemanja Matić 3) Nemanja Vidić

Sep 8: 1) Lev Yashin 2) Joe Mercer 3) Angelo Schiavio

Sep 9: 1) Antonio Conte 2) Roberto Mancini 3) Dino Zoff

Sep 10: 1) Marko Arnautović 2) Christian Fuchs 3) Alex Manninger

Sep 11: Brazil's Mário Zagallo and France's Didier Deschamps

Sep 12: Don Mackay, George Curtis, John Sillett, Don Howe, Terry Butcher, Bobby Gould, Phil Neal, Ron Atkinson, Gordon Strachan

Sep 13: 1) Gerd Müller, Miroslav Klose 2) Lukas Podolski 3) Paul Pogba, Kylian Mbappé

Sep 14: 1) Berti Vogts 2) Marco Reus

Sep 15: Vavá and Garrincha: Brazil, Leonel Sánchez: Chile, Dražan Jerkovi: Yugoslavia, Valentin Ivanov: Soviet Union

Sep 16: 1) Liverpool and Fulham 2) Denmark 3) Juventus

Sep 17: 1) Kolo and Yaya Touré 2) Salomon Kalou 3) Gervinho

Sep 18: 1) Southampton, Derby County, Plymouth Arfyle, Wimbledon, Bolton Wanderers, Coventry City, West Ham United, Leyton Orient 2) Plymouth Argyle 3) Southampton

Sep 19: 1) Queens Park Rangers 2) Bobby Robson, Graham Taylor, Terry Venables, Glenn Hoddle, Howard Wilkinson, Kevin Keegan, Sven-Göran Eriksson 3) Manchester City

Sep 20: John Guidetti, Magnus Hedman, Freddie Ljungberg, Mikael Lustig, Daniel Majstorovic, Johan Mjällby

Sep 21: 1a) Stanley Matthews b) Eamonn Collins 2) Stan Mortensen 3a) Alan Ball b) Nigel Worthington

Sep 22: 1) Bobby Robson at Barcelona, Roy Hodgson at Internazionale 2) Corinthians 3) Real Valladolid

Sep 23: 1) Just Fontaine 1958, Gerd Müller 1970 2) Gabriel Batistuta 1994, 1998 3) Geoff Hurst

Sep 24: Gaetano Scirea, Antonio Cabrini, Arnold Mühren, Stefano Tacconi, Sergio Brio, Danny Blind, Gianluca Vialli, Vítor Baía

Sep 25: 1) Lothar Matthäus (75 times), Michael Ballack (55 times), Philipp Lamm (53 times) 2) Italy (1982) and Argentina (1986) 3) Leeds United, Saint-Étienne

Sep 26: 1) One with 1. FC Kaiserslautern, three with Bayern Munich 2) Three 3) 13

Sep 27: 1) Leeds United 2) Dynamo Moscow 3) Boca Juniors 4) AC Milan 5) Bolton Wanderers 6) Liverpool 7) Blackburn Rovers 8) Everton 9) Celtic

Sep 28: 1) Eddie Gray 2) George Graham 3) Gary McAllister

Sep 29: 1) Harald "Toni" Schumacher 2) Tony Woodcock 3) Pierre Littbarski

Sep 30: Netherlands, Sparta Rotterdam, Barcelona, Galatasaray, Saudi Arabia

OCTOBER

Oct 1: 1) Roger Byrne, David Pegg, Tommy Taylor, Frank Swift 2) Reuben Noble-Lazarus, 15 years, 45 days 3) Matthew Briggs, 16 years and 68 days

Oct 2: 1) Geoff Hurst 2) Stanley Matthews 3) Bobby Charlton 4) Kenny Dalglish

Oct 3: 1) Ajax 2) Juventus, Internazionale, AC Milan 3) Los Angeles Galaxy

Oct 4: 1) Patrik Berger 2) Milan Baroš 3) Karel Poborský

Oct 5: 1) Júlio César 2) Robinho 3) Kaká

Oct 6: 1) "Mean Machine" 2) "The Damned United" 3) "When Saturday Comes" 4) "Escape to Victory"

Oct 7: 1) José Mourinho, Steve Holland, Guus Hiddink, Antonio Conte 2) Vicente del Bosque and Fernando Hierro 3) Diego Simeone

Oct 8: 1) Dino Zoff, Claudio Gentile, Gaetano Scirea, Marco Tardelli, Paolo Rossi 2) Liverpool 1-0 3) Enzo Bearzot

Oct 9: 1) Daniel Passarella 2) Jorge Valdano 3) Diego Maradona

Oct 10: 1) Mark Hughes 2) Internazionale 3a) Jupp Heynckes b) Pep Guardiola

Oct 11: 1) Preston North End 2) Waterford United 3) Bobby Moore

Oct 12: 1) George Graham 2) Ron Greenwood, Bobby Robson, Terry Venables 3) Wimbledon

Oct 13: Michel Platini, Jean-Pierre Papin, Zinedine Zidane

Oct 14: 1) Eddie McCreadie 2) Peter Osgood 3) Peter Bonetti

Oct 15: 1) Hull City, Aston Villa, Chelsea 2) Argentina 1-0 3) Fenerbahçe

Oct 16: 1) Jürgen Klinsmann 2) Jürgen Kohler 3) Thomas Häßler

Oct 17: 1) Gordon Davies 2) Bobby Robson 3) Tommy Trinder

Oct 18: 1) Frank Lampard 2) Cristiano Ronaldo 3) Gunnar Nordahl 4) Jimmy Greaves

Oct 19: 1) Zlatan Ibrahimović 2) Tomas Brolin 3) Glenn Strömberg

Oct 20: 1) Gareth Bale 2) Juventus, Leeds United, Newcastle United, Sheffield United, Wrexham, Sydney Olympic 3) Chester City

Oct 21: 1) Liverpool, Middlesbrough, Wolverhampton Wanderers, Swindon Town, Macclesfield Town 2) Macclesfield Town, Milton Keynes Dons, Blackburn Rovers, Notts County, Blackpool 3) Tom Ince

Oct 22: 1) Oleg Blokhin, Igor Belanov 2) Michael Preud'homme, Fabien Barthez, Oliver Kahn, Gianluigi Buffon 3) Yugoslavia

Oct 23: 1) Franz Beckenbauer 2) Carlos Alberto 3) Dennis Tueart

Oct 24: 1) Sven-Göran Eriksson, Steve McClaren, Fabio Capello, Roy Hodgson, Sam Allardyce, Gareth Southgate 2) Peter Shilton, Stanley Matthews 3) Steven Gerrard

Oct 25: David Gaskell: 1963; Alex Stepney: 1976, 1977; Gary Bailey: 1979, 1983, 1985; Jim Leighton: 1990; Les Sealey: 1990 replay; Peter Schmeichel: 1994, 1995, 1996, 1999; Tim Howard: 2004; Roy Carroll: 2005; Edwin van der Sar: 2007; David de Gea: 2016, 2018

Oct 26: 1) Argentina 2) France 3) Netherlands 4) Brazil 5) Germany 6) Italy 7) Ireland

Oct 27: Arthur Rowe, Bill Nicholson, Terry Venables, Ray Clemence, Osvaldo Ardiles, Steve Perryman, Chris Hughton, Clive Allen, Tim Sherwood

Oct 28: 1) Cafu 2) Kaká 3) Robinho

Oct 29: 1) Juventus and Fulham 2) Clarence Seedorf with Ajax, Real Madrid and AC Milan 3) David De Gea

Oct 30: 1) Sergio Agüero 2) Hernán Crespo 3) Lionel Messi 4) Gabriel Batistuta

Oct 31: 1) 1958, 1962, 1970, 1994, 2002 2) Vicente Feola, Aymoré Moreira, Mário Zagallo, Carlos Alberto Parreira, Luiz Felipe Scolari 3) Bellini, Mauro Ramos, Carlos Alberto, Cafu

NOVEMBER

Nov 1: 1) Neville Southall 2) Southampton, Everton, Blackburn Rovers 3) Blackburn Rovers, Manchester City, Fulham, Queens Park Rangers, Stoke City, Southampton

Nov 2: 1) Venezuela 2) Scotland 3) Senegal 4) Serbia 5) Belgium

Nov 3: Angelo Schiavio (Italy, 1934), Alcides Ghiggia (Uruguay, 1950), Helmut Rahn (West Germany, 1954), Andreas Brehme (West Germany, 1990), Andrés Iniesta (Spain, 2010), Mario Götze (Germany, 2014)

Nov 4: 1) Bernd Schuster 2) Luis Enrique 3) Gheorghe Hagi

Nov 5: 1) Davor Šuker 2) Eduardo da Silva 3) Mario Mandžukić

Nov 6: Wilf McGuinness, Frank O'Farrell, Tommy Docherty, Dave Sexton, Ron Atkinson, David Moyes, Louis van Gaal, José Mourinho, Ole Gunnar Solskjær

Nov 7: 1) John Fashanu 2) Carl Hoddle 3) Bradley Wright-Phillips 4) Aaron Lescott 5) Peter Springett

Nov 8: 1) Chris Waddle 2) David Beckham 3) Mark Hateley

Nov 9: 1) Robbie Fowler 2) Damien Duff 3) Romário

Nov 10: 1) Marc-André ter Stegen 2) Manuel Neuer 3) Oliver Kahn

Nov 11: Bobby Robson, Graham Taylor, Terry Venables, Glenn Hoddle, Howard Wilkinson, Kevin Keegan, Peter Taylor, Sven-Göran Eriksson, Steve McClaren, Fabio Capello, Stuart Pearce, Roy Hodgson, Sam Allardyce, Gareth Southgate

Nov 12: Racing Club Paris, Olympique Marseille, Cagliari, Torino

Nov 13: Germany (3), Spain (3), France (2), Soviet Union, Italy, Netherlands, Denmark, Greece, Portugal

Nov 14: 1) Johnny Haynes 2) Mick Mills 3) Bryan Robson 4) Alan Shearer 5) David Beckham 6) Steven Gerrard 7) Harry Kane

Nov 15: 1) Mohamed Salah (twice), El Hadji Diouf, Sadio Mané 2) They are the only European born players to win the award 3) Monaco, Paris Saint-Germain, AC Milan

Nov 16: 1) Derek Dooley 2) Darío Silva 3) David Busst

Nov 17: 1) Real Madrid 2) Southampton 3) Sporting CP 4) Real Madrid

Nov 18: 1) Christian Eriksen 2) Pierre-Emile Højbjerg 3) Daniel Agger

Nov 19: 1) Spain 2) Uruguay 3) Germany

Nov 20: 1) Charlton Athletic 2) Norman Whiteside 3) Didier Drogba

Nov 21: Thierry Henry, Ian Wright, Cliff Bastin, John Radford, Jimmy Brain, Ted Drake, Doug Lishman, Robin van Persie, Joe Hulme, David Jack, Dennis Bergkamp, Reg Lewis, Jack Lambert, Frank Stapleton, Theo Walcott, David Herd, Olivier Giroud, Joe Baker

Nov 22: 1) Scotland 2) Portugal 3) Australia

Nov 23: 1) Tony Brown 2) Dixie Dean 3) Mick Channon

Nov 24: Ally MacLeod, Alex Ferguson, Craig Brown

Nov 25: 1) Benni McCarthy 2) Siphiwe Tshabalala 3) Shaun Bartlett

Nov 26: 1) Trevor Francis 2) David Platt 3) Graeme Souness

Nov 27: Galatasaray, Internazionale, Zenit Saint Petersburg, Italy

Nov 28: 1) Dick Nanninga 2) Rudi Völler 3) Mario Götze

Nov 29: Mark Hughes, Lee Sharpe, David Beckham, Wayne Rooney (2), Cristiano Ronaldo

Nov 30: Jimmy Greaves (Chelsea, Tottenham Hotspur), Alan Shearer (Blackburn Rovers, Newcastle United), Jack Southworth (Blackburn Rovers, Everton), Malcolm MacDonald (Newcastle United, Arsenal), Jimmy Floyd Hasselbaink (Leeds United, Chelsea), Robin van Persie (Arsenal, Manchester United)

DECEMBER

Dec 1: 1) Andrés Iniesta 2) Dunga 3) Andrés Iniesta

Dec 2: 1) Alfredo Di Stéfano 2) Hungary, Czechoslovakia and Spain 3) Ferenc Puskás

Dec 3: 1) The Black Stars 2) Avram Grant 3) 2006

Dec 4: 1) Ivor Allchurch 2) Norman Hunter 3) Stuart Pearce

Dec 5: 1972: Gerd Müller 1976: Dieter Müller 1992: Karlheinz Riedle (joint top scorer) 2012: Mario Gómez (joint top scorer)

Dec 6: 1) Mark Schwarzer 2) Terry Venables 3) Harry Kewell

Dec 7: 1) Kenny Dalglish 2) Alan Shearer 3) Chris Sutton

Dec 8: 1) French Guiana 2) Australia 3) Jamaica

Dec 9: Norman Hunter, David O'Leary, Eddie Gray, Gary McAllister, Simon Grayson

Dec 10: Willy Caballero, Hernán Crespo, Franco Di Santo, Juan Sebastián Verón

Dec 11: Hungary, Great Britain

Dec 12: Brendan Rodgers, Kenny Dalglish, Roy Hodgson, Rafa Benítez

Dec 13: 1) Northern Ireland 2) Tommy Lawton 3) San Marino

Dec 14: 1) Stanley Matthews, Bobby Charlton, Kevin Keegan 2) Real Madrid, Newcastle United, Manchester United, Stoke City 3) Ian Rush, Roger Hunt, Gordon Hodgson, Billy Liddell, Steven Gerrard, Robbie Fowler, Kenny Dalglish

Dec 15: 1) Leeds United, Manchester United, AC Milan, Hellas Verona, Southampton, Bristol City 2) Lou Macari 3) Harry Redknapp

Dec 16: 1984

Dec 17: Gylfi Sigurðsson

Dec 18: 1) Nobby Stiles 2) Alf Common 3) Juninho

Dec 19: Manuel Pellegrini, José Mourinho, Carlo Ancelotti, Rafa Benítez, Santiago Solari, Julen Lopetegui, Zinédine Zidane

Dec 20: Unai Emery, Thomas Tuchel, Mauricio Pochettino

Dec 21: Alf Ramsey, Joe Mercer, Don Revie, Bobby Robson, Terry Venables, Kevin Keegan, Peter Taylor, Stuart Pearce, Gareth Southgate

Dec 22: Trevor Francis

Dec 23: 1) Antonio Valencia 2) Felipe Caicedo 3) Christian Benítez

Dec 24: Alexis Sánchez, Eduardo Vargas

Dec 25: Pelé, Neymar, Ronaldo, Romário, Zico, Bebeto, Rivaldo

Dec 26: 1a) Bert Trautmann b) Joe Corrigan c) Joe Hart d) Ederson 2) Peter Shilton 3) Portsmouth 2-1

Dec 27: Ian Rush, Aaron Ramsey

Dec 28: 1) Coventry City, Sunderland, Motherwell, Sydney FC, Partick Thistle, Brentford, Inverness Caledonian Thistle, Hibernian, Newport County, Philippines 2) Clydebank 3) Ron Greenwood

Dec 29: Ron Atkinson

Dec 30: Peter Shilton, Ray Clemence, Phil Parkes, Jimmy Rimmer, Joe Corrigan, Nigel Spink, Gary Bailey, Chris Woods, David Seaman, Dave Beasant, Nigel Martyn, Tim Flowers, Ian Walker, David James, Richard Wright, Paul Robinson, Rob Green, Chris Kirkland, Ben Foster, Scott Carson, Joe Hart, Jack Butland, John Ruddy, Fraser Forster, Tom Heaton, Jordan Pickford, Nick Pope, Alex McCarthy, Dean Henderson, Sam Johnstone

Dec 31: Huddersfield Town, Wigan Athletic, Crystal Palace, Birmingham City, Sunderland, Hull City, Aston Villa, Sheffield Wednesday

TRIVQUIZ
FROM ABBA TO ZAPPA, AMÉLIE TO ZULU, AND AGÜERO TO ZIDANE
NEW FOOTBALL AND POP CULTURE QUIZZES EVERY DAY AT TRIVQUIZ.COM
trivquiz.com
trivquiz
trivquiz
trivquizcomic

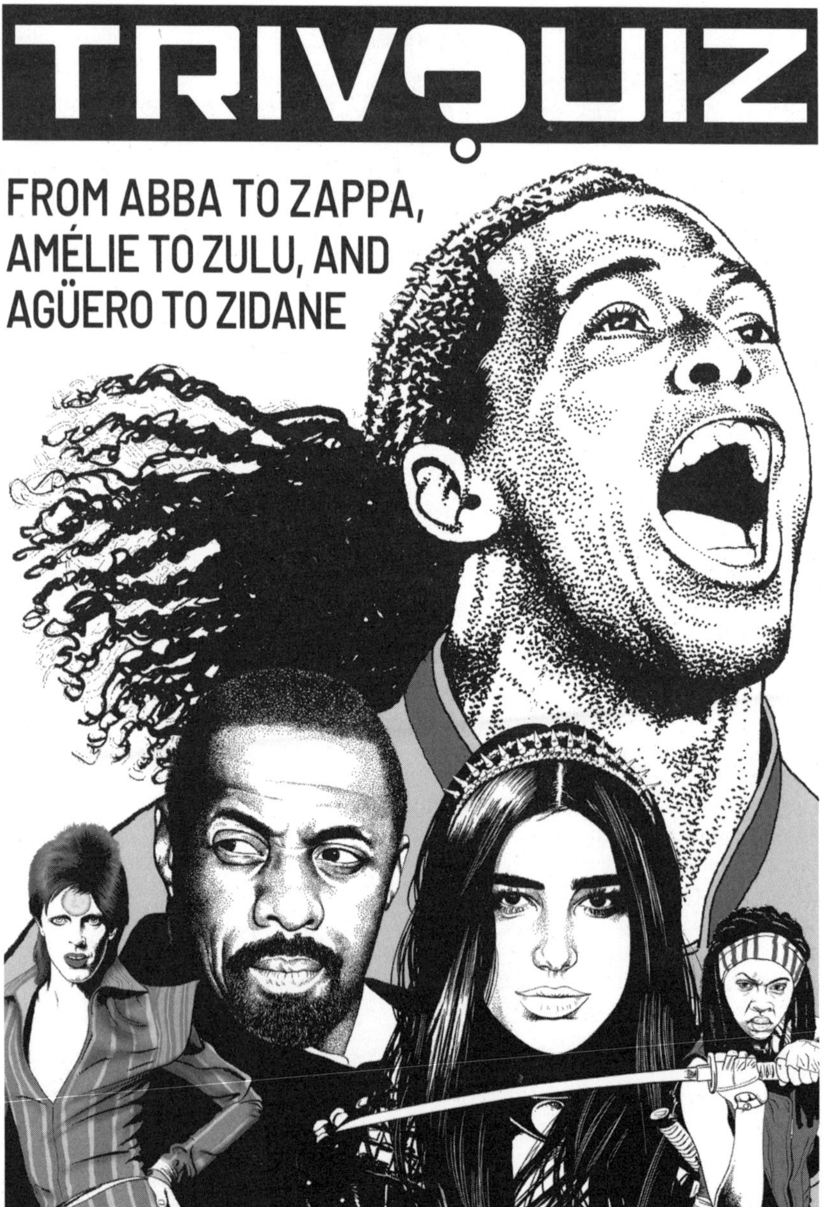

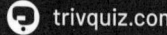

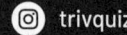